South University Library
Richmond Campus
2151 Old Brick Road
Glen Allen, Va 23060

MAR 1 3 2018

Workplace Bullying and Mobbing in the United States

Workplace Bullying and Mobbing in the United States

Volume 1

Maureen Duffy and David C. Yamada, Editors

Foreword by Gary Namie

An Imprint of ABC-CLIO, LLC
Santa Barbara, California • Denver, Colorado

Copyright © 2018 by ABC-CLIO, LLC

All rights reserved. No part of this publication may be reproduced, stored in a retrieval system, or transmitted, in any form or by any means, electronic, mechanical, photocopying, recording, or otherwise, except for the inclusion of brief quotations in a review, without prior permission in writing from the publisher.

Library of Congress Cataloging-in-Publication Data

Names: Duffy, Maureen P., editor. | Yamada, David C., editor.
Title: Workplace bullying and mobbing in the United States / Maureen Duffy and David C. Yamada, editors ; foreword by Gary Namie.
Description: Santa Barbara, California : Praeger, 2018. | Includes bibliographical references and index.
Identifiers: LCCN 2017013247 (print) | LCCN 2017031060 (ebook) | ISBN 9781440850240 (ebook) | ISBN 9781440850233 (set : alk. paper) | ISBN 9781440850257 (volume 1) | ISBN 9781440850264 (volume 2)
Subjects: LCSH: Bullying in the workplace—United States. | Harassment—United States.
Classification: LCC HF5549.5.E43 (ebook) | LCC HF5549.5.E43 W67168 2018 (print) | DDC 331.25/6—dc23
LC record available at https://lccn.loc.gov/2017013247

ISBN: 978-1-4408-5023-3 (set)
      978-1-4408-5025-7 (vol. 1)
      978-1-4408-5026-4 (vol. 2)
      978-1-4408-5024-0 (ebook)

22 21 20 19 18   1 2 3 4 5

This book is also available as an eBook.

Praeger
An Imprint of ABC-CLIO, LLC

ABC-CLIO, LLC
130 Cremona Drive, P.O. Box 1911
Santa Barbara, California 93116-1911
www.abc-clio.com

This book is printed on acid-free paper ∞

Manufactured in the United States of America

Contents

VOLUME 1

Foreword ix
Gary Namie

Preface xiii
Maureen Duffy and David C. Yamada

PART I: UNDERSTANDING WORKPLACE BULLYING AND MOBBING

1. Workplace Bullying and Mobbing: Definitions, Terms, and When They Matter 3
   David C. Yamada, Maureen Duffy, and Peggy Ann Berry

2. Prevalence of Workplace Bullying and Mobbing among U.S. Working Adults: What Do the Numbers Mean? 25
   Loraleigh Keashly

3. Risk Factors for Becoming a Target of Workplace Bullying and Mobbing 53
   Gary Namie and Ruth Namie

4. Organizational Risk Factors: An Integrative Model for Understanding, Treating, and Preventing Mobbing and Bullying in the Workplace 75
   Len Sperry

PART II: EXAMINING THE IMPACT OF WORKPLACE BULLYING AND MOBBING

5 Workplace Bullying and Mobbing and the Health of Targets   101
  Melody M. Kawamoto

6 The Psychosocial Impact of Workplace Bullying and
  Mobbing on Targets   131
  Maureen Duffy

7 Workplace Bullying and Mobbing: A Neuropsychotherapeutic
  Perspective   151
  Pieter J. Rossouw

8 Vicarious and Secondary Victimization in Adult Bullying
  and Mobbing: Coworkers, Target-Partners, Children,
  and Friends   171
  Pamela Lutgen-Sandvik

9 When Workplace Bullying and Mobbing Occur:
  The Impact on Organizations   201
  Renee L. Cowan

PART III: PREVENTION OF WORKPLACE BULLYING AND MOBBING

10 How Awareness and Education Can Help with Recognition of
   Workplace Bullying and Mobbing   221
   Gary Namie, Ruth Namie, and Carol Fehner

11 The Role of Human Resources in Bullying and
   Mobbing Prevention Efforts   235
   Teresa A. Daniel

12 Innovative Practices in Workplace Conflict Resolution   265
   John-Robert Curtin

VOLUME 2

PART IV: UTILIZING EFFECTIVE INTERVENTIONS IN RESPONDING TO WORKPLACE BULLYING AND MOBBING

13 Best Practices in Psychotherapy for Targets of Workplace Bullying and Mobbing   291
    Maureen Duffy and Jessi Eden Brown

14 Best Practices in Coaching for Targets of Workplace Bullying and Mobbing   315
    Jessi Eden Brown and Maureen Duffy

15 Best Practices in Coaching for Aggressors and Offenders in Workplace Bullying and Mobbing   335
    Benjamin M. Walsh

16 The Role of the Consultant in Assessing and Preventing Workplace Bullying and Mobbing   357
    Gary Namie and Ruth Namie

17 The Role of the Ombuds in Addressing Workplace Bullying and Mobbing   387
    Tony Belak

PART V: THE LEGAL LANDSCAPE IN THE UNITED STATES FOR WORKPLACE BULLYING AND MOBBING

18 The American Legal Landscape: Potential Redress and Liability for Workplace Bullying and Mobbing   413
    David C. Yamada

19 Comparing and Contrasting Workplace Bullying and Mobbing Laws in Other Countries with the American Legal Landscape   435
    Ellen Pinkos Cobb

PART VI: WORKPLACE BULLYING AND MOBBING WITHIN SPECIFIC EMPLOYMENT SECTORS

20 Workplace Bullying and Mobbing in the Health Care Sector   457
    Susan Johnson

21 Workplace Bullying and Mobbing in K–12 Settings:
    School Principal Mistreatment and Abuse of Teachers   481
    Jo Blase and Joseph Blase

22 Workplace Bullying and Mobbing in U.S. Higher Education   507
    Loraleigh Keashly and Joel H. Neuman

23 Workplace Bullying and Mobbing in the Public Service
    Sector and the Role of Unions   539
    Gregory Sorozan

24 Workplace Bullying and Mobbing in the Corporate Sector   561
    Kelly H. Kolb and Mary Beth Ricke

25 Workplace Bullying and Mobbing in the Nonprofit Sector   589
    Vega Subramaniam

Epilogue: An Agenda for Moving Forward   611
David C. Yamada and Maureen Duffy

About the Editors and Contributors   619

Index   627

Foreword

These volumes build upon a strong foundation. American researchers, educators, practitioners, and advocates in the arena of workplace bullying, mobbing, and abuse are in debt to the foundational theories and practices developed by our European friends and colleagues. Our research and commentary in these volumes flows from their significant work in the field of workplace bullying and mobbing.

I marvel at the breadth and depth of the chapters that follow in this two-volume set. The impressive anthology is a testament to the abilities of this mostly American contingent of writers to address every aspect of the workplace bullying and mobbing phenomenon—from definition to impact to solutions to charting a future course. On a personal note, I am proud to have collaborated with many of the invited authors.

The societal context of this project is critical. Academics, practitioners, and advocates alike stand against abusive conduct at work that creates almost insurmountable problems for individuals, coworker relationships, families, and organizations. Nevertheless, combating work abuse in America is not uncritically accepted. Though our society has made other forms of abuse taboo—child abuse, domestic violence, student-age bullying—bullying and mobbing at work remain widespread, acceptable, and even promoted. For example, many Americans revere corporate leaders and politicians who have well-known bullying reputations.

Though abusive workplace conduct is universal across cultures, American solutions must necessarily take into account the unique characteristics of our lived experiences. We are not a democratic socialist nation as are many European countries, and our people are not collectivist by nature. Our heritage is more that of rugged individualism and personal resourcefulness. However, this enterprising nature of ours can sometimes devolve into ruthless competition. Television reality shows that feature cutthroat competitive backstabbing among participants, culminating in elimination, enjoy strong ratings. When the public gets a say in declaring winners, it typically rewards the most cunning, Machiavellian person who has exploited kind or trusting others to win. In myriad ways, we are a winner-take-all society. We condemn second place finishers as losers.

Our dominant culture socializes us to believe that we are different from others in the world. This accounts for our sometimes myopic nationalistic views that connote superiority. Putting aside my disdain for cultural narcissism, I readily admit we are different from the other nations that have identified workplace mobbing and bullying as problematic and taken national or state-level actions to ameliorate the problems. The reasons for the difference are varied and complex.

First, to date, American lawmakers have not shown the political will to fund research that could remotely implicate employer responsibility for psychologically unsafe, and therefore unhealthy, workplaces. We live in a time of unprecedented hostility to science and fact-driven decision making. Heinz Leymann's clinic for those abused in the workplace would not likely be funded by any government grant in the United States today.

A second difference is that our European predecessors have made it clear in all statutory laws and occupational health regulations that employers are primarily responsible for harm suffered by employees. Abusive employees or managers are seen as agents of their employers. In America, blaming corporations for anything—criminal acts, large-scale environmental damage, or havoc wreaked on the global financial system—is often equated with a lack of patriotism. We are among the most, if not *the* most, corporate-driven capitalistic cultures on earth. Asking that human factors be included in the capitalistic equation is tantamount to sacrilege.

Rather than holding employers accountable, American workers turn on each other in internecine feuds. We blame victims (bullied targets in the context of these volumes), people who, in fact, are just like ourselves. We commit the fundamental attribution error of minimizing the role of environments over behavior and overestimate personalities as causal factors. The individualism for which we Americans are known lets organizations off the hook. When we pin responsibility on victims, it ostensibly lends order to a chaotic world. We adopt the delusion that "bad things only happen to bad people," accounting for a third difference.

It seems reasonable that trade unions are a solution to worker powerlessness in bullying scenarios. They could and should be. However, in America, sympathy for unions is undermined by a 40-year corporate campaign against joining or forming unions. Sadly, America's unionization rate ranks among the lowest in the world, thus adding a fourth contrast between the world and America to the list.

A subtle, but fundamental, difference between us and much of the rest of the world is that personal dignity in America is considered something that one must "earn." Europeans, in their codification of antimobbing and antibullying regulations, proclaim that workers have an inherent dignity. The dignitarian doctrine protects employees' privacy, personal integrity, or identity and self-esteem. Here, self-esteem is mocked.

Employers' duty of care, an extension of dignitarianism, mandates employer vigilance over workers' safety—both physical and psychological. Bullying and mobbing and abuse at work should rightly be considered assaults on the dignity of workers. Dignitarian principles are not reflected in our employment laws. There is no mainstream dignity movement in America, notwithstanding pioneering efforts to create one. Outside of the workplace bullying movement, we have a long journey ahead to gain widespread acceptance of the importance of personal dignity.

Workplace bullying, mobbing, and abuse are phenomena that make for a chaotic, unpredictable, cruel, and fearful world for those targeted and their families. Orderly explanations are unavailable. The bullying work environment is a world turned upside down. All too often, good souls are targeted for abuse, while those who exploit others garner rewards. Coworkers shrink with anticipatory fear rather than help their abused colleagues. And executives and administrators all too often ignore clear reports of bullying and mobbing, sometimes preferring to rationalize aggressive acts as natural and indispensable parts of a successful workplace climate.

We need evidence-based solutions that effectively address the core issues underlying bullying, mobbing, and abuse at work. These volumes provide hope and confirmation that progress is being made toward those goals. Despite our shortcomings, Americans are innovators and social entrepreneurs. From our ranks will surely emerge the unique American answers we seek.

I was personally inspired by many of the authors between the covers of this book. It is my hope that the publication of this collection of research studies and commentaries on the 20th anniversary of the launch of the U.S. workplace bullying movement inspires future generations of academics, practitioners, and advocates. We all must strive to make America a kinder, more compassionate place to work, and these volumes provide an important blueprint.

Gary Namie
Workplace Bullying Institute

Preface

Maureen Duffy and David C. Yamada

Joined by our tremendous group of chapter contributors and colleagues, we are pleased to offer this two-volume book set that explores workplace bullying and mobbing from multidisciplinary perspectives, with a dual focus on research and practice. We hope that it will serve as a useful educational and reference work not only for researchers, practitioners, and students in many fields that call for an understanding of bullying and mobbing at work, but also for members of the general public who seek to comprehend these behaviors and potential responses to them.

Workplace bullying and mobbing inflict destructive effects on immediate targets, coworkers, witnesses, family members, and host organizations. The costs of these forms of interpersonal mistreatment can be measured in terms of harm to physical and emotional health, anxious and distressed family relationships, diminished trust in coworkers and organizations, reduced workplace productivity and morale, and actual dollar costs for everything from treatment to retraining to litigation.

In a little over three decades, research about workplace bullying and mobbing has been conducted in many countries around the world. The implications of this growing body of research, knowledge, and practice concerning workplace bullying and mobbing in the United States form the bases for these volumes. In this preface, we would like to share with readers the roots of this project, its overall purpose and scope, and a preview of what to expect in the pages to come. We close with our acknowledgments.

SEEDS PLANTED

The biennial Work, Stress and Health conference is a welcomed contrast to the dreary sense of obligation and hierarchy that pervades all too many academic and professional events. Sponsored by the American Psychological Association, the National Institute for Occupational Safety and Health, and the Society for Occupational Health Psychology, Work, Stress and Health attracts a diverse array of academicians, practitioners, and students who are interested in applying research and best practices to the fostering of healthier workplaces.

The May 2015 conference in Atlanta not only exemplified the compelling draw of this gathering, but in many ways, it also planted the seeds for this project. During the conference, a multidisciplinary cohort of scholars and practitioners interested in workplace bullying and mobbing naturally coalesced. We attended each other's workshops, talked between formal sessions, and exchanged ideas over meals at local eateries. We got to know each other better, learned more about the work that each of us was doing, and enjoyed a shared sense of professional community and camaraderie. At some point, a couple of those present commented that there was an awful lot of talent in the area of workplace bullying and mobbing represented at the conference and that we ought to put together a book showcasing this work from a distinctly American perspective. Eighteen months later, we were able to send this book to publication. It has been our honor and privilege to shepherd it along.

PURPOSE

Our primary purpose in developing this book set was to bring together important research and thinking about workplace bullying and mobbing from leading and emerging American researchers, theorists, and practitioners and to present that work in a comprehensive and systematic way. (For a chapter on applications from neuroscience, we did go half-way around the world to Australia to find the relevant expertise.) We assure our readers, especially those from outside the United States, that we were not being provincial or ethnocentric in choosing this focus. Rather, we understood that the employment context in the United States is very different from that in European nations, Australia, and Canada—countries that have produced so much foundational, high-quality research, scholarship, and commentary about workplace bullying and mobbing. For better and for worse, these American differences cover the major employment sectors (private, public, and nonprofit); systems of employee relations; and mechanisms for resolving legal and labor disputes.

In the context of this American focus, we perceived a need for an encyclopedic treatment of workplace bullying and mobbing that embraces multidisciplinary and multifaceted examination and analysis. We intended these volumes to be theoretically inclusive and to present a range of policy, practice, and research perspectives. We also wanted to showcase the accumulated wisdom of practitioners in the area of workplace bullying and mobbing so that readers would be able to juxtapose practitioner understandings and perspectives with those of researchers and scholars. In so doing, we tried to stay true to the most robust and comprehensive interpretation of evidence-based practice, namely, reliance on a combination of research and practice evidence with stakeholder values, priorities, and preferences.

The mutual informing of research and practice is evident throughout each of the contributions to the book set. Furthermore, where appropriate, research gaps needing attention are identified, along with the tagging of ongoing challenges in the areas of practice and policy. Finally, careful readers will identify respectful differences of opinion and viewpoint among the chapter authors. We did not recruit authors for the purpose of fomenting disagreement, but we did want to include a variety of analyses, interpretations, and framings to provide looks at workplace bullying and mobbing from different vantage points. In this sense, we hope that this project contributes to our overall understanding of the subject matter in ways that respect the complexities of the various topics.

PREVIEWING THESE VOLUMES

The book set is divided into six parts. Part I focuses on understanding and describing workplace bullying and mobbing. In this section, topics such as terminology and prevalence rates are discussed as well as risk factors for becoming a target and organizational risk factors for the development of bullying and mobbing. In part II, we examine the effects of workplace bullying and mobbing. Health impairments experienced by targets and broader psychosocial impacts are described. The effects of bullying and mobbing on the brains of targets and the resulting implications are discussed in the contribution on neuroscience and bullying. The effects of vicarious victimization on family members and coworkers are examined. We also examine the impacts of bullying and mobbing on the host organizations. In part III, we focus on the prevention of workplace bullying and mobbing. This includes the role of human resources (HR) and applications of various conflict resolution tools.

In part IV, we center on effective interventions to respond to workplace bullying and mobbing. This section includes discussions of best practices in psychotherapy and in coaching for targets of workplace bullying and mobbing as well as possibilities for coaching aggressors and offenders. The potential roles of workplace consultants and the ombudsperson are also examined. In part V, we consider the legal landscape for workplace bullying and mobbing in the United States. This includes an examination of relevant legal developments in the United States, followed by a comparative look at how legal systems in other countries address bullying and mobbing behaviors, the latter being especially relevant to multinational employers.

Finally, in part VI, we focus on workplace bullying and mobbing within specific employment sectors. Health care, K–12 educational settings, higher education, public service and the role of unions, the corporate sector, and the nonprofit sector all receive individual treatments. We close with an epilogue in which the coeditors share final thoughts and impressions about the overall subject matter and provide commentary about how awareness of bullying and mobbing will continue to affect the nature of workplace interactions and relationships.

We hope that these volumes will be useful in different ways, depending on the individual reader's needs. For some, this material will yield specific research summaries or potential good practices. For others, single chapters or groups of chapters will be worth cover-to-cover reads to obtain topical overviews. For those who want a comprehensive overview of workplace bullying and mobbing, a full reading of both volumes will provide a useful, comprehensive starting point. In any event, we trust that engaging with these volumes will be time well spent.

ACKNOWLEDGMENTS

We are deeply grateful for the knowledge, expertise, and experiences that have been generously shared by our contributors, and we cannot thank them enough for their hard work and patience with our recurring demands as editors. We specially thank Drs. Ruth and Gary Namie for their pioneering leadership in bringing the problem of workplace bullying to national attention in the United States. It is hard to imagine where we would be in the United States had they not come along and helped to put this social problem before us.

On a broader scale, we express our appreciation and gratitude to scholars, practitioners, workers, and advocates around the world who are devoting time and energies toward helping us understand and respond to bullying and mobbing at work. The fellowship of those who understand the destructiveness of these behaviors and want to prevent and stop them is a special one. We are especially appreciative of the signature contributions of researchers and theorists outside of the United States who have helped to build foundations for our work today. Many of their writings are cited in our various chapters.

We also wish to thank Jessica Gribble, our editor at Praeger/ABC-CLIO, and the production and marketing teams there. Jessica has been a staunch supporter of this project from the outset and has guided it with a deft hand. It has only been a pleasure to work with her and to benefit from her ideas and creativity. Daniel Glass, our APA guru, peerless editorial assistant, and Suffolk University doctoral candidate, helped to make the technical side of editing this book set seem easy.

In addition to our joint acknowledgments, I (M.D.) have a few individual expressions of thanks that I wish to share. People from all over the country and, indeed, from many other countries have communicated with me over the years about their own experiences of workplace bullying and mobbing. To them, and to my clients, I offer my sincerest appreciation for their trust. I hope that in the pages of this book set, they will continue to find resources for their own recovery and positive reengagement in the world of work. My coeditor, colleague, and friend, David Yamada, has been an amazing partner in this project. He is a wonderful collaborator and has made doing this book set rewarding in ways too many to list. Finally, to my husband, with gratitude as always for your unconditional support, and for your many surprise cups of tea, coffee, and glasses of wine.

I (D.Y.) want to express my gratitude to several institutions and individuals. Suffolk University Law School and Valparaiso University provided welcomed support and space to work on this project. Maureen Duffy, who graciously invited me to join her as coeditor—a leap of faith to be sure—has gifted me with her wisdom and expertise, attention to detail, good humor, and friendship. To put it in a lawyer's vernacular, it has been an honor to "second chair" the planning and editing of this book set with her. Furthermore, I dedicate my work on the project to dear friends Mary Louise Allen, Denise McCrane, and Brian McCrane, as well as to my late mom, Betty Yamada, who was the antithesis of a bully.

PART I

Understanding Workplace Bullying and Mobbing

1

Workplace Bullying and Mobbing: Definitions, Terms, and When They Matter

David C. Yamada, Maureen Duffy, and Peggy Ann Berry

Since the late 1980s, when the terms *workplace mobbing* and *workplace bullying* began to appear in the research and professional literature, scholars and practitioners in fields as diverse as psychology, organizational behavior, and law have attempted to define these terms or have suggested other labels for naming the underlying behaviors. Three decades later, the concepts of workplace bullying and mobbing are fully entering the mainstream vocabularies of employee relations and interpersonal mistreatment.

The process of labeling and defining human interactions can be a tricky and sometimes touchy business, as many researchers and theorists have come to realize. In what is now a multidisciplinary field of study, with multiple disciplinary lexicons simultaneously in use, labeling and defining workplace bullying and mobbing remains a sometimes fraught activity. Nonetheless, what is common to these efforts to label and define these behaviors is the shared interest in understanding the underlying social and neurobiological processes involved; the damaging effects on targets and an increasingly wide range of other stakeholders; and the development of effective means to both prevent workplace bullying and mobbing and offer treatments, interventions, and legal relief to those affected.

Naming something is a powerful epistemological act with real-world significance. Drawing a distinction by naming and defining something brings that something from the background into the foreground, thereby enabling it to be studied and investigated. Keeney (1983) stated that "drawing any distinction necessarily leaves us with an altered, expanded universe for further investigation" (p. 23). It would be a safe bet to say that there are very few professionals, especially practitioners, working in the area of workplace bullying and mobbing who have not heard clients express huge relief upon learning that the abuse they have been experiencing at work has a name and is studied in the professional literature. The naming of their experiences of bullying and mobbing provides validation, opportunities for understanding, and avenues for healing. John Dewey (1910/2007), the American philosopher, psychologist, and educational reformer, also paid attention to the importance of naming. He said,

> Every one has experienced how learning an appropriate name for what was dim and vague cleared up and crystallized the whole matter. Some meaning seems distinct almost within reach, but is elusive; it refuses to condense into definite form; the attaching of a word somehow (just how, it is almost impossible to say) puts limits around the meaning, draws it out from the void, makes it stand out as an entity on its own account. (p. 173)

Thus, we begin these volumes with what may appear to be an obligatory chapter on terms and definitions. However, we do so with aspirations that go beyond checking a box. In addition to providing and explaining basic terms and definitions, we will highlight when, why, and how they matter, while acknowledging that people will have their own opinions as to which ones best capture the underlying behaviors. As we see it, these behaviors are so damaging and destructive to individuals and organizations that we should not get too caught up in debates over who is "right" on the question of preferred terminology. Rather, we embrace and call for a "big tent" approach that focuses on understanding, preventing, and responding to these behaviors on individual, organizational, and public policy levels.

Accordingly, this chapter will identify and discuss varying terms and definitions related to our focus on workplace bullying and mobbing. We begin by focusing on a representative sampling of definitions used for our primary terms of workplace bullying and workplace mobbing, followed by a look at other terms that have been invoked to cover the same or similar behaviors. We then discuss the key elements of the definitions, followed by a brief consideration of the most common bullying and mobbing behaviors. Finally, we offer an examination of the implications of these terms and definitions for important stakeholder interests. Before proceeding, we wish to acknowledge that no core definition can possibly cover all the relevant dynamics of bullying and mobbing at work. In parsing and distinguishing them, we are not finding fault with what is or is not contained in a given definition. In many cases, a factor that one author includes in a basic definition may be covered by another author elsewhere in a commentary.

DEFINING WORKPLACE BULLYING

Three representative definitions of workplace bullying are provided here. They include definitions from Andrea Adams, the British journalist who first popularized the term *workplace bullying* in the 1980s and early 1990s; Gary and Ruth Namie, the cofounders of the American-based Workplace Bullying Institute, who were most responsible for bringing the term *workplace bullying* to the United States; and leading European researchers Stale Einarsen, Helge Hoel, Dieter Zapf, and Cary Cooper.

Andrea Adams

The late Andrea Adams used a series of BBC radio documentaries to bring the topic to a more public audience. In 1992, she authored what may have been the first book to use "bullying" at work as its operative term (Adams, 1992). She observed that even though workplace bullying is "like a malignant cancer" and that "the majority of the adult population spends more waking hours at work than anywhere else," the manifestations of this form of abuse "are widely dismissed" (Adams, 1992, p. 9). In a 1994 speech to the trade union Manufacturing, Science and Finance, she defined bullying this way:

> Workplace bullying constitutes offensive behaviour through vindictive, cruel, malicious or humiliating attempts to undermine an individual or groups of employees. And these persistently negative attacks on their personal and professional performance are typically unpredictable, irrational and often unfair. This abuse of power or position can cause such chronic stress and anxiety that the employees gradually lose belief in themselves, suffering physical ill-health and mental distress as a result. (Ellis, 2011, p. 2)

Adams was a journalist, not a researcher or theorist. However, her early explanation of workplace bullying captured many of the elements found in more academic definitions. Furthermore, by emphasizing a public audience rather than an academic one for her work, she helped to lay the groundwork for mainstreaming workplace bullying as an employee relations concern.

Gary Namie and Ruth Namie

In 1997, Gary and Ruth Namie, both holders of PhDs in psychology, founded the Campaign Against Workplace Bullying, the first major initiative designed to import the term *workplace bullying* into the vocabulary of American employee relations and mental health treatment. This effort would evolve into the creation of the Workplace Bullying Institute and the publication of several books (Namie & Namie, 1999, 2009, 2011).

The Namies define workplace bullying as the "repeated, health-harming mistreatment of a person by one or more workers that takes the form of verbal abuse; conduct or behaviors that are threatening, intimidating, or humiliating; sabotage that prevents work from getting done; or some combination of the three" (Namie & Namie, 2009, p. 1). They go on to characterize workplace bullying as a form of "psychological violence" that mixes "verbal and strategic assaults to prevent the Target from performing work well," thus undermining "an employer's legitimate business interests" (Namie & Namie, 2009, p. 1). They add that bullying includes an aggressor's "personal agenda of controlling another human being," typically via "a combination of deliberate humiliation and the withholding of resources" required to perform a job (Namie & Namie, 2009, p. 1).

Working in conjunction with Zogby Analytics pollsters, the Workplace Bullying Institute has conducted periodic national scientific surveys on workplace bullying using various measures that build off this basic definition. Further discussion of those surveys may be found in chapter 2, which examines the prevalence of workplace bullying and mobbing behaviors.

Stale Einarsen, Helge Hoel, Dieter Zapf, and Cary Cooper

Leading European researchers and theorists Stale Einarsen, Helge Hoel, Dieter Zapf, and Cary Cooper have been examining bullying, mobbing, and related behaviors at work going back to the 1990s. While acknowledging the complexities and "many shapes and shades" of this topic (Einarsen, Hoel, Zapf, & Cooper, p. 4), they define workplace bullying this way: "At a basic level it is about the systematic mistreatment of a subordinate, a colleague, or a superior, which, if continued and long-lasting, may cause severe social, psychological, and psychosomatic problems in the target" (Einarsen et al., 2011, p. 4). They further expound on this definition: "Bullying at work is about repeated actions and practises that are directed against one or more workers; that are unwanted by the victim; that may be carried out deliberately or unconsciously, but clearly cause humiliation, offence, and distress; and that may interfere with work performance and/or cause an unpleasant working environment" (Einarsen et al., 2011, p. 9).

DEFINING WORKPLACE MOBBING

Now we offer three representative definitions of *workplace mobbing*. They include definitions from Heinz Leymann, the first to adopt and develop the term *mobbing* in a workplace context; Noa Davenport, Ruth Distler Schwartz, and Gail Elliott, whose 1999 book helped to introduce workplace mobbing to American audiences; and Maureen Duffy and Len Sperry, coauthors of two leading books on workplace mobbing behaviors.

Heinz Leymann

During the 1980s, the late Swedish psychologist Heinz Leymann adopted the term *mobbing* to describe the kinds of abusive, hostile behaviors that were being directed at employees by their coworkers. This pioneering expert on mobbing behaviors built on the work of ethologist Konrad Lorenz, who studied the behaviors of birds and other animals when they ganged up to drive a target animal out of their territory. Here is his "operational definition" of workplace mobbing (Leymann, 1990):

> Psychical terror or mobbing in working life means hostile and unethical communication which is directed in a systematic way by one or a number of persons mainly toward one individual.... These actions take place often (almost every day) and over a long period (at least for six months) and, because of this frequency and duration, result in considerable psychic, psychosomatic and social misery. (p. 120)

Leymann (1990, 1996) fleshed out the above definition through his development of a multiphase model of workplace mobbing: namely, Phase 1: the precipitating conflict; Phase 2: the escalation of abusive behaviors against a target; Phase 3: the involvement of management or administration into the conflict; Phase 4: the acceleration of negative acts and labeling of the target; and Phase 5: the elimination of the target from the workplace or unit within it.

Kenneth Westhues, the Canadian sociologist, built on the work of Heinz Leymann and investigated multiple cases of workplace mobbing, in particular among academics in higher education. In a highly regarded series of books on workplace mobbing, Westhues (1998, 2004, 2005a, 2005b, 2005c) extended and applied Leymann's definition and understanding of workplace mobbing to his analysis of multiple actual cases.

Noa Davenport, Ruth Schwartz, and Gail Elliott

Noa Zanolli Davenport, Ruth Distler Schwartz, and Gail Pursell Elliott (1999) introduced workplace mobbing into the U.S. employee relations vocabulary via their 1999 book, *Mobbing: Emotional Abuse in the American Workplace*. They defined mobbing this way:

> The mobbing syndrome is a malicious attempt to force a person out of the workplace through unjustified accusations, humiliation, general harassment, emotional abuse, and/or terror.

It is a "ganging up" by the leader(s)—organization, superior, coworker, or subordinate—who rallies others into systematic and frequent "mob-like" behavior.

. . . The result is always injury—physical or mental distress or illness and social misery and, most often, expulsion from the workplace. (Davenport et al., 1999, p. 40)

In America, *bullying* gained a stronger foothold than *mobbing* as a preferred term for employee relations stakeholders and the general public during the first decade of the century. However, the work of these authors would help to keep mobbing in the U.S. work abuse vocabulary as well.

Maureen Duffy and Len Sperry

Maureen Duffy and Len Sperry (2012) define workplace mobbing this way:

Workplace mobbing is nonsexual harassment of a coworker by a group of members of an organization for the purpose of removing the targeted individual(s) from the organization or at least a particular unit of the organization. Mobbing involves individual, group, and organizational dynamics. It predictably results in the humiliation, devaluation, discrediting, and degradation; loss of professional reputation; and, often, removal of the victim from the organization through termination, extended medical leave, or quitting. The results of this typically protracted traumatizing experience are significant financial, career, health, and psychosocial losses or other negative consequences. (p. 52)

Duffy and Sperry's (2012, 2014) definition of workplace mobbing is based on a systemic, integrative approach to understanding workplace abuse and includes the interaction of the individual with the group and with the larger organization—all elements that they see as crucial in the development of workplace mobbing and, hence, as necessary for inclusion in a comprehensive definition. Like other definitions, Duffy and Sperry's includes the fact that workplace mobbing is physically and psychologically health harming. Unlike other definitions, they include the reputational damage and other psychosocial losses that follow workplace mobbing.

In expanding on the inclusion in their definition of the fact that workplace mobbing is a typically traumatizing experience, Duffy and Sperry (2014) state that "it leaves the victim reeling, not knowing what has happened, why it happened, and, most important, what will happen in the future. Being mobbed can take away a victim's sense of safety and security in the world" (p. 1).

BULLYING VS. MOBBING

Researchers and commentators about bullying and mobbing behaviors at work have expressed different views about the relationship between the two terms. At times, these discussions have yielded (usually respectful) differences of opinion.

Einarsen, Hoel, Zapf, and Cooper (2011) recommend avoiding "the trap, often observed in social sciences, where new issues are coming into focus and a plethora of competing terms and concepts are introduced" (pp. 4–5), while gently chiding the United States for falling into it. They further suggest that "in practice, only minor differences exist between the concepts of bullying, harassment, and mobbing" (Einarsen et al., 2011, p. 5). Accordingly, they endorse a more or less interchangeable use of the terms in referring to "the systematic exhibition of aggressive behavior at work directed towards a subordinate, a coworker, or even a superior, as well as the perception of being systematically exposed to such mistreatment while at work" (Einarsen et al., 2011, p. 5).

Duffy and Sperry (2012, 2014) make the case for not conflating mobbing with bullying. They see the primary conditions differentiating mobbing from bullying in the workplace as (1) ganging up or group aggression that is always characteristic of mobbing and (2) organizational participation in mobbing through acts of commission or omission or both against the target. In Leymann's (1990, 1996) multiphase model, organizational involvement in mobbing is specified in Phase 3, and Duffy and Sperry see organizational culture, climate, and leadership as a central feature of this destructive social process. On the other hand, bullying can involve one-on-one aggression and not include the process of ganging up by multiple actors. Additionally, definitions of bullying are silent on the issue of organizational involvement—a basic element of both Leymanns's (1990, 1996) and Duffy and Sperry's (2012, 2014) definitions.

Martin and Peña Saint Martin (2012) prefer the use of the term *mobbing* over *bullying* to avoid conceptual confusion between mobbing and bullying. They suggest that the concept of bullying is most clearly associated for many, especially for those in Latin America and other Spanish-speaking countries, with aggression among schoolchildren. Because of differences in languages and in cultural understandings, it has so far not been possible to arrive at a global consensus of what the best term to describe workplace aggression is. Like Duffy and Sperry (2012, 2014) they also point out that the term *mobbing* always refers to group or collective aggression and is, therefore, more theoretically precise.

For Duffy and Sperry (2014), not conflating bullying and mobbing is particularly important when thinking about interventions to reduce and prevent workplace mobbing. They state, "Understanding the difference between workplace bullying and workplace mobbing is important because you can't solve workplace mobbing by only addressing the bullying behaviors of individuals. Since organizations are the incubators of workplace mobbing, solving the problem of mobbing requires awareness and change at the organizational level as well as at the individual level" (Duffy & Sperry, 2014, p. 17). For Duffy and Sperry, the value of theoretical precision and sensitivity makes the case for distinguishing between mobbing and bullying and not conflating the differences between them.

OTHER TERMS RELATED TO BULLYING AND MOBBING AT WORK

Many other terms have been used to describe behaviors typically associated with, or related to, bullying and mobbing. Perhaps the earliest American treatment of this general subject is Carroll M. Brodsky's *The Harassed Worker* (1976), describing workers who had been subjected to mental cruelty on the job that escaped safety protections designed to prevent physical workplace hazards. Other labels have included abusive supervision (Tepper, 2000); lateral violence, horizontal violence, and oppressed group behavior (Roberts, 1984; Vessey, Demarco, Gaffney, & Budin, 2009); emotional abuse (Keashly, 1997); indirect, relational, and social aggression (Archer & Coyne, 2005); disruptive behaviors (The Joint Commission, 2008); chronic work trauma (Stennett-Brewer, 1997); relational aggression (Dellasega, 2009); and incivility (Pearson & Porath, 2009). Below is a closer look at several terms that have been offered during the past two decades.

Work Abuse

On the eve of workplace bullying and mobbing entering the lexicon of American employee relations, therapists Judith Wyatt and Chauncey Hare invoked the term *work abuse* to largely describe the same cluster of behaviors (Wyatt & Hare, 1997). In their 1997 book, they define work abuse as the "demeaning or brutalizing of a person through patterned ways of interacting at work that are mostly denied" (Wyatt & Hare, 1997, p. 373). These behaviors generally fall into four categories: "Ongoing (Neglectful) Abuse," "Chronic Scapegoating," "Acute Scapegoating," and "Denial of Due Process" (Wyatt & Hare, 1997, p. 8).

Wyatt and Hare (1997) are especially critical of any tendency to conflate work stress and work abuse. Work stress is often a euphemism for work abuse and is invoked when people who are "routinely misused within a work system" blame the effects on themselves (Wyatt & Hare, 1997, p. 373). The term *work stress*, they believe, "carries society's false implication of self-blame for one's abusive situation" (Wyatt & Hare, 1997, p. 373).

Emotional Abuse

In an early comprehensive literature review and commentary, Loraleigh Keashly (1997) uses the term *emotional abuse* to capture varieties of verbal and nonverbal workplace aggression. She derived from the research seven common dimensions to form an overall definition of emotional abuse at work:

- "'Behavior' can include verbal and nonverbal/physical modes of expression";
- "Constitutes a pattern (vs. a single event)";
- "Includes behavior that is unwelcomed, unwanted, or unsolicited by the target";
- "Involves a violation of a standard of conduct towards or treatment of others or of a person's rights";
- "Results in harm to the target";
- "There is intent or controllability of the action"; and
- "Involves power differences" (Keashly, 1997, pp. 94–96).

Abusive Work Environment

The Healthy Workplace Bill (HWB), authored by David Yamada, serves as the template workplace antibullying legislation for law reform efforts in the United States (Yamada, 2013). The HWB does not use the terms *bullying* or *mobbing* in its key operational and definitional language. Rather, use of the term *abusive work environment* as a proxy for workplace bullying reflects the author's decision to make the proposed bill language more legally congruent with protections against harassment based on protected class status, such as sexual harassment.

The Healthy Workplace Bill defines its primary cause of action as follows: "It shall be an unlawful employment practice under this Chapter to subject an employee to an abusive work environment as defined by this Chapter" (Yamada, 2013, p. 352). Within the bill language, the critical definition is "abusive work environment," which "exists when an employer or one or more of its employees, acting with intent to cause pain or distress to an employee, subjects that employee to abusive conduct that causes physical harm, psychological harm, or both" (Yamada, 2013, p. 351). As explained in chapter 18, "abusive conduct" is further defined in ways that capture bullying and mobbing behaviors (Yamada, 2013, p. 351).

Abusive Supervision

Abusive supervision is a term used to describe a type of workplace abuse that occurs between a supervisor and subordinate, in which the abuse is top-down and carried out within the context of a relationship in which there are clear power differentials. The characteristic behaviors are excessive criticism, faultfinding, nitpicking, micromanagement, and excessive supervision or scrutiny. Ben Tepper (2000) defines abusive supervision as "subordinates' perceptions of the extent to which supervisors engage in the sustained display of hostile verbal and nonverbal behaviors, excluding physical contact" (p. 178). Tepper's (2000) definition is based on the subjective assessment of the subordinate under supervision. However, the concept of abusive supervision has evolved to the point that certain supervisory behaviors (i.e., excessive criticism, faultfinding, etc.) are now generally regarded as intrinsically hostile or abusive, irrespective of whether the subordinate views them that way or not.

Workplace Violence and Psychological Violence

American conceptualizations of *workplace violence* commonly emphasize physical aggression, physical harm, and criminal behavior. For example, here is one of the early contemporary framings of the topic, courtesy of workplace violence expert Raymond Flannery:

> Offices, courts, schools, and healthcare settings are no longer safe havens from crime. The four major societal crimes of homicide, assault, rape, and robbery have now become frequent visitors to the workplace.... While we shall look more closely at the specific nature of these crimes, ... the general national statistics suggest that violence in society and in the workplace has become a major public health problem for our country. (Flannery, 1995, p. 5)

Some definitions leave room for purely verbal and nonverbal, nonphysical behavior, while continuing to focus on physically violent behavior that overlaps with criminal activity. For example, the U.S. Occupational Safety and Health Administration (2002) uses this definition: "Workplace violence is violence or the threat of violence against workers. It can occur at or outside the workplace and can range from threats and verbal abuse to physical assaults and homicide, one of the leading causes of job-related deaths" (p. 1).

Also, the National Institute for Occupational Safety and Health (2006), the workplace-safety research arm of the federal government, has a classification system that labels "worker-on-worker" violence as Type III Violence, which may include "verbal violence (e.g., threats, verbal abuse, hostility, harassment) and other forms, such as stalking" (p. 4).

The Namies, among others in the United States, have attempted to bridge the gap by using the term *psychological violence* to describe bullying (Namie & Namie, 2009, p. 1). They appear to be on strong international ground, with both the International Labour Organization (Chappell & DiMartino, 2006) and the World Health Organization (Cassitto, Fattorini, Gilioli, & Rengo, 2003) also referring to bullying and mobbing behaviors as psychological violence and including them under the workplace violence rubric. While this may be an accurate characterization of forms of severe nonphysical aggression, the term is not widely used in the American employment context.

Workplace Incivility

Workplace incivility has been defined as "the exchange of seemingly inconsequential inconsiderate words and deeds that violate conventional norms of workplace conduct" (Pearson & Porath, 2009, p. 12). Incivility researchers Christine Pearson and Christine Porath give as examples "interrupting a conversation," "talking loudly in common areas," "arriving late," "not introducing a newcomer," "failing to return a phone call," and "showing little interest in another individual's opinion" (Pearson & Porath, 2009, p. 12).

At times, incivility has been conflated with bullying and mobbing, and sometimes it has been used interchangeably, especially in the popular media. Furthermore, incivility research is sometimes used to buttress analyses of more severe forms of workplace mistreatment. In logical terms, it could be argued that while not every act of incivility rises to the level of bullying or mobbing, many bullying or mobbing behaviors would surely qualify as acts of incivility. Increasingly, however, researchers are distinguishing between incivility on one hand and bullying and mobbing on the other.

Harassment and Hostile Work Environment

Hostile work environment is a legal term used to describe a common form of harassment grounded in protected class status, such as sex or race. Most of the leading case law has developed in the context of sexual harassment (Yamada, 2000). Chapter 18 sets out the U.S. Supreme Court's standard for defining what constitutes a hostile work environment under Title VII of the Civil Rights Act.

At times, those who are not versed in employment discrimination law will invoke this term to describe workplace bullying, aggression, and incivility. This is understandable, for combinations of these behaviors can surely make for hostile work environments. However, this may also create the misleading impression that all bullying-type behaviors are prohibited under employment discrimination laws, which is not the case. Unless it can be shown that harassing behaviors are motivated by the target's protected class status, they do not fall within the prohibitions of the Civil Rights Act and similar protective statutes (Yamada, 2000).

COMMON WORKPLACE BULLYING AND MOBBING BEHAVIORS

As a whole, workplace bullying and mobbing situations cover a gamut of overt and covert behaviors directed at targets. However, none of the core definitions examined here lists the more common bullying and mobbing behaviors. Although these behaviors may be self-evident to many who are consulting these volumes, it may be useful for those who are newer to the general subject matter to see a catalogue of some of the more common forms of workplace abuse. This also helps to put the definitions in context and build a foundation for the remaining chapters.

Workplace Bullying Institute U.S. Survey

The Workplace Bullying Institute's 2007 U.S. scientific survey of workplace bullying provides a useful snapshot of common abusive behaviors at work (WBI, 2007). Under WBI's guidance, the polling firm Zogby International conducted some 7,700 online interviews of a survey group representative of the U.S. population. Among those who indicated they had been subjected to forms of workplace bullying:

- 53 percent reported verbal abuse including "shouting, swearing, name calling, malicious sarcasm, threats to safety, etc.";
- 53 percent reported behaviors and actions, private or public, including "threatening, intimidating, humiliating, hostile, offensive, inappropriately cruel conduct, etc.";
- 47 percent reported abuse of authority, including "undeserved evaluations, denial of advancement, stealing credit, tarnished reputation, arbitrary instructions, unsafe assignments, etc.";
- 45 percent reported "interference with work performance," including "sabotage, undermining, ensuring failure, etc."; and,
- 30 percent reported "destruction of workplace relationships"..."among co-workers, bosses, or customers." (WBI, 2007, p. 12)

Other frequent bullying behaviors reported by survey participants included sexual harassment, defamation and misrepresentation, physical assault, pay and benefit reductions, and terminations without cause (WBI, 2007).

Leymann's Critical Incident Model

Heinz Leymann identified frequent workplace mobbing behaviors as part of a multi-phase critical-incident model leading from mobbing to expulsion (Leymann, 1990). Phase 1 is the critical incident itself, usually an unresolved work conflict that leads supervisors and/or coworkers to resent or dislike the victim. Phase 2 is the actual mobbing or stigmatizing of the victim, which includes a range of negative acts against the victim, including removal from the workplace. Specific behaviors may include:

- Injuring the victim's personal reputation, including "rumor mongering, slandering, holding up to ridicule";
- Directing or limiting communications, such as undermining the victim's ability to communicate, giving the silent treatment, or "continual loud-voiced criticism and meaningful [hostile] glances";
- Physical and social isolation of the victim;
- Undermining the victim's ability to work, including withholding work assignments or giving the victim "humiliating or meaningless work tasks"; and,
- Directing "violence and threats of violence" at the victim. (Leymann, 1990, p. 121)

Phase 3 involves more formal management activity that "turns the person into a marked individual" through negative formal evaluations of job performance and negative assessments of suitability for continued employment. Phase 4 is the acceleration of abuse and the negative labeling of the target. Finally, phase 5 culminates in the expulsion of the victim from the organization.

Individual Situations May Vary

Individual aggressors may have their favored tactics and strategies, and patterns of abusive behaviors may emerge in certain types of work settings. Many of the negative acts and patterns of negative acts in bullying and mobbing are sadly predictable. However, it would be risky to presume that there are uniform sets of bullying and mobbing behaviors for given situations. Indeed, while some occurrences of work abuse are ordinary and foreseeable in terms of the behaviors described above, we are continually amazed and appalled at the inventive combinations of mistreatment that can be directed at targets.

Accordingly, specific instances of mobbing and bullying typically involve varying combinations of these hostile behaviors and negative acts. Based on our familiarity with hundreds of bullying and mobbing situations, a multitude of contextual factors shapes the choices of abusive behaviors enacted by aggressors. These include, among other things, power relationships grounded in organizational hierarchies and interpersonal dynamics, legal relationships, the number and nature of key actors, institutional resources available to aggressors, and motivations driving the mistreatment. Furthermore, in given situations the types of bullying and mobbing behaviors may change over time, depending upon the status of those targeted and the roles of those enlisted to participate in the abuse.

KEY ELEMENTS OF DEFINITIONS

Obviously, the foregoing definitions of bullying, mobbing, and related terms vary in some ways. Taken as a whole, however, they lead us to a largely shared cluster of key elements.

Negative Acts

All of the core definitions of bullying and mobbing include negative acts. For example, Adams refers to "vindictive, cruel, malicious or humiliating attempts to undermine" targets (Ellis, 2011, p. 2). Namie and Namie (2009) cite "verbal abuse; conduct or behaviors that are threatening, intimidating, or humiliating; sabotage that prevents works from getting done; or some combination of the three" (p. 1). And Duffy and Sperry (2012) describe "devaluation, discrediting, and degradation; loss of professional reputation; and, often, removal of the victim from the organization" (p. 52). Lists of specific negative behaviors, however, are usually reserved for subsequent commentary following the definitions.

Many commentators would readily acknowledge that bullying and mobbing are dignity-denying forms of mistreatment. However, only Keashly's (1997) definition expressly describes the harm in terms of societal norms and rights, noting that workplace emotional abuse "involves a violation of a standard of conduct towards or treatment of others or of a person's rights" (p. 95).

Intention

Most definitions and explanations of workplace bullying and mobbing, as well as definitions of related terms, include an element of intent by an aggressor, either explicitly or implicitly. For example, in defining workplace bullying, Namie and Namie (2009) refer to an aggressor's "personal agenda of controlling another human being" (p. 1). Duffy and Sperry (2014), in describing workplace mobbing, refer to how "individuals, groups, or organizations target a person for ridicule, humiliation, and removal from the workplace" (p. 1). Yamada's (2013) legal conceptualization of an abusive work environment includes "intent to cause pain or distress to an employee" (p. 351). By contrast, Einarsen, Hoel, Zapf, and Cooper state that bullying "may be carried out deliberately or unconsciously" (2011, p. 9).

A 2009 survey of human resources practitioners by Teresa Daniel and Gary Metcalf (2016) exploring distinctions between perceived workplace bullies and tough bosses suggested that intent matters. Interviews of survey respondents indicated that the presence of malice created a dividing line between bullying and tough management: "Participants were able to articulate clear distinctions between a bully and a tough boss. The 'so what' of this study was our finding that it is the presence or absence of *malice* that determines whether a conflict at work is actually workplace bullying, with malice defined as "the desire to cause pain, injury, or distress to another" (Daniel & Metcalf, 2016, p. 31).

Frequency and Duration

Under Leymann's definition (1990, p. 120), "these actions take place often (almost every day) and over a long period (at least for six months)." Other core definitions are less specific, with the Namies (2009, p. 1) referring to "repeated" behaviors and Einarsen, Hoel, Zapf, and Cooper (2011, p. 9) referring to "repeated actions and practises." Furthermore, as noted by Keashly (1997), the behaviors present a pattern as opposed to being a single event. In general, we may presume that the greater the frequency and duration of the mistreatment, the more likely it is to be considered a form of bullying or mobbing. Specifications of frequency and duration are also likely to appear in survey instruments measuring prevalence rates.

Negative Impacts

Virtually every definition of bullying, mobbing, or similar terms includes negative health impacts on targets. Namie and Namie (2009) refer to "health-harming" effects (p. 1), while Einarsen and colleagues (2011) describe "severe social, psychological, and psychosomatic problems" (p. 4). Duffy and Sperry (2014) include "deteriorating physical and mental health" (p. 1), and add to that the disorientation experienced by targets who are left "reeling, not knowing what has happened, why it happened, and . . . what will happen in the future" (p. 1). In the legal context, Yamada's conceptualization of an "abusive work environment" requires "physical harm, psychological harm, or both" to state a valid cause of action (2013, p. 351).

The core definitions tend not to delve into forms of collateral damage facing targets, including psychosocial impacts such as vocational and professional identities, future employability and career prospects, and impairment of family and personal relationships. They also tend to omit the significant costs of these behaviors to employers and organizations. However, the cited commentators and researchers discuss these factors at length in their major works.

Number and Roles of Actors

Most of the core definitions anticipate a single target. However, Adams refers to attempts to undermine an "individual or groups of employees" (Ellis, 2011, p. 2), and Einarsen, Hoel, Zapf, and Cooper (2011) refer to behaviors "that are directed against one or more workers" (p. 9). This raises the question of whether negative acts directed at a larger number of workers somehow lose "eligibility" to be deemed bullying or mobbing, perhaps at some stage falling into the category of very bad management rather than targeted aggression.

In terms of aggressors, both the bullying and mobbing definitions generally anticipate the possibility of more than one actor participating in the abusive behaviors. Davenport, Schwartz, and Elliott (1999) invoke the more emotionally laden "ganging up" (p. 40) in their definition of mobbing.

FRAMING CONCEPTS FOR TERMS AND DEFINITIONS

Organizational Culture and Responsibility

The basic definitions provided here focus on central actors, intentions, behaviors, and impacts. Most of the core definitions do not branch into the roles of organizational cultures in discouraging or enabling the underlying behaviors, nor do they address questions of institutional responsibility when such behaviors occur. Duffy and Sperry (2012) are unique in this respect in that they include "mobbing involves individual, group, and organizational dynamics" (p. 52) in their definition. Nonetheless, learned researchers and commentators readily acknowledge the organizational implications of bullying and mobbing, including the central role of top leadership in establishing workplace cultures. These behaviors are especially prevalent in organizations with more pronounced hierarchical structures (Grubb, Roberts, Swanson, Burnfield, & Childress, 2005).

Power Imbalances and Differentials

Of the core definitions shared here, Keashly (1997) expressly mentions power differentials between aggressors and targets; Adams refers to the "abuse of power or position" (Ellis, 2011, p. 2); and Leymann includes the inevitable role of management or administration (1990, 1996). Surveys covering workplace bullying in America consistently show supervisors and bosses as the most likely aggressors by a significant margin over peers and coworkers, with subordinates coming a distant last (Namie & Namie, 2009). More fundamentally, bullying and mobbing behaviors are, by their very nature, exercises of power over another because of organizational rank and culture, individual personalities, demographics, and perceived target vulnerabilities.

IMPLICATIONS OF TERMS AND DEFINITIONS

The public at large, academic researchers, labor and employee relations practitioners, legal and dispute resolution institutions, and mental health providers are among the stakeholders whose interests are implicated by how we label and define workplace bullying, mobbing, and related behaviors.

Public Education, Dialogue, and Understanding

The benefits of naming, labeling, and defining behaviors can be considerable. Both authors can attest to having people targeted by workplace bullying and mobbing reporting that they had no idea what they were enduring until they discovered articles, Web sites, and blogs using these terms and explaining the underlying behaviors and their impacts. The terms and definitions resonated with these individuals and often captured their experiences.

Whether dealing with individuals, organizations, or society as a whole, the naming of recurring behaviors in our lives may help us to develop a contextual understanding of our experiences. Consider, for example, how the term *sexual harassment* has changed our understanding of employment relations, discrimination, and gender. Until the underlying behaviors were named, women so targeted had no easy way to refer to them. Today, however, the term *sexual harassment* is well understood and has significant personal, societal, and legal meanings.

Of course, there are risks that come with using such familiar words as *bullying* and *mobbing*. Both terms carry differing cultural connotations that may add emotional components to the definitions offered above and elsewhere. For example, over the years, the authors have fielded claims that bullying is too soft a label to adequately capture the damage wrought by the underlying behaviors, while encountering others who believe the term is too heavy-handed. To further illustrate, mobbing may conjure up images of angry assemblies of people carrying pitchforks, whereas workplace mobbing may actually be much more strategic and multidirectional in nature.

Furthermore, adapting these terms to label workplace aggressors involves potential stigmatization. Most would not want to be branded a bully or a mobber, and some may face retaliation, retribution, or ostracism after being publicly tagged as such.

Research

In designing and conducting research studies about workplace bullying and mobbing, definitions may play a significant role. For example, definitions will help to inform lists of behaviors or scales used by researchers in prevalence surveys. Furthermore, definitions may shape questions posed to survey respondents or interviewees in qualitative studies. Further evidence of this will be found in chapter 2 (prevalence of bullying and mobbing).

The use of labels or terms in survey research may be more problematic. As discussed above, *bullying* and *mobbing* may carry strong connotations. Invoking terms (e.g., "Have you ever been bullied at work?") rather than behaviors may project meanings to respondents or invite them to make up their own, thus subjectively influencing their answers to survey questions.

Mental Health Care

If a client or patient approaches a mental health care provider with a personal account about, say, domestic abuse or sexual harassment, then using the label will likely provide a common base of understanding for both parties that can inform further discussion and eventual therapeutic and treatment options. It can potentially be so with workplace bullying and mobbing.

However, for two reasons, we are not quite there yet. First, unlike sexual harassment, the terms are not sufficiently well-known that workers will necessarily invoke them when confronted by the behaviors. Second, the mental health community is not adequately informed on this overall topic, resulting in too many situations being dismissed or misunderstood as ordinary conflicts and stressors of a job (see chapters 13 and 14 for a fuller discussion). However, levels of understanding are widening and deepening, and it is eminently foreseeable that targets of bullying and mobbing will get more hospitable and understanding receptions from mental health providers in the years to come.

Labor and Employee Relations

Terms and definitions matter greatly for ground-level applications in labor and employee relations. As explained in chapter 18, collective bargaining agreements and, in many jurisdictions, employee handbooks have contractual force. If provisions covering bullying and mobbing behaviors are included in such documents, then nearly every key word or phrase carries potential legal significance for employees and employers. If an employment policy refers to generic bullying or mobbing but does not define the term in terms of conduct or behavior, then in the event of litigation, it may be left to a legal tribunal to adopt a definition.

Law and Public Policy

Specific words and phrases matter greatly in law and public policy, including those covering bullying and mobbing behaviors. Courts and administrative tribunals will look first to specific terms and definitions in legislation and regulations to clarify the scope of coverage of legal protections and obligations. In the case of laws that explicitly cover bullying and mobbing behaviors, definitions contained within will be controlling.

Conflict Resolution

Labels, definitions, and accompanying legal norms may significantly influence the roles of conflict resolution mechanisms, including alternative dispute resolution modalities. If bullying and mobbing are acknowledged as forms of interpersonal mistreatment or abuse, then conflict resolution systems are more likely to recognize the possibilities of wrongful behavior and exploitation of power differentials. If these behaviors are classified as forms of interpersonal conflict, then parties are more likely to be treated as equals who cannot resolve their differences privately.

MAKING ROOM FOR A BIG TENT

In this chapter, we set out a basic landscape of terms and definitions that will inform and help to frame subsequent chapters in these two volumes. We hope that we have done so in a way that creates room for different preferences and opinions on terminology related to these destructive workplace behaviors.

REFERENCES

Adams, A. (1992). *Bullying at work: How to confront and overcome it*. London: Virago.
Archer, J., & Coyne, S. M. (2005). An integrated review of indirect, relational, and social aggression. *Personality and Social Psychology Review, 9*(3), 212–230.
Brodsky, C. M. (1976). *The harassed worker*. Lexington, MA: Lexington Books.
Cassitto, M. G., Fattorini, E., Gilioli, R., & Rengo, C. (2003). *Raising awareness of psychological harassment at work*. R. Gilioli & M. A. Fingerhut (Eds.). Retrieved from http://www.who.int/occupational_health/publications/en/oehharassmentc.pdf
Chappell, D., & DiMartino, V. (2006). *Violence at work* (3rd ed.). Geneva, Switzerland: International Labour Office.
Daniel, T. A., & Metcalf, G. S. (2016). *Stop bullying at work: Strategies and tools for HR, legal, & risk management professionals* (2nd ed.). Alexandria, VA: Society for Human Resource Management.
Davenport, N., Schwartz, R. D., & Elliott, G. P. (1999). *Mobbing: Emotional abuse in the American workplace*. Ames, IA: Civil Society Publishing.

Dellasega, C. A. (2009). Bullying among nurses: Relational aggression is one form of workplace bullying: What can nurses do about it? *American Journal of Nursing, 109*(1), 52–58.

Dewey, J. (2007). *How we think.* New York: Cosimo Classics. (Original work published 1910.)

Duffy, M., & Sperry, L. (2012). *Mobbing: Causes, consequences, and solutions.* New York: Oxford University Press.

Duffy, M., & Sperry, L. (2014). *Overcoming mobbing: A recovery guide for workplace aggression and bullying.* New York: Oxford University Press.

Einarsen, S., Hoel, H., Zapf, D., & Cooper, C. L. (Eds.). (2011). *Bullying and harassment in the workplace: Developments in theory, research, and practice* (2nd ed.). London: CRC Press.

Ellis, A. (2011). *Andrea Adams, British pioneer: Bio and text of 1994 speech.* Retrieved from http://workplacebullying.org/multi/pdf/adams.pdf

Flannery, R. B., Jr. (1995). *Violence in the workplace.* New York: Crossroad.

Grubb, P. L., Roberts, R. K., Swanson, N. G., Burnfield, J. L., & Childress, J. H. (2005). Organizational factors and psychological aggression: Results from a nationally representative sample of US companies. In V. Bowie, B. S. Fisher, & C. L. Cooper (Eds.), *Workplace violence issues, trends, strategies* (pp. 37–59). Portland, OR: Willan Publishing.

The Joint Commission. (2008). Behaviors that undermine a culture of safety. *Sentinel Event Alert, 40.* Retrieved from https://www.jointcommission.org/assets/1/18/SEA_40.PDF

Keashly, L. (1997). Emotional abuse in the workplace: Conceptual and empirical issues. *Journal of Emotional Abuse, 1*v1), 85–117.

Keeney, B. P. (1983). *Aesthetics of change.* New York: Guilford Press.

Leymann, H. (1990). Mobbing and psychological terror at workplaces. *Violence and Victims, 5*(2), 119–126.

Leymann, H. (1996). The content and development of mobbing at work. In D. Zapf & H. Leymann (Eds.), *Mobbing and victimization at work* (pp. 165–184). Hove, England: Psychology Press.

Martin, B., & Peña Saint Martin, F. (2012). Mobbing and suppression: Footprints of their relationships. *Social Medicine, 6*(4), 218–226.

Namie, G., & Namie, R. (1999). *Bullyproof yourself at work!: Personal strategies to recognize and stop the hurt from harassment.* Benicia, CA: DoubleDoc Press.

Namie, G., & Namie, R. (2009). *The bully at work.* Naperville, IL: Sourcebooks.

Namie, G., & Namie, R. (2011). *The bully-free workplace: Stop jerks, weasels and snakes from killing your organization.* Hoboken, NJ: John Wiley & Sons.

National Institute for Occupational Safety and Health. (2006). *Workplace violence prevention strategies and research needs: Report from the conference partnering in workplace violence prevention, translating research into practice* (DHHS NIOSH Publication No. 2006-144). Retrieved from https://www.cdc.gov/niosh/docs/2006-144/pdfs/2006-144.pdf

Occupational Safety and Health Administration. (2002). *OSHA fact sheet: Workplace violence* Retrieved from https://www.osha.gov/OshDoc/data_General_Facts/factsheet-workplace-violence.pdf

Pearson, C., & Porath, P. (2009). *The cost of bad behavior: How incivility is damaging your business and what to do about it*. New York: Portfolio.

Roberts, S. J. (1983). Oppressed group behavior: Implications for nursing. *Advanced Nursing Science, 5*(3), 21–30.

Stennett-Brewer, L. (1997). *Trauma in the workplace: The book about chronic work trauma*. Decatur, IL: Nepenthe Publications.

Tepper, B. J. (2000). Consequences of abusive supervision. *Academy of Management Journal, 43*(2), 178–190.

Vessey, J., Demarco, R., Gaffney, D., & Budin, W. (2009). Bullying of staff registered nurses in the workplace: A preliminary study for developing personal and organizational strategies for the transformation of hostile to healthy workplace environments. *Journal of Professional Nursing, 25*(5), 299–306. doi:10.1016/j.profnurs.2009.01.022

Westhues, K. (1998). *Eliminating professors: A guide to the dismissal process*. Lewiston, NY: Edwin Mellen Press.

Westhues, K. (2004). *Workplace mobbing in academe: Reports from twenty universities*. Lewiston, NY: Edwin Mellen Press.

Westhues, K. (2005a). *The envy of excellence: Administrative mobbing of high-achieving professors*. Lewiston, NY: The Tribunal for Academic Justice/Edwin Mellen Press.

Westhues, K. (2005b). *The pope versus the professor: Benedict XVI and the legitimation of mobbing*. Lewiston, NY: The Tribunal for Academic Justice/Edwin Mellen Press.

Westhues, K. (Ed.) (2005c). *Winning, losing, moving on: How professionals deal with workplace harassment and mobbing*. Lewiston, NY: The Edwin Mellen Press.

Workplace Bullying Institute (WBI). (2007). *2007 U.S. workplace bullying survey*. Retrieved from http://workplacebullying.org/multi/pdf/WBIsurvey2007.pdf

Wyatt, J., & Hare, C. (1997) *Work abuse: How to recognize and survive it*. Rochester, VT: Schenkman Books.

Yamada, D. C. (2000). The phenomenon of "workplace bullying" and the need for status-blind hostile work environment protection. *Georgetown Law Journal, 88*(3), 475–536.

Yamada, D. C. (2013). Emerging American legal responses to workplace bullying. *Temple Political & Civil Rights Law Review, 22*(2), 329–354.

2

Prevalence of Workplace Bullying and Mobbing among U.S. Working Adults: What Do the Numbers Mean?

Loraleigh Keashly

Aggression and hostility are unfortunately part of the workplace landscape for many people (Kelloway, Barling, & Hurrell, 2006). The U.S. Centers for Disease Control and Prevention through their workplace arm, the National Institute of Occupational Health and Safety (NIOSH), have identified workplace aggression as a significant risk to workers (Wiegand et al., 2012). National surveys such as the General Social Survey (GSS) and the National Health Interview Survey (NHIS) include items regarding exposure to workplace violence, aggression, harassment, and bullying, which permits tracking of the rates of these experiences over time in the general population. These data inform public policy and responding. A 2002 representative national survey of over 2,500 U.S. wage and salary workers found that 6 percent experienced workplace violence and 41.4 percent experienced psychological aggression at work during the previous 12 months (Schat, Frone, & Kelloway, 2006). Such exposure is harmful for the individual, other workers, the organization, and beyond (Einarsen, Hoel, & Zapf, 2011).

Workplace bullying and mobbing are unique phenomena in the domain of workplace aggression in that they are not discrete events or behaviors; rather, they are grounded in ongoing relationships with particular others, and thus are enduring and persistent forms of aggression (Keashly & Jagatic, 2011). Numerically, these relationships are not as frequent as general exposure to aggressive behavior; however, their effects are stronger, more wide-ranging, and longer lasting (McGinley, Richman, & Rospenda, 2011). Over the past two decades in the United States, there has been an increasing interest in understanding and addressing workplace bullying and mobbing from a variety of quarters, for example, researchers, governmental agencies, employee advocate groups, professional organizations, and service providers. This is an exciting development and bodes well for the political and public will to address this pressing public health problem.

In this chapter, we will explore the prevalence, or size, of the workplace bullying and mobbing problem in the United States. To fully understand the numbers, we need to consider how bullying and mobbing are operationalized and measured, the time referent utilized (e.g., past month, 6 months, a year, working career), and the source, as well as the nature of the samples upon which prevalence estimates are based. To give you a sense of why understanding the basis for the numbers is important, the studies reviewed here provide rates for bullying and mobbing ranging from 7 percent to 96 percent among U.S. workers (see table 2.1). Thus, what is "real," and why is it important to know that? Understanding what these numbers reflect has implications for how workplace bullying and mobbing are perceived and ultimately addressed.

DEFINING ELEMENTS OF WORKPLACE BULLYING AND MOBBING: WHAT DISTINGUISHES THEM FROM THE REST?

To ensure that our measurement captures workplace bullying and mobbing, the distinctive features of these phenomena need to be incorporated in our assessment. In addition to negative behavior, our measurement needs to permit or include the assessment of repetition, duration, pattern or variety, and the power differential between actor and target (Hershcovis, 2011; Keashly & Jagatic, 2003; Lutgen-Sandvik, Tracy, & Alberts, 2007; Nielsen, Matthiesen, & Einarsen, 2010; Yamada, Duffy, & Berry, this volume). Repetition is often assessed through frequency of occurrence, duration through the chosen time referent, and pattern through a number of different behaviors and occasionally the severity or intensity of behaviors. The power differential is relevant because of how it influences the target's ability to effectively cope or respond. Some measurement assesses the organizational or social power differences between the actor and target, with the implication that the coping abilities of the target are impeded. Other measures specifically include the impact of not being able to defend oneself. While critical to distinguishing workplace bullying and mobbing conceptually, these elements (individually and together) have also been tied to the nature of the impact on and experience of the target and others in the environment (Fox & Stallworth, 2010; Hershcovis, 2011; Keashly & Neuman, 2002). Yamada, Duffy, and Berry (this volume) argue that intent is an element of workplace bullying and mobbing.

Conceptually, intent is relevant in the distinction between occasional aggressive exposure and bullying and mobbing, and it is also notoriously difficult to verify and thus measure (Matthiesen & Einarsen, 2010). Perceived intentionality is thus not often included in measurement. For this chapter,

Table 2.1 Studies of Workplace Bullying and Mobbing in the United States

Study and Data Collection Date	Sample	Method/Operationalization	Time Frame Duration	Rates	Actors
Schat et al., 2006 Collected in 2002–2003	U.S. workers (representative random sample) N = 2,508 (57% response rate)	Telephone interview Behavioral checklist (5 items psychological aggression; 4 items physical aggression)	Prior 12 months	Psych aggression: 41.4% ≥ 1 event 13% ≥ 1 event/weekly Physical aggression: 6% ≥ 1 event 1.3% ≥ 1 event/weekly	All aggression: Customers ≥ Coworkers ≥ Superior
Lutgen-Sandvik et al., 2007 Collected in 2006	U.S. workers; N = 403;	Online survey NAQ-R (behavioral checklist; 22 items) + single item def'n Def'n: "... bullying as a situation where one or several individuals perceive themselves to be on the receiving end of negative actions from one or more persons persistently over a period of time, in a situation where the targets have difficulty defending themselves against these actions. We do not refer to a one-time incident as bullying."	Prior 6 months Prior 6–12 months	46.8% ≥ 1 event/weekly 28% ≥ 2 events/weekly **Self-identify:** 9.7% prior 6–12 months 29.8% prior working career **Witness:** 10.9% prior 6–12 months	Not asked
Rospenda et al., 2008 Collected in 2003–2004	U.S. workers (representative random sample) N = 2151 (52% response rate)	Phone survey GWH (behavioral checklist) scale + single item "In the past 12 months at work, have you been discriminated or harassed for any other reason (excluding race and sex)?"	Prior 12 months	63% ≥ 1 event during 12 months **Self-identify:** 12% prior 12 months Females ≥ males	Not asked

(Continued)

Table 2.1 Continued

Study and Data Collection Date	Sample	Method/Operationalization	Time Frame Duration	Rates	Actors
Workplace Bullying Institute, 2007 (Lutgen-Sandvik & Namie, 2009) Collected in 2007	U.S. workers (representative random sample) N = 7,740	Online survey Single item def'n "At work, have you experienced or witnessed any or all of the following types of repeated mistreatment: sabotage by others that prevented work being done, verbal abuse, threatening conduct, intimidation, humiliation?"	Prior 12 months; working career	**Self-identify:** 12.6% prior 12 months 24.2% working career excl. prior 12 months **Witness:** 12.3% in working career **Actor:** 0.4%	Superior 72.5% Peer 17.4% Subordinate 8.5%
Workplace Bullying Institute, 2010 Collected in 2010	U.S. workers (representative random sample) N = 2,092	Online survey Single item def'n "At work, have you experienced or witnessed any or all of the following types of repeated mistreatment: sabotage by others that prevented work being done, verbal abuse, threatening conduct, intimidation, humiliation?"	Prior 12 months; working career	**Self-identify:** 8.8% prior 12 months 25.7% working career excl. prior 12 months **Witness:** 15.5% in working career **Actor:** 0.3%	Males ≥ Females Same-sex bullying 64% in 12 months
Workplace Bullying Institute, 2014 Collected in 2014	U.S. workers (representative random sample) N = 1,000	Online survey Single item def'n "At work, what has been your personal experience with the following types of repeated mistreatment: abusive conduct that is threatening, intimidating, humiliating, work sabotage or verbal abuse?"	Prior 12 months; working career	**Self-identify:** 7% prior 12 months 20% working career excl. prior 12 months People of color ≥ Whites **Witness:** 21% • 11% saw it • 10% know it happened **Actor:** 0.5%	Superior 56% Peer 33% Subordinate 11% Multiple actors 23% Males ≥ Females Same-sex bullying 77% in 12 months

Lipscomb et al., 2015 **Collected in 2009–2010**	State unionized public sector employees (4 agencies; NE state) N = 11,874 (response rate 71.8%)	Online survey NAQ-R (behavioral checklist; six items) + single item def'n "Bullying can be described as having taken place when abusive behavior is repeated over a period of time and when the victim experiences difficulties in defending himself or herself in this situation. It is not bullying if the incident does not occur repeatedly."	Prior 6 months	44.2% ≥ 1 event in 6 months • 35.4% less than weekly • 8.8% ≥ 1 event/weekly **Self-identify:** 10% in 6 months • 7.6% less than weekly (occasional bullying) • 2.4% at least weekly (regular bullying) *Rate of self-identification varies by agency.	Superior ≥ Peer ≥ Subordinate
VitalSmarts, 2014 **Collected in 2014**	U.S. workers N = 2,283	Online survey Behavioral checklist (8 items)	Currently and in working career	63% ≥ 1 event currently 96% ≥ 1 event ever	Superior 52% Peer 36% Subordinate 11%
CareerBuilder, 2014 **Collected in 2014**	U.S. private sector workers (representative probability sample) N = 3,372	Online survey Single item def'n "Bullying has been defined as unwanted, aggressive behavior that involves a real or perceived power imbalance. The behavior is often repeated over time. Bullying includes actions such as making threats, spreading rumors, attacking someone physically or verbally, and excluding someone from a group on purpose."	Currently and in working career	**Self-identify:** 7% currently 28% in working career Females 34% self-identify Males 22% self-identify	Superior 33% Peer 19% Customer 19% Multiple actors 29% Note: Multiple responses were permitted.

(Continued)

Table 2.1 Continued

Study and Data Collection Date	Sample	Method/Operationalization	Time Frame Duration	Rates	Actors
Keashly & Jagatic, 2000 Collected in 1999	U.S. adults in Michigan (stratified random representative sample) N = 1,189 N = 898 worked in prior 12 months	Telephone interview Behavioral checklist (17 items) + single item "Have you felt mistreated by someone at work?"	Prior 12 months and working career	65.4% at least one event • 47% monthly or less • 18.4% at least weekly **Self-identify:** 27% prior 12 months • 16.7% bothered them a lot • 42% working career • 26.8% bothered them a lot	Supervisors 43.9% Coworkers 41.4% Subordinate 4.0% Other 9.7% Males = Females Same race Supervisor 65.2% Coworker 24.8% Subordinate 2.6% Other 9.4% Male = Female Same race
Burnazi, Keashly, & Neuman, 2005 Collected in 2004	U.S. working adults in Michigan (stratified random representative sample) N = 438	Telephone survey Behavioral checklist (top 10 WAR-Q items) + single item "Have you felt repeatedly or persistently mistreated by someone at work?"	Prior 12 months and working career	71% ≥ 1 event • 57% monthly or less • 14% at least weekly **Self-identify:** 10% prior 12 months • 6.8% bothered them a lot • 3.5% mistreated at least weekly	Supervisor 70.7% Coworker 9.8% Subordinate 2.4% Customer 2.4% Male = Female
National Health Interview Survey; DHHS, 2010; Alterman et al., 2013 Collected in 2010	U.S. workers N = 17,524	In-person interview; Single item "Were you threatened, bullied, or harassed by anyone while you were on the job?"	Prior 12 months	**Self-identify:** 7.8% in overall sample • industry differences	Not asked

General Social Survey Quality of Worklife Module (2014) **Collected in 2002, 2006, 2010, 2014**	U.S. adults ≥ 18 years (representative sample); those who worked in past 12 months 2002 N = 1,796 2006 N = 1,734 2010 N = 1,187 2014 N = 1,250	In-person interview Single item "Were you threatened or harassed in any other way by anyone while you were on the job?" (Excluding harassment due to sex, race, and age)	Prior 12 months	**Self-identify:** 2002 11.2% 2006 8.7% 2010 9.4% 2014 8.1% Not asked
Grubb et al., 2004 (NIOSH) **Collected in 2002–2003**	U.S. organizations N = 516 (62% response rate); key informant responded	Telephone survey Single item def'n "How often in the past year has bullying occurred at your establishment, including repeated intimidation, slandering, social isolation, or humiliation by one or more persons against another?"	Prior 12 months	24.5% some degree of bullying 7.1% frequent incidents Targets: Employees 55.2% Supervisor 7.7% Customer 10.5% Nonprofit ≥ Profit Unionized ≥ Nonunion Large org'n ≥ Small Supervisor 14.7% Coworker 39.2% Customer 24.5%
Society for Human Resource Management, 2012 **Collected in 2011**	HR professionals with SHRM membership N = 401 (15% response rate)	Single item def'n "Persistent, offensive, abusive, intimidating or insulting behavior or unfair actions directed at another individual, causing the recipient to feel threatened, abused, humiliated or vulnerable. Workplace bullies and targets may be employees, clients or vendors of the affected organization."	In experience with current organization In own career	51% bullying incidents in org'n Large org'n ≥ Small 27% of respondents indicated being bullied in career

(Continued)

Table 2.1 Continued

Study and Data Collection Date	Sample	Method/Operationalization	Time Frame Duration	Rates	Actors
USPS; Califano et al., 2000 Collected in 1999	1. USPS workers $N = 11,932$ (65.1% response rate) 2. U.S. workers (random representative sample) $N = 3,009$ (63.3% response rate)	Paper survey **Experienced:** Behavioral checklist (six items) on verbal abuse **Witnessed:** Single item def'n "About how often did you see someone at work do ... verbal abuse such as shouting, swearing trying to provoke an argument calling someone a name putting them down in front of others, making intimidating or threatening gestures?"	Prior 12 months; working career	**Experienced:** **USPS Sample** 61.2% ≥ 1 event ever 37% in past year • 75.3% notably upset **National Sample** 47.6% ≥ 1 event ever 35.7% in past year • 67.1% notably upset **Witnessed:** **USPS Sample** 36.9% at least monthly • 26.7% at least weekly • 10.2% monthly **National Sample** 32.9% at least monthly • 21.5% at least weekly • 11.4% monthly	Supervisor 40.4% Coworker 42.6% Subordinate 3.6% Customer 11.2% Male ≥ Female Supervisor 36.8% Coworker 37% Subordinate 4.2% Customer 13.8% Male ≥ Female

then, we will utilize the elements of repetition, duration, pattern or variety, and the power differential to evaluate the types of measurement that have been used in surveys of U.S. working adults so we can understand what is being measured and thus interpret the statistics accurately.

MEASUREMENT: HOW WE ASK THE QUESTION SHAPES THE ANSWER WE GET

For the purpose of prevalence estimates, there are two primary ways of identifying who has been bullied or mobbed in a survey: self-labeling and behavioral classification. This is a matter of from whose perspective the identification is made.

Self-labeling: I Am a Victim

Known as the *subjective* approach, self-labeling involves asking respondents whether they have been a target of bullying or mobbing at work. As can been seen in table 2.1, some surveys provided a specific definition of bullying or mobbing incorporating, to varying degrees, key definitional elements, and others did not, relying on respondent's own definition of these phenomena. For example, Lipscomb et al. (2015) and Lutgen-Sandvik et al. (2007) utilize the definition developed by well-known bullying researcher Staale Einarsen and his colleagues (Einarsen, Raknes, & Matthiesen, 1994). This definition references negative behaviors, repetition, duration, and an inability to defend oneself. The CareerBuilder (2014) definition includes these elements and also specifically references the power imbalance. These definitions are consistent with those used in scholarly research (Nielsen et al., 2010). The Workplace Bullying Institute (WBI) surveys (e.g., 2007, 2010, 2014) and the 2004 Michigan survey (Burnazi, Keashly, & Neuman, 2005) reference repetitive negative actions, but they do not reference duration or the power or ability to defend oneself. The remaining studies using self-identification invoke the construct label (bullied, harassed, mistreated, threatened), leaving the meaning of the construct up to the respondent.

In all these studies, respondents are self-identifying, but the difference in specificity of the construct raises the question of what precisely is being assessed. For example, laypersons and researchers agree that negative behavior and negative impact or harm are critical components of the experience of "feeling bullied" (Keashly, 2001; Saunders, Huynh, & Goodman-Delahunty, 2007). However, laypeople focus less on repetition, persistence, and power imbalance as key in discerning their experiences. Thus, with very specific definitions, there may be conflicts with the respondents' definitions, and people may not identify themselves as being victims (Saunders et al., 2007).

Alternatively, by not providing a definition, respondents may self-identify as being bullied or mobbed based on their experiences, which may be more accurately captured under conflict, occasional aggression, or incivility, thus potentially inflating the prevalence rates (Nielsen et al., 2010). Contrary to findings in other countries (Nielsen et al., 2010), the specificity of the definition does not appear to have substantially influenced the prevalence rate for these U.S.-based studies.

Studies utilizing detailed definitions (CareerBuilder, 2014, Lipscomb et al., 2015; Lutgen-Sandvik et al., 2007) suggest rates of current bullying (6–12 months prior) ranging from 7–10 percent, while those asking respondents whether they had been bullied or harassed in the prior 12 months, that is, personal definitions, report rates ranging from 8.1 percent (General Social Survey, 2014) to 12 percent (Rospenda, Richman, & Shannon, 2008). The GSS is particularly interesting because data have been collected on self-labeling (without definition) since 2002. Examination of the rates in table 2.1 appear to show a decline from a high of 11.2 percent in 2002 to 8.1 percent in 2014. Looking only at data from 2014 (e.g., CareerBuilder, 2014; GSS, 2014; WBI, 2014), the rate of prevalence by self-identification appears to be around 7–8 percent in the prior 12 months. To provide a sense of how these rates map to other countries, Scandinavian countries have rates of 5–6 percent for self-labeling (with or without a definition), and other European countries have rates of 14 percent (with definition) and 25 percent without definition (see Nielsen et al., 2010 for detailed breakdown). With regard to the United Kingdom, Hoel and Cooper (2000) report a self-labeling (with definition) rate of 10.6 percent.

The types of scales used range from yes/no/don't know (e.g., WBI surveys) to scales where the yes option requires some indication of frequency (yes; rarely, yes; now and then, yes; several times per month, yes; several times per week, yes; daily (NAQ-R); Einarsen, Hoel, & Notelaers, 2009; Lipscomb et al., 2015; Lutgen-Sandvik et al., 2007). The latter response format recognizes that bullying and mobbing are not either/or phenomena but progressive, developing and intensifying over time (Einarsen et al., 2011). This response format allows the determination of the degree of bullying or mobbing (Fox & Stallworth, 2010; Lutgen-Sandvik et al., 2007; Nielsen et al., 2010). Although the studies reported here did not provide rates of occasional versus regular bullying (Hoel, Cooper, & Faragher, 2001), these are important indicators, as the evidence on the process of bullying suggests that occasional bullying, if left unaddressed, could move toward frequent or regular bullying (Rospenda, Richman, Wislar, & Flaherty, 2000; Zapf & Gross, 2001).

There are two interesting twists on the self-labeling approach: as a witness and as an actor. What we could call *other-labeling*, witnessing, or *vicarious aggression* (Barling, 1996) concerns workers reporting whether they have seen or are aware of others in their workplace being bullied or mobbed. Research finds that witnesses show similar negative effects to targets (Hoel & Einarsen, 1999; Vartia, 2001). Discussions of prevalence are enriched by considering the rates of witnessing because they provide information regarding (1) the extent of the impact or "victim" net (e.g., work team, unit, organization)—VitalSmarts (2014) reports that 97 percent of their respondents indicated that the bully's behavior impacted several people beyond themselves; (2) the quality of work climate, specifically a hostile work environment; (3) the possibility for mobbing, as some of the witnesses may join in the process (Namie & Lutgen-Sandvik, 2010); and (4) possible resources for leveraging early and effective responding, that is, *bystander action* (Keashly & Neuman, 2007). Thus, a combination of perceived victimization rates and witnessing rates provides an idea of the overall degree of involvement and impact in the workplace. Studies that queried respondents' experiences as witnesses find rates (in the prior 12 months) ranging from 11 percent (Lutgen-Sandvik et al., 2007) to 21 percent (WBI, 2014), with higher witness rates in the Califano et al. (2000) comparative study of verbal abuse (a subset of bullying behaviors) of the United States Postal Office (USPS; 36.9% at least monthly; 26.7% weekly) and a national working sample (32.9% at least monthly; 21.5% weekly). The most recent WBI survey (2014) identified categories of respondents who, in their working careers, had been bullied (not witnessed) and had witnessed (not bullied), resulting in an overall rate of 48 percent perceived victimization prevalence. Utilizing U.S. Labor Department statistics, WBI (2014) projected that 65.6 million U.S. workers have some experience with workplace bullying and mobbing in their working careers.

In terms of identifying as an actor, few surveys include this perspective. A key reason is that social desirability suggests that people would be less willing to frame what they do as bullying and mobbing, particularly given the increasingly public evaluation of these phenomena as bad and unjustified (see Ferris, Zinko, Brouer, Buckley, & Harvey, 2007, for another perspective). Of the studies reviewed here, only the WBI (2007, 2010, 2014) surveys asked respondents whether they had engaged in bullying. Endorsement rates were approximately 0.4 percent (roughly 75,000 workers). The huge disparity between those who identify as bullies and those who identify as having been bullied or seen someone bullied supports the idea that asking people to self-identify as actors likely results in an underestimate. We know relatively little about those who engage in these behaviors beyond what targets and witnesses perceive. Understanding the actors has implications for intervention and action. That may suggest coming at it from another method, such as the behavioral classification method, to which we will now turn our attention.

Behavioral Classification: I Have Experienced These Behaviors

Behavioral classification is an *objective* approach that involves providing respondents with a list of negative behaviors and asking them how frequently they have experienced each of these behaviors from someone at work over a specified period of time. The items are written in behavioral terms, and there is typically no reference to bullying, mobbing, or harassment (Lutgen-Sandvik et al., 2007). An exception is the VitalSmarts (2014) survey, which specifically refers to the behaviors included as "forms of workplace bullying." Some studies reviewed here utilized established behavioral measures, such as the Negative Acts Questionnaire–Revised (NAQ-R; Einarsen et al., 2009; Lipscomb et al., 2015; Lutgen-Sandvik et al., 2007); Generalized Workplace Harassment (Rospenda & Richman, 2004; Rospenda et al., 2008); and the Workplace Aggression Research Questionnaire (WAR-Q; Neuman & Keashly, 2004; Keashly & Jagatic, 2000; Burnazi et al., 2005), while others developed their inventories by drawing from various scales and focus group and interview data. The domain of possible behaviors is (sadly) enormous and beyond the scope of this chapter to discuss in detail (for more detail, see Keashly & Jagatic, 2003; Rodriguez-Caballeira, Solanelles, Vinacua, García, & Martín-Peña, 2010).

To provide a flavor of the behavioral domain, a useful categorization is based on the focus of the behaviors, specifically person-related, work-related, and physical intimidation (Einarsen et al., 2009). Examples of person-related behaviors include being humiliated or ridiculed, being ignored or excluded, and being the subject of gossip, rumors, and insulting remarks. Work-related behavior examples include withholding information needed to do the job, being ordered to do work below the worker's level of competence, and excessive monitoring of work. Examples of physical intimidation behaviors include being shouted at or the target of rage, intimidating gestures, and threats of physical violence.

A recently recognized set of behaviors acknowledges the use of electronic media as the means for bullying or mobbing others, that is, *cyberbullying*. While cyberbullying has been the subject of much research attention among teens, it has only recently become the subject of research in workplaces (Privitera & Campbell, 2009). These specific behaviors have not yet made their way into the established behavioral inventories and need to be included. Evidence suggests that cyberbullying may have even more profound implications for workers than "traditional" bullying because of its boundaryless, permanent, and invisible nature (D'Cruz & Noronha, 2013).

Regardless of the specific set of behaviors used, the identification of a respondent as "being bullied or mobbed" is based on the researcher applying a set of criteria. The types of criteria that have been utilized include:

1. number of discrete behaviors endorsed;
   a. at least one behavior regardless of frequency;
   b. at least one or two behaviors of prespecified frequency, most often at least weekly, mapping on Leymann's (1996) definition of workplace mobbing. Utilizing the criterion of at least two behaviors reflects the patterning/variety feature of workplace bullying and mobbing (Matthiesen & Einarsen, 2010);
   c. total number of behaviors of a prespecified frequency. This indicator provides evidence of patterning as well as the opportunity to discern the degree of bullying exposure, similar to the self-labeling method of occasional vs. regular bullying (Hoel et al., 2001; Lipscomb et al., 2015; Lutgen-Sandvik et al., 2007);
2. the overall sum of frequency of behaviors with predetermined cutoffs (see Notelaers & Einarsen, 2013 regarding NAQ-R cutoffs); and
3. mean frequency of behaviors in the inventory.

The behavioral inventory as a measure allows classification via all of the above criteria, that is, several indicators are possible from this one set of data. For the purpose of prevalence, classification into discrete categories of not bullied or bullied is the number of behaviors endorsed (1a and/or 1b), in essence treating bullying and mobbing as either/or kinds of phenomena. Given that bullying and mobbing are characterized as progressive processes, relying on these indicators alone does not give us a full picture of the nature of these phenomena.

Not surprisingly, the rates of prevalence vary depending on the specific behavioral criteria utilized. Defining exposure as at a least one negative act regardless of frequency produces rates (e.g., 41.4%, Schat et al., 2006, to 96%, VitalSmarts, 2014) notably higher than when the categorization is based on one behavior occurring at least weekly (e.g., 8.8%, Lipscomb et al., 2015, to 46.8%, Lutgen-Sandvik et al., 2007). Looking at European data using at least one behavior per week, Nielsen et al. (2010) report prevalence estimates of 10 percent in Scandinavian countries and 16–17 percent in other European countries. When the criterion of two or more behaviors is utilized, the rates drop notably.

The single behavior exposure indicator is problematic for at least two reasons. First, bullying and mobbing are rarely manifested in a single incident, let alone a single behavior. Thus, to be true to the patterning nature of bullying and mobbing, at minimum two behaviors should be the criterion. An even more precise indicator of patterning and, indeed, degree, would be the number of behaviors endorsed. In our early work (Keashly, Harvey, & Hunter, 1997), we found that the number of behaviors uniquely influences people's experiences beyond what was accounted for by frequency of exposure. The second limitation is that reliance on a single behavior as the cutoff for classification is heavily influenced by the number and variety of behaviors included in the inventory. For example, both Lutgen-Sandvik et al. (2007) and Lipscomb et al. (2015) used items from the Negative Acts Questionnaire-Revised, which includes person-related, work-related, and physical intimidation behaviors (Einarsen et al., 2009). This questionnaire has 22 items. Lutgen-Sandvik et al. (2007) used all 22 items, while Lipscomb et al. (2015) chose a subset of six based on overall perceived seriousness, encompassing only person-related and physical intimidation behaviors. The authors argued that the other (work-related) behaviors reflected conduct other than bullying. Indeed, the most frequent behaviors reported by Lutgen-Sandvik et al. (2007) were work-related behaviors, with person-related and physical intimidation behaviors reported at much lower levels. Thus, by restricting the types of behaviors to exclude work-related items (which tend to be more frequently occurring) and also by having fewer behaviors overall, Lipscomb et al. (2015) have created a more conservative estimate of exposure prevalence.

An advantage of the behavioral classification method relative to the self-labeling method is the opportunity to identify types of bullying and mobbing behaviors and thus to examine their connection to impact and experience as well as to different actors or relationships between actor(s) and target(s) (Neuman & Keashly, 2004; Hershcovis & Reich, 2013). Einarsen (1999) has argued that, as noted above, bullying and mobbing are not so much about the behaviors themselves but rather the frequency, duration, patterning, and the inability to respond effectively. However, other research has found that exposure to different types of behavior have differential effects (Cooper, Hoel, & Faragher, 2004). This suggests that behavioral inventories should include a variety of behaviors (direct-indirect, active-passive, verbal-physical; Buss, 1961; Neuman & Baron, 1998; Notelaers & Einarsen, 2013) to more fully capture the prevalence and nature of exposure.

Referring back to the actor perspective, the behavioral inventory measure may be more revealing in terms of prevalence of enacted bullying or mobbing, as it does not require the actor to identify himself or herself as a bully. When this approach is taken, rates of enacting aggressive behaviors by workers toward others at work is quite high, with rates of 50–75 percent, indicating that they have engaged in at least one aggressive behavior (Brotheridge, Lee, & Power, 2012; Glomb, 2002; Greenberg & Barling, 1999).

Comparison of Methods

Rates of victimization prevalence based on self-labeling tend to be lower than prevalence based on behavioral endorsement (Nielsen et al.,

2010: for exceptions, see Keashly & Neuman, this volume). One interpretation of this difference is that these two methods are addressing different aspects of workplace bullying and mobbing. Self-labeling is about the experience of victimization, and the behavioral classification method is about assessing exposure to specific negative behaviors that may (or may not) constitute bullying and mobbing (Keashly & Jagatic, 2011; Nielsen et al., 2010). The two are expected to be related, but the correlation is not a perfect one (Einarsen et al., 2009). The decision to self-identify as being a bullying or mobbing victim reflects influences beyond actual exposure, including a desire not to appear weak or unable to cope or a personal definition of bullying not coinciding with the research definition (Nielsen et al., 2010; Saunders et al., 2007). Having said this, research shows that those who self-identify as bullied have higher rates of exposure to a variety of behaviors than those who do not self-identify (Jennifer, Cowie, & Ananiadou, 2003; Lutgen-Sandvik et al., 2007).

Another influence on self-labeling is the nature of behaviors included in the inventory. Behavioral inventories are composed of behaviors of varying severity, and perceived severity is an important influence on a person's evaluation and labeling of his or her experience (Lipscomb et al., 2015; Lutgen-Sandvik et al., 2007; Price Spratlen, 1994). For example, Keashly and Jagatic (2000) and Burnazi et al. (2005) asked respondents the extent to which they were upset by their experience (a proxy indicator of severity). They found people varied in their degree of upset and that this was linked to the resultant impact and perceived harm.

Examination of the severity of behaviors included in inventories reveals that not all behaviors are of equal merit in the experience of feeling bullied (Cooper et al., 2004). Behaviors directed at the person, such as rumors, threats, and humiliation, are perceived as more severe than work-focused behaviors, such as exclusion from meetings, stealing work, and manipulating information (Escartín, Rodríguez-Carballeira, Zapf, Porrúa, & Martín-Peña, 2009; Meglich, Faley, & DuBois, 2012). In addition, perceptions of severity are influenced by cultural definitions of appropriate and inappropriate behavior (Escartín et al., 2009; Power et al., 2013) as well as the source of the behavior, a point we will return to later. To the extent that the behaviors endorsed are not experienced as severe or upsetting, the respondent is less likely to label his or her experience as being bullied or mobbed. This pattern of findings is similar to what has been found in the sexual harassment literature (Schneider, Pryor, & Fitzgerald, 2011). This literature also notes that experiencing harm did not require labeling oneself as a victim. That is, exposure to negative behaviors is sufficient to have a notable negative impact (Hoel & Cooper, 2000).

The distinctiveness of these two measurement approaches suggests the value of utilizing both in surveys, permitting more nuanced and finer distinctions among people's experiences. For example, connecting respondents' answers to these two methods reveals a number of discrete categories, including the "bullied/nonvictim," which is someone who does not self-identify as bullied but based on his or her exposure to behaviors would be characterized this way (Jennifer et al., 2003). Lutgen-Sandvik et al. (2007) and Lipscomb et al. (2015) determined the degree of bullying and tied it to differential nature and degree of impact. Further, by including different perspectives (target, witness, and even actor), we can get an indication of the nature and extent of the impact of bullying and mobbing in workplaces and beyond.

TIME REFERENT: THE LONGER THE TIME FRAME, THE HIGHER THE RATE

An influence on prevalence rates is the time frame within which we are asking respondents about their experiences. As can be seen in table 2.1, the studies vary from experiences in the prior 6 months, prior 12 months, or in the entire working career. It may well be that people have not had any experiences of being bullied or mobbed in the past 6–12 months but have had experiences prior to this. The studies that included the time referent of "entire working career" show higher rates of prevalence, indicating that these phenomena are sadly a notable part of many people's work lives.

There are methodological concerns with having extended time frames because of concerns about recall: the longer time over which one is recalling, the less accurate the estimate (Bowling, Camus, & Blackmore, 2015). However, it can be argued that being bullied or mobbed is a highly salient experience and thus more easily recalled. Of note here is that many of these studies are snapshots of a particular period of time rather than a tracking over time. Tracking over time would permit us to get a sense of duration, which is a core element of bullying and mobbing. The one exception is the work of Judy Richman and her colleagues and their multiwave study of *generalized workplace harassment* in a university, which occurred over a 10-year period (McGinley et al., 2011). Some studies reviewed did ask respondents who self-identified as being bullied or mobbed about the duration of their experiences. The results are stunning. In earlier work, Namie's (2000) survey of bullying victims reported an average duration of 16.5 months. VitalSmarts (2014) reports a duration of more than 5 years for 53 percent of respondents, and McGinley et al. (2011), in their longitudinal study of university employees, identified employees of chronic abuse over 10 years! Thus, the time frame for specific responding merely provides us with the ability to distinguish between bullying and mobbing and exposure to aggressive behavior. To capture the truly enduring quality of bullying and mobbing and its effects requires gathering information about the length of the experience.

SAMPLE: WHOM WE ASK AND HOW WE RECRUIT THEM SHAPES PREVALENCE AND PROFILE

Given that this chapter is focused on the prevalence of workplace bullying and mobbing in the United States, I chose to look at studies that purported to reflect the U.S. working population rather than those in specific industries. If the goal is to develop a picture of the experience of the U.S. working adult population, then representative random sampling is key to permitting such generalizability. A representative sample reflects the key characteristics of the population we are seeking to understand. A random sample increases the chances that we will achieve representativeness. Thus, to generalize to the U.S. working adult population, we want samples that reflect the profiles of working adults, such as sex, race/ethnicity, industry, occupation, and other key aspects.

Several studies included here utilized the random representative approach, namely, the national working force samples: Califano et al. (2000); GSS (2014); National Health Interview Survey (Alterman, Luckhaupt, Dahlhamer, Ward, & Calvert, 2013; Department of Health and Human Services (DHHS, n.d.); Schat et al. (2006); and WBI (2007, 2010, 2014); the Michigan workforce: Burnazi et al. (2005) and Keashly and Jagatic (2000); the private sector workforce of CareerBuilder (2014); and the state unionized public sector of Lipscomb et al. (2015). Developing such samples is a massive undertaking requiring substantial resources to be able to do it effectively and appropriately. Other studies included in this review used nonrandom samples either as convenience samples or through other mechanisms. Nonrandom samples cannot be assumed to accurately reflect the U.S. working population, and, thus, the results may not generalize working adults' experiences writ large. Rates in random samples tend to be lower than rates in nonrandom samples (Nielsen et al., 2010).

Another influence regarding the sample is how the recruitment was accomplished. For example, Burnazi et al. (2005), Califano et al. (2000), GSS (2014), NHIS (2010), Keashly and Jagatic (2000), Lutgen-Sandvik et al. (2007), Schat et al. (2006), and Rospenda et al. (2008) embedded their items on bullying and mobbing in a broader survey of quality of working life or general employment issues. This is an important consideration, as surveys that explicitly focus on workplace bullying and mobbing may face self-selection by the respondents. That is, once told the survey is about bullying, some respondents may choose not to respond for a variety of reasons, and thus their voices are lost. On the other side, those who have had experiences may be more inclined to participate. Thus, prevalence rates from these studies are affected by the respondents' connection to the topic. Rates in samples of workplace experience surveys tend to be lower than samples whose surveys focus exclusively on workplace bullying (CareerBuilder, 2014; VitalSmarts, 2014; WBI, 2007, 2010, 2014).

Specific Industry and Occupational Samples

Within some surveys of the working population, data were collected on the industry or occupation of the respondents (DHHS, n.d.; Schat et al., 2006), or the survey was directed at a specific industry or occupation, for example, Califano et al. (2000), USPS; Lipscomb et al. (2015), state unionized public sector; and CareerBuilder (2014), private sector. Rates of prevalence based on exposure to bullying and mobbing behaviors and the experience of being victimized are higher in some industries and occupations than others. For example, the National Health Interview Survey (DHHS, n.d.) reports a rate in the overall U.S. working population of 7.8 percent in the prior 12-month period, and rates of 9.1 percent in health care (over 10% for nurses alone); 10.1 percent in retail trade; and 9.4 percent in transportation, in contrast to 5 percent in construction and 3.6 percent in mining and oil.

Who the actors are may be particularly important to discern, as several of these industries are service intensive and thus clients, customers, or patients may be key actors. An interesting example of an industry-specific study is the Califano et al. (2000) study of the USPS. In their report, the authors compared the postal service sample to a national sample of U.S. workers, often denoting that the postal service was no worse and often better in terms of experiences on the job. An exception was verbal abuse, with postal workers reporting higher levels than the national working sample. Thus, considering the representation of industries and occupations in a sample is important in discerning the accuracy of a prevalence statistic for the U.S. working population as a whole. Industry- or occupation-specific prevalence rates are valuable, and they reveal the influence of context and expectations and norms on the enactment of and exposure to bullying and mobbing. This information has implications for the design and implementation of actions to address bullying and mobbing.

Whom Do We Ask? Individuals and Organizations

The majority of the studies included in this chapter focused on individual workers and their experiences, mostly as targets, occasionally as witnesses, and rarely as actors. These data give us a sense of the spread of bullying and mobbing in workplaces. Another set of respondents is organizations. For example, the Society of Human Resource Management (SHRM; 2012) and NIOSH (Grubb, Roberts, Grosch, & Brightwell, 2004) gathered their information from organizations and their experiences with bullying. Fully one-quarter of the organizations surveyed by NIOSH indicated that bullying was present, with 7 percent indicating that it was frequent (Grubb et al., 2004). More recently, the SHRM (2012) found that over half of the HR managers surveyed indicated that bullying had been and was an issue in their organizations. As stunning as these rates are, they are likely underestimates, as individuals (targets and witnesses) are often reluctant to formally report these experiences for fear of retaliation or that nothing will be done (Keashly, 2001). What is exciting is that organizational awareness of bullying and mobbing has implications for addressing these pernicious problems.

SOURCE: WHO DOES IT SHAPES THE EXPERIENCE AND THE IMPACT

Another element that is critical is who the actor is vis-à-vis the target. As noted earlier, the NHIS study (DHHS, n.d.) found that industry rates are likely influenced by the sources of the bullying, particularly in the service-related industries where customers and clients are notable sources. Source is an important consideration in terms of differentiating bullying and mobbing from other related phenomena, such as hostile or aggressive work environments, as well as understanding the experience of feeling bullied and mobbed and the nature and extent of the impact (Hershcovis & Reich, 2013; Keashly & Jagatic, 2011).

Ultimately, the true prevalence rate of bullying and mobbing in the U.S. working population is influenced by the source. In terms of distinctiveness, by virtue of its persistence and enduring nature, bullying and mobbing occur in the relationship between a specific target and a specific actor. If a survey utilizes the self-labeling method, respondents are often queried about the actor. Most research utilizing behavioral inventories do not ask who the source of the behaviors is (for an exception, see Neuman & Keashly, 2004). Thus, it is impossible to distinguish between exposure based on different behaviors coming from different actors and different behaviors coming from the same actor (Keashly, 2013). The former reflects a hostile work environment with aggressive behaviors, while the latter is more specifically workplace bullying or mobbing.

Another important reason for identifying sources is that bullying and mobbing at the hands of superiors, peers, and subordinates is enacted and experienced differently (Hershcovis & Barling, 2010). Several studies reviewed here did gather data on who the actors were vis-à-vis the target. As can be seen in table 2.1, the prevalence rate varies depending on who is the actor. In the earlier discussion about samples, how people were recruited (quality of work life survey vs. a bullying survey) was identified as influential in prevalence rates. This is also true in terms of who gets identified as the source of workplace bullying and mobbing. Studies whose survey was focused on bullying (CareerBuilder, 2014; Lipscomb et al., 2015; VitalSmarts, 2014; WBI, 2007, 2010, 2014) were more likely to identify the actor as a superior, then as a peer, and least often as a subordinate. In contrast, those studies whose workplace bullying and mobbing questions were embedded in a broader "quality of work life survey" (Burnazi et al., 2005; Califano et al., 2000; DHHS, 2010; GSS, 2014; Keashly & Jagatic, 2000; Rospenda et al., 2008; Schat et al., 2006) report similar rates for superiors and peers and much less for subordinates. It may be that when respondents are cued to "workplace bullying and mobbing" for their initial participation, the public image of these being boss-enacted phenomena may prime these experiences, making them more salient when responding. We do know that bullying behaviors at the hands of superiors are experienced more negatively than such behaviors from other sources, and thus the boss as actor may more readily come to mind (Keashly & Neuman 2002).

Some studies also collected data on the sex of the actor, revealing that men are more often identified as actors. By examining the sex of the target and actor together, we know that bullying and mobbing tend to be predominantly same-sex phenomena (WBI, 2007, 2010, 2014).

Gathering data on the number of actors involved allows us to assess the presence and prevalence of mobbing. The CareerBuilder (2014) survey did include a question regarding the identity of the actors that allowed respondents to choose more than one. Of those who indicated they were currently being bullied, almost a third reported being bullied (or mobbed) by several actors (L. Nikravan, personal communication, November 11, 2016). With this exception, the prevalence rates of other studies mask mobbing from view.

Although knowing the overall prevalence of workplace bullying and mobbing is important, being able to drill down to look at who is doing what to whom gives us further insight into the faces and nuances of workplace bullying and mobbing. Understanding what happens in these relationships opens the door to crafting relevant and effective actions and interventions.

PURPOSE FOR STUDY: WHY WE WANT TO KNOW SHAPES HOW WE ASK THE QUESTION

The studies reviewed here reflect a variety of interests that include academic research; public health (GSS, NHIS); employee advocacy (WBI, CareerBuilder, VitalSmarts); professional organizations (SHRM); and industry (USPS). Understanding the purpose of the study provides insight into the measurement utilized, which in turn shapes the prevalence rate. For academic research (e.g., Burnazi et al., 2005; Keashly & Jagatic, 2000; Lipscomb et al., 2015; Lutgen-Sandvik et al., 2007; Rospenda et al., 2008, Schat et al., 2006), survey data provides the opportunity to articulate the distinct nature of bullying and mobbing vis-à-vis other negative workplace phenomena (e.g., incivility, general aggression, hostile work environment) and to test explanatory theories and models. Measurement needs to more precisely capture the distinctive features of workplace bullying and mobbing, hence the utilization of self-labeling and psychometrically reliable and valid behavioral inventories. For public health (GSS, 2014; DHHS, 2010), the purpose is to have an estimate of the size of the problem relative to other workplace problems (like harassment and discrimination) that impacts quality of life for U.S. citizens to garner support for spending scarce public health dollars. Thus, measurement needs to clearly focus on the respondents' experiences of victimization, that is, self-labeling as bullied or mistreated.

For employee advocacy groups (CareerBuilder, 2014; VitalSmarts, 2014; WBI, 2007, 2010, 2014), the focus is on demonstrating that employees are being victimized systematically and that organizations have a responsibility to take action. For this purpose of mobilizing for action, the self-labeling method that utilizes the distinct feature of repeated and persistent aggression is useful, and the resultant statistics are attention-grabbing. A dramatic example of this is VitalSmarts' (2014) claim that 96 percent of workers have experienced bullying in their working career, with 63 percent currently experiencing bullying. Such statistics grab our attention and make us want to learn more, an important goal for employee advocate organizations. Given that Human Resources is often the unit that is expected to engage with workplace problems such as bullying and mobbing, SHRM's (2012) survey of their members' experiences gives a sense of the scope of the problem for these professionals, and thus the need for member support and training. Measurement here then needs to clearly distinguish bullying and mobbing from other negative behaviors and situations, which demonstrates the value of self-labeling using a precise definition.

Finally, the USPS (2000) survey is distinctive among the studies reviewed here in that it was motivated by a need to address a public perception of the USPS as a violent place ("going postal"). The comparative study was conducted by the well-respected National Center on Addiction and Substance Abuse at Columbia University and reflects the academic value of precise construct measurement of relevant phenomena by definition and specific behavioral examples.

IN SUM: WHAT IS THE "REAL" PREVALENCE?

In this chapter, we have examined the ways in which the prevalence rate of workplace bullying and mobbing is shaped by the measurement approach, time frame, sample, and source. We have also recognized how the purpose of the study influences the metric chosen and the resultant profile of workplace bullying and mobbing. Somehow, though, the answer of "it depends" does not seem satisfying, does it? We want specific numbers. So here goes: utilizing the self-labeling with precise definition measurement, 7–8 percent of U.S. working adults will feel they are currently (prior 6–12 months) being bullied or mobbed by someone at work, and over a quarter of all working adults will identify as having been bullied or mobbed in their working career. Depending on occupation and industry, the risks for being bullied and mobbed may be higher than the overall prevalence. Broadening the impact net further, one-quarter to one-third of all working adults have witnessed others being bullied or mobbed. Translating these percentages to numbers of workers using the Bureau of Labor Statistics (n.d.) nonfarm labor force for 2014 (most recent data collection reported here) of 137.5 million workers, 9.8 million workers are currently being bullied or mobbed, 35–40 million have experienced bullying and mobbing in their working careers, and 35–45 million have witnessed the bullying and mobbing of others.

No matter how you cut it, that is a lot of workers who are being affected by persistent and repeated aggression in relationships of consequence (with superiors, coworkers, and clients/customers), not to mention their family and friends who are primary supports for them. Beyond persistent aggression, these studies reveal that one-third to one-half of American workers in any 12-month period are exposed to aggressive behavior from someone with whom they work. Measuring and tracking these occasional acts of aggression are important; if left unaddressed, they could develop into bullying or mobbing situations.

To end on a more hopeful note, the good news from this review is that there is increasing interest from a variety of stakeholders in identifying and understanding workplace bullying and mobbing, with evidence that the public writ large, and public health agencies and other organizations more specifically, perceive these as major workplace issues that must be addressed. Recognizing there is a problem and realizing the size of it is a critical step in taking workplace bullying and mobbing seriously and builds the will for developing and implementing strategies for managing and eradicating these very destructive workplace experiences that touch us all.

REFERENCES

Alterman, T., Luckhaupt, S. E., Dahlhamer, J. M., Ward, B. W., & Calvert, G. M. (2013). Job insecurity, work-family imbalance, and hostile work environment: Prevalence data from the 2010 National Health Interview Survey. *American Journal of Industrial Medicine*, 56(6), 660–669.

Barling, J. (1996). The prediction, experience, and consequences of workplace violence. In G. R. VandenBos & E. Q. Bulatao (Eds.), *Violence on the job: Identifying risks and developing solutions* (pp. 29–49). Washington, D.C.: American Psychological Association.

Bowling, N. A., Camus, K. A., & Blackmore, C. E. (2015). Conceptualizing and measuring workplace abuse: Implications for the study of abuse's predictors and consequences. In P. L. Perrewé, J. R. B. Halbesleben, & C. C. Rose (Eds.), *Mistreatment in organizations* (pp. 225–263). Bingley, England: Emerald Group Publishing Limited.

Brotheridge, C. M., Lee, R. T., & Power, J. L. (2012). Am I my own worst enemy? The experiences of bullying targets who are also aggressors. *Career Development International, 17*(4), 358–374.

Bureau of Labor Statistics, United States Department of Labor (n.d.). Retrieved from http://data.bls.gov/pdq/SurveyOutputServlet?request_action=wh&graph_name=CE_cesbref1

Burnazi, L., Keashly, L., & Neuman, J. H. (2005). *Aggression revisited: Prevalence, antecedents, and outcomes.* Paper presented as part of the symposium on Workplace Bullying and Mistreatment, Academy of Management, Oahu, Hawaii.

Buss, A. H. (1961). *The psychology of aggression.* New York: Wiley.

Califano, J. A., Fraser, D. A., Hamburg, B. A., Hamburg, D. A., Robson, J. E., & Zoellick, R. B. (2000). *Report of the United States Postal Service Commission on a safe and secure workplace.* Retrieved from http://permanent.access.gpo.gov/lps12068/33994.pdf

CareerBuilder (2014). *Office bullying plagues workers across races, job levels and educational attainment.* Retrieved from http://www.careerbuilder.com/share/aboutus/pressreleasesdetail.aspx?sd=9%2f18%2f2014&siteid=cbpr&sc_cmp1=cb_pr842_&id=pr842&ed=12%2f31%2f2014

Cooper, C. L., Hoel, H., & Faragher, B. (2004). Bullying is detrimental to health, but all bullying behaviours are not necessarily equally damaging. *British Journal of Guidance & Counselling, 32*(3), 367–387.

D'Cruz, P., & Noronha, E. (2013). Navigating the extended reach: Target experiences of cyberbullying at work. *Information and Organization, 23*(4), 324–343.

Department of Health and Human Services (DHHS). (n.d.). Retrieved November 1, 2016 from http://www.cdc.gov/niosh/topics/nhis/pdfs/NHISinfo.pdf

Einarsen, S. (1999). The nature and causes of bullying at work. *International Journal of Manpower, 20*(1/2), 16–27.

Einarsen, S., Hoel, H., & Notelaers, G. (2009). Measuring exposure to bullying and harassment at work: Validity, factor structure and psychometric properties of the Negative Acts Questionnaire–Revised. *Work & Stress, 23*(1), 24–44.

Einarsen, S., Hoel, H., & Zapf, D. (2011). *Bullying and harassment in the workplace: Developments in theory, research and practice* (2nd ed.). Boca Raton, FL: CRC Press.

Einarsen, S., Raknes, B. R. I., & Matthiesen, S. B. (1994). Bullying and harassment at work and their relationships to work environment quality: An exploratory study. *European Journal of Work and Organizational Psychology, 4*(4), 381–401.

Escartín, J., Rodríguez-Carballeira, A., Zapf, D., Porrúa, C., & Martín-Peña, J. (2009). Perceived severity of various bullying behaviours at work and the relevance of exposure to bullying. *Work & Stress, 23*(3), 191–205.

Ferris, G. R., Zinko, R., Brouer, R. L., Buckley, M. R., & Harvey, M. G. (2007). Strategic bullying as a supplementary, balanced perspective on destructive leadership. *The Leadership Quarterly, 18*(3), 195–206.

Fox, S., & Stallworth, L. E. (2010). The battered apple: An application of stressor-emotion-control/support theory to teachers' experience of violence and bullying. *Human Relations, 63*(7), 927–954.

General Social Survey. (2014). Quality of work life module. Retrieved from https://gssdataexplorer.norc.org/variables/2825/vshow

Glomb, T. M. (2002). Workplace anger and aggression: Informing conceptual models with data from specific encounters. *Journal of Occupational Health Psychology, 7*(1), 20–36.

Greenberg, L., & Barling, J. (1999). Predicting employee aggression against coworkers, subordinates and supervisors: The roles of person behaviors and perceived workplace factors. *Journal of Organizational Behavior, 20*(6), 897–913.

Grubb, P. L., Roberts, R. K., Grosch, J. W., & Brightwell, W. S. (2004). Workplace bullying: What organizations are saying. *Employee Rights & Employment Policy Journal, 8*, 407–422.

Hershcovis, M. S. (2011). "Incivility, social undermining, bullying... oh my!": A call to reconcile constructs within workplace aggression research. *Journal of Organizational Behavior, 32*(3), 499–519.

Hershcovis, M. S., & Barling, J. (2010). Towards a multi-foci approach to workplace aggression: A meta-analytic review of outcomes from different perpetrators. *Journal of Organizational Behavior, 31*(1), 24–44.

Hershcovis, M. S., & Reich, T. C. (2013). Integrating workplace aggression research: Relational, contextual, and method considerations. *Journal of Organizational Behavior, 34*(S1), S26–S42.

Hoel, H., & Cooper, C. L. (2000). *Destructive conflict and bullying at work*. Manchester, England: Manchester School of Management, UMIST.

Hoel, H., Cooper, C. L., & Faragher, B. (2001). The experience of bullying in Great Britain: The impact of organizational status. *European Journal of Work and Organizational Psychology, 10*(4), 443–465.

Hoel, H., & Einarsen, S. (1999). *Workplace bullying*. New York: John Wiley & Sons.

Jennifer, D., Cowie, H., & Ananiadou, K. (2003). Perceptions and experience of workplace bullying in five different working populations. *Aggressive Behavior, 29*(6), 489–496.

Keashly, L. (2001). Interpersonal and systemic aspects of emotional abuse at work: The target's perspective. *Violence and Victims, 16*(2), 211–245.

Keashly, L. (2013). Hostile work relationships. In B. Omdahl & J. Fritz (Eds.), *Problematic relationships at work* (Vol. 2; pp. 43–67). New York: Peter Lang Publishing.

Keashly, L., Harvey, S., & Hunter, S. (1997). Emotional abuse and role state stressors: Relative impact on residence assistants' stress. *Work and Stress, 11*, 35–45.

Keashly, L., & Jagatic, K. (2000, August). *The nature, extent and impact of emotional abuse in the workplace: Results of a statewide survey*. Paper presented at the Academy of Management Conference, Toronto, Canada.

Keashly, L., & Jagatic, K. (2003). By any other name: American perspectives on workplace bullying. In S. Einarsen, H. Hoel, D. Zapf, & C. Cooper (Eds.), *Bullying and emotional abuse in the workplace: International research and practice perspectives* (pp. 31–61). Boca Raton, FL: CRC Press.

Keashly, L., & Jagatic, K. (2011). North American perspectives on workplace hostility and bullying. In S. Einarsen, H. Hoel, D. Zapf, & C. Cooper (Eds.), *Bullying and harassment in the workplace: Developments in theory, research and practice* (2nd ed.; pp. 41–71). Boca Raton, FL: CRC Press.

Keashly, L. & Neuman, J. H. (2002, August 12). *Exploring persistent patterns of workplace aggression.* Paper presented at the Workplace Abuse, Aggression, Bullying, and Incivility: Conceptual and Empirical Insights symposium, Meeting of the Academy of Management, Denver, Colorado.

Keashly, L. & Neuman, J. H. (2007, November). *Stepping up: Developing peer strategies for addressing bullying.* Paper presented as part of a training and development session, "Building Workplace Bullying Seminars: Grounding Training and Development in Strong Communication Scholarship," National Communication Association Annual Meeting, Chicago, Illinois.

Kelloway, E. K., Barling, J., & Hurrell, J. J., Jr. (Eds.). (2006). *Handbook of workplace violence.* Thousand Oaks, CA: Sage Publications.

Leymann, H. (1996). The content and development of mobbing at work. In D. Zapf & H. Leymann (Eds.). *Mobbing and victimization at work* (pp. 165–184). Hove, England: Psychology Press.

Lipscomb, J., London, M., McPhaul, K. M., Ghaziri, M. E., Lydecker, A., Geiger-Brown, J., & Johnson, J. V. (2015). The prevalence of coworker conflict including bullying in a unionized US public sector workforce. *Violence and Victims, 30*(5), 813–829.

Lutgen-Sandvik, P., Tracy, S. J., & Alberts, J. K. (2007). Burned by bullying in the American workplace: Prevalence, perception, degree and impact. *Journal of Management Studies, 44*(6), 837–862.

Matthiesen, S. B., & Einarsen, S. (2010). Bullying in the workplace: Definition, prevalence, antecedents and consequences. *International Journal of Organization Theory and Behavior, 13*(2), 202–248.

McGinley, M., Richman, J. A., & Rospenda, K. M. (2011). Duration of sexual harassment and generalized harassment in the workplace over ten years: Effects on deleterious drinking outcomes. *Journal of Addictive Diseases, 30*(3), 229–242.

Meglich, P. A., Faley, R. H., & DuBois, C. L. (2012). The influence of actions and actors on the perceived severity of workplace bullying. *Journal of Management Policy and Practice, 13*(1), 11.

Namie, G. (2000, October 27–28). *U.S. hostile workplace survey 2000.* Paper presented at the New England Conference on Workplace Bullying, Suffolk University Law School, Boston, Massachusetts.

Namie, G., & Lutgen-Sandvik, P. E. (2010). Active and passive accomplices: The communal character of workplace bullying. *International Journal of Communication, 4,* 343–373.

Neuman, J. H., & Baron, R. A. (1998). Workplace violence and workplace aggression: Evidence concerning specific forms, potential causes, and preferred targets. *Journal of Management, 24*(3), 391–419.

Neuman, J. H., & Keashly, L. (2004, April 4). *Development of the workplace aggression research questionnaire (WAR-Q): Preliminary data from the Workplace Stress and Aggression Project.* Paper presented at the Theoretical Advancements in the Study of Anti-Social Behavior at Work symposium, meeting of the Society for Industrial and Organizational Psychology, Chicago, Illinois.

Nielsen, M. B., Matthiesen, S. B., & Einarsen, S. (2010). The impact of methodological moderators on prevalence rates of workplace bullying: A meta-analysis. *Journal of Occupational and Organizational Psychology, 83*(4), 955–979.

Notelaers, G., & Einarsen, S. (2013). The world turns at 33 and 45: Defining simple cutoff scores for the Negative Acts Questionnaire–Revised in a representative sample. *European Journal of Work and Organizational Psychology, 22*(6), 670–682.

Power, J. L., Brotheridge, C. M., Blenkinsopp, J., Bowes-Sperry, L., Bozionelos, N., Buzády, Z., . . . Madero, S. M. (2013). Acceptability of workplace bullying: A comparative study on six continents. *Journal of Business Research, 66*(3), 374–380.

Price Spratlen, L. (1994). Interpersonal conflict which includes mistreatment in a university workplace. *Violence and Victims, 10*(4), 285–297.

Privitera, C., & Campbell, M. A. (2009). Cyberbullying: The new face of workplace bullying? *CyberPsychology & Behavior, 12*(4), 395–400.

Rospenda, K. M., & Richman, J. A. (2004). The factor structure of generalized workplace harassment. *Violence and Victims, 19*(2), 221–238.

Rospenda, K. M., Richman, J. A., & Shannon, C. A. (2008). Prevalence and mental health correlates of harassment and discrimination in the workplace: Results from a national study. *Journal of Interpersonal Violence, 24*(5), 819–843.

Rospenda, K. M., Richman, J. A., Wislar, J. S., & Flaherty, J. A. (2000). Chronicity of sexual harassment and generalized workplace abuse: Effects on drinking outcomes. *Addiction, 95*(12), 1805–1820.

Saunders, P., Huynh, A., & Goodman-Delahunty, J. (2007). Defining workplace bullying behaviour professional lay definitions of workplace bullying. *International Journal of Law and Psychiatry, 30*(4), 340–354.

Schat, A. C., Frone, M. R., & Kelloway, E. K. (2006). Prevalence of workplace aggression in the U.S. workforce: Findings from a national study. In E. K. Kelloway, J. Barling, & J. J. Hurrell (Eds.), *Handbook of workplace violence* (pp. 47–89). Thousand Oaks, CA: Sage Publications.

Schneider, K. T., Pryor, J. B., & Fitzgerald, L. F. (2011). Sexual harassment research in the United States. In S. Einarsen, H. Hoel, D. Zapf, & C. L. Cooper (Eds.), *Bullying and harassment in the workplace: Developments in theory, research and practice* (2nd ed.; pp. 143–265). Boca Raton, FL: CRC Press.

Society of Human Resource Management. (2012). *Workplace bullying.* Retrieved from https://www.shrm.org/hr-today/trends-and-forecasting/research-and-surveys/pages/workplacebullying.aspx

Vartia, M. A. (2001). Consequences of workplace bullying with respect to the well-being of its targets and the observers of bullying. *Scandinavian Journal of Work, Environment & Health, 27*(1), 63–69.

VitalSmarts. (2014). *How to confront the workplace bully.* Retrieved from https://www.vitalsmarts.com/resource-center/research

Workplace Bullying Institute. (2007). *The WBI U.S. Workplace Bullying Survey 2007.* Retrieved from http://workplacebullying.org/multi/pdf/WBIsurvey2007.pdf

Workplace Bullying Institute. (2010). *The WBI U.S. Workplace Bullying Survey 2010.* Retrieved from http://workplacebullying.org/multi/pdf/WBIsurvey2007.pdf

Workplace Bullying Institute. (2014). *The WBI U.S. Workplace Bullying Survey 2014.* Retrieved from http://www.workplacebullying.org/multi/pdf/WBI-2014-US-Survey.pdf

Wiegand, D. M., Chen, P. Y., Hurrell, J. J., Jr., Jex, S., Nakata, A., Nigam, J. A., . . . Tetrick, L. E. (2012). A consensus method for updating psychosocial measures used in NIOSH health hazard evaluations. *Journal of Occupational and Environmental Medicine, 54*(3), 350–355.

Zapf, D., & Gross, C. (2001). Conflict escalation and coping with workplace bullying: A replication and extension. *European Journal of Work and Organizational Psychology, 10*(4), 497–522.

3

Risk Factors for Becoming a Target of Workplace Bullying and Mobbing

Gary Namie and Ruth Namie

The chapter title implies that a host of personal characteristics can be identified that predict why one person is targeted for bullying and others are not. We sort the identification into three components: (1) the search for a dispositional or personality trait profile, (2) behaviors that tend to lead to aggression directed against targets, and (3) characteristics of perpetrators that operate either unilaterally or interactively with targeted workers' actions. Next, we explore how certain emotional consequences of being bullied exacerbate the harm endured by targets. They are predictors of impact severity rather than being selected for bullying and mobbing. Finally, we close with our predictions for a brighter future for targets of bullying.

DO TARGET PERSONALITIES PREDICT BULLYING?

We begin with dispositional approaches to explain why certain individuals might be targeted.

Business school researchers like to include "victim precipitation" in their list of variables explored in bullying-related studies. For example, Tepper, Duffy, Henle, and Lambert (2006) defined *victim precipitation* as "the idea that some individuals may become at risk of being victimized by provoking the hostility of potential perpetrators" (p. 104). The authors explicitly borrowed victim precipitation from criminal justice. For this particular study, with a sample of military supervisors and National Guard members, the authors incorporated an omnibus dispositional tendency—*negative affectivity* (NA): people who experience high levels of distress, feeling upset, afraid, or jittery—as a predictor of being abused by supervisors. High NA individuals are less able to defend themselves against aggression or they are perceived by coworkers as annoying, not likeable, and thus provocative. Tepper and colleagues (2006) confirmed that those high in NA indeed perceived being treated more abusively. They concluded that abusive supervision is a trickle-down phenomenon and called for organizations to first treat *supervisors* more fairly if subordinates are not to be subjected to abuse. (The lay term "sh** flows downhill," known to nearly everyone, comes to mind.)

If the form of abuse under examination had been domestic violence, the analogous recommendation would have been to first provide services for the batterers to satisfy their needs with the hope that it mitigates battering. Thankfully, domestic violence advocates appropriately focused first on alleviating harm done to victims and then attending to the needs of batterers. Social justice movements are driven by the unmet needs of victims, underdogs, and the disadvantaged—not the coddling of abusers, typically those who already enjoy the privileges of societal support.

Our methodological criticism of the Tepper et al. (2006) study is that subordinates' NA tendencies were queried contemporaneously with all other measures. In other words, subordinates who had already experienced abusive supervision by one or more of the other participants could have been made distressed, upset, afraid, and jittery specifically *as the result* of the abuse. The researchers instead treated the NA trait cluster as an immutable preexisting characteristic of subordinates' personalities.

In another study (Tepper, Moss, & Duffy, 2011), the researchers invoked *moral exclusion theory*, which states that some targets deserve fair treatment (each person has a "scope of justice") and others are excluded from moral rules (assuming justice concerns for them are inapplicable). *Scope of justice* refers to the range or boundaries for psychological fairness that an individual holds with respect to how others should be treated (Opotow, 2012). Two ostensibly objective variables—supervisors' perceptions of emotional conflict with subordinates and work performance of subordinates—were correlated with supervisors' perceived dissimilarity from subordinates. The findings demonstrated that subordinates targeted for abuse are those from whom supervisors felt most dissimilar. Abuse was also more likely for those considered "poor performers." In the concluding discussion section of the study, there was an alarming call to study rank-and-file employees' acts of workplace deviance as a related predictor of abusive supervision. This seems to further reflect a cool indifference toward targeted workers as somehow less worthy.

Choosing victim precipitation as a research variable in bullying-related studies in the 21st century is odd because it was deemed outdated as long ago as 1984 by researchers in its original field of origin: criminal justice (Timmer & Norman, 1984). The sociology of criminal victimization demonstrates how U.S. crime is structurally precipitated. The analogy for bullying is that sophisticated studies place the dyadic relationship between perpetrator and target in the broader context of organizational politics and leadership.

Ignoring system factors is misguided. In brief, criminology has abandoned victim precipitation.

The premier source of social science research on the topic is the Bergen Bullying Research Group at the University of Bergen, Norway, run by Stale Einarsen, a clinical and organizational psychologist. Lind, Glaso, Pallesen, and Einarsen (2009) challenged the predictive power of personality of the target as the antecedent to bullying: do targets possess flawed personalities? They administered the Neuroticism-Extraversion-Openness Five-Factor Inventory (NEO-FFI), a five-factor model of personality assessment instrument, to workers who had been bullied and those who had not been bullied. Targets did not score higher on the neuroticism scale. They were no more anxious, worried, easily upset, or insecure than nontargets. However, targets did score higher on the conscientiousness scale, meaning they were self-disciplined, organized, hardworking, moralistic, and rule-bound. The authors ruled out a general victim personality profile.

BLAMING VICTIMS

Our American societal tendency to blame victims for their fate is worse than business school myopia on the topic. The underlying process is part of normal person perception principles and a form of automatic thinking that, if left unchecked, blames victims. Social psychologists call it the *fundamental attribution error* (Jones, 1979). There is a significant difference in how targets explain the reasons for the social misery that bullying has inflicted on them and how outsiders (HR, coworkers, managers distant from the incidents) explain it.

Inculcated in American mythic culture is reverence for the power of the individual over situations. Strong personal will is expected to overcome all obstacles. Conversely, research into attribution biases shows that outsiders (*observers*, in research jargon) automatically, without deliberate thought or malice, tend to overestimate the role of personality, or dispositional factors, when explaining the actions of others (*actors*). Individuals themselves (the "actors") see themselves as behaving responsively to the push and pull of external environmental factors. They are adaptive and flexible.

From the target's perspective, perpetrators and perpetrator support systems are part of the environment, not aspects of who they are. Investigators who arrive at the ubiquitous finding in bullying cases of simple "personality conflict" between the accused and complainant commit the fundamental attribution error. They overestimate the contributory role of target personalities (internal factors) to explain bullying. It is a way of perceiving targets as broken people. As Tepper et al. (2011) concluded, bullied targets may be precluded from moral treatment based on their personality.

UNWANTED, UNINVITED ASSAULT

No rational person thinks that anyone invites upon themselves repeated waves of psychological assaults involving verbal abuse, threats to one's identity, and paralyzing intimidation that creates excessive distress over long periods of time. Bullying is an irrational process. A variant of victim blaming is the assumption that the mistreatment was wanted or invited. As with sexual harassment, bullying's illegal cousin, no mistreatment is invited in the eyes of the law. Just because bullying in the United States is currently legal does not make it less abusive or disruptive to the targeted individuals and the organization.

WHY NOT FIGHT BACK?

We now share observations about behaviors exhibited across targets that could also trigger targethood. Given these are generalities, not every target exhibits all the behaviors.

Targets do not defend themselves in the immediacy of the initial assault during which bullies are probing for defenses or the lack thereof. They do not fight back because they cannot. If they could have employed a combative defensive reply for immediate use, they would not be targets. They would be one of the 73 percent of adult Americans who have never experienced bullying (Namie, 2014c). And if they could have, they would have.

Ironically, targets do confront their bullies in 69 percent of cases (Namie, 2013c). However, because they wait more than a month, the confrontation is ineffective. To effectively rebuff a perpetrator, the response must be immediate and clearly contingent upon the assault directed at the target. Delay dilutes the power of countermeasures by breaking the connection between assault and response. Waiting creates a lost opportunity to stop the bullying.

Target countermeasures are also rendered ineffective because the target operates in isolation, often without any institutional support. The perpetrators and management have an alliance, formal or informal, against the target. Human resources tends to promise support and then fails to engage senior management to stop it. In fact, once HR alerts senior managers, the target is disbelieved and discounted (D'Cruz & Noronha, 2010). In another study, D'Cruz and Noronha (2011), recorded instances where coworkers who were friends with bullied targets helped their beleaguered colleagues. This voluntary help refuted the do-nothing bystander effect typical of so many coworker actions. Then, HR, on behalf of the employer, reversed the helping. The authors called this "helpless helpfulness" invoked by the institution. The finding helps the reader understand why targets are relatively powerless when bullying happens.

GENDER AND TARGETHOOD

Workplace bullying is defined by the Workplace Bullying Institute (WBI) in its most recent national survey of a representative sample of all adult Americans (Namie, 2014c) as "repeated mistreatment of an employee by one or more employees: abusive conduct that takes the form of verbal abuse, threats, intimidation, humiliation or sabotage of work performance" (p. 3). Respondents were queried about their personal experiences with abusive conduct. The term *workplace bullying* did not appear in the survey. The prevalence was 27 percent: 7 percent describing themselves as currently experiencing the mistreatment, and 20 percent reporting it as part of their work history. Witnesses, whose experience was vicarious rather than direct, comprised 21 percent of respondents. Rounding out the sample were a group purportedly aware of bullying without personally experiencing it (19%), and 28 percent who neither acknowledged bullying nor had any experience with it.

From that 2014 survey, we also know that 60 percent of all targets are women. Women are also perpetrators, but only a minority of them (31%). Women bullies disproportionately pursue women as their targets (in 68% of cases). Twenty-one percent of all bullying is defined by the woman-on-woman dyad. The male bully and male target pair represents 30 percent of all bullying.

The woman-on-woman aggression has also been called the *queen bee phenomenon*. The rationale of authors Derks, Van Laar, and Ellemers (2016) is that the internecine hostility is a reaction to being members of a marginalized group—women in male-dominated organizations. In this way, woman-on-woman psychological violence is the same construct as horizontal (or lateral) violence, a term used in the nursing profession (Purpora, Blegen, & Stotts, 2012). In both spheres, senior women distance themselves from, and even aggress against, younger women that observers could argue need and deserve help from their mentors.

Feminist Phyllis Chesler (2009) explored women's inhumanity to women in an important book. She concluded that much of the cruelty shown to women by women is partly a remnant of human evolution. At its core is internecine competition among females of most species. Female humans have dense cortexes that can override impulses or instincts. Societal civility can cover antisocial action. However, competition among women does occur.

We asked targets to contrast currently being bullied with having been bullied before but not now. Same-gender pairings comprise 77 percent of the cases when only current bullying is considered (Namie, 2014c). These pairings fairly often preclude targets invoking their employers' nondiscrimination policies, which are based on state and federal civil rights laws. From a previous national survey, we know that 80 percent of all cases of mistreatment would not meet Equal Employment Opportunity (EEO) complaint eligibility criteria (Namie, 2007).

In 2014, women targets were more likely to report being currently bullied when their perpetrator was a woman (27%) than when the perpetrator was a man (15%). Women reported much higher rates of historical bullying (47%) than did men (27%).

Anecdotally, the majority of calls to WBI from targets seeking advice were historically from women. Respondents completing online surveys at the WBI Web site are typically women (80%–84%). We posit that women feel the pain from bullying and are motivated to reverse their circumstances. Bullying comes with stigma attached. Men may be more reluctant to admit the powerlessness that targethood connotes than women.

Salin and Hoel (2013) challenged the notion that workplace bullying is gender neutral (as in it affects everyone similarly) by considering it a "gendered phenomenon." That is, the experience is different for women than men. Women are more likely to label negative acts bullying and rate them more severely than men. This is partly explained by the lower status women have in most organizations. In turn, lower power compels silence by targets and a reliance on passive conflict resolution strategies at work, avoidance, or denial. Women are more likely to seek social support outside work rather than confront their bullies. Hence, the preponderance of women callers to WBI for help.

RACE AND TARGETHOOD

Individuals who are members of historically disadvantaged groups enjoy civil rights protections codified in state and federal laws. That is, if they are members of a protected status group, such as women, minority races, older workers, or disabled individuals, they may be eligible to file a complaint with their employer when nondiscrimination policies are believed to have been violated.

For the WBI national survey (Namie, 2014c), the polling organization provided data on four races of adult Americans surveyed: Hispanics, African Americans, Asian Americans, and Whites. Each of the minority groups experienced a higher rate of abusive conduct than Whites (24%): 33 percent of Hispanics, 33 percent of African Americans, and 33 percent of Asian Americans. Despite workers' familiarity with the illegality of racial discrimination in contemporary workplaces, that knowledge seems to have not mitigated the mistreatment for members of those minority groups. The data do not allow us to ascertain whether bullying supplements existing discrimination or supplants it.

When we combine the prevalence rates for those who directly experienced bullying with those who only witnessed it, we estimate the total proportion of individuals "affected" by bullying. The national, whole sample, rate was

48 percent (Namie, 2014c). Hispanics were the most affected (57%), African Americans second (54%), and Asian Americans third (53%), compared to Whites at 44 percent.

There were differences across the racial groups in which particular factors best explained the bullying. The four factors across which survey respondents were asked to apportion a percentage of responsibility for abusive conduct were target characteristics, perpetrator characteristics, the employer, and society. African Americans assigned the high percentages to employers (32%) and society (30%). Of all the racial groups, Hispanics blamed targets the most, assigning 33 percent of responsibility. Perpetrators were blamed most by Whites (47%). Asian Americans placed the most responsibility on employers (46%) of all the groups. The two groups with the highest "external" explanatory factor percentages were African Americans (62%) and Asian Americans (50%). Whites and Hispanics preferred "internal" personality factors to explain bullying (68% and 65%, respectively).

WHEN THERE IS A HISTORY OF PRIOR ABUSE

Targets of bullying completed an online WBI survey asking when they had first experienced abuse of any kind in their lives. Forty-four percent reported their first abuse happening in their family of origin (Namie, 2013b). In a more detailed study of targets, WBI found that 20 percent had been subjected to partner violence, 20 percent abuse from siblings, 17 percent physical child abuse, 11 percent sexual child abuse, and 10 percent adult sexual assault or rape (Namie, 2011c).

To be clear, prior abuse does not put a "kick me" sign on an adult's back. However, it does mean that the adult workplace target of abuse is more likely to recognize the mistreatment than a person without historical experience. The emotional consequences of the emotional abuse will not likely be delayed. Retraumatization repeats the horrific feelings from prior experiences. In fact, trauma victims can have their symptoms triggered by traumatizing events not related to their original experiences.

Targets who have never been traumatized can be bullied for weeks or months and not recognize it. How? The American workplace can be toxic in so many ways that the mistreatment directed at them could be considered routine, the "way business is done" in that organization. Also, targets tend to be rule followers, not mavericks (or "social deviants," as business school researchers characterize them). Targets would not reflexively report wrongdoing without first looking inward to explore how they might have caused a problem for their bully. This misdirection postpones correctly identifying it for what it is. It is often family or coworkers who convince the target that the perpetrator's actions are not normal nor acceptable.

Targets late to recognize their bullying are at high risk for great harm, according to Janoff-Bulman's (1989) model. They are the ones with the most idealistic and optimistic views of the world, having never been significantly mistreated. Prior abuse may serve to accelerate recognition. The earlier recognition happens, the quicker resolution steps can be taken. In this way, victims of prior abuse may be quicker to mobilize into action.

TARGET BEHAVIORS AS PREDICTORS

We now explore a set of behaviors that workers exhibit that increase the likelihood that they will be targeted for bullying and mobbing. We begin with actions that appear on the surface to be counterintuitive triggers. That is, they are all positive. The three we discuss are (1) targets' superior technical skills at the job, (2) targets' popularity within the organization, and (3) targets' aversion to political gamesmanship.

From our experiences with targets, the oft-repeated mantra is, "I just want to be left alone to do my job." This plea to stop meddling comes from workers with a strong work ethic. They feel obligated to perform well in exchange for a paycheck. They are not the socially deviant workers; their workplace citizenship behaviors are above reproach. They are the exemplars—honest, independent, ethical, team players, and the go-to experts about work procedures for coworkers (Namie, 2003). From a hiring employer's perspective, they are ideal conscientious employees.

STRENGTH AND OPTIMISM ARE LIABILITIES

WBI asked self-described targets of bullying to state why they were targeted. First in 2003 and then again in 2012 (Namie, 2012b), targets said bullying was partly triggered by their strengths, not their weaknesses. The two strengths were technical and social skills of a higher level than their assailants. Making the social comparison with a stronger person creates tension for some perpetrators. Rather than be comfortable with another person's talent, regardless of rank—subordinate, peer, or superior—some individuals choose to displace or torment the threatening person. This is especially true when the target is known to be more intelligent than her or his bully (Kim & Glomb, 2010).

In an experimental study (Parks & Stone, 2010), group members resented the most altruistic member for making a greater contribution to the group. That effort was construed by others as a superior, though unexpressed, morality than theirs. The least selfish members were banished, second in unpopularity only to the most selfish group members.

It seems that possessing a cluster of positive work-related traits can get an American worker in trouble, notwithstanding employer calls for engaged employees right under their noses. Behavioral patterns gleaned from court cases with which we have been involved, coupled with the thousands of telephone tales we have heard, confirm that strong performers are the individuals targeted. But why does performance strength not translate to the social skill of rebuffing targeted psychological assaults?

We could as easily ask why nurses who tirelessly care for the health of others typically ignore the impact of bullying on their personal health. Teachers who are effective with the children of strangers often cannot teach their own children. Lawyers who advise clients regarding legal conduct can commit unethical acts without self-restraint. It is paradoxical.

It is possible that the attention of targets is placed solely on work tasks with little time or desire to focus on potentially destructive people in their work environment. In other words, limits to one's cognitive load may put the target at risk.

Janoff-Bulman's (1989) theory of traumatization is a better explanation. She sorts individuals who have been exposed to potentially traumatizing life events into two groups: those who experience symptoms of trauma and those who do not. A belief in the benevolence (equity, fairness) of the world is the key determinant of group membership. Holding such an optimistic belief, an assumption about the surrounding world is shattered when bullying invades that person's life. It overwhelms the person's ability to cope. It is dissonant with a lifetime of positive experiences and expectations—that people are fair, that hard work will be rewarded, and that respect is reciprocated. When those assumptions are shattered, trauma can result.

So, it is the optimist who is at risk. Cynical, pragmatic, and nonidealistic individuals recognize workplace political game playing as normal. The latter group is less shocked, less surprised, less disappointed, and hence less likely to be traumatized. Targets we have known were all surprised, bushwhacked. They never saw the assaults coming at them.

Targets can stubbornly remain optimistic, even in the face of years of brutal abuse. One-quarter of targets cling to the belief that their employer will save them once it learns the extent of the emotional abuse they suffer (Namie, 2013a). While they wait for the impossible, their health is further compromised from unremitting exposure to distress.

Targets tell us via all channels of communication with the WBI that they are not political game players (Namie, 2012b). Some would see this as naiveté, a liability. Kramer (2006) asks us to place a higher value on political intelligence than emotional intelligence in organizations. People without political intelligence, being unaware of power relationships and consequences for exercising power over others, have a harder time recognizing manipulative Machiavellian behavior by others. It also makes it impossible for them to mount a successful counter to the sophisticated campaign of destruction engineered by one or more perpetrators intent on displacing the target. The requisite skills are not in their personal repertoire.

Of course, we never advise targets to lower themselves and act like bullies themselves. If every person was driven purely by office politics, no work would ever get done.

BEHAVIORAL ANTECEDENTS TO TARGETHOOD

From our two decades of work in bullying and mobbing, we have observed the following behaviors to be typical of targets. Some targets are "nice." Unfortunately, this is not a compliment as we commonly use the term. Look up the definition. The word's Latin root, *nescius*, means to be ignorant. It evolved into being foolish or stupid. So, it's better to be kind than nice. To be nice can make one easily exploited.

Many targets exhibit behaviors that make them *high self-disclosers*. They voluntarily offer their future enemies ammunition with which to assassinate their character in the early stages of their relationships, including those with potential perpetrators. They consider personal information to be building blocks of new relationships. That is, they share intimate facts about their lives expecting their bosses and coworkers to reciprocate with secrets of their own. Sadly, such disclosures enable the exploitation around which future bullying is centered. Bullies are not open, disclosing types. They solicit information from open targets only for the purpose of using it against them later.

The risk from a strong attachment to a beloved job is *an overinvestment of one's identity in that job*. When work and identity become inseparable, a vulnerability opens for others to see. One need not be a sadistic perpetrator to notice that the targeted individual may lack a balance between life at work and life outside work. But sadistic bullies, especially those in management, can leverage that overinvestment into maximizing the distress that accompanies the threat of job or career loss.

It is difficult enough for targets to resume their lives after the bullying incidents have been resolved, favorably or not. Starting over in another department at the same firm or finding work at another employer is tough. But generating a new narrative for one's life is a much larger task (Lutgen-Sandvik, 2008). It essentially requires reinventing oneself after first grieving the loss of the original self. When both job and identity are lost to bullying, the task is doubly hard.

Perfectionism is stressful and impossible to attain (Wirtz et al., 2007). High-achieving bullied targets can fall prey to this demanding self-imposed form of criticism. In some cases, targets tell us they won't leave their job until they prove to their bully that the lies about their incompetence are false. They will work harder to produce a result that will never satisfy the abuser. Nor will it satisfy themselves. As they push harder, lose more sleep, grow more fatigued, and experience neurological changes from the prolonged stress, they become less capable of their former performance level. They are chasing an unattainable standard.

Ironically, perfectionism is used by bullies to justify their arbitrary and capricious work assignments with floating, unachievable standards.

PERPETRATORS' CHARACTERISTICS

Bullying can be partially explained as being a compensatory process. Garcia, Restubog, Kiewitz, Scott, and Tang (2014) traced the practice of abusive supervision to perpetrators' history of aggression learned in their family of origin, mediated by states of angry rumination as adults. And in that angry mental state, threat perception is more likely. Bullies may be adults physically with an immaturity with respect to moral development and emotional intelligence.

Targets in a WBI online survey (Namie, 2012b) rated the abusive-toxic personality of perpetrators as the second most important factor in why bullying happened to them. It was ranked behind the target's superior technical skill. Clearly, bullying is predicated upon perpetrators' need to control the lives of others. Perpetrators unilaterally choose whom to target, the choice of tactics, timing—including onset, cessation and resumption—and location. Targets lack the power to alter those choices. The process is in no way a voluntary collaboration.

The non-WBI literature supports our conclusion about targets being good performers. Fast and Chen (2009) believe a bully's aggression is cover for supervisory incompetence. Treadway, Shaughnessy, Breland, Yang, and Reeves (2013) documented that politically skilled bullies hide their lack of performance skill from their superiors. This is done through ingratiation up the chain of command. Ingratiation cements the bond between perpetrator and management sponsor. This allows bullies to abuse with impunity (Namie, 2009). When and if the bully is ever exposed, the sponsor (as senior manager in the organization) often denies the facts and retains the favored, albeit brutal, bully. A longitudinal five-year study bolsters our impunity claim (Glambek, Skogstad, & Einarsen, 2016). Bullies are rarely punished.

There are two sources—one anecdotal and one empirical—that suggest that bullying could be an interaction between dominating predators and their prey. The first is derived from our consulting work in organizations. The work requires assessing and counseling identified perpetrators. From that group comes a rationale for bullying that defies rationality. Many bullies have told us that they preferred not to act abusively but that some individuals who could not counter initial aggression deserved mistreatment. "Why?" we inquired. Because she or he could not be respected by virtue of "allowing" themselves to be intimidated and humiliated. In this way, bullying and mobbing were warranted by the unwilling perpetrator. This perverse reasoning mirrors explanations based on provocative victims.

The empirical evidence for an interaction between abusers and abused victims comes from a study of Canadian prisoners only obliquely related to bullying and mobbing. Book, Costello, and Camilleri (2013) asked maximum-security prisoners—some psychopathic and some not—to choose from among videotaped men and women the ones they deemed easiest to mug (with intent to rob or steal from) and to describe their selection criteria. The videotaped people had described whether they had previously been victimized or assaulted in a way greater than bullying. One woman had been the victim of sexual assault. Psychopathic prisoners showed the highest accuracy in selecting the participants who had actually been victimized. Within the psychopathic group, prisoners who scored high in the interpersonal/affective characteristics of psychopaths—manipulativeness, superficial charm, and lack of empathy—were the ones with greatest identification accuracy. These are the people most likely to exploit others. The psychopathic traits of lack of behavioral control and impulsivity were not predictors of victim identification accuracy.

Psychopaths high in the interpersonal traits of psychopathy based their selection of a victim primarily on gait. In other words, they attended to how the videotaped person walked, either with confidence or "like an easy target." Gait was the principal cue connoting vulnerability. As it turns out, the videotaped people who displayed vulnerable body language were more likely to have had a history of victimization in the past. Psychopaths then chose those same people for future victimization. The authors suggest this may account for bullied targets' inability to escape repeating their targethood across situations and employers over time.

This study informs the literature on bullying and mobbing with its demonstration that some victims do exhibit external displays of vulnerability. Some predators can sense it, while other observers cannot. But shouldn't we distinguish everyday perpetrators of bullying and mobbing in workplaces from imprisoned psychopaths?

Robert Hare, the North American authority on psychopathy, found in one study of managers and executives that the prevalence of the traits in corporate America matched the proportion in the general population (Babiak, Neumann, & Hare, 2010). The psychopaths at work tended to be the highest-ranking executives. The most psychopathic managers in the study scored highest in the affective and interpersonal domains of psychopathy (and not in the lifestyle and antisocial domains). Researchers had performance evaluation data from subordinates and managers of those individuals. They were rated the most charismatic by others even when performance skill was low. The researchers' conclusion was that the pairing of psychopathic abilities and intelligence enables managers to manipulate and con others. This finding matches the Book et al. (2013) finding above with psychopathic prisoners.

OSTRACISM, ISOLATION, AND SELF-HARM

Bullying polarizes witnesses in the workforce. When bosses give explicit orders to exclude the targeted worker from work production activities, they are playing the "divide and conquer" game. Exclusion from social life with coworkers typically follows.

Coworkers sort themselves into supporters of either the target or perpetrators. Approximately 15 percent of coworkers publicly side with the bully and act aggressively toward the target, their former friend (Namie, 2008). Once the target has been ostracized by peers, those peers go to extraordinary lengths to rationalize their antisocial actions. They even muster anger at the target for not having stood up and confronted the bully (Diekmann, Walker, Galinsky, & Tenbrunsel, 2012). Thus, the target is made to appear undeserving of help in coworkers' eyes.

The targets most at risk of self-harm or suicide are people who live alone. The bullying experience is extremely distressful. Social support is an important—perhaps the most important—antidote to that distress. Family and friends become the only sources of validation and continuity once colleagues from work sever ties with their bullied coworker (Namie, 2011b). Pets are an inadequate buffer against the sea of overwhelming misery that bullying can bring.

Social isolation of the distressed target allows irrational, delusional, and self-destructive thoughts to emerge unchallenged. For years, the relationship between bullying and suicide among adults was simply correlational. That is, the fact that bullying caused targets to consider suicide could not be confirmed. In a longitudinal study spanning five years with a sample of bullied and nonbullied workers, it was found that bullied targets were twice as likely to consider suicide even after five years (Nielsen, Nielsen, Notelaers, & Einarsen, 2015).

In one case with which this author is familiar, the target took great pains to draw the link between the years of managerial abuse and the suicide. The target wrote multiple letters explaining the reasons for the suicide. Police found the blood-stained letters near the body after the shooting. No misinterpretation could be made by those who found the target. This is rare. It is more likely that bullied workers lose their jobs, became estranged from family and children over time, lose homes to foreclosure, live in their cars, begin to binge on alcohol, and decide to take their lives when all perceived viable options run out. With this pattern of decline, it is difficult to connect suicides to former workplaces. Yet, it was the abusive workplace that unraveled the once complete and satisfying lives of targets.

POWERFUL BULLYING-RELATED EMOTIONS—SHAME AND GUILT

There are many synonyms for workplace bullying: abusive conduct, psychological violence, status-blind harassment, mobbing, abusive supervision, workplace aggression, and emotional abuse. Emotional abuse evokes the most common harm associated with bullying, psychological injury. Bullying is nonphysical workplace violence.

The principal emotions related to bullying are shame and guilt. Targets universally experience shame. Abusers are keen to generate that sense of shame, feelings of utter worthlessness as a human being. When parents and teachers abuse children, the adults tell the children they will never amount to anything. They are a big "nothing." When spouses emotionally abuse their partners, they say how unlovable the person is and how lucky he or she is to be with her or him.

When workplace abusers disrespect another person at work, they treat them with contempt. They treat them with utter disregard reserved for subhumans, for those not on the same level as the perpetrator. The bully's narcissism provides the sought-after contrast. The bully wants to convince the target that the bully is a "somebody" while the target is a "nobody." When targets come to believe the lie—it only needs to be repeated enough without the bully held accountable—it starts to define the target's reality. Shame is the result. Healing from shame takes longer than it takes to simply remove the bully or to transfer the target to safety.

Guilt is a different emotion. Targets feel guilty for not having the courage, wits, or ability to counter the perpetrator's initial onslaught. Once the domination begins, it is impossible for the target to get to safety alone. Conscientious targets wish they had done more. In fact, it requires either a large group of coworkers (a rare occurrence) or a benevolent and caring employer to provide the requisite psychological safety.

PERCEIVED INJUSTICE AND OBSESSIVENESS

Two interrelated behaviors dominate the bullying experience throughout the prolonged ordeal—sensing grave injustice and an obsessiveness over case details. Bullying is unjust because it is primarily noncontingent punishment. There is no rational explanation for why the target was selected and then subjected to the barrage of negative acts over such a long period of time. If the bullying is primarily done behind closed doors, there are no witnesses. Perpetrators who torment their prey in private know that if the description of events emerges as a tie—"he said, he said"—managers win. The targets' sense of injustice ensues.

The injustices of bullying can be characterized as procedural (the rules not being applied fairly or consistently for all employees, the target is singled out for exclusion of rules); distributive (resources needed to succeed are denied to the target and not to other employees, guaranteeing failure); and retributive (fairness in punishment, it is meted out only to the target, not others, and for no rational reason). Injustice nags the target, often long after the employer's incomplete resolution. Injustice is rooted in the violation of the target's expectations about the work world that are shattered by the bully and the employer who backs the bully.

Obsessiveness is the inability to let go of the feelings of injustice. The comparative, and objectively verifiable, data related to the differential treatment received by the target should not be ignored. Targets' thinking goes as follows: if only people would listen and if they would read the voluminous accumulated documentation of years of incidents, justice could be won. Justice is unlikely when the employer acts as both judge and jury and does not fully understand the nuances of bullying and mobbing.

Without independent investigations, the truth is difficult to discover. Employers rely on independent outsiders only in cases involving high-ranking managers and executives accused of harassment whom they wish to retain. In fact, most bullied targets never see an investigation in response to their complaints. Why? Because the vast majority of events, however destructive or disgusting, fail to meet EEO criteria. Without illegality and the exposure to liability, employers do not feel compelled to respond to mere bullying complaints.

Another explanation for targets' obsessiveness is that they are not believed by authorities with whom the sordid details are eventually shared. In only 9 percent of cases are targets believed, according to a WBI online survey (Namie, 2014a). For 53 percent of targets, the employer needed to discredit the person as a liar. About 20 percent were believed until the perpetrator gave an opposing tale ("he said, he said"), and 18 percent of targets were not believed because the misconduct described sounded too outrageous to be possible. From the perspective of the senior manager hearing a report that one of his favorite supervisors is a tyrant, it is more important to retain the bullying supervisor, his personal friend, and to save face rather than to believe a worker he doesn't know. It's not rational, but it's understandable. This is exactly what happens in many cases.

When the case details are rejected by HR or the EEO officer for ineligibility (as happens in most same-race or same-gender cases) and the target is not believed, the target feels delegitimized. She or he is told that no response by the employer is compelled by law. This triggers the downward emotional spiral characteristic of the bullying experience.

ANGER AND EMBITTERMENT

Consider a bullying case months after the bullying started. After shock from the employer's denial of responsibility subsides, targets tend to grow angrier. In many ways, their mental health is better. They are less vulnerable and emotionally fragile. However, they seem to have become more like the social deviant from business school research studies. They certainly did not start that way, but over time, they evolved from the kind, patient, hardworking, naïve worker into a one-person social movement hell-bent on finding justice for themselves.

Linden (2003), a German psychiatrist, described a subtype of adjustment disorder and defined it as the mental reaction to exceptional negative life events. He called it embitterment, *posttraumatic embitterment disorder* (PTED). PTED has three core factors: a strong sense of injustice, deterioration of psychological well-being, and a desire for revenge. In a study gauging PTED levels for bullied and nonbullied workers, Karatuna and Gok (2014) found consistently higher scores by bullied workers on all dimensions. With prolonged exposure to distress, changes in economic status, and strained family relations, the nastiness of embitterment becomes understandable.

WHAT STOPS THE BULLYING?

Bullying is demeaning, ostracizing, disempowering, cruel, threatening, humiliating, untruthful, and unrelated to the work itself. Yet, it persists. In an online WBI survey (Namie, 2014b), 1,000 respondents rank ordered the aspects of bullying that upset them the most. Ranked from first to sixth are the following: (1) Being accused of incompetence when I possessed more technical skills than my accuser; (2) Being humiliated in front of coworkers; (3) Feeling ashamed though I did nothing wrong; (4) Management ignoring my complaint; (5) Having coworkers ostracize, exclude, and reject me; and (6) Retaliation that followed my complaint.

In a large sample WBI survey online, we asked targets whether their bullying had stopped, and, if it had, what had made it stop (Namie, 2012a). It had stopped for 25 percent of targets when they were terminated; another 25 percent had been made so miserable at work that they had been constructively discharged; 28 percent had voluntarily quit, typically for their health's sake; and 11 percent had transferred to a different job with the same employer (also perceived as unjust because "Why should I be the one to move? I did nothing"). Remarkably, perpetrators suffered some negative consequences—5 percent were fired, and 6 percent were punished (but actions taken remained confidential and unknown to the target). It is clear that targets pay the price to end the bullying. Once targeted for bullying, individuals have a 7 in 10 chance of losing their jobs.

Given the high rate of displacement from bullying, what is the financial and safety aftermath for targets? WBI asked the questions in 2011. The financial impact is slightly more negative than positive—53 percent earned less money in a subsequent job; 39 percent did earn more. One-quarter of the displaced targets never got a next job. With respect to safety from bullying, 37 percent escaped and were safe; 31 percent were bullied in the next job. The best outcome—higher pay with safety—was the fate of only 12 percent of targets. The rest got higher pay but were bullied again (17%) or lower pay but were safe from bullying (25%) (Namie, 2011a).

Much of our advice to targets centers on raising their awareness of the importance of avoiding irreversible stress-related health problems. Health and well-being need to be made prominent when making decisions about staying with an employer who refuses to ensure psychological safety for its workers. Too often, only fiscal matters factor into decisions. How can one not "afford to leave" if the risk of stress-related lifetime impairments is 100 percent?

AN IMAGINED FUTURE UNDERSTANDING OF BULLYING AND TARGETS

Here is our modest proposal for how workplace bullying in America could and should be understood:

- It is a natural, sometimes unavoidable, phenomenon that thrives only when ignored or treated with indifference. When noticed and made transparent, it will lose its harmful impact.
- Measure the prevalence in organizations and work together to attenuate the rate. There need be no organizational shame. The only shame is knowing and failing to act.
- Hold executive leadership responsible for eradicating it. It is not an "HR issue." Only the culture shapers can have lasting impact and force change quickly.
- Tie the absence of abusive conduct to requisite managerial performance evaluations and criteria for promotions and retention.
- Calculate the preventable costs associated with bullying. Monitor reductions in risk management expenditures.
- Destigmatize bullying for targets. Deny its power to shame. Encourage targets to meet and be agents of change for the organization.

- Name perpetrators without demonizing them. Grant that they acted first out of ignorance. Launch training in key management skills. Allow them to change their behavior at work to avoid dismissal. If they don't change, terminate.
- Adopt correction techniques using proper methods, not the misapplication of conflict resolution tools. Focus on restorative justice for all affected employees.
- Make changes in hiring procedures that once made abusers appear attractive. Change reference checking processes.
- Do not block hiring talented people if they were once targeted for bullying. Make it easy to be honest about the necessity of leaving a toxic workplace.
- Recognize the competitive advantages to the employer bold enough to recruit talent promising a psychologically safe workplace. Make the designation as coveted as being one of the "Best Places to Work."

TARGETS ARE THE BEST OF US

We compliment targets for representing the "better nature" of us all, as humans. The exploited ones are the most sensitive among us. Regardless of the occupation they rely on for a paycheck, they are our society's artists, creative innovators, practitioners of peaceful relations, the orchestrators of social networks at work based on kindness and loyalty, and the opposition to the societal coarseness fostered by our capitalist culture. It's a zero-sum competitive, winner-take-all regimen that demands hypervigilance and constant attention to self-preservation, with little time left for compassion for others. And in that dark side of the world of work, targets shine the rare light. For this, they are mocked and selected for abuse.

> Work is, by its very nature, about violence to the spirit as well as the body. . . . It is, above all (or beneath all), about daily humiliations. To survive the day is triumph enough for the walking wounded among the great many of us.—Studs Terkel (1974, p. xi)

Most employees in most workplaces are not doing anything close to what they love. They are dispirited. We have found targets to have been very adaptive prior to their bullying. For one-third of adult targets, the abuse sustained at work is the first time they had faced such humiliation, intimidation, and threats (Namie, 2013b). Only one-fifth had been bullied during their school years. So, before bullying, they believed in a fair world. Fueled by a strong work ethic and optimism, they had managed to find joy in their work. They deserve our admiration.

And they deserve thanks from every coworker for being the pioneers in a toxic workplace. Targets are the sacrificial "canaries in the mine" who pay with their jobs, careers, health (and sometimes their lives) as they live, and then report, the terror of a workplace lacking psychological safety for all workers. Each target story is a tragedy. It is worse when many workers are allowed to suffer while the repeating, chronic abuser is allowed to operate without accountability. Targets are sacrificed needlessly as the employer dodges responsibility by effectively blaming the displaced workers, falsely branded as poor performers.

Not all bullied targets are whistle-blowers in the technical sense. The facts they reveal are not only about fraud or waste. However, they do reveal abuse—abusers and abusive practices—that a good employer should neither tolerate nor encourage. Whistle-blowers are incorrigible truth tellers. Targets are the same. Organizations could learn lessons from both targets and whistle-blowers. In America, it is common to shoot messengers who bring unsolicited news that all is not well in the trenches. Alas, that is the current fate of bullied targets.

UNIQUENESS OF THE WBI PERSPECTIVE

We based information in this chapter on four sets of data.

First, we used our direct anecdotal experience with individuals who had sought advice from us about extricating themselves from their bullying workplaces. We stopped counting the telephone sessions at 10,000. From those typical hour-long harangues, we came to recognize patterns common to bullying incidents and to patiently listen for the unique and innovatively cruel twists adopted by perpetrators. The calls flooded the Workplace Bullying Institute's toll-free line in WBI's early years. Eventually, Jessi Eden Brown, the counseling professional whose chapters (chapters 13 and 14) can be found elsewhere in this volume, handled those desperate callers for WBI.

Our other deep engagement with targets derives from nearly two decades of training and consulting to organizations and unions. This work intimately connects us to people and their workplaces.

Second, we have gathered empirical data about the nuances of targets' experiences from nearly 50 online WBI surveys. The studies relied on self-selected (nonscientific) respondent samples with results that can be extrapolated only to targets. The results are informative and useful regarding the lives of targets.

Third, we used our experiences with legal cases as expert witnesses. It is a smaller sample than the two above sources. In this role, the author derives in-depth knowledge about real-world incidents within complex organizations.

Fourth, and finally, the academic scientific literature on bullying has grown exponentially since the movement's founding by Heinz Leymann in the late

1980s (Leymann, 1990). Most articles published in peer-reviewed journals on the topic rely on targets as research participants simply because they are the most readily available. Most articles are not experiments based on randomization. Instead, they are descriptive by necessity. We cite works that best describe the target experience.

REFERENCES

Babiak, P., Neumann, C. S., & Hare, R. D. (2010). Corporate psychopathy: Talking the walk. *Behavioral Sciences and the Law, 28*(2), 174–193.

Book, A., Costello, K., & Camilleri, J. A. (2013). Psychopathy and victim selection: The use of gait as a cue to vulnerability. *Journal of Interpersonal Violence, 28*(11), 2368–2383.

Chesler, P. (2009). *Woman's inhumanity to woman*. Chicago: Chicago Review Press.

D'Cruz, P., & Noronha, E. (2010). Protecting my interests: HRM and targets' coping with workplace bullying. *Qualitative Report, 15*(3), 507–534.

D'Cruz, P., & Noronha, E. (2011). The limits to workplace friendship: Manageralist HRM and bystander behavior in the context of workplace bullying. *Employee Relations, 33*(3), 269–288.

Derks, B., Van Laar, C., & Ellemers, N. (2016). The queen bee phenomenon: Why women leaders distance themselves from junior women. *Leadership Quarterly, 27*(3), 456–469.

Diekmann, K. A., Walker, S. D. S., Galinsky, A. D., & Tenbrunsel, A. E. (2012). Double victimization in the workplace: Why observers condemn passive victims of sexual harassment. *Organization Science, 24*(2), 614–628.

Fast, N. J., & Chen, S. (2009). When the boss feels inadequate: Power, incompetence, and aggression. *Psychological Science, 20*(11), 1406–1413.

Garcia, P., Restubog, S. L. D., Kiewitz, C., Scott, K. L., & Tang, R. L. (2014). Roots run deep: Investigating psychological mechanisms between family aggression and abusive supervision. *Journal of Applied Psychology, 99*(5), 883–897.

Glambek, M., Skogstad, A., & Einarsen, S. (2016). Do the bullies survive? A five-year, three-wave prospective study of indicators of expulsion in working life among perpetrators of workplace bullying. *Industrial Health, 54*(1), 68–73.

Janoff-Bulman, R. (1989). Assumptive worlds and the stress of traumatic events: Application of the schema construct. *Social Cognition, 7*(2), 111–136.

Jones, E. E. (1979). The rocky road from acts to dispositions. *American Psychologist, 34*(2), 107–117.

Karatuna, I., & Gok, S. (2014). A study analyzing the association between post-traumatic embitterment disorder and workplace bullying. *Journal of Workplace Behavioural Health, 29*(2), 127–142.

Kim, E., & Glomb, T. M. (2010). Get smarty pants: Cognitive ability, personality and victimization. *Journal of Applied Psychology, 95*(5), 889–901.

Kramer, R. M. (2006, February). The great intimidators. *Harvard Business Review, 84*(2), 88–96.

Leymann, H. (1990). Mobbing and psychological terrorization. *Violence and Victims*, 5(2), 119–126.

Lind, K., Glaso, L., Pallesen, S., & Einarsen, S. (2009). Personality profiles among targets and nontargets of workplace bullying. *European Psychologist*, 14(3), 231–237.

Linden, M. (2003). Posttraumatic embitterment disorder. *Psychotherapy and Psychosomatics*, 72(4), 195–202.

Lutgen-Sandvik, P. (2008). Intensive remedial identity work: Responses to workplace bullying trauma and stigmatization. *Organization*, 15(1), 97–119.

Namie, G. M. (2003). *2003 Report on abusive workplaces*. Retrieved from http://www.workplacebullying.org/multi/pdf/N-N-2003C.pdf

Namie, G. M. (2007). *2007 WBI U.S. workplace bullying survey*. Retrieved from http://workplacebullying.org/multi/pdf/WBIsurvey2007.pdf

Namie, G. M. (2008). *How coworkers respond to workplace bullying*. Retrieved from http://www.workplacebullying.org/multi/pdf/N-N-2008A.pdf

Namie, G. M. (2009). *Still bullying with impunity*. Retrieved from http://www.workplacebullying.org/multi/pdf/N-N-2009D.pdf

Namie, G. M. (2011a). *Post-bullying financial woes for bullied targets*. Retrieved from http://www.workplacebullying.org/multi/pdf/2011-IP-B.pdf

Namie, G. M. (2011b). *Who supports bullied targets?* Retrieved from http://www.workplacebullying.org/multi/pdf/2011-IP-L.pdf

Namie, G. M. (2011c). *Workplace bullying and prior experiences with abuse*. Retrieved from http://www.workplacebullying.org/multi/pdf/2011-IP-All.pdf

Namie, G. M. (2012a). *Effectiveness of bullied target resolution strategies*. Retrieved from http://www.workplacebullying.org/multi/pdf/WBI-2012-StrategiesEff.pdf

Namie, G. M. (2012b). *How bullies select their targets*. Retrieved from http://www.workplacebullying.org/multi/pdf/WBI-2012-IP-I.pdf

Namie, G. M. (2013a). *Barriers to bullied targets leaving their jobs*. Retrieved from http://www.workplacebullying.org/multi/pdf/WBI-2013-IP-C.pdf

Namie, G. M. (2013b). *First-time abusers in bullied targets' lives*. Retrieved from http://www.workplacebullying.org/multi/pdf/WBI-2013-IP-H.pdf

Namie, G. M. (2013c). *The timing and results of targets confronting bullies at work*. Retrieved from http://www.workplacebullying.org/multi/pdf/WBI-2013-IP-D.pdf

Namie, G. M. (2014a). *Believe it or not: Impugning the integrity of targets of workplace bullying*. Retrieved from http://www.workplacebullying.org/multi/pdf/WBI-2014-IP-F.pdf

Namie, G. M. (2014b). *The many ways workplace bullying offends its targets*. Retrieved from http://www.workplacebullying.org/multi/pdf/WBI-2014-IP-C.pdf

Namie, G. M. (2014c). *2014 WBI U.S. workplace bullying survey*. Retrieved from http://www.workplacebullying.org/multi/pdf/WBI-2014-US-Survey.pdf

Nielsen, M. B., Nielsen, G. H., Notelaers, G. & Einarsen, S. (2015). Workplace bullying and suicidal ideation: A 3-wave longitudinal Norwegian study. *American Journal of Public Health*, 105(11), e23–e28.

Opotow, S. (2012). The scope of justice, intergroup conflict, and peace. In L. R. Tropp (Eds.), *The Oxford Handbook of Intergroup Conflict* (pp. 72–88). New York: Oxford University Press. doi:10.1093/oxfordhb/9780199747672.013.0005

Parks, C. D., & Stone, A. B. (2010). The desire to expel unselfish members from the group. *Journal of Personality and Social Psychology, 99*(2), 303–310.

Purpora, C., Blegen, M. A., & Stotts, N. A. (2012). Horizontal violence among hospital staff nurses related to oppressed self or oppressed group. *Journal of Professional Nursing, 28*(5), 306–314.

Salin, D., & Hoel, H. (2013). Workplace bullying as a gendered phenomenon. *Journal of Managerial Psychology, 28*(3), 235–251.

Tepper, B. J., Duffy, M. K., Henle, C. A., & Lambert, L. S. (2006). Procedural injustice, victim precipitation, and abusive supervision. *Personnel Psychology, 59*(1), 101–123.

Tepper, B. J., Moss, S. E., & Duffy, M. K. (2011). Predictors of abusive supervision: Supervisor perceptions of deep-level dissimilarity, relationship conflict, and subordinate performance. *Academy of Management Journal, 54*(2), 279–294.

Terkel, S. (1974) *Working*. New York: Pantheon.

Timmer, D. A., & Norman, W. H. (1984). The ideology of victim precipitation. *Criminal Justice Review, 9*, 63–68.

Treadway, D. C., Shaughnessy, B. A., Breland, J. W., Yang, J., & Reeves, M. (2013). Political skill and the job performance of bullies. *Journal of Managerial Psychology, 28*(3), 273–289.

Wirtz, P. H., Elsenbruch, S., Emini, L., Rudisuli, K., Groessbauer, S., & Ehlert, U. (2007). Perfectionism and the cortisol response to psychosocial stress in men. *Psychosomatic Medicine, 69*(3), 249–255.

4

Organizational Risk Factors: An Integrative Model for Understanding, Treating, and Preventing Mobbing and Bullying in the Workplace[1]

Len Sperry

This chapter reviews three intersecting sets of organizational dynamics and offers an integrative model of mobbing and bullying that integrates them and provides a useful basis for the assessment, conceptualization, treatment, and prevention of mobbing and bullying. This model is illustrated with a case example of organizational dynamics operative in a case of mobbing. It begins with the limitations of zero tolerance and related policies. After a brief description of the integrative model, it describes each component: organizational, team, and individual dynamics. Before delving into the substance of this chapter, I would like to share a few words about what informs this model.

One of my responsibilities as vice chair of the Department of Psychiatry and Behavior Medicine at the Medical College of Wisconsin was to lead the Division of Organizational Psychiatry and Corporate Health. This division provided training and consultation to organizations dealing with various corporate issues. An issue of increasing concern then was violence, including mobbing and workplace bullying, which the division understood as rooted in organizational dynamics. At the time, this was a minority perspective, the opposite of the prevailing perspective, which was that mobbing and bullying were caused by individual dynamics, that is, the perpetrator was a "bad apple." A second perspective was that mobbing and bullying could best be understood as interpersonal conflict or the result of interpersonal violence, the "bad apples" explanation. At the time, there was less receptivity to organizational dynamics or the "bad barrel" explanation, and even less to the integrative perspective, the individual, team, and organizational dynamics explanation.

My research, consulting, clinical work, and writing on mobbing and bullying (Duffy & Sperry, 2012; Duffy & Sperry, 2014; Sperry, 2009) has reflected the organizational dynamics (Sperry, 1993, 1996a, 1996b, 1998, 2002) and the integrative model (Sperry, 2009). It was not uncommon for others to comment that while my conceptualization on mobbing and bullying is interesting, it is too complex and not essential in explaining, treating, or preventing these forms of violence. Until very recently, the sentiment was that policies and interventions should be based on the simplest possible explanation, that is, individual or interpersonal dynamics. As research would soon reveal, the simplest explanation turned out to be a simplistic explanation.

A case in point is the *zero-tolerance policy*, which for the past two decades has been adopted by nearly all school organizations. This policy is based on the premise that individual dynamics or interpersonal dynamics are the primary antecedents of mobbing and bullying. The corporate world would later follow that lead with zero tolerance for mobbing and bullying behavior with timely and consistent punishment, such as termination. Sutton's (2007) provocatively titled book, *The No Asshole Rule*, reflects the belief that zero tolerance and related policies provide the best explanation and most effective way to deal with and to prevent mobbing and bullying. However, mounting research, reports of national organizations and advisory groups, and the everyday experience of administrators and executives have increasingly pointed to the failure of such individually and interpersonally based policies.

Then as now, the organizational dynamics viewpoint has been proposed as essential in understanding, treating, and preventing mobbing and bullying (Sperry, 2009). In fact, taken together, these three perspectives—the individual dynamics along with the interpersonal or work team dynamics and the organizational dynamics—intersect in an integrative fashion. A basic premise of this chapter is that organizational dynamics are the basic perspective for understanding, treating, and preventing mobbing and bullying, and when augmented by the individual perspective and the interpersonal work team perspectives, together, all three perspectives provide a much fuller, more comprehensive, more compelling explanation of mobbing and bullying than any single perspectives.

THE FAILURE OF ZERO-TOLERANCE POLICIES AND THE CASE FOR AN INTEGRATIVE MODEL

As the tide of negative effects of mobbing and bullying escalated in both school and corporate organizations, there was great hope that a decisive administrative solution, zero-tolerance policies, would stem this tide. Across the United States, school districts moved quickly to implement this "solution." Corporations moved slower in implementing it.

Zero-tolerance policies in school organizations are a punitive response to mobbing and bullying. These policies are based on the premise that individuals (students) are perpetrators of violence and that the prospect of punishment serves as a deterrent and that failure to strongly punish such misbehavior sends the message that schools are not serious about the safety of students and staff. A related premise is that nonpunitive interventions allow disruptive students to remain in the classroom and prevent other students from learning.

Both of these premises have been repeatedly challenged over the past two decades, even though most school districts have adopted such policies. For example, in 2011, the National Education Association (NEA), in a widely publicized report (Boccanfuso & Kuhfeld, 2011), endorsed several effective, nonpunitive alternatives to zero tolerance. These included both targeted behavioral programs as well as a preventive approach to violence and misbehavior. Rigorous evaluations of these programs have shown them to have significant, positive impacts on student behaviors and academic achievement. All promote positive youth development and skills. In contrast, this report indicated that there was little research to support zero-tolerance policy-based programs.

In May 2016, the National Academies of Sciences, Engineering, and Medicine, the influential independent government advisory group of researchers, issued the book-length report *Preventing Bullying through Science, Policy, and Practice* (NASEM, 2016). In the report, they review all research on zero-tolerance policies and conclude that such policies are ineffective in combating bullying. They recommend ending all such policies that automatically suspend or expel students for bullying. In fact, the conclusion of their review was that such policies can do more harm than good because they fail to provide skill training or replacement behaviors to those who are suspended or expelled. The report also noted that zero-tolerance policies lead to an underreporting of bullying because many people—teachers, administrators, and targets—commonly view suspensions as overly punitive.

In contrast to school organizations, there is relatively little research on the impact of zero-tolerance policies in corporate organizations. This lack of research support is perplexing given that many such organizations have incorporated punitive policies in their codes of conduct and employee handbooks. Nevertheless, a critical review of zero-tolerance and related policies in corporate settings is necessary. An important research study concluded that organizational dynamics rather than individual or interpersonal dynamics underlie mobbing and bullying in work organizations (Hutchinson, Wilkes, Jackson, & Vickers, 2010). Even though organizations have zero-tolerance and in-house reporting policies on mobbing and bullying behavior in place, "informal organizational alliances may serve to counteract these policies and ensure reports are minimized, ignored or denied. Further, the absence of interpersonal conflict as a factor in bullying, suggests the reliance upon mediation premised upon resolving interpersonal conflict maybe an inappropriate response" (Hutchinson et al., 2010, p. 179).

This is not to say that zero-tolerance policies are never effective nor appropriate, because in some circumstances they may be (McKay, Ciocirlan, & Chung, 2010). However, there is no research evidence supporting the premise that mobbing and bullying are exclusively caused by individual or interpersonal dynamics. In fact, evidence strongly supports the premise that organizational dynamics underlie mobbing and bullying, and as described in the following sections, it is probably more accurate to say that there are three intersecting sets of dynamics—individual, interpersonal, and organizational dynamics—that best explain this distressing and destructive phenomena (Samnani & Singh, 2012).

RESEARCH SUPPORT FOR THE INTEGRATIVE MODEL

As previously noted, the basic premise of the integrative model (Sperry, 2009) is that integrating or incorporating organizational dynamics, individual dynamics, and work dynamics together provides a more comprehensive and compelling explanation of mobbing and bullying than any one of the dynamics alone. Until recently, there has only been a limited research basis for such a model. However, research on mobbing and bullying in the workplace has grown significantly over the past 20 years. Taken together, this research provides considerable support for the integrative model.

An extensive review of the existing research literature on workplace mobbing and bullying has recently been compiled and published by Samnani and Singh (2012). Based on their review of this literature, these researchers have developed a conceptual model of the antecedents and consequences of mobbing and bullying. They have concluded that there are interrelated levels of antecedents or dynamics of workplace mobbing and bullying: individual, group (work team), and organizational. They also posit a societal level, although they note that there is considerably less research on its impact than on the other three levels. In addition, based on their review and conceptual model, they have identified several critical areas for future research that will extend the current literature (Samnani & Singh, 2012).

Additional research support for the integrative model comes from research on the multidimensional model of bullying and mobbing described by the research team headed by Hutchinson (Hutchinson et al., 2010). Distinct from the just-described model based on a review of research (Samnani & Singh, 2012), the multidimensional model was derived from structural equation modeling (SEM) and confirmatory factor analysis (CFA) of randomized survey data. Their multidimensional model was the best fit model derived from these sophisticated analyses by both SEM and CFA. Of the three sets of dynamics—individual, work group, and organizational factors—organizational characteristics were confirmed to be the critical antecedents of mobbing and bullying. They were found to influence both the occurrence of mobbing and bullying and the resultant consequences.

The following sections review the theory and research on each of the three intersecting sets or levels of the model. These include organizational dynamics, individual dynamics, and work team dynamics.

ORGANIZATIONAL DYNAMICS

Organizational dynamics refers to the interplay of influences among an organization's subsystems. An organization can be visualized as a set of five overlapping concentric circles, wherein each circle represents the subsystems of an organization: structure, culture, strategy, leaders, and personnel within a larger circle representing the organization's external environment (Sperry, 1996a). Organizations also have a history and developmental trajectory. Each of these six subsystems plus the developmental trajectory is briefly described along with its potential for fostering or preventing abusive actions, that is, mobbing.

Structure

Structure refers to mechanisms that aid an organization to achieve its intended task and goals (Sperry, 1993). It specifies the reporting relationship of all roles, their span of control and scope of authority, and their location in a hierarchy of roles, that is, an organizational chart. Structure also specifies the expectations of each role along with the policies, procedures, and routines for interacting and communicating with others in the performance of the task. A key component of an organization's structure is its policies and procedures, which are written documents that specify how the day-to-day duties of the organization are carried out and by whom. Because the internal and external environments of the organization continue to change, new policies or revisions of existing policies are needed. For example, federal law led to the addition of anti–sexual harassment policies in employee handbooks throughout corporate America.

Another element of structure involves the number of hierarchical levels within an organization. Bureaucratic organizations typically have four hierarchical levels: entry-level workers, the supervisory level, the middle management level, and the top management or the executive level. In contrast, flatter and more nonbureaucratic organizations typically have as few as two levels:

the worker level and the management level. Certain types of abusiveness are more likely to occur at given levels of an organization. For example, although teasing and goading, name calling, physical contact, and overt accusations may occur at any level of the organization, they are more common at lower levels. In the middle levels of the organization, abusiveness can manifest as attacks on professional or managerial skills and abilities and is often accompanied by political maneuvering to discredit others. On the other hand, abusiveness at the executive level can be more subtle and exclusionary (Sperry, 1998). Depending on the level of the organization, abusiveness can function as a means of degrading, controlling, discrediting, or excluding an individual.

One of the most tangible structural components of an organization is a given job. Several aspects of a job that can trigger abusiveness include occupational selection, standards of productivity, work pressure, and job stress as well as role conflict, ambiguity, and overload. Certain occupations and organizations are inherently more aggressive, and potentially abusive, than others. This is particularly the case with the construction, mining, and timber industries as well as police forces and football teams (Brodsky, 1976).

Defined standards of productivity can also foster abusive behavior. Increased demands for productivity lead to work pressure that can result in abusiveness. Productivity standards are utilized in business because they provide an objective standard against which to measure an employee's work behavior or a work team's outputs. Accordingly, a worker may be slow or sloppy and become a target for abusiveness by supervisors (Brodsky, 1976). Or, a worker may be too productive and become a target for abusive behavior by coworkers for being a rate buster, that is, an overperformer.

Work pressure refers to externally imposed work demands or pressures exerted on employees to achieve maximum productivity. Increasingly, the private sector is based on maximization of profits through high productivity. Accordingly, the demand is for workers to increase production so that the organization can become even more competitive. Work pressure results and is the inherent tension in a production system. Work pressure is threatening because workers realize that they may lose rewards or control over their environment and that punishment may be imposed if they fail to measure up. Such punishments might be threats, reprimands, job transfers, dismissal, or disruption of friendship patterns (Brodsky, 1976).

A recent review of research on organizational factors involved in mobbing and bullying highlights four dimensions of structure. These dimensions are changes in one's position, work pressure and job stress, performance demands, role conflict, and lack of role clarity. All are identified as antecedents of workplace mobbing and bullying (Agervold, 2009).

More recent empirical research found that reward is the aspect of organizational structure that is the most predictive antecedent of mobbing and bullying. In an organization, reward takes several forms: salary, benefits, promotions, and personal and professional recognition. Various sanctions, including fines, suspension, and termination, are the reverse side of reward. Teams also reward team members, particularly for their loyalty and willingness to follow group norms and leader initiatives, both positive and negative. The Hutchinson research team found that mobbing and bullying is "more prevalent in environments where actors who engage in the behavior do not receive effective sanctions, and may, instead, be awarded through perks, promotion or favorable treatment. These forms of tolerance and rewards may function to influence the occurrence of bullying and enable repetitive, patterned and escalated forms of the behavior" (Hutchinson et al., 2010, pp. 177–178).

Strategy

Strategy refers to the organization's overall plan or course of action for achieving its identified goals (Sperry, 1993). Corporate strategy is based on the organization's core values, vision, and mission statements. Strategic planning and implementation is essential for an organization in achieving its goals. These results will also be manifested in job productivity, satisfaction, and morale instead of complaints of bullying or mobbing.

A basic axiom is that structure should follow strategy, which is to say that the structure of an organization should be designed to be compatible with its strategy. When the strategy of an organization emphasizes productivity and competitiveness at the expense of the well-being and respect for employees, such a strategy—and its supporting structure—can foster abusiveness in the workplace.

Organizations that are serious about being a mobbing-proof organization and whose goal is to create a mobbing-free environment are advised to think strategically. This means integrating this goal into the organization's strategy. Specifically, this means specifying respect and caring as core values, revising the mission and vision of the organization to reflect those values, and specifying human resources policies that foster a mobbing-free environment. It also requires that the strategy is implemented by addressing the goal in a proactive manner and exemplifying it through management behavior (McKay et al., 2010).

Culture

Culture refers to the constellation of shared experiences, beliefs, assumptions, stories, customs, and actions that characterize an organization (Deal & Kennedy, 1982). The major determinants of culture are the *actual* core values manifested by senior executives, the history of the corporation, and the senior executive's vision of the organization. While an organization's *stated* core values are likely to be described in its vision statement, its *actual* core values are reflected in the corporate culture. Too often, there is a disconnect between stated and actual or manifested core values—what an organizations says it values and what values are actually experienced by the organization's personnel and its customers.

The culture of an organization may be sufficiently offensive, intimidating, or hostile such that it interferes with the ability of certain workers to perform their jobs effectively. In addition, culture can also be offensive and harmful to women, minorities, and other potential targets, such as off-color or ethnic jokes and various kinds of harassing or abusive behavior (Friedland & Friedland, 1994).

Organizational climate is a specific facet of an organizational culture. It refers to the shared perceptions or experiences of employees of the policies, practices, and procedures of their organization as well as the behaviors that are expected, supported, and rewarded (Cooper, 2016). While the broad concept of culture is difficult to measure, it is much easier to accurately assess organizational climate, particularly with survey instruments. A recent study of organizational factors found that a poor social climate was an identified antecedent of mobbing and bullying.

Leadership

Leadership refers to a process of influence whereby a leader persuades, enables, or empowers others to pursue and achieve the intended goals of the organization (Sperry, 2002). An effective leader can create a vision that tells members where the corporation is going and how it will get there and then galvanizes members' commitment to the vision by being ethical, open, empowering, and inspiring (Bennis & Nanus, 1986). Furthermore, the leadership subsystem plays a critical role in shaping themes that harmonize the subsystems of structure, culture, and strategy (Kets de Vries & Miller, 1984).

For abusiveness to occur in an organization, the aggressive elements must exist within a culture that permits and rewards abusiveness, and leadership must allow or permit the abusiveness. Accordingly, both the type and degree of abusiveness are a function of the extent to which there is a pervading sense of "permission to act abusively" on the part of the abuser (Sperry, 1998). Without this sense of permission, the individual who undertakes to abuse another will himself or herself become the target of ostracism, another kind of abusiveness, by his or her fellows. Abusiveness in the work setting requires some level of acquiescence by management. Typically, supervisors tacitly support one worker's abuse of another by looking the other way or failing to discipline the perpetrator. Other times, supervisors participate in or actually initiate the abusive behavior. Occasionally, a superior may know of a lower-level supervisor's harassment of employees but will not intervene, believing that to put an end to it would undermine that supervisor's authority (Brodsky, 1976).

Among the various leadership styles are the transformational, the transactional, and the authoritarian. *Transformational leadership* is characterized by the leader who motivates and inspires a work team to perform tasks and to achieve the desired goal. *Transactional leadership* is characterized by a leader's use of authority to reward or sanction team members depending on their results. *Authoritarian leadership*, also called *autocratic leadership*, is characterized by the leader's control over all decisions with little or no input from team members.

Recent research findings on the role of organizational leadership style as an antecedent of mobbing and bullying are particularly telling. It was found that while transformational and transactional leadership styles decreased the likelihood of mobbing, the authoritarian leadership style increased it. Furthermore, the paternalistic or authoritarian leadership style was mildly and negatively associated with mobbing (Ertureten, Cemalcilar, & Aycan, 2013). These researchers also found that the more employees perceived downward mobbing, that is, mobbing supported by leadership, the more employees were likely to report lower job satisfaction, lower job engagement and commitment, and a higher turnover intention, that is, a desire to leave the organization (Ertureten et al., 2013). This research confirms earlier findings that an autocratic leadership style fosters mobbing and bullying actions (Agervold, 2009). Finally, Hutchinson and colleagues (2010) found that misuse of legitimate leadership authority was a key antecedent of workplace mobbing and bullying.

Personnel

Personnel refers to the members of an organization, particularly employees but not those in formal leadership positions. Since a leader's success is largely a function of the productivity and behavior of the employees that report to him or her, personnel is an important subsystem in any organization. Personnel function best when the leadership style is responsive and supportive of personnel needs and expectations (Uris, 1964). For example, personnel with an affinity for the autocratic approach may respond favorably to the autocratic leadership style, whereas personnel seldom respond favorably to an abusive leadership style. The lack of match between leadership and personnel can account for conflict, decreased productivity and performance, and the health consequences of workplace abusiveness.

Recent research on the impact of mobbing on employees who were targets of or knew about mobbing and bullying in their organization found that these employees experienced lower job satisfaction and higher turnover intention (Akar, Anafarta, & Sarvan, 2011). Related research found that increased burnout, lower job satisfaction and a perceived decrease in organizational support were noted among such employees. Decreased engagement and organizational commitment were noted in another study (Gülle & Soyer, 2016).

External Environment

These internal subsystems interact and mutually influence one another. The configuration of these five subsystems is also greatly affected by its external subsystem, the environment (Sperry, 2002). The environmental subsystem refers to those factors outside the organization's internal subsystems that influence it and interact with it. The environment includes economic, legal, political, and sociocultural factors. It also includes technological factors, such as community relations, workforce availability, competitors, shareholders and other stakeholders, market saturation, customers' demands and changes, government statutes, environmental policies, other regulatory requirements, and standard industrial practices. In times of turbulence and rapid social and technological changes, the environmental subsystem may exert as much or more influence on organizational direction and functioning as other subsystems. Federal legislation, or its absence, in the case of mobbing and bullying, has and will continue to significantly impact the health and well-being of an organization's personnel.

Developmental Trajectory

Organizational dynamics provide a cross-sectional view of an organization but reveal little about an organization's developmental history or longitudinal view. Just as a person grows and develops and then declines, so do organizations. Six stages of organizational development and decline are described here (Sperry, 1993, 2002). They are new venture, expansion, professionalization, consolidation, early bureaucratization, and late bureaucratization. These stages of organizational development are important in understanding the development of mobbing. Organizations have periods in their growth and development where, during times of expansion, transition, and decline related to increasing external threats, the organization is more likely to create conditions giving rise to the emergence of mobbing.

New Venture

The first stage of an organization's development involves the conception of a *new venture*. The critical tasks at this stage include defining a target group (e.g., pet lovers, students, computer users) and developing a product or service that targets such a group. Accomplishing these tasks requires the ability to extend or create a market need; the willingness to make a risky investment of time, energy, and money to create an organization that satisfies the unmet need; and the ability to create an embryonic organizational structure that can provide that service to the target group. These abilities are characteristic of the entrepreneurial leader, and the entrepreneurial leadership style is most compatible with this stage.

Expansion

The second stage of development involves rapid growth. This stage commences very quickly or after the organization has been in new venture for a number of years. The major problems that occur in *expansion* involve growth rather than survival. Organizational resources are stretched to their limits as a new wave of members joins the organization, as demands for services increase, and as the organization's original, often primitive, day-to-day operating system becomes overwhelmed. Organizational growing pains are painfully present. Growing pains signal that changes are needed and cannot be ignored; they imply that the organization has not been fully successful in developing the internal system it needs at a given stage of growth.

Professionalization

The first two stages represent the entrepreneurial organization. Even though they may have lacked well-defined goals, policies, plans, or controls, these organizations prospered. However, as this critical size is being achieved, the organization begins experiencing growing pains as its members outgrow its initial structure and operating systems (Flamholtz & Randle, 2000). New structures and operating systems must be implemented. Another wave of new members requires more formal planning, defined roles and responsibilities, performance standards, and control systems. Developing a strategic planning and management system then becomes the critical task of the *professionalism* stage. This in turn requires organizational development efforts that provide the concurrent level of skill training needed to implement this management system.

Consolidation

After transitioning to a professionally managed system, the organization can focus its efforts on *consolidation*. Consolidation means maintaining a reasonable increase in growth while developing the organizational culture. Culture becomes a critical concern in this stage because current members may no longer share the organization's original core values, vision, and mission of what the organization is or where it is going. At this stage, the knowledge base and skills of members are regularly upgraded. Leadership that combines entrepreneurship and integration is most compatible with this stage. Individual members who are able to function interdependently with superiors, coworkers, and subordinates are most compatible with the organization's collaborative or participative styles.

Early Bureaucratization

As the organization transitions to the *early bureaucratization* stage, there is a subtle but clear shift from substance to form. Status seeking, business as usual, and appearances characterize the behavior of members. Later in this stage, the focus shifts to internal turf wars. Backbiting, coalition building, and paranoia are common. Growing pains are particularly intense as members' dissatisfaction mounts. In some organizations, negativity threatens to poison the organization's climate. At first, leadership was content to rest on the organization's laurels, but now it shifts to a self-protective mode. Cliques become the usual mode of communication, and the best and brightest start leaving the organization.

The emphasis has clearly shifted from growth and maintenance to decline. The structures and the planning and development functions are much less responsive than in previous stages. Leadership is marked by administration and, in the later part of this stage, by inefficient administration. Decentralization and delegation become increasingly threatening to leadership, and efforts to recentralize power are frequent behaviors during this stage. Counterdependency behavior, including passive-aggression, becomes commonplace, reflecting demoralization among workers as well as managers.

Late Bureaucratization

Many of the subunits and subsystems of the organization become clearly dysfunctional during the final stage of *late bureaucratization*. Miscommunication is commonplace, and two-way communication is limited or nonexistent. Coordination and follow-through are the exception rather than the rule: "My right hand is seldom aware that my left hand exists, much less knows what it is doing." New members are no longer informed of the mission statement and strategy, and, for all members, the organizational culture reflects a sense of helplessness and a lack of common direction. "Come late, leave early," "do as little as you have to," "don't try to change anything," and "protect job security at all costs" are attitudes reflecting the organizational culture in late bureaucratization.

The critical function at this stage is to forestall and avoid extinction, as the organization is figuratively in intensive care and is being maintained by external life-support systems. The corporate subsystems are conflictual and nonresponsive to the needs of both members and clientele. Little if any training and development occur. Administrators struggle to buy time and prolong the organization's life. But inefficiency and ineffectiveness are to be expected. Clients find access to responsive subsystems the exception rather than the rule. Not surprisingly, the reemergence of dependency among members complements the autocratic style of leaders. The eventual demise of the organization seems inevitable, and consultants report that the prognosis for organizations at this stage for even heroic interventions is poor (Adizes, 1999).

Organizations are particularly sensitive to mobbing and other forms of abusiveness during periods of transition between stages, particularly as an organization attempts to reorganize and restructure. Strandmark and Hallberg (2007) found that periods of workplace reorganization or restructuring often give rise to workplace abuse. In my experience, mobbing is also likely to occur in the expansion and bureaucratization stages.

INDIVIDUAL DYNAMICS

The view that individual dynamics, that is, factors such as personality traits, experiences, motivations, and other psychological dynamics, can be sufficient to cause aggressive and abusive behavior has been challenged by considerable research on situational factors, that is, group or team dynamics. While many clinicians and psychotherapists favor this individual dynamics orientation, some researchers consider that an individual's behavior in an organization is more likely to be influenced by powerful situational and systemic or organizational determinants (Zimbardo, 2007). In fact, in specific circumstances, otherwise morally good individuals engage in abusive behaviors because of situation and systemic factors. Because society is overly invested in the individualistic view of abusive behavior, it should not be surprising that it attempts to treat or manage such behavior by subjecting individuals to therapy, rehabilitation, or incarceration rather than address situational or systemic factors. However, if the principal cause is group or organizational dynamics, such individual interventions are likely to fail or be less effective than if the interventions included these other causal factors.

It should be noted that organizational dynamics can provide a useful marker in understanding the likelihood that bullying and mobbing will occur within a given organization. However, while organizational dynamics may be a necessary condition for workplace mobbing and bullying, it is not a sufficient condition. In other words, being employed in an organization with a mobbing or bully-prone strategy, structure, culture, and leadership does not, in and of itself, predict that such abusive behavior will occur.

Personality

Organizational dynamics appear to affect employees differentially. Accordingly, an employee's personality style and level of psychological maturity interacts with the organization's dynamics and differentially influences that employee's response to mobbing and bullying (Mantell, 1994). Because some targets experience more health consequences of mobbing and bullying than others (Einarsen, Hoel, & Cooper, 2003), the hope was that understanding the personality structure of a target would be useful in predicting such consequences. Unfortunately, there has been little research addressing this consideration.

However, it has been established that there are at least three different psychological profiles of targets of mobbing and bullying (Matthiesen & Einarsen, 2001). One profile involves an extreme range of severe psychological problems and personality disturbances, that is, depressive, anxious, suspicious, uncertainty, and confusion. A second profile is characterized by depression and suspiciousness. And the third profile reflects a quite normal personality, despite having experienced mobbing. The researchers conclude that specific vulnerabilities and hardiness factors exist among some targets. Specifically, those with psychological problems, low self-esteem, and a high degree of anxiety may be more likely to feel bullied and harassed and find it difficult to defend themselves from such behavior (Matthiesen & Einarsen, 2001). Given the small sample sizes and methodological shortcomings and no replication of the results, the findings of this study are quite preliminary.

Other research has consistently found that those with higher levels of neuroticism and higher levels of negative affect (anger, fear, and sadness) are more likely to experience workplace mobbing and bullying. Ethnicity seems to also be a factor in that Hispanics have been reported to be more likely to be targets than Blacks, Asians, and Whites (Samnani & Singh, 2012).

Similarly, there is very little research on the psychological profile of those perpetrating workplace bullying and mobbing. In one study, bullies described themselves as being high on aggressiveness and were found to be low on social competence and high on social anxiety (Einarsen, et al., 2003). Based on survey data and clinical observation, Namie (2003) suggests that all bullies are narcissistic and egocentric. Although these individuals may not meet all the criteria for a DSM-5 (American Psychiatric Association, 2013) diagnosis of narcissistic personality disorder, they do exhibit some narcissistic features. Other research has found that being male rather than female, facing job insecurity, and experiencing high job strain, that is, stress from high job demands and low control over their work, are each predictive of perpetrating mobbing actions (Samnani & Singh, 2012).

Work Orientation

In addition to personality, work orientation may explain why some targets are more vulnerable to the consequences of mobbing and bullying. *Work orientation* is defined as an individual's attitude toward work reflected in his or her thoughts, feelings, and behaviors about work (Wrzesniewski, McCaukley, Rozin, & Schwartz, 1997). Research has identified three work orientations: job, career, and calling. Individuals with a job orientation view their work as simply a job, a means to a financial end so they can engage in nonwork activities such as hobbies. Individuals with a career orientation value prestige, promotion, pay, and status. They work because it leads to higher self-esteem, higher social standing, and increased power (Bellah, Madsen, Sullivan, Swidler, & Tipton, 1985). Not surprisingly, their personal identity is tied to their work, and so their professional identity becomes their personal identity. For individuals with a calling orientation, work is their passion. They value the sense of fulfillment it provides while achieving their personal mission to make the world a better place. They also tend to have higher levels of job engagement and organizational commitment (Davidson & Caddell, 1994). Research finds that most professionals adopt a career orientation, while those who adopt a calling orientation report higher job satisfaction and life satisfaction compared to those with job and career orientations (Wrzesniewski et al., 1997).

Work orientation might suggest the extent to which a target is physically and psychologically impacted by mobbing as a function of his or her attitude about work. Targets with a career orientation typically experience considerably more distress and disability than those with other work orientations. Because their personal-professional identity is so closely tied to their work, targets with career orientations might view the abusive behavior of others and the threat of job loss as a significant invalidation of their personal-professional identity. Accordingly, they might conclude that they no longer have a purpose in living, and they may die or commit suicide soon afterward (Westhues, 2005). Recent research indicates that individuals with a high level of organizational commitment are less likely to engage in mobbing, perhaps suggestive that those with a calling orientation are the least likely to perpetrate mobbing (Gülle & Soyer, 2016).

WORK TEAM DYNAMICS

In contrast to individual dynamics that are central in clinically oriented psychology, organizational psychology presumes that situational factors are the primary determinants of an employee's behavior. In the workplace, employees function as members of a formal work team, or of a group led by a manager, or as a member of an informal group. Whatever the situation, work team dynamics can serve as a powerful antecedent in workplace mobbing and bullying.

Group or Team Cohesiveness

A group of individuals in the workplace tend to function as a unit, or as an in-group, because of group cohesiveness and other powerful forces that keep such individuals together and focused on the same goals. As these cohesive forces fail, disintegration begins to occur, and the group ceases to exist. Among the most powerful of these group cohesive forces are dependency and narcissism (Mantell, 1994). In its most benign form, narcissism is recognizable as group pride. When individual members feel proud of their group, the group itself experiences pride. A universal but less benign form of group narcissism is animosity toward an out-group, that is, the creation of an enemy. A surefire way of increasing group cohesiveness is to incite a group's hatred of an external enemy. Not surprisingly, shortcomings within the in-group are easily overlooked by focusing attention on the shortcomings of the out-group.

Formal versus Informal Groups

Work groups or teams may be formal work teams or informal groups. The informal group is also known as the informal organization (Leavitt & Bahrami, 1987). It is formed by personnel around a workplace issue or an outside activity. In reality, informal groups can perform many of the organization's duties. Chance meetings at the water cooler, informal lunch meetings, and impromptu telephone calls can effectively implement the organization's strategy. In contrast, these informal groups can have an agenda contrary to the organization's stated mission. They could disrupt work production in a given unit within the organization, or they could harass a particular individual, that is, mobbing. In short, a disgruntled or hostile informal group can effectively undermine the organization's strategy (Mantell, 1994).

Referring to informal groups as *informal organizational alliances*, Hutchinson's research (Hutchinson et al., 2010) emphasizes the role of these informal alliances as a central mechanism through which a work team's mobbing and bullying actions are mediated. Furthermore, this research suggests that the nature and extent of informal alliances significantly influence the likelihood that work team members will tolerate or engage in mobbing and bullying as a function of being socialized into group norms that are tolerant and facilitative of this behavior (Hutchinson et al., 2010).

ILLUSTRATION OF INDIVIDUAL, GROUP, AND ORGANIZATIONAL DYNAMICS IN A CASE OF MOBBING

The following case illustrates how three sets of dynamics intersect: individual, group or team, and organizational. It demonstrates how these dynamics foster workplace mobbing and its impact on the target despite the organization's policies against harassment.

Teresa "Terry" Lopez is a married 25-year-old Mexican American who had worked as a registered nurse for a group medical practice for the past six months. The practice included six physicians, eight nurses, and four support staff. Terry had worked as a floor nurse at a university teaching hospital for two years prior to starting at the group practice. Although she liked the challenge of working with adult medical and surgical patients and got excellent performance reviews, she found the stress of working rotating 10-hour shifts was seriously affecting her health. She experienced chronic insomnia and other health concerns.

The group practice offered her regular hour shifts with no nights or weekends and a high salary, which was important given her husband's unemployed status. Terry was considerably younger than the other nurses and support staff, and she had replaced a well-liked older nurse who it was said "had issues" with the medical director and was apparently forced to "retire." Needless to say, the nursing staff was not particularly happy to welcome Terry. Initially, most of them were cordial but distant, but two were anything but cordial.

Mobbing began almost from the first day Terry arrived at the practice. She soon sensed that two nurses wanted her gone. Soon afterward, two more nurses and three support staff joined that group. After three months, the situation had become intolerable. Terry not only found it very difficult to do her job amid the sabotaging behaviors, but she was unable to be very supportive to her husband who was depressed about his recent job layoff. Terry began experiencing tension headaches and increased asthma symptoms. She reviewed the employee handbook, and after reading the policy on harassment and zero tolerance, she decided it made the most sense to file a complaint with the human resources (HR) director. Soon thereafter she would come to regret this decision.

After a week of no response from Claire Radnor, the HR director, Terry at first asked and then later demanded a meeting with Ms. Radnor. The director arranged for them to meet in the lunchroom, which was empty at the time. Terry was surprised to learn that the director downplayed the situation, saying, "These nurses have been here a long time and get along with everyone. Maybe you're a little thin-skinned. It may take a while longer to feel a part of the group, so hang in there." The director got up and left. Terry was confused and hurt and began to cry. Her first thoughts were that her future at the practice looked grim and that she would probably have a hard time finding a similar position because she could not see herself returning to hospital nursing.

For the next few weeks, Terry felt greatly distressed at work and increasingly symptomatic. She got the silent treatment from some, negative comments from others, and harassing unsigned notes. On two occasions, her nursing notes on patients "disappeared," leading her to stay after her shift ended to rewrite them. No one would talk to her at lunch, and she was not invited to off-site social activities. Any effort on her part to "feel part of the group" seemed to be rebuffed or ignored. She became increasingly depressed and was unable to give emotional support to or receive emotional support from her husband, who remained unemployed and depressed himself.

Fortunately, a friend told her about a psychological consultant who worked with people like Terry who had work issues. They arranged to meet, and Terry explained her circumstances. The consultant, Dr. Patricia Danzinger, undertook an investigation of individual, work group, and organizational dynamics. Terry was surprised that the practice was not receptive to the consultant's request for information and to interview staff members, beyond that of a short meeting with the HR director. Nevertheless, Dr. Danzinger was able to develop an understanding and conceptualization of why and how mobbing behavior occurred and was fostered within the practice. Besides information from Terry and the HR director, the consultant reviewed information from the practice's Web site, patient brochure, and employee handbook. Here is a brief summary of her notes of that assessment and conceptualization.

Assessment of Organizational Dynamics

Strategy

The stated mission of the practice was "quality medical care provided by a highly trained and committed professionals." The actual mission appeared to be meeting profit projections and limiting malpractice and negligence. The stated core values were competency, efficiency, and putting patients first. It is noteworthy that also putting staff first was not mentioned, nor was respect for staff.

Structure

The medical practice had three organizational levels consisting of management, the medical director, nursing director, and HR director (first level); physicians (second level); and nurses and office staff (third level). The practice had reasonably adequate policies and procedures for business transactions. However, its employee manual only addressed discrimination based on ethnicity, religion, and age, in addition to an anti–sexual harassment policy. While there was a zero-tolerance policy with stipulations for suspension and termination, there was no indication that the policy had been implemented or used. Specifically, there were no procedures in place for reporting complaints of harassment nor for investigating or adjudicating them. Training in prevention of harassment was not part of new employee orientation nor for existing employees.

Leadership

The medical director was an older physician who had been a MASH surgeon during the Vietnam War. His leadership reflected both the autocratic and paternalistic styles. The leadership styles of the nursing director and the HR director appeared to be autocratic. All three seemed to focus on efficiency with a minimum of problems and the belief that employee concerns would either solve themselves or be resolved by termination.

Culture

The medical practice's culture reflected the personality of the medical director, a paternalistic older physician who demanded results and was impatient to have patient problems resolved quickly and quietly, and he expected the same for staff issues. For him, the practice was doing well when there were no reported problems. Accordingly, the nursing director and HR director saw to it that the practice was doing well.

Personnel

Most of the physicians, nurses, and support staff had been employed at the practice for several years and were quite loyal to the medical director and his way of running the practice. Terry was the newest employee and did not appear to understand and accept the prevailing culture nor share the medical director's vision for how personnel issues were to be resolved.

External Environment

Because of the changing health care environment, it was unlikely that the medical practice would be able to continue its current operation, particularly as other similar practices had been bought out by hospital corporations or affordable care organizations. There was speculation among the physician staff that the medical director would soon sell the practice and retire.

Developmental Trajectory

The practice appeared to be at the early bureaucratization stage, and at the same time, it was facing major restructuring. It has been pointed out that workplace reorganization or restructuring can engender workplace abuse (Strandmark & Hallberg, 2007). Workplace abuse is also likely to occur in the early bureaucratization stages. In this respect, the practice is quite vulnerable to mobbing.

Assessment of Individual Dynamics

Terry's personality pattern is that of being hardworking, conscientious, and pleasing of authority figures. Because of her need to please and be accepted by others, she was particularly sensitive to the abusive remarks and behaviors of her coworkers. Her work orientation appears to be more job-oriented than career-oriented or calling-oriented. It was not always this way, but insomnia and other health problems, as well as family concerns, that is, her husband's unemployment, have influenced her work values.

Assessment of Group Dynamics

The in-group involved in the mobbing consisted of most of the nurses and support staff. Interestingly, the physicians did not seem to be involved in colluding or stopping the abuse. It not known whether the medical director was even aware of Terry's situation. The nursing and HR directors appeared to have misused their authority by colluding rather than resolving the abuse.

Conceptualization and Recommendations

An assessment of the medical practice's dynamics revealed an organization that seemed to focus on the profit and patient outcomes and not on developing staff or resolving staff issues. Consequently, forces that fostered abusiveness were allowed to develop unchecked and even unwittingly reinforced. It appears that Terry's need to attend to her health and family concerns increased her proneness to the abusiveness of the nursing and support staff. At the same time, the practice's strategy, structure, leadership style, culture, environmental factors, and developmental trajectory seemed to support and reinforce the mobbing behavior. It is noteworthy that the zero-tolerance policy had no apparent impact on either dealing with or preventing mobbing in this case.

CONCLUDING NOTE

In sum, an individual employee's response to abusiveness in a workplace setting is influenced and mediated by individual dynamics, group dynamics, and organizational dynamics. Furthermore, individual, group, and organizational dynamics can either foster or reduce the likelihood of mobbing and bullying in the workplace. Of the six organizational dynamics described, the organization's structure, leadership, and culture appear to exert considerable influence on group members, both formal work team and informal group, to act in a healthy, supportive way toward fellow workers or to engage in mobbing or bullying behavior. The case of Terry illustrated these three intersecting dynamics.

Research was presented that supports this integrative model and discredits more simplistic models. Presumably, this integrative model can be useful to consultants and others in dealing with and preventing abusive behaviors in workplace settings.

NOTE

1. Portions of this chapter have been adapted from Sperry, L. (2009). Mobbing and bullying: The influence of individual, work group, and organizational dynamics on abusive workplace behavior. *Consulting Psychology Journal, 61*(3), 190–201; and Sperry, L. (1998). Organizations that foster inappropriate aggression. *Psychiatric Annals, 28*(5), 279–284.

REFERENCES

Adizes, I. (1999). *Managing corporate lifecycles: An updated and expanded look at the corporate lifecycles.* Upper Saddle River, NJ: Prentice Hall.

Agervold, M. (2009). The significance of organizational factors for the incidence of bullying. *Scandinavian Journal of Psychology, 50*(3), 267–276.

Akar, N. Y., Anafarta, N., & Sarvan, F. (2011). Causes, dimensions and organizational consequences of mobbing: An empirical study. *Ege Akademik Bakis, 11*(1), 1467–1479.

American Psychiatric Association (2013). *Diagnostic and statistical manual of mental disorders* (5th ed.). Arlington, VA: American Psychiatric Association.

Bellah, R., Madsen, R., Sullivan, W., Swidler, L. & Tipton, S. (1985). *Habits of the heart: Individualism and commitment in American life.* New York: Harper & Row.

Bennis, W., & Nanus, B. (1986). *Leaders: Strategies for change* (2nd ed.). New York: Harper.

Boccanfuso, C., & Kuhfeld, M. (2011, March). Multiple responses, promising results: Evidence-based, non-punitive alternatives to zero tolerance. *Child Trends, 2011*(9). Retrieved from http://www.nea.org/assets/docs/alternatives-to-zero-tolerance.pdf

Brodsky, C. (1976). *The harassed worker.* Lexington, MA: Lexington Books.

Cooper, C. (2016). *The Blackwell encyclopedia of management.* Blackwell Publishing, Blackwell Reference Online. Retrieved from http://www.blackwellreference.com/public/book.html?id=g9780631233176_9780631233176

Davidson, J., & Caddell, D. (1994). Religion and the meaning of work. *Journal for the Scientific Study of Religion, 33,* 135–147.

Deal, J., & Kennedy, A. (1982). *Corporate cultures: The rites and rituals of corporate life.* Reading, MA: Addison-Wesley.

Duffy, M. & Sperry, L. (2012). *Mobbing: Causes, consequences, and solutions.* New York: Oxford University Press.

Duffy, M., & Sperry, L. (2014). *Overcoming mobbing: A recovery guide for workplace aggression and bullying.* New York: Oxford University Press.

Einarsen, S., Hoel, H., & Cooper, C. (Eds.). (2003). *Bullying and emotional abuse in the workplace: International perspectives in research and practice.* London: Taylor & Francis.

Ertureten, A., Cemalcilar, Z., & Aycan, Z. (2013). The relationship of downward mobbing with leadership style and organizational attitudes. *Journal of Business Ethics, 116*(1), 205–216.

Flamholtz, E. and Randle, Y. (2000) Growing Pains: Transitioning from an Entrepreneurship to a Professionally Managed Firm, new rev. ed. Jossey-Bass, San Francisco.

Friedland, L. & Friedland, D. (1994). Workplace harassment: What mental health practitioners need to know. In L. Vandecreek, S. Knapp, & T. Jackson (Eds.), *Innovations in clinical practice: A sourcebook* (pp. 237–253). Sarasota, FL: Professional Resource Press.

Gülle, M., & Soyer, F. (2016). Examining mobbing perceptions and organizational commitment levels of physical education and sport teachers. *Journal of Physical Education and Sport, 16*(1), 210–216.

Hutchinson, M., Wilkes, L., Jackson, D., & Vickers, M. H. (2010). Integrating individual, work group and organizational factors: Testing a multidimensional model of bullying in the nursing workplace. *Journal of Nursing Management, 18*(2), 173–181.

Kets de Vries, M., & Miller, D. (1984). *The neurotic organization: Diagnosing and changing counterproductive styles of management.* San Francisco, CA: Jossey-Bass.

Leavitt, H., & Bahrami, H. (1987). *Managerial psychology: Managing behavior in organizations* (5th ed.). Chicago: University of Chicago Press.

Mantell, M. (1994). *Ticking bombs: Defusing violence in the workplace.* Burr Ridge, IL: Irwin.

Matthiesen, S. B. & Einarsen, S. (2001). MMPI-2 configurations among victims of bullying at work. *European Journal of Work and Organizational Psychology, 10,* 467–484.

McKay, R., Ciocirlan, C. E., & Chung, E. (2010). Thinking strategically about workplace bullying in organizations. *Journal of Applied Management and Entrepreneurship, 15*(4), 73–93.

Namie, G. (2003). Workplace bullying: Escalated incivility. *Ivey Business Journal, 68*(2), 1–6.

National Academies of Sciences, Engineering, and Medicine (NASEM). (2016). *Preventing bullying through science, policy, and practice.* Washington, D.C.: The National Academies Press. doi:10.17226/23482

Samnani, A. K., & Singh, P. (2012). 20 years of workplace bullying research: A review of the antecedents and consequences of bullying in the workplace. *Aggression and Violent Behavior, 17*(6), 581–589.

Sperry, L. (1993). *Psychiatric consultation in the workplace.* Washington, D.C.: American Psychiatric Press.

Sperry, L. (1996a). *Corporate therapy and consulting.* New York: Brunner/Mazel.

Sperry, L. (1996b). Leadership dynamics: Character and character structure in executives. *Consulting Psychology Journal, 48,* 268–280.

Sperry, L. (1998). Organizations that foster inappropriate aggression. *Psychiatric Annals, 28*(5), 279–284.

Sperry, L. (2002). *Effective leadership: Strategies for maximizing executive productivity and health.* New York: Brunner-Routledge.

Sperry, L. (2009). Mobbing and bullying: The influence of individual, work group, and organizational dynamics on abusive workplace behavior. *Consulting Psychology Journal, 61*(3), 190–201.

Strandmark, M., & Hallberg, L. (2007). Being rejected and expelled from the workplace: Experiences of bullying in the public service sector. *Qualitative Research in Psychology, 4*(1–2), 1–14.

Sutton, R. (2007). *The no asshole rule.* New York: Warner Business Books.

Uris, A. (1964). *Techniques of leadership.* New York: McGraw-Hill.

Westhues, K. (2005). *The envy of excellence: Administrative mobbing of high-achieving professors.* Lewiston, NY: Edwin Mellen Press.

Wrzesniewski, A., McCaukley, C. Rozin, P. & Schwartz, B. (1997). Jobs, careers, and callings: People's relations to their work. *Journal of Research in Personality, 31,* 21–33.

Zimbardo, P. (2007). *The Lucifer effect: Understanding how good people turn evil.* New York: Random House.

PART II

Examining the Impact of Workplace Bullying and Mobbing

5

Workplace Bullying and Mobbing and the Health of Targets

Melody M. Kawamoto

Contrary to the childhood rhyme, "Sticks and stones may break my bones, but words will never hurt me," hurtful words can trigger a spectrum of negative health outcomes. At the mild end of the spectrum, the response may barely be noticeable, such as a fleeting sense of discomfort. However, when hurtful words are repeated and sustained, when attacks evolve into increasingly abusive actions, and when perpetrators use the power of authority or of the group against a target, what might have begun as mild discomfort can progress to severe consequences with respect to the three dimensions of the World Health Organization's (WHO) definition of health: "a state of complete physical, mental and social well-being and not merely the absence of disease or infirmity" (World Health Organization, 1948, para. 1). Unfortunately, bullying, like hurtful words, is often not recognized as harmful, particularly when it appears to be within cultural, social, and organizational norms.

Based on a review of publication dates on PubMed, a database of scholarly biomedical and life sciences literature, research on psychological stressors has increased dramatically since the 1930s, when they were reported to cause negative health outcomes in laboratory animals. Research on workplace bullying, a psychosocial stressor, began to increase in the 1980s, after it was linked to negative health outcomes among workers. The stressors and outcomes are varied and complex. Despite decades of research and hundreds of articles published yearly, many questions remain unanswered, and many issues are still being debated. Thus, as new knowledge from ongoing research is continuously revealed and understanding evolves, summaries of the state of current knowledge quickly become obsolete. For this reason, this chapter will not cover all negative health outcomes of workplace bullying. Instead, it presents examples that illustrate important or unresolved issues, such as the evolution of knowledge and understanding, debates about diagnostic criteria and interpretations of findings, and implications for treatment and prevention.

In an attempt to avoid debates about language and to promote common understanding, this chapter begins by clarifying words and terms that can easily be misunderstood. This chapter focuses on post-traumatic disorders, cardiovascular outcomes, and musculoskeletal disorders because of their clinical and public health importance and because the issues they illustrate are relevant to other negative health outcomes. This chapter closes with an occupational and public health approach to identify and control workplace bullying and prevent its negative health outcomes while also addressing clinical issues.

DEFINITIONS OF WORDS AND TERMS

Misunderstandings arise when words and terms are not clear or the meanings are not shared by all. Different groups, such as employees, managers, lawyers, and health care providers, use words and terms that tend to reflect their particular perspectives and frameworks. A word or term may have a commonly accepted definition within a group, such as a profession or discipline, but may not be understood by outsiders. Differences may also exist within a single group. For example, a word or term may be used long after its historical meaning is no longer relevant, while new words and terms arising from new observations and concepts may undergo years of research and debate before acceptance.

Workplace Bullying

Mobbing, hostile work environment, harassment, disruptive behavior, incivility, and other terms have been used as synonyms for *bullying,* making communication confusing. Different groups have different preferences. For example, employees typically use more informal everyday language, such as *bullying,* while managers tend to use more formal language or jargon, such as *disruptive behavior* or *incivility,* which can be misunderstood and misleading. Legal terms, such as *harassment* and *hostile work environment,* are defined by very specific laws, resulting in a legal use much narrower than what the general public understands. In addition to multiple words and terms, multiple definitions have been proposed to capture the complexity of workplace bullying. Although definitions used in research on workplace bullying have varied, they have been similar to the Workplace Bullying Institute (WBI) definition: "Workplace bullying is repeated, health-harming mistreatment of one or more persons (the targets) by one or more perpetrators. It is abusive conduct that is (1) threatening, humiliating, or intimidating; (2) work interference or sabotage which prevents work from getting done; or (3) verbal abuse" (WBI, 2015, para. 1).

Stressors and Stress

The word *stress*, which is important when discussing workplace bullying, can be confusing. In 1936, Selye, a medical researcher, reported the syndrome that we now know as stress, the stereotypic biological responses seen after exposure to a variety of harmful agents. Initially, the word *stress* was used for both the agent and the body's response. To clarify the difference, Selye (1975) proposed that the agent be called a *stressor* and the response *stress*. Some dictionaries ("Stress," n.d.) and some journal articles still define stress as both the agent and the response. This chapter will use *stressor* for the agent and *stress* for the response, whether psychological or physical.

Psychosomatic Illnesses and Somatoform Disorders

Before the late 19th century, *physical* pertained to the body and what was observable. *Psychological* pertained to the mind and emotions, which were considered to be separate from the body. Definitions of *psychosomatic illness* included "hysteria," "imaginary disease," and "neurosis" (National Institutes of Health, 2011). By the early 20th century, new therapies, psychology experiments, and clinical observations of patients diagnosed with hysteria led to hypotheses that the physical and the psychological were interrelated (NIH, 2011). Subsequently, scientific and technological advances led to observations of what was previously unobservable, showing interactions between physical and psychological processes. The breakdown of the separation between mind and body led to a reconceptualization of psychosomatic disorders. Diagnoses of "hysteria" and "imaginary disease" are no longer made. The term "neurosis" was phased out of the third edition of the American Psychiatric Association (APA) *Diagnostic and Statistical Manual of Mental Disorders* (*DSM-III*) in 1980, although it remains in the WHO publication, *The ICD-10 Classification of Mental and Behavioural Disorders: Diagnostic Criteria for Research* (Bienvenu, Wuyek, & Stein, 2009). Earlier connotations of *neurosis* still persist in the popular media ("Neurosis," 2011) and the general population.

Multidisciplinary collaborations among the medical specialties, psychology, and the social sciences now focus on experimental and clinical studies of biological, psychological, behavioral, and social factors that affect health and disease (American Psychosomatic Society, 2016). This is broader and different from the medical specialty of psychosomatic medicine, which focuses on psychiatric disorders, somatoform disorders, and psychological factors that affect medical, surgical, and other patients (Accreditation Council for Graduate Medical Education, 2015). The term *somatoform disorders* is still used for conditions with physical symptoms that suggest a physical illness but have no demonstrable biological cause or mechanism and have evidence of a relationship with psychological factors ("Somatoform disorder," n.d.). Uses of *psychological* and *psychosomatic* have evolved to reflect changes in scientific knowledge and will likely continue to evolve as research uncovers previously unknown biological causes and their mechanisms.

Injury, Illness, and Health Outcomes

While definitions of a single word may be similar from one dictionary to another, they also vary. *Injury* is harm or damage. Some dictionaries specify infliction by an external force ("Injury," n.d.). One definition specifies that the harm is physical ("Injury," 2014), while another includes psychological harm ("Injury," 2005). The definition of *illness* also varies, and some definitions include pathological conditions of the mind or body ("Illness," 2009, 2011). Both *injury* and *illness* indicate harm to health with physical or psychological outcomes. The word *injury* is probably best understood when the harm is caused by an external factor and the relationship between exposure and harm to health is direct in time and space. *Illness* is probably best understood when the outcome is ill health or a pathological condition, such as a clinical syndrome or disease, that would not be considered an injury.

In this chapter, *negative health outcomes* will refer to negative states of personal health that could be the result of an exposure to the causal factor of interest. Whether an outcome is called an injury or an illness is not as important as the fact that the outcome is a harm to health. Research studies about relationships between workplace bullying and certain observed health outcomes have shown negative or conflicting results; not all suspected outcomes have been studied, and some true effects may still be unsuspected. Thus, while outcomes could be effects, *effects* may not be the correct term for all outcomes.

Symptoms, Signs, and Syndromes

A *symptom* is subjective evidence of a health problem that is perceived only by the person experiencing it. A *sign* or *finding* is objective evidence of a health problem that can be observed by health care professionals and others as well as the affected individual. A *syndrome* is a combination of symptoms or signs that may be unrelated but, when they occur together, create a distinct clinical picture that suggests a specific health condition or its cause ("Syndrome," n.d.).

Comorbidities

Morbid refers to disease or pathological state ("Morbid," n.d.), and *comorbid* refers to disease or condition that occurs simultaneously with another ("Comorbid," n.d.).

Other words and terms will be defined as needed where they are used.

NEGATIVE HEALTH OUTCOMES ASSOCIATED WITH WORKPLACE BULLYING

Symptoms and Diagnoses

In Europe in the 1980s, Leymann (1990) recognized that psychological abuse and terror in the workplace were causing severe psychological consequences for targets. He noted that a variety of stressors triggered the same physiological response and that different individuals experienced different health outcomes. He also noted that secondary consequences, such as loss of job and social support, were additional stressors that magnified the harm. When introducing this phenomenon he called *workplace mobbing* to the English-speaking world, the negative outcomes he listed included feelings of desperation and total helplessness, rage, anxiety, and despair; depression, hyperactivity, compulsion, and suicide; psychosomatic illnesses; and possible immune system effects. He suspected that the large number of psychiatric diagnoses might have been related to the absence of information about social factors that would have suggested work-relatedness (Leymann, 1990). He commented that the misdiagnosed conditions could have been "psychosocial occupational illness[es]" (Leymann, 1990, p. 122). He listed social isolation, stigma, job loss, and loss of coping resources as some of the negative social outcomes of workplace mobbing (Leymann, 1990). Social well-being, it should be remembered, is a dimension in the WHO definition of *health* (World Health Organization, 1948).

Leymann & Gustafsson (1996) looked at a representative sample of the Swedish workforce and found 350 employees (15%) who were identified as targets of workplace mobbing. The reported symptoms fell into recognizable categories of stressor-related outcomes, such as cognitive effects, psychosomatic symptoms, symptoms of the neuroendocrine stress response, muscular tension, sleep problems, and symptoms that suggested post-traumatic stress disorder (PTSD) and general anxiety disorder.

A WBI online health survey of self-identified targets found that the most frequently reported diagnoses and conditions noted by health care professionals were uncontrollable mood swings (70%), heart palpitations (61%), high blood pressure (60%), clinical depression (49%), and migraine headaches (48%; Workplace Bullying Institute, 2012). A diagnosis of PTSD was reported by 30 percent and a diagnosis of acute stress disorder by 19 percent. Survey participants reported PTSD-like symptoms, such as anticipation of next negative event (83%), agitation or anger (66%), obsession over personal circumstances (59%), and intrusive thoughts such as flashbacks and nightmares (50%). Other frequently reported symptoms included overwhelming anxiety (80%), difficulty falling asleep or too little sleep (77%), insomnia (60%), loss of concentration or memory (76%), pervasive sadness (64%), panic attacks (52%), loss of affect (50%), and tension headaches (44%). Suicidal thoughts were reported by 29 percent, and 16 percent reported that they had planned how to commit suicide (WBI, 2012). Although these results do not prove that workplace bullying was the cause, they overlap with those of other reports (e.g., Bonde et al., 2016; Leymann, 1990; Leymann & Gustafsson, 1996; Mikkelsen & Einarsen, 2002).

Post-Traumatic Disorders

The post-traumatic disorders deserve attention because they can be severely disabling, with consequences for physical and social health as well as psychological health. Leymann and Gustafsson (1996) extensively interviewed 64 patients who had been subjected to workplace mobbing and were being treated for PTSD at a rehabilitation clinic. The results showed that almost all of the interviewed clinic patients had severe PTSD. They also had secondary diagnoses of anxiety, psychosomatic problems, and depression, but not psychosis (Leymann & Gustafsson, 1996). From Germany, Groeblinghoff and Becker (1996) reported a case study of two targets of workplace mobbing. Both targets had symptoms that fit *DSM-III-R* diagnostic criteria for PTSD. More than 15 years later, the WBI (2012) health survey of self-identified targets found that 30 percent had a diagnosis of PTSD, and higher percentages reported PTSD-like symptoms (e.g., 83% anticipation of next negative event and 50% flashbacks or nightmares).

Post-traumatic stress disorder

Physicians caring for soldiers and veterans of the American Civil War, World War I, and World War II described clinical syndromes that they called "shell shock," "war neurosis," "combat fatigue," "battle fatigue," and other terms (Andreasen, 2010; DiMauro, Carter, Folk, & Kashdan, 2014; Friedman, 2015a; Jones & Wessely, 2007). Debates about causes included exposure to trauma versus personal shortcoming, combat versus noncombat experience, and the possibility of a pension as an incentive. Debates about symptoms and findings included single or disparate conditions, normal or psychopathological responses, and short- or long-term duration of symptoms (Andreasen, 2011; DiMauro et al., 2014). The historical documentation and debates laid the groundwork for the recognition of similar clinical findings among large numbers of soldiers and veterans of the Vietnam War. Similar findings were also recognized among those who had experienced other types of trauma, such as Nazi concentration camps, natural disasters, life-threatening injuries, and sexual assault. At the same time, the sociopolitical climate favored recognition of trauma-related health conditions (Andreasen, 2011; DiMauro et al., 2014).

In 1980, in its third *DSM* revision *(DSM-III)*, APA officially recognized PTSD as a diagnosis. It required a traumatic triggering factor, such as war-related trauma, imprisonment in a concentration camp, natural disasters, life-threatening injuries, and sexual assault (Andreasen, 2011; DiMauro et al., 2014). Since 1980, *DSM* criteria for PTSD have undergone several changes. In a review of *DSM-IV* criteria for PTSD, the Institute of Medicine (IOM) concluded that the core clinical features and diagnostic criteria were well-established and useful for guiding the diagnosis and assessment of patients (Institute of Medicine, 2006, p. 24). It also noted that "a person might not meet full criteria for a diagnosis of PTSD and yet still be highly symptomatic and in need of treatment. PTSD symptoms might be mild to severe, and functioning might be influenced by other factors, such as comorbid conditions or social support. Severe symptoms might be disabling even in the absence of a full diagnosis" (IOM, 2006, p. 18). The IOM recommended that diagnostic criteria be based on best evidence and that criteria be revised as new evidence becomes available (IOM, 2006, p. 44).

Major changes to the diagnostic criteria for PTSD appeared in *DSM-5*, released in 2013. Changes included moving PTSD from the anxiety disorder cluster to a new diagnostic cluster for trauma- and stressor-related disorders, removing subjective symptoms as stressor criteria, and separating avoidance and numbing into two diagnostic clusters (Friedman, 2015b). The stressor triggering the new onset or significant exacerbation of symptoms could be an exposure to a catastrophic event involving actual or threatened death or injury or a threat to the physical integrity of oneself or others. Symptoms were categorized into four diagnostic clusters: (1) intrusive recollection of the traumatic event, such as intrusive daytime images of the event, traumatic nightmares, and flashbacks that evoke panic, terror, dread, grief, or despair; (2) avoidance and behavioral strategies to reduce the likelihood of exposure to trauma-related stimuli or, if exposed, to minimize the intensity of the psychological response; (3) negative cognitions and mood, such as erroneous appraisals of the causes or consequences of the traumatic event, which can result in a wide variety of negative emotional states, such as anger, guilt, or shame; dissociative psychogenic amnesia; diminished interest in significant activities; feeling detached or estranged from others; and inability to experience positive feelings; and (4) alterations in arousal or reactivity, including symptoms resembling those of panic and general anxiety disorders, such as insomnia and cognitive impairment; hypervigilance (which may appear to be paranoia) or a startle response; and irritability or outbursts of anger with emotional and behavioral components that include aggressive, reckless, and self-destructive behaviors. The remaining criteria are symptoms lasting at least one month; significant social, occupational, or other distress as a result of the symptoms; and the absence of another explanation, such as medications, substance use, or other illness (Friedman, 2015b).

In the 1990s, WHO included PTSD as a diagnosis in *ICD-10* (Friedman, 2015b; World Health Organization, 1993) with a definition intended for international use. The *ICD-10* definition of PTSD is similar to the diagnostic criteria in *DSM-IV* (IOM, 2006; World Health Organization, 1993). Proposals for *ICD-11*, the next revision, are under review. In a large study with samples from multiple nations, the proportions of individuals identified with PTSD were similar when using *DSM-5* diagnostic criteria and the proposed *ICD-11* definition (Stein et al., 2014). In contrast, studies of three sample U.S. populations (national community [online]; military veterans [online]; and veterans and partners) showed that using the proposed *ICD-11* definition resulted in lower prevalence rates than when using *DSM-IV* and *DSM-5* criteria and the *ICD-10* definition (Wisco et al., 2016). These differences raised concerns that individuals with clinically significant symptoms might not meet the diagnostic requirements of *ICD-11* (Wisco et al., 2016).

The importance of this issue is related to the U.S. government's obligation to implement *ICD-11* when it is finalized and the required use of *ICD* codes for billing and reimbursement transactions covered by the U.S. Health Insurance Portability and Accountability Act (HIPPA) of 1996 (Wisco et al., 2016). Thus, severely symptomatic individuals who do not meet the definition of PTSD may not be able to access the treatment they need. The *ICD-11* proposals for PTSD have not yet been accepted, and the working group on stress-related disorders was instructed to focus on improving the clinical utility of relevant diagnostic categories (Keeley et al., 2016).

Complex post-traumatic stress disorder

Herman (1997) summarized studies about individuals entrapped in prolonged and repeated trauma (such as politically organized mass murder, domestic violence, and childhood abuse). Their symptoms did not fit diagnoses of ordinary anxiety disorders, ordinary psychosomatic disorders, ordinary depression, or PTSD. She noted that, in the context of earlier social attitudes, particularly about women, victims were misdiagnosed, mislabeled, and blamed for their conditions. She suggested that victims' responses to trauma would be best understood as a spectrum of disorders rather than a single one and proposed that the syndrome related to chronic trauma have its own name, *complex PTSD* (Herman, 1997). This proposal was not accepted for *DSM-5* because field trials for *DSM-IV* indicated that almost all individuals who met the proposed diagnosis for complex PTSD also met diagnostic criteria for PTSD (National Center for PTSD, 2016). A nonspecific diagnostic option was Disorders of Extreme Stress Not Otherwise Specified (DESNOS).

In contrast, WHO surveys of psychiatrists and psychologists showed that the most frequently recommended addition to *ICD-11* was complex PTSD (Keely et al., 2016). Clinicians wanted recognition of severe and enduring responses to exceptionally high levels of trauma (Maercker et al., 2013). The *ICD-11 Beta Draft* (WHO, 2016) proposes that complex PTSD be defined as a disorder arising "after exposure to a stressor typically of an extreme or prolonged nature and from which escape is difficult or impossible." In addition to core PTSD symptoms, the definition includes persistent and pervasive disturbances of affect, self-concept, and relational functioning (WHO, 2016).

A study of self-referred trauma survivors seeking treatment at a trauma clinic in New York City found three different symptom profiles: PTSD, complex PTSD, and low symptoms (Cloitre, Garvert, Brewin, Bryant, & Maercker, 2013). Differences were based on symptoms rather than type of trauma. Studies of two Internet-based samples, a community sample representative of the U.S. adult population and a sample of trauma-exposed veterans, raised concerns about the *ICD-11* proposal to differentiate complex PTSD from PTSD (Wolf et al., 2015). Using a different model, the severity of symptoms explained differences better than symptom profiles. Those with high severity PTSD symptoms had high severity complex PTSD symptoms, and those with low severity PTSD symptoms had low severity complex PTSD symptoms.

As with PTSD, many issues about complex PTSD are still under debate. However, clinicians still have to make practical decisions about diagnoses and treatments while awaiting the scientific and epidemiological evidence they need to guide them. The U.S. Department of Veterans Affairs National Center for PTSD recognized that special treatment considerations may be needed and included complex PTSD as an outcome of prolonged, repeated trauma (National Center for PTSD, 2016).

Embitterment disorder

After the German reunification in the 1990s, embitterment was recognized as a severe condition of persistent mental illness related to social and economic disruptions (Reiman, 2011). Linden (2003), in Germany, studied this condition and proposed a new diagnosis, *post-traumatic embitterment disorder* (PTED), as a subgroup of adjustment disorders. Core criteria differed from those of PTSD. The triggering event could be an exceptional but not extreme life event or a negative but not life-threatening life event that the patient considered unjust or insulting and a violation of basic beliefs and values (Linden, 2003). The patient's reactions included prolonged feelings of embitterment.

In an interview study of 48 patients diagnosed by clinical judgment as having PTED, 73 percent identified a work-related trigger as the critical life event (Linden, Baumann, Rotter, & Schippan, 2007). Sensky (2010), working in occupational health in the United Kingdom, wrote an editorial about embitterment and organizational justice. He pointed out that occupational health clinicians readily recognized the embitterment syndrome. He noted that some cases appeared to be related to a series of adverse events of a similar nature rather than a single event. Thus, he proposed calling the syndrome *chronic embitterment* instead of PTED. He identified organizational aspects of embitterment, such as nonexplicit psychological work contracts and conflicts between professional and organizational values.

Muschalla and Linden (2011) categorized workplace triggers into three types of injustice: (1) organizational, such as discrimination, unfair promotion rules, and unfair pay; (2) informational, such as untruthful communications or unjustified decisions by individuals within the organization, with increased risk for personal insults and humiliation; and (3) interpersonal or interactional, such as undeserved or irrational treatment, including abusive or aggressive supervision. In a questionnaire study of consecutive individuals seen over a three-month period at an occupational health department in the United Kingdom, chronic embitterment was associated with perceived breaches of procedural justice (Sensky, Salimu, Ballard, & Pereira, 2015).

Linden and Maercker (2011) defined embitterment in easy-to-understand language: "a complex emotion, typically comprising a sense of having been let down or been insulted and a feeling of being a loser, combined with a desire to fight back and, at the same time, a feeling of being cornered and helpless, which subsequently causes an individual to have fantasies of revenge and aggression towards him or herself and the environment" (p. 1).

However, agreement has not yet been reached about whether or how to diagnose embitterment. In an interview study of 48 patients diagnosed with PTED, 48 percent met criteria for major depression, and 98 percent reported persistent negative mood (Linden et al., 2007). However, a diagnosis of major depression was considered unlikely because 92 percent had normal affect when distracted and unimpaired modulation of affect. Dobricki and Maercker (2010) reviewed three studies by Linden and coworkers, including the study reported in 2007. They noted that the proposed core symptoms for PTED are the main characteristics of other categories of mental disorders. Therefore, they recommended classifying embitterment disorders in accordance with *ICD-10* definitions for adjustment disorders and anxiety disorders, which include PTSD.

Sensky (2010) recognized overlaps between chronic embitterment and depression, anxiety, and PTSD but pointed out distinct features, such as anger, frustration, and a sense of injustice. He suggested that, in earlier studies of workplace bullying, a diagnosis of chronic embitterment would have fit targets who had PTSD symptoms but did not meet full diagnostic criteria for PTSD. Ege (2010), in Italy, evaluated 18 individuals who were suffering from workplace conflicts and found that 91.5 percent met PTED criteria. Many had been incorrectly diagnosed with depression or phobia and had been ineffectively treated. In the previously mentioned three-month-long questionnaire study of consecutive individuals at an occupational health department in the United Kingdom, the majority of those with chronic embitterment were not depressed or anxious; however, they were more frequently depressed or anxious than those without embitterment (Sensky et al., 2015).

Post-traumatic disorders and workplace bullying

Obvious similarities are seen between the post-traumatic disorders and the health outcomes of workplace bullying, suggesting that research findings in one area can be relevant to the other. For both, the trigger is an external trauma. Some triggers overlap, such as the interpersonal or interactional injustices in the definition of embitterment disorder and the extreme or prolonged trauma from which escape is difficult or impossible in the *ICD-11* proposed definition of complex PTSD. Some outcomes overlap, such as avoidance, negative cognitions and mood, and alterations of arousal and reactivity in the diagnostic criteria for PTSD.

Workplace bullying is likely to be recognized as an exceptional though commonplace, negative life event rather than as a life-threatening one, favoring a diagnosis of embitterment disorder over PTSD. However, outcomes related to workplace bullying can be life-threatening, the most obvious being suicide. (Chapter 13 of this book discusses workplace bullying as a life-threatening stressor more fully.) Cognitive impairment can contribute to potentially life-threatening acute physical injuries. However, injury investigations typically focus on immediate causes and find easily accepted explanations in physical and personal factors while overlooking psychosocial stressors, such as workplace bullying.

Other disabling psychological conditions, such as depression and anxiety disorders, can result from exposure to psychological stressors, including workplace bullying. They can also exist with post-traumatic disorders as comorbid conditions. These are discussed in chapter 13.

Physical Health Outcomes

Stressors, stress responses, biological pathways, and health outcomes

Selye (1936) discovered that laboratory animals subjected to different acute noxious physical or chemical stimuli, such as cold temperatures, surgical injury, excessive exercise, or sublethal doses of drugs, developed the same pathological physical changes, which included stomach ulcerations, shrinkage of lymphoid tissue, and enlargement of the adrenal glands. The variety of unpleasant stressors causing the same biological responses suggested that specific stimuli were not as important as the stressfulness of the situation. Selye attributed this to the body's nonspecific response to any stressor. He later demonstrated that the stimuli could also be psychological and did not have to be unpleasant (Selye, 1973). Rather, the body's response depended on the intensity of the demand on the body to adapt to a new situation. While the biological and physiological responses to stressors were stereotypic, they could produce different syndromes or lesions in different people, such as headaches, gastrointestinal symptoms and ulcers, cardiovascular diseases, and kidney diseases.

In the tradition of Selye's pioneering work, subsequent research has continued to uncover the biological bases for the variety of stressor-related negative health outcomes. McEwen and other researchers studying communications between the brain and the body discovered that the metabolic and immune systems act together with the neuroendocrine system in response to stressor-induced imbalances (e.g., McEwen, Bowles, et al., 2015; McEwen, Gray, & Nasca, 2015a). The responses affect cognition, decision making, anxiety, and mood; can change behaviors and behavior states; and affect physiological processes. (Chapter 7 of this book discusses neuroscience more fully.) Although these biological responses are protective in the short term, when stressors increase beyond the body's adaptive capacity or when regulatory mechanisms are impaired, the responses become maladaptive. Both structure (such as brain neurons) and function (such as neurotransmitter and hormone activity) are affected. Studies of nonprimate animals and of nonhuman primates in captivity and in the wild have shown that exposures to stressors lead to outcomes such as chronic anxiety and depression, chronic inflammation, atherosclerosis, obesity, and diabetes (e.g., McEwen, Bowles, et al., 2015; Meyer & Hamel, 2014; Sapolsky, 1990; Shively & Day, 2015).

Telomeres are DNA-protein caps at the ends of chromosomes that keep chromosomes from deteriorating or fusing with other chromosomes during DNA transcription. They lose a few base pairs with each transcription. Over time, this loss can be observed as telomere shortening, making telomere length a useful biological marker of cell aging. Accelerated telomere shortening has been associated with levels of perceived psychological stress and chronicity of stress (Epel et al., 2004; Puterman & Epel, 2012). Telomere length was found to be a predictor of mortality in patients with stable coronary heart disease (Goglin et al., 2016). A study of telomere length and life span adversity of a nationally representative sample of adults over 50 years of age and their spouses showed that lifetime cumulative adversity predicted shorter telomere lengths and that childhood adversity affects cellular aging into later adulthood (Puterman et al., 2016).

Thus, many adverse factors, such as early childhood experiences, gene-environment interactions (*epigenetics*), socioeconomic factors, physical activity, and diet, may contribute to negative health outcomes. Although they may not be the sole or direct causal factor, they can influence an individual's vulnerability or resilience on exposure to stressors (e.g., Mathur et al., 2016; McEwen, Bowles, et al., 2015; Puterman et al., 2016; Shively & Day, 2015).

Employees in 55 workplaces who reported being bullied frequently or who were exposed to direct harassment and intimidating behavior had significantly reduced levels of cortisol compared with levels among employees who did not report such experiences (Hansen, Hough, & Persson, 2011; Hogh, Hansen, Mikkelsen, & Persson, 2012). These findings show that human responses to stressors of workplace bullying are similar to the findings of animal studies and begin to explain how workplace bullying could lead to chronic negative health outcomes.

Workplace stressors and cardiovascular disorders

The Whitehall I studies of British civil servants, which began in the mid-1960s, showed that, after 10 years of follow-up, men in the lowest employment grade level had the highest mortality from coronary heart disease (atherosclerosis of the coronary arteries, also called ischemic heart disease in some other studies) and that mortality decreased as grade level increased (Marmot, Shipley, & Rose, 1984). Similar relationships between employment grade and cardiovascular morbidity and risk factors were seen in Whitehall II studies of a subsequent cohort (generation) of British civil servants (Ferrie, Shipley, Davey Smith, Stansfeld, & Marmot, 2002). Whitehall I and other research findings in the 1960s and 1970s suggest a relationship between psychosocial stressors and the development of heart disease (e.g., Karasek, Baker, Marxer, Ahlbom, & Theorell, 1981; Marmot, 1986). However, stressors of interest varied from study to study. Multiple possible risk factors, such as workload and job satisfaction, were studied, but some were not applicable to all workplaces.

To address this, Karasek (1979) proposed a job strain model that focused on two types of job characteristics relevant to any workplace: high psychological demands of the job and low decision latitude (or control) at work. In a study of male Swedish workers, Karasek et al. (1981) found that a psychologically demanding job increased the risk of symptoms and signs of coronary heart disease and increased the risk of premature death related to cardiovascular or cerebrovascular disease. They also found that low decision latitude was associated with increased risk of cardiovascular disease.

Since then, many studies have shown job strain to predict increased cardiovascular outcomes (e.g., Belkić, Schnall, Landsbergis, & Baker, 2000; Chandola et al., 2008; Kivimäki & Kawachi, 2015; Theorell et al., 2016). Job strain has also been associated with increases in ambulatory blood pressure, an early and objective indicator of cardiovascular risk (e.g., Joseph et al., 2016; Landsbergis, Schnall, Warren, Pickering, & Schwartz, 1994).

Despite the consistency of findings over the years, many issues remain unresolved (see section on Research and Clinical Issues, this chapter).

Workplace stressors and musculoskeletal disorders

Physical work-related stressors, such as repetitive motion, excessive force, and awkward postures, are known to contribute to musculoskeletal disorders. However, research findings have suggested that psychosocial and organizational factors also contribute. In a study of a representative sample of the U.S. population, Yang et al. (2016) found *hostile work environment* (a term sometimes used as a synonym for *workplace bullying*) to be one of the workplace risk factors for neck pain. In a cross-sectional survey at a large retail company in Italy, Vignoli, Guglielmi, Balducci, and Bonfiglioli (2015) found that while physical stressors predicted musculoskeletal symptoms, the more workers were exposed to workplace bullying, the more they reported symptoms of the low back, upper back, and neck. Bullying also contributed indirectly through job-related strain. Studies on the role of psychosocial and organizational factors on musculoskeletal disorders are ongoing (E. Hitchcock, personal communication, May 23, 2016).

Physical health outcomes and workplace bullying

The role of workplace bullying is likely to be overlooked when evaluating physical health outcomes. Linking cardiovascular diseases, musculoskeletal disorders, and other possible outcomes to work-related factors is difficult when these health conditions are commonly found in the general population and when well-known risk factors, such as individual characteristics or personal habits, are accepted as sufficient and satisfactory explanations. However, ignoring workplace bullying as a possible risk factor ignores the findings of decades of stress research that have shown negative physical health outcomes. No mention of workplace bullying in a medical evaluation does not mean that bullying did not take place, but it does suggest that the relevant questions might not have been asked. Lack of knowledge or understanding about biological mechanisms does not mean that bullying can be ruled out as a contributing factor, but it does reflect the current state of scientific knowledge.

Since Selye's discovery that multiple different stressors can cause negative physical changes in nonprimate laboratory animals, research evidence about such relationships has been growing. Subsequent studies of nonhuman primates in captivity and in the wild, recent and current studies about biological mechanisms to explain outcomes, and epidemiological studies about organizational stressors, job strain, and workplace bullying are building a body of knowledge about the relationships between stressors, including workplace bullying, and negative health outcomes.

OTHER FORMS OF ABUSIVE SOCIAL PHENOMENA

Workplace bullying is only one form of abusive social phenomena that can trigger biological responses that negatively affect health. Other forms include violence against children and intimate partners, childhood bullying, and sexual harassment. While some features, such as the use of physical violence, are different, a feature in common is the use of nonphysical power and humiliation. Unfortunately, another feature they share is that they are often hidden or not recognized.

Research has shown that significant adversity in early childhood can affect the development of the body's stress response systems; affect development of the brain, cardiovascular system, immune system, and metabolic regulatory controls; impair learning and behavior; and lead to lifelong chronic, stress-related physical and mental illness (Shonkoff et al., 2012). A review of studies on bullied children showed serious negative effects on physical, mental, and social health in adulthood (Wolke & Lereya, 2015). A long-term study showed that children who were bullied had greater increases of a biological marker of low-grade inflammation from childhood to young adulthood than was found in other children (Copeland et al., 2014). *Cyberbullying*, defined as "willful and repeated harm inflicted through the use of computers, cell phones, and other electronic devices" (Sabella, Patchin, & Hinduja, 2013, p. 2704), has also been shown to increase health risks (Mishna et al., 2016).

RESEARCH ISSUES, CLINICAL ISSUES

While useful for designing research, determining preventive measures or treatment modalities, and managing insurance payments, case definitions and diagnostic criteria are constructs based on hypotheses that may be incomplete or incorrect. In fact, scenarios for workplace bullying are variable and complex, with different combinations of multiple possible triggering, risk, and protective factors. Health outcomes also vary and may be complicated by comorbid conditions. Among the post-traumatic disorders, diagnostic criteria vary, even for the same diagnosis: criteria for different diagnoses overlap, proposed diagnoses and their criteria are not universally accepted, and concerns about underdiagnosis and overdiagnosis affect decisions about diagnostic criteria. These complexities complicate the interpretation of research findings and affect clinical practice. Despite agreement that research should inform decisions about diagnosis and care, study criteria may be excluding the most vulnerable individuals, such as those with preexisting risk factors or comorbidities.

The issues about cardiovascular conditions and musculoskeletal disorders are relevant to all negative outcomes of workplace bullying, whether physical or psychological. Workplace bullying may not be recognized as a triggering or contributing factor. Even when workplace bullying is recognized, its relationship with negative outcomes may not be obvious, particularly when the time from exposure to outcome (called *latency*) is long. Factors unrelated to workplace bullying are easily accepted as sufficient explanations, and the need for further evaluation remains unrecognized. As a result, even if the clinical diagnosis is correct, overlooking bullying as a possible causal or contributing factor can affect treatment, prevention, and future research.

In clinical settings, ignoring workplace bullying as a possible causal or contributing factor would be similar to relying solely on medications to treat type 2 diabetes while not recognizing the importance of diet and physical activity. In the workplace, identifying, addressing, and eliminating bullying are important for the recovery of affected individuals and preventing negative health outcomes. The importance is magnified when outcomes are potentially life-threatening, disabling, or chronic and when they affect not only the well-being of the individual target but also the well-being of their family and friends.

In epidemiological research, the variety and complexity of workplace bullying scenarios and negative outcomes present multiple possibilities for hypotheses and models; selection of variables, their definitions, and measurement methods; type of study; and statistical methods (e.g., Choi et al., 2015; Hershcovis, 2011; Hershcovis & Reich, 2013). For example, job strain questions and measurements vary from study to study, and some psychosocial factors, such as effort-reward imbalance and job insecurity, are not captured by the job strain model. Results of studies that focus on specific populations, situations, or outcomes cannot be generalized (universally applied) to other populations and situations, such as studies in countries with progressive social and workplace health policies to countries without the same protections; studies of white-collar workers to other types of workers; and studies of workers with lower levels of exposure to workers with higher levels of exposure (Choi et al., 2015). The same subjective responses may have different meanings in different study populations (e.g., Burr, Formazin, & Pohrt, 2016). Prospective studies, which can examine causal relationships, take longer to carry out than cross-sectional surveys, which can show associations but not causation (e.g., Hershcovis & Reich, 2013).

These issues explain why current knowledge and understanding are far from satisfactory. However, overlapping results of studies of stressors and health outcomes in different mammalian species, different scenarios, and different types of studies suggest that the findings are relevant despite the unresolved issues. Moreover, research on the biological effects of stressors on the body and the brain is beginning to uncover physiological mechanisms to explain how exposure to stressors affects health. Nevertheless, whether and how soon issues about diagnosis, classifications, and clinical relevance are resolved will depend not only on research goals, priorities, funding, and findings, but also on social, organizational, and economic issues. For example, decisions about overdiagnosis or underdiagnosis and whether workplace bullying is a hazardous workplace exposure will likely be influenced by those who will be held responsible for the economic costs.

PUBLIC HEALTH AND OCCUPATIONAL HEALTH

Public health focuses on the health of populations through surveillance, research, interventions, and the promotion of policies and programs. Occupational health, the part of public health that focuses on worker populations, works with employers, managers, employee representatives, government agencies, health care and insurance providers, and researchers to address exposures, risk factors, health outcomes, and preventive measures. With such resources, the occupational health framework offers an established approach to address workplace bullying.

Bullying as a Hazardous Workplace Exposure

Workplaces are recognized as potential sources of hazardous exposures to chemical, physical, and biological agents and safety hazards that are not commonly found in the home or community, or, if present in those environments, the potential for harm is minimal. Some well-recognized workplace hazards are regulated to reduce the health risk to workers. Other exposures may not be universally recognized as a hazard or may be difficult to detect or measure. Certain workplace exposures, such as ergonomic factors and stressors, are encountered outside as well as in the workplace, making it difficult to determine whether and how much work contributed to the harm.

Recognizing workplace bullying

Workplace violence is recognized as a potential hazardous workplace exposure (Occupational Safety and Health Administration, 2011; Romano, Levi-Minzi, Rugala, & Van Hasselt, 2011; Rugala & Isaacs, 2004). Nonphysical threats, harassment, bullying, emotional abuse, and intimidation are included in the spectrum of violence. However, guidelines on workplace violence focus on physical violence, particularly those that result in death and serious injury. They categorize acts of nonphysical violence as warning signs of possible future physical violence, not as real exposures that could harm health. Yet, the negative health outcomes of nonphysical violence can be just as real as the harm caused by physical violence or by well-recognized chemical and safety hazards in the workplace.

Linking outcomes to workplace bullying is a challenge when workplace bullying is not recognized or outcomes are not immediately obvious, are heterogeneous in nature, or could be explained by other causes. Often, targets do not feel safe enough to report bullying or do not feel economically secure enough to leave their jobs voluntarily despite deteriorating health. Even when supervisors, managers, or employers are not active perpetrators of workplace bullying, they participate in bullying if they encourage it; do nothing to stop it (i.e., allow it); or do not recognize it. Coworker perpetrators can interpret management's inaction as approval to continue the abuse. Under any of these circumstances, workplace bullying can become a stressor that triggers biological processes of the stress response and can harm health.

Consequences of unrecognized workplace bullying

Repeated or sustained abuse can lead to negative secondary work, social, and economic outcomes that become additional stressors, triggering additional symptoms that could range in severity from mild discomfort to an alarming multisymptom stress response. The symptoms and the alarm can lead to deteriorating work performance, which can provoke further bullying, leading to a self-perpetuating downward spiral in which negative effects become new stressors that trigger new or worsening negative outcomes. (See the discussion of "victimology" in Mikkelsen & Einarsen, 2002, p. 398). Thus, these cumulative negative outcomes affect all three dimensions of the WHO (1948) definition of health: physical, mental, and social well-being. The downward spiral can continue even after the target leaves the workplace because of ill health; involuntary termination (i.e., dismissal from employment or firing); or voluntary termination (e.g., leaving because of intolerable work conditions, also known as *constructive discharge*).

From Recognition to Prevention: Public Health and Occupational Health

Identifying and naming workplace bullying as a hazardous workplace exposure, as Leymann (1990, 1996) did, makes it possible for employees, managers, employers, health care providers, family, and friends to respond appropriately. Thus, recognition is the necessary first step to prevent future negative health outcomes and promote the recovery of affected targets. While some health outcomes may respond to clinical treatment, focusing on specific outcomes does not address the role of stressors. Continued exposure to workplace bullying will continue to have a negative impact on health.

In the occupational health framework, a fundamental principle for preventing negative health outcomes is to address the root cause by controlling harmful exposures. When the exposure is a tangible agent, such as a chemical, physically removing the hazard from the workplace (elimination) is the most effective measure. Alternative measures (in order of decreasing effectiveness) include replacing the hazard (substitution); controlling exposures through design and technology, such as redesigning the process or the worker-process interface, reengineering machinery or equipment, and improving ventilation; administrative measures, such as scheduling and training; and the use of personal protective equipment by individual workers. As the number of points of control increases, so does the number of opportunities for breaches in protection.

Controlling psychosocial stressors is much less straightforward than controlling biological, chemical, or physical agents. Organizational factors play a role, such as when workplace bullying is ignored, allowed, or encouraged by the organization's leadership, culture, and climate (for more on organizational culture and climate, see Schneider, Ehrhart, & Macey, 2013; also chapter 4 this volume). People within workplace organizations have varying levels of individual competencies in emotional and social intelligence (for more on emotional and social intelligence, see Goleman, 1995, 2006). Organizational issues need to be addressed with preventive measures and restorative approaches that create a safe workplace environment. Making sure that targets of workplace bullying are protected from further harm should be a priority. (Chapters 4 and 9 focus on organizational considerations more fully.)

Gallup, Inc., has studied employee engagement internationally as well as in the United States for decades. Over the years, hundreds of organizations and millions of employees have participated (Gallup, 2016). Although the Gallup employee engagement surveys do not specifically address bullying, they are relevant because targets of workplace bullying would likely give negative responses to survey questions, such as "I have received recognition or praise for doing good work," "My supervisor, or someone at work, seems to care about me as a person," and "At work, my opinions seem to count." Meta-analyses of employee survey results and performance outcomes provided by participating organizations have shown that lower employee engagement is associated with higher employee turnover, more safety incidents, and higher absenteeism (Gallup, 2013; Gallup, 2016). These negative outcomes can also be organizational outcomes of workplace bullying. Organizations that participated in the education of managers and collaborated with Gallup on change initiatives experienced measurable incremental and cumulative increases of employee engagement (Gallup, 2016). Current research and plans for future research include health-related variables, such as sick days and biological markers (e.g., cholesterol, triglycerides, and cortisol; Gallup, 2016). Results of such studies will be important to show whether improving employee engagement can lead to improved health. Adding variables about workplace bullying may show how much of a role workplace bullying plays in poor employee engagement.

Choi et al. (2015) also advocate improving workplace conditions. They point out that workplace stressors may be contributing to personal risk factors, such as tobacco smoking, and cite WHO, National Institute for Occupational Safety and Health, and American Heart Association recommendations for health promotion approaches that include improving the work organization and work environment. They justify such changes on the basis of the "precautionary principle," arguing that "when existing evidence, even if incomplete, strongly suggests that job, organizational and legislative changes are beneficial for worker and organization health, it is imperative to act and evaluate" (Choi et al., 2015, p. 306).

Protective Factors and Resilience

When workplace bullying is a stressor, its causal or contributory role in the development of negative health outcomes may be unrecognized or ignored, especially when other stressors or risk factors, such as adverse childhood experiences and domestic violence, are identified. These factors do not negate or diminish the contributions of workplace bullying and may add to the risk. Therefore, addressing workplace bullying by suspecting its possibility, identifying it, and addressing it is important. Eliminating workplace bullying would be ideal, but organizationally initiated control measures may not be timely or effective. Because of this, measures to reduce risk at the individual level become important.

Many researchers are now studying *resilience*, the ability to adapt and thrive when facing adversity (e.g., McEwen, Gray, et al., 2015b; Puterman & Epel, 2012; Puterman et al., 2013; Reul et al., 2015; Rossouw & Rossouw, 2016). One of the most hopeful discoveries is that even "mature and aging individuals continue to show the results of experiences, including opportunities for redirection of unhealthy tendencies through a variety of interventions" (McEwen, Gray, et al., 2015b, p. 7). Interventions such as physical activity (exercise), good sleep quality, social connections, and healthy emotional regulation have been shown to change the structures and functions in the brain and have been associated with clinical improvements (e.g., Puterman et al., 2013; Reul et al., 2015, Rossouw & Rossouw, 2016). The journal *Neurobiology of Stress* devoted its inaugural issue to stress resilience, thus acknowledging the importance of research in this area (McEwen, 2015; Valentino, Sheline, & McEwen, 2015).

Role of Clinicians and the Health Care System

When workplace bullying leads to severe and chronic health outcomes, restoring health is a priority. In clinical settings, recognizing bullying as a factor is important but challenging. Comprehensive clinical evaluations include a differential diagnosis, a list of possible diagnoses and their causes, to be ruled in or out. Omitting workplace bullying from the differential diagnosis allows it to remain unsuspected and undiscoverable, and it can lead to misdiagnoses and inappropriate treatment choices, as noted by Leymann (1990). Clinicians routinely screen clients and patients for personal and social risk factors for preventable diseases. Adding screening questions about workplace bullying to the routine clinical evaluation should improve diagnoses and lead to appropriate therapeutic and preventive measures. To improve the quality of responses, questions should be asked in a way that minimizes bias, blame, and shame.

Some pharmacological agents have been shown to be effective in treating the post-traumatic disorders, and neuroscientific findings can help guide therapeutic decisions (e.g., Arnsten, Raskind, Taylor, & Connor, 2015). However, therapeutic effects may last only as long as medications are continued (e.g., Carlson, Chemtob, Rusnak, Hedlund, & Muraoka, 1998; van der Kolk et al., 2007). A Veterans Administration review of evidence-based psychotherapies showed that *cognitive processing therapy* and *prolonged exposure therapy* improved mean scores on the PTSD Checklist (Rosen et al., 2016). Barriers to patient acceptance of treatment included the demanding tasks of trauma-focused therapy, low distress intolerance, and poor affect management (Rosen et al., 2016). Pharmacologic targeting of physiological contributors to patient nonacceptance may improve psychotherapeutic outcomes (Rosen et al., 2016).

Research in alternative treatment modalities also show promise. For example, *eye movement desensitization and reprocessing* (EMDR) to treat PTSD has been found to be as successful as routine therapy and standard pharmaceutical agents and appears to have longer-lasting effects than relaxation-based treatment or medication alone (Carlson et al., 1998; van der Kolk et al., 2007; van der Kolk, 2014). Other body-based therapies, such as yoga, also appear to be useful (e.g., van der Kolk, 2014; van der Kolk et al., 2014). Because of the complexity of possible exposures, outcomes, clinical features, and treatment effects and acceptance, treatments should be personalized to the individual's needs (McEwen, Gray, et al., 2015b; van der Kolk, 2014). Thus, clinicians have to be knowledgeable about workplace bullying, its diversity of adverse health outcomes, the appropriateness and limitations of available treatments, and the usefulness of integrating different types of treatment.

IN CLOSING

In all its complexity and variety, workplace bullying is a psychosocial stressor that can severely harm health in all three dimensions of the WHO definition of health, physical, mental, and social well-being. Research is beginning to uncover the physiological mechanisms of the body's responses to stressors, leading to possibilities of improved preventive and therapeutic measures. While additional research is necessary to address many unresolved issues, sufficient evidence exists to recommend addressing bullying in the workplace.

Bullying is not required for workplace functioning. Rather, it is a hazardous exposure that affects workers and their work. Elimination is the most logical measure for controlling exposure to this nonessential hazard. Unfortunately, elimination is not the easiest measure to undertake. First, the highest organizational levels have to acknowledge that workplace bullying is a harmful work exposure that should be eliminated. Then, they need to have the will to eliminate it. As long as exposure continues, measures should be taken to prevent its negative outcomes.

Despite the challenges, the future is hopeful. During the preparation of this chapter, hundreds of relevant articles with new findings and new understandings appeared in the research literature. They provide evidence for future improvements in efforts to minimize and prevent the negative health outcomes related to workplace bullying.

REFERENCES

Accreditation Council for Graduate Medical Education. (2015). *ACGME program requirements for graduate medical education in psychosomatic medicine*. Retrieved from https://www.acgme.org/Portals/0/PFAssets/ProgramRequirements/409_psychosomatic_med_07012015_1-YR.pdf

American Psychosomatic Society. (2016). *About APS*. Retrieved from http://www.psychosomatic.org/about/index.cfm

Andreasen, N. C. (2010). Posttraumatic stress disorder: A history and a critique. *Annals of the New York Academy of Sciences, 1208*(1), 67–71.

Andreasen, N. C. (2011). What is post-traumatic stress disorder? (Guest editorial). *Dialogues in Clinical Neuroscience, 13*(3), 240–243.

Arnsten A. F. T., Raskind, M. A., Taylor, F. B., & Connor, D. F. (2015). The effects of stress exposure on prefrontal cortex: Translating basic research into successful treatments for post-traumatic stress disorder. *Neurobiology of Stress, 1*, 89–99.

Belkić, K., Schnall, P., Landsbergis, P., & Baker, D. (2000). The workplace and cardiovascular health: Conclusions and thoughts for a future agenda. *Occupational Medicine: State of the Art Reviews, 15*(1), 307–321.

Bienvenu, O. J., Wuyek, L. A., & Stein, M. B. (2009). Anxiety disorders diagnosis: Some history and controversies. In M. B. Stein & T. Steckler (Eds.), *Behavioral neurobiology of anxiety and its treatment* (pp. 1–19). Berlin, Germany: Springer-Verlag.

Bonde, J. P., Gullander, M., Hansen, Å. M., Grynderup, M., Persson, R., Hogh, A., . . . Kolstad, H. A. (2016). Health correlates of workplace bullying: A 3-wave prospective follow-up study. *Scandinavian Journal of Work, Environment & Health, 42*(1), 17–25.

Burr, H., Formazin, M., & Pohrt, A. (2016). Methodological and conceptual issues regarding occupational psychosocial coronary heart disease epidemiology. *Scandinavian Journal of Work, Environment & Health, 42*(3), 251–255.

Carlson, J. G., Chemtob, C. M., Rusnak, K., Hedlund, N. L., & Muraoka, M. Y. (1998). Eye movement desensitization and reprocessing (EDMR) treatment for combat-related posttraumatic stress disorder. *Journal of Traumatic Stress, 11*(1), 3–24.

Chandola, T., Britton, A., Brunner, E., Hemingway, H., Malik, M., Kumari, M., . . . Marmot, M. (2008). Work stress and coronary heart disease: What are the mechanisms? *European Heart Journal, 29*(5), 640–648.

Choi, B., Schnall P., Landsbergis, P., Dobson, M., Ko, S., Gómez-Ortiz, V., . . . Baker, D. (2015). Recommendations for individual participant data meta-analyses on work stressors and health outcomes: Comments on IPD-Work Consortium papers. *Scandinavian Journal of Work, Environment & Health, 41*(3), 299–311.

Cloitre, M., Garvert, D. W., Brewin, C. R., Bryant, R. A., & Maercker, A. (2013). Evidence for proposed *ICD-11* PTSD and complex PTSD: A latent profile analysis. *European Journal of Psychotraumatology, 4*. doi:10.3402/ejpt.v4i0.20706

Comorbid. (n.d.). In *The free dictionary*. Retrieved from http://www.thefreedictionary.com/comorbid

Copeland, W. E., Wolke, D., Lereya, S. T., Shanahan, L., Worthman, C., & Costello, E. J. (2014). Childhood bullying involvement predicts low-grade systemic inflammation into adulthood. *Proceedings of the National Academy of Sciences of the USA, 111*(21), 7570–7575.

DiMauro, J., Carter, S., Folk, J. B., & Kashdan, T. B. (2014). A historical review of trauma-related diagnoses to reconsider the heterogeneity of PTSD. *Journal of Anxiety Disorders, 28*(8), 774–786.

Dobricki, M., & Maercker, A. (2010). (Post-traumatic) embitterment disorder: Critical evaluation of its stressor criterion and a proposed revised classification. *Nordic Journal of Psychiatry, 64*(3), 147–152.

Ege, H. (2010). Different typologies of workplace conflict and their connections with post traumatic embitterment disorder (PTED). *Health, 2*(3), 234–236.

Epel, E. S., Blackburn, E. H., Lin, J., Dhabhar, F. S., Adler, N. E., Morrow, J. D., & Cawthon, R. M. (2004). Accelerated telomere shortening in response to life stress. *Proceedings of the National Academy of Sciences of the United States of America, 101*(49), 17312–17315.

Ferrie, J. E., Shipley, M. J., Davey Smith, G., Stansfeld, S. A., & Marmot, M. G. (2002). Change in health inequalities among British civil servants: The Whitehall II study. *Journal of Epidemiology & Community Health, 56*(12), 922–926.

Friedman, M. J. (2015a). *History of PTSD in veterans: Civil War to DSM-5*. Retrieved from http://www.ptsd.va.gov/public/PTSD-overview/basics/history-of-ptsd-vets.asp

Friedman, M. J. (2015b). *PTSD history and overview*. Retrieved from http://www.ptsd.va.gov/professional/PTSD-overview/ptsd-overview.asp

Gallup. (2013). *State of the global workplace: Employee engagement insights for business leaders worldwide*. Omaha, NE: Gallup, Inc.

Gallup. (2016). *The relationship between engagement at work and organizational outcomes: 2016 Q^{12} meta-analysis* (9th ed.). Omaha, NE: Gallup, Inc.

Goglin, S. E., Farzaneh-Far, R., Epel, E. S., Lin, J., Blackburn, E. H., & Whooley, M. A. (2016). Change in leukocyte telomere length predicts mortality in patients with stable coronary heart disease from the Heart and Soul Study. *PLOS ONE, 11*(10), e0160748. doi:10.1371/journal.pone.0160748

Goleman, D. (1995). *Emotional intelligence: Why it can matter more than IQ*. New York: Bantam Books.

Goleman, D. (2006). *Social intelligence: The new science of human relationships*. New York: Bantam Books.

Groeblinghoff, D., & Becker M. (1996). A case study of mobbing and the clinical treatment of mobbing victims. *European Journal of Work and Organizational Psychology, 5*(2), 277–294.

Hansen, Å. M., Hogh, A., & Persson, R. (2011). Frequency of bullying at work, physiological response, and mental health. *Journal of Psychosomatic Research, 70*(1), 19–27.

Herman, J. (1997). *Trauma and recovery: The aftermath of violence from domestic abuse to political terror*. New York: Basic Books.

Hershcovis, M. S. (2011). "Incivility, social undermining, bullying . . . oh my!": A call to reconcile constructs within workplace aggression research. *Journal of Organizational Behavior, 32*(3), 499–519.

Hershcovis, M. S., & Reich, T. C. (2013). Integrating workplace aggression research: Relational, contextual, and method considerations. *Journal of Organizational Behavior, 32*(S1), S26–S42.

Hogh, A., Hansen, Å. M., Mikkelsen, E. G., & Persson, R. (2012). Exposure to negative acts at work, psychological stress reactions and physiological stress response. *Journal of Psychosomatic Research, 73*(1), 47–52.

Illness. (2009). In *Mosby's medical dictionary* (8th ed.). Retrieved from http://medical-dictionary.thefreedictionary.com/illness

Illness. (2011). In *American Heritage dictionary of the English Language* (5th ed.). Retrieved from http://www.thefreedictionary.com/illness

Injury. (n.d.). In *The free dictionary.* (n.d.). Retrieved from http://www.thefreedictionary.com/injury

Injury. (2005). In *Collins dictionary of medicine.* Retrieved from http://medical-dictionary.thefreedictionary.com/injury

Injury. (2014). In *Collins English dictionary—Complete and unabridged* (12th ed.). Retrieved from http://www.thefreedictionary.com/injury

Institute of Medicine (IOM). (2006). *Posttraumatic stress disorder: Diagnosis and assessment.* Washington, D.C.: National Academies Press.

Jones, E., & Wessely, S. (2007). A paradigm shift in the conceptualization of psychological trauma in the 20th century. *Journal of Anxiety Disorders, 21*(2), 164–175.

Joseph, N. T., Muldoon, M. F., Manuck, S. B., Matthews, K. A., Macdonald, L. A., Grosch, J., & Kamarck, T. W. (2016). The role of occupational status in the association between job strain and ambulatory blood pressure during working and nonworking days. *Psychosomatic Medicine, 78*(8), 940–949.

Karasek, R. (1979). Job demands, job decision latitude, and mental strain: Implications for job redesign. *Administrative Science Quarterly, 24*(2), 285–308.

Karasek, R., Baker, D., Marxer, F., Ahlbom, A., & Theorell, T. (1981). Job decision latitude, job demands, and cardiovascular disease: A prospective study of Swedish men. *American Journal of Public Health, 71*(7), 694–705.

Keeley, J. W., Reed, G. M., Roberts, M. C., Evans, S. C., Robles, R., Matsumoto, C., . . . Maercker, A. (2016). Disorders specifically associated with stress: A case-controlled field study for ICD-11 mental and behavioural disorders. *International Journal of Clinical and Health Psychology, 16*(2), 109–127.

Kivimäki, M., & Kawachi, I. (2015). Work stress as a risk factor for cardiovascular disease. *Current Cardiology Reports, 17*(9), 630–638.

Landsbergis, P. A., Schnall, P. L., Warren, K., Pickering, T. G., & Schwartz, J. E. (1994). Association between ambulatory blood pressure and alternative formulations of job strain. *Scandinavian Journal of Work, Environment & Health, 20*(5), 349–363.

Leymann, H. (1990). Mobbing and psychological terror at workplaces. *Violence and Victims, 5*(2), 119–126.

Leymann, H. (1996). The content and development of mobbing at work. *European Journal of Work and Organizational Psychology, 5*(2), 165–184.

Leymann, H., & Gustafsson, A. (1996). Mobbing at work and the development of post-traumatic stress disorders. *European Journal of Work and Organizational Psychology, 5*(2), 251–275.

Linden, M. (2003). Posttraumatic embitterment disorder. *Psychotherapy and Psychosomatics, 72*(4), 195–202.

Linden, M., Baumann, K., Rotter, M., & Schippan, B. S. (2007). The psychopathology of posttraumatic embitterment disorders. *Psychopathology, 40*(3), 159–165.

Linden, M., & Maercker, A. (2011). Introduction. In M. Linden & A. Maercker (Eds.), *Embitterment: Societal, psychological, and clinical perspectives* (pp. 1–3). Vienna, Austria: SpringerWienNewYork.

Maercker, A., Brewin, C. R., Bryant, R. A., Cloitre, M., van Ommeren, M., Jones, L. M., . . . Reed, G. M. (2013). Diagnosis and classification of disorders specifically associated with stress: Proposals for ICD-11. *World Psychiatry, 12,* 198–206.

Marmot, M. G. (1986). Does stress cause heart attacks? *Postgraduate Medical Journal, 62*(729), 683–686.

Marmot, M. G., Shipley, M. J., & Rose, G. (1984). Inequalities in death—Specific explanations of a general pattern? *Lancet, 323*(8384), 1003–1006.

Mathur, M. B., Epel, E., Kind, S., Desai, M., Parks, C. G., Sandler, D. P., & Khazeni, N. (2016). Perceived stress and telomere length: A systematic review, meta-analysis, and methodologic considerations for advancing the field. *Brain, Behavior, and Immunity, 54*, 158–159.

McEwen, B. (Ed.). (2015). Stress resilience [Special issue]. *Neurobiology of Stress, 1*.

McEwen, B. S., Bowles, N. P., Gray, J. D., Hill, M. N., Hunter, R. G., Karatsoreos, I. N., & Nasca, C. (2015). Mechanisms of stress in the brain. *Nature Neuroscience 18*(10), 1353–1363.

McEwen, B. S., Gray, J. D., & Nasca, C. (2015a). 60 years of neuroendocrinology: Redefining neuroendocrinology: Stress, sex and cognitive and emotional regulation. *Journal of Endocrinology, 226*(2), T67–T83.

McEwen, B. S., Gray, J. D., & Nasca, C. (2015b). Recognizing resilience: Learning from the effects of stress on the brain. *Neurobiology of Stress, 1*, 1–11.

Meyer, J. S., & Hamel, A. F. (2014). Models of stress in nonhuman primates and their relevance for human psychopathology and endocrine dysfunction. *Institute for Laboratory Animal Research Journal, 55*(2), 347–360.

Mikkelsen, E. G., & Einarsen, S. (2002). Relationships between exposure to bullying at work and psychological and psychosomatic health complaints: The role of state negative affectivity and generalized self-efficacy. *Scandinavian Journal of Psychology, 43*(5), 397–405.

Mishna, F., McInroy, L. B., Lacombe-Duncan, A., Bhole, P., Van Wert, M. Schwan, K., . . . Johnston, D. (2016). Prevalence, motivations, and social, mental health and health consequences of cyberbullying among school-aged children and youth: Protocol of a longitudinal and multi-perspective mixed method study. *JMIR Research Protocols, 5*(2), e83. doi:10.2196/resprot.5292

Morbid. (n.d.). In *The free dictionary*. Retrieved from http://www.thefreedictionary.com/morbid

Muschalla, B., & Linden, M. (2011). Embitterment and the workplace. In M. Linden & A. Maercker (Eds.). *Embitterment: Societal, psychological, and clinical perspectives* (pp. 154–167). Vienna, Austria: SpringerWienNewYork.

National Center for PTSD, U.S. Department of Veterans Affairs (2016). *Complex PTSD*. Retrieved from http://www.ptsd.va.gov/professional/PTSD-overview/complex-ptsd.asp

National Institutes of Health (NIH) U.S. National Library of Medicine. (2011). *Psychosomatic medicine: "The puzzling leap."* Retrieved from https://www.nlm.nih.gov/exhibition/emotions/psychosomatic.html

Neurosis. (2011). In *American Heritage dictionary of the English language* (5th ed.). Retrieved from http://www.thefreedictionary.com/neurosis

Occupational Safety and Health Administration. (2011). *OSHA issues compliance directive to address workplace violence* [Trade release]. Retrieved from https://www.osha.gov/pls/oshaweb/owadisp.show_document?p_table=NEWS_RELEASES&p_id=20637

Puterman, E., & Epel, E. (2012). An intricate dance: Life experience, multisystem resiliency, and rate of telomere decline throughout the lifespan. *Social and Personality Psychology Compass, 6*(11), 807–825.

Puterman, E., Epel, E. S., Lin, J., Blackburn, E. H., Gross, J. J., Whooley, M. A., & Cohen, B. E. (2013). Multisystem resiliency moderates the major depression-telomere length association: Findings from the Heart and Soul Study. *Brain, Behavior, and Immunity, 33*, 65–73.

Puterman, E., Gemmill, A., Karasek, D., Weir, D., Adler, N. E., Prather, A. A., & Epel, E. S. (2016). Lifespan adversity and later adulthood telomere length in the nationally representative US Health and Retirement Study. *Proceedings of the National Academy of Sciences of the USA, 113*(42), e6335–e6342.

Reiman, A. (2011). Preface. In M. Linden & A. Maercker (Eds.), *Embitterment: Societal, psychological, and clinical perspectives* (pp. v–vi). Vienna, Austria: SpringerWienNewYork.

Reul, J. M. H. M., Collins, A., Saliba, R. S., Mifsud, K. R., Carter, S. D., Gutierrez-Mecinas, M., ... Linthorst, A. C. E. (2015). Glucocorticoids, epigenetic control and stress resilience. *Neurobiology of Stress, 1*, 44–59.

Romano, S. J., Levi-Minzi, M. E., Rugala, E. A., & Van Hasselt, V. B. (2011). Workplace violence prevention: Readiness and response. Retrieved from https://leb.fbi.gov/2011/january/workplace-violence-prevention-readiness-and-response

Rosen, C. S., Matthieu, M. M., Stirman, S. W., Cook, J. M., Landes, S., Bernardy, N. C., ... Watts, B. V. (2016). A review of studies on the system-wide implementation of evidence-based psychotherapies for posttraumatic stress disorder in the Veterans Health Administration. *Administration and Policy in Mental Health and Mental Health Services Research, 43*(6), 957–977.

Rossouw, P. J., & Rossouw, J. G. (2016). The predictive 6-factor resilience scale: Neurobiological fundamentals and organizational application. *International Journal of Neuropsychotherapy, 4*(1), 31–45.

Rugala, E. A., & Isaacs, A. R. (Eds.). (2004). *Workplace violence: Issues in response.* Retrieved from https://www.fbi.gov/stats-services/publications/workplace-violence

Sabella, R. A., Patchin, J. W., & Hinduja, S. (2013). Cyberbullying myths and realities. *Computers in Human Behavior, 29*(6), 2703–2711.

Sapolsky R. (1990). Stress in the wild. *Scientific American, 262*(1), 116–123.

Schneider, B., Ehrhart, M. G., & Macey, W. H. (2013). Organizational climate and culture. *Annual Review of Psychology, 64*, 361–388.

Selye, H. (1936). A syndrome produced by diverse nocuous agents. *Nature, 138*(3479), 32.

Selye, H. (1946). The general adaptation syndrome and the diseases of adaptation. *Journal of Allergy and Clinical Immunology, 17*(4), 231–247.

Selye, H. (1973). The evolution of the stress concept: The originator of the concept traces its development from the discovery in 1936 of the alarm reaction to modern therapeutic applications of syntoxic and catatoxic hormones. *American Scientist, 61*(6), 692–699.

Selye, H. (1975). Confusion and controversy in the stress field. *Journal of Human Stress, 1*(2), 37–44.

Sensky, T. (2010). Chronic embitterment and organisational justice. *Psychotherapy and Psychosomatics, 79*(2), 65–72.

Sensky, T., Salimu, R., Ballard, J, & Pereira, D. (2015). Associations of chronic embitterment among NHS staff. *Occupational Medicine, 65*(6), 431–436.

Shively, C. A., & Day, S. M. (2015). Social inequalities in health in nonhuman primates. *Neurobiology of Stress, 1,* 156–163.

Shonkoff, J. P., Garner, A. S., Siegel, B. S., Dobbins, M. I., Earls, M. F., Garner, A. S., . . . Wood, D. L. (2012). The lifelong effects of early childhood adversity and toxic stress. *Pediatrics, 129*(1), e232–e246.

Somatoform disorder. (n.d.). In *The free dictionary.* Retrieved from http://medical-dictionary.thefreedictionary.com/somatoform+disorder

Stein, D. J., McLaughlin, K. A., Koenen, K. C., Lukoye, A., Friedman, M. J., Hill, E. D., . . . Kessler, R. C. (2014). DSM-5 and ICD-11 definitions of posttraumatic stress disorder: Investigating "narrow" and "broad" approaches. *Depression and Anxiety, 31*(6), 494–505.

Stress. (n.d.). In *The free dictionary.* Retrieved from http://www.thefreedictionary.com/stress

Syndrome. (n.d.). In *The free dictionary.* Retrieved from http://www.thefreedictionary.com/syndrome

Theorell, T., Jood, K., Järvholm, L. S., Vingård, E., Perk, J., Östergren, P. O., & Hall, C. (2016). A systematic review of studies in the contributions of the work environment to ischaemic heart disease development. *The European Journal of Public Health, 26*(3), 470–477.

Valentino, R., Sheline, Y, & McEwen, B. (2015). Editorial introduction to the special issue on stress resilience. *Neurobiology of Stress, 1,* 80.

van der Kolk, B. A. (2014). *The body keeps the score: Brain, mind, and body in the healing of trauma.* New York: The Penguin Group.

van der Kolk, B. A., Spinazzola, J., Blaustein, M. E., Hopper, J. W., Hopper, E. K., Korn, D. L., & Simpson, W. B. (2007). A randomized clinical trial of eye movement desensitization and reprocessing (EMDR), fluoxetine, and pill placebo in the treatment of posttraumatic stress disorder: Treatment effects and long-term maintenance. *Journal of Clinical Psychiatry, 68*(1), 37–46.

van der Kolk, B. A., Stone, L., West, J., Rhodes, A., Emerson, D., Suvak, M., & Spinazzola, J. (2014). Yoga as an adjunctive treatment for posttraumatic stress disorder: A randomized controlled trial. *Journal of Clinical Psychiatry, 75*(6), e559–e565.

Vignoli, M., Guglielmi, D., Balducci, C., & Bonfiglioli, R. (2015). Workplace bullying as a risk factor for musculoskeletal disorders: The mediating role of job-related psychological strain. *BioMed Research International, 2015,* Article ID 712642. doi:10.1155/2015/712642

Wisco, B. E., Miller, M. W., Wolf, E. J., Kilpatrick, D., Resnick, H. S., Badour, C. L, . . . Friedman, M. J. (2016). The impact of proposed changes to ICD-11 on estimates of PTSD prevalence and comorbidity. *Psychiatry Research, 240,* 226–233.

Wolf, E. J., Miller, M. W., Kilpatrick, D., Resnick, H. S., Badour, C. L., Marx, B. P., . . . Friedman, M. J. (2015). ICD-11 complex PTSD in U.S. national and veteran samples: Prevalence and structural associations with PTSD. *Clinical Psychological Science 3*(2), 215–229.

Wolke, D., & Lereya S. T. (2015). Long-term effects of bullying. *Archives of Disease in Childhood*, 100(9), 879–885.

Workplace Bullying Institute (WBI). (2012). *The WBI website 2012 instant poll D—Impact of workplace bullying on individuals' health.* Retrieved from http://www.workplacebullying.org/multi/pdf/WBI-2012-IP-D.pdf

Workplace Bullying Institute (WBI). (2015). *The WBI definition of workplace bullying.* Retrieved from http://www.workplacebullying.org/individuals/problem/definition

World Health Organization (WHO). (1948). *WHO definition of health.* Retrieved from http://www.who.int/about/definition/en/print.html

World Health Organization (WHO). (1993). *The ICD-10 classification of mental and behavioural disorders: Diagnostic criteria for research.* Geneva, Switzerland: World Health Organization.

World Health Organization (WHO). (2016). ICD-11 *beta draft.* Retrieved from http://apps.who.int/classifications/icd11/browse/f/en

Yang, H., Hitchcock, E., Haldeman, S., Swanson, N., Lu, M.-L., Choi, B., . . . Baker, D. (2016). Workplace psychosocial and organizational factors for neck pain in workers in the United States. *American Journal of Industrial Medicine*, 59(7), 549–560.

6

The Psychosocial Impact of Workplace Bullying and Mobbing on Targets

Maureen Duffy

The effects of workplace bullying and mobbing on targets are not limited to negative health effects. Targets can experience multiple and spiraling psychosocial effects, including effects on personal and professional identity, damage to reputation, feelings of betrayal, loss of social and friendship networks at work, increased family problems, issues with loss of trust, and loss of belief in the world as a fair and just place. If the bullying and mobbing result in job loss, the negative impact is compounded, and targets can experience difficulties with reemployability in addition to the basic losses associated with job loss, which include financial losses and loss of health and retirement benefits.

With some exceptions (Duffy & Sperry, 2014; Lutgen-Sandvik, chapter 8 this volume), the literature to date has primarily focused on the negative physical and psychological consequences to bullying and mobbing targets. While this focus has been essential in helping to understand the damaging effects of bullying and mobbing on targets, it has been incomplete. A broader focus that includes a discussion of this wider array of psychosocial effects and losses is necessary—not for the purposes of painting a gloomy picture for targets but to realistically present the myriad layered effects of workplace bullying and mobbing that targets, their family members, and their health care providers must address to promote sustainable recovery. In this chapter, these psychosocial impacts of workplace bullying and mobbing will be examined.

The concept *psychosocial* refers to the relationship between the individual and the environment within which the individual lives and functions and is the basis of major approaches to understanding the individual (Woodward, 2015). It is a person-in-context approach and includes the influence on the individual of such social factors as school, work, family and friendship relationships, and larger structural social factors such as poverty, education, gender, race and ethnicity, income, and social class.

For most Americans, having a "good job" is a source of personal pride and satisfaction and is a foundation for faith in the future. Therefore, it is no surprise that when things go wrong at work through bullying and mobbing, the impact goes well beyond work-related concerns and affects every dimension of a target's life. Self-confidence, self-esteem, faith in a secure future, beliefs about fairness and justice in the world, physical health, mental health, family relationships, social relationships, finances and financial security, health and life insurance, retirement planning, and the ability to obtain other jobs are all potentially impacted when bullying or mobbing happens.

When a target first becomes aware that he or she is a target of workplace bullying or mobbing, confusion and disbelief are very common initial reactions. Over time, this confusion and disbelief give way to a flood of emotions, including sadness and anger. Once a person becomes a target of bullying or mobbing, life at work is qualitatively changed, and the target's feelings and relationships are also changed. Work is no longer normal or routine, and the target knows that he or she has been singled out for very unwanted attention. While most targets ultimately become aware of the profound unfairness of the experience of bullying and mobbing, many initially feel embarrassment and blame themselves for what they might have done or could have done differently. Self-confidence plummets, and the foundation at work that the target relied upon to do an effective job is no longer stable or predictable. For the target of bullying or mobbing, showing up for work is no longer normal or routine. The target is faced with a surge of very strong emotions on a daily basis as well as uncertainty about his or her work future and often experiences compromised self-esteem and self-confidence as a result.

Bullying and mobbing are health-harming behaviors. The most widely known harm to targets and victims of bullying and mobbing are the physical and psychological injuries that frequently arise during and after episodes of workplace bullying and mobbing (Duffy & Sperry, 2012). However, harm is not limited to damage to physical and mental health. Harm includes the experience of exclusion that is an inherent part of workplace bullying and mobbing, the social pain that goes along with the experience of exclusion, and the resulting disruptions and loss of workplace friendships and social networks.

In the case of the significant numbers of bullying and mobbing targets who ultimately lose their jobs, issues of reemployability and faith and confidence in the future are important concerns that must be addressed by all those involved in helping targets to recover. The degree to which occupational or professional identity is salient to a person also determines the degree to which that person is likely to be overwhelmed and distressed by the experience of workplace bullying or mobbing. Additionally, the intertwining of occupational or professional identity with one's larger personal identity complicates both the experience of bullying and mobbing and recovery from it. Finally, whether an individual sees the world as generally fair and just or sees it as more unjust and capricious is influenced by the experience of bullying and mobbing, which, in turn, influences that person's ongoing adjustment and contentment in the world. All of these psychosocial effects potentially accruing to targets of workplace bullying and mobbing broaden the range of harms beyond damage to physical and psychological health and will be addressed in this chapter.

WORK AND PERSONAL IDENTITIES

Work is central to a person's identity. Occupational or professional identity and personal identity are tied up with the work that a person does every day. "There is an emergent consensus that *identity* refers to the meanings that individuals attach reflexively to themselves, and which are developed and sustained through processes of social interaction as they seek to address the question 'who am I?'" (Brown, 2015, p. 23). In more everyday language, identity refers to how self-definition and self-appraisal arises out of ongoing social interactions. Self-definitions and self-appraisals are an assessment of personal qualities and characteristics, past and present contributions, and future potential around a particular social position, for example, work identity or identity as a parent. Individuals shape these self-appraisals and self-definitions into stories about who they are and about how and why they perform and function in various relational positions and roles in the way that they do. These stories of one's identity can also be thought of as narratives of identity. Individuals develop narratives through interactions with others and tell themselves stories of who they are as people in the conduct of roles in their lives that are important to them.

People have more than one identity in their lives. Most people have many identities, and these identities are associated with the various and important (to the individual) relational positions that they occupy in life. The same person can have a work identity, a spousal identity, a parental identity, a friend identity, a political identity, an athletic identity, an intellectual identity, a religious or spiritual identity, and many more. Together, these multiple identities make up the larger self or personal identity, and all of these identities are mutually informing. Changes in one identity influence and shape the other identities and the overall sense of self or personal identity. As any of these identities change or shift, the stories or narratives that go along with them also change and shift. It is through these narratives of identity that people know and understand their own experiences. Identity work, according to Sveningsson and Alvesson (2003), is the activity of "being engaged in forming, repairing, maintaining, strengthening or revising the constructions that are productive of a sense of coherence and distinctiveness" (p. 1165) about the self. Identify work, therefore, is basic adaptational work that a person does continuously and that facilitates the person's engagement in the world with others.

Identity stories or narratives change as a result of what happens in interactions with other people who are central to the performing of particular roles or identities. Think, for example, of a mother who defined her identity as a parent as the most important of the many roles or identities she occupied. She spent her life devoted to her child, whom she nurtured, taught, and guided throughout childhood and adolescence. As her child approached early adulthood and independence, this child failed in university and at work and got into moderate trouble with the law. The mother, in significant personal distress, negatively reevaluated her parenting contributions and was distraught over how she could help her child become more productive and successful at this point in her parenting life. She was left with the choice of repairing her parent identity, lowering its priority in her life, or remaining more or less frozen in grief—hard choices all.

Like the identity of parent, work identity is also changed by ongoing experiences. A person's work identity "refers to a work-based self-concept, constituted of a combination of organizational, occupational, and other identities that shapes the roles a person adopts and the corresponding ways he or she behaves when performing his or her work" (Walsh & Gordon, 2008, p. 47). Workplace bullying or mobbing subverts work identity and thrusts a target into a position of having to reevaluate his or her narrative about life as a worker while simultaneously having to justify and defend workplace decisions, interactions, and other behaviors. Lutgen-Sandvik (2008) describes the identity work required of bullying and mobbing targets as difficult and exhausting.

Consider the following. A highly regarded physician hired by the senior partners in a large practice and research group was never fully accepted by his colleagues in the new group. The day-to-day practice administrator denied him the same level of clerical and technical support routinely provided to the other group members and moved his office to an isolated location. The administrator, together with other colleagues, consistently demeaned his research and clinical practice priorities, gave him excessive on-call assignments, made arranging time off for professional conferences and vacation extremely difficult, accused of him being abrupt with colleagues and not collegial, and, ultimately, banded together and signed a petition for his removal from the group practice. Then they went further and accused the physician of patient mismanagement and violation of research protocols, thereby jeopardizing his previously unblemished career and threatening his livelihood. No one could go through such an experience without feeling the deep sting of humiliation and reputational damage and without questioning the meanings and purpose that had previously given shape to one's professional life. After such an experience, one's work identity and work narratives would never be the same again. This is what happens to targets of workplace bullying and mobbing; they are faced with having to reconstruct a work identity that incorporates the painful facts of bullying and mobbing and integrate that reconstructed work narrative of identity into their larger self-identity.

For example, prior to being bullied or mobbed, a worker enjoyed the benefits of a good reputation among her colleagues. When she contributed to the discussions in staff meetings, people listened to what she had to say and took her point of view seriously. Her ideas and perspectives were valued, and she was asked for her input. She was consulted about how she thought proposed changes would impact her coworkers and the company's clients. That she and her opinion mattered in her workplace was something that she had been able to take for granted. After being bullied, that was no longer the case. Her perspective was devalued just as her reputation had been devalued during the bullying. Now when she offered her point of view during staff meetings, if she had the nerve to even do so, her coworkers clearly did not listen, rolled their eyes, and moved on to someone else as quickly as possible. Where before bullying her actions and decisions were trusted and her coworkers had confidence in them, now every action and decision was called into question and scrutinized. Such dramatic changes in how a target of bullying or mobbing is viewed in the workplace are not uncommon. In the face of such changes, how one thinks about one's work identity and the meaning of work will inevitably change.

Tom Fryers, a visiting professor of public mental health at the University of Leicester in the United Kingdom, described the profound impact on him of an experience in which he was badly mistreated that resulted in his reworking of his personal and work identities:

> Having free-lanced as a public health physician for over a decade, with the inevitable variation in both the availability and type of work, "retirement" is, perhaps, a vaguer concept than for those with conventional full time jobs. In my middle sixties, I was drifting towards retirement, thinking that I should soon refuse any new work, when an incident occurred quite unconnected with work. Many have experienced being treated by someone with utter contempt, but a dramatic confrontation in which I was made to feel a worthless "nothing" forced me to reflect on my immediate future, my social status in retirement, and the importance of work. I abandoned thoughts of full retirement and took up new research commitments, having concluded that, for me, it was important to be a "something," whatever that "something" was. (Fryers, 2006, para. 1)

After being humiliated, Fryers totally reworked his previous plans for retirement to "be something," demonstrating with his life choices the wrongness of the person who had made him feel worthless. Similarly, bullying and mobbing targets will go to great lengths to challenge their damaged work identities and ultimately to repair and revise them.

Bullying and mobbing subvert work identities, and this undermining has effects for both the individual target and his or her wider relational network. For many, work is the principal component of personal identity and serves as a basic source of social legitimacy (Fryers, 2006). When work is threatened through bullying or mobbing, one's personhood, legitimacy in the world, way of making a living, financial security, source of meaning and purpose, and way of being valued by others are all threatened. Work identity, personal identity, and self-esteem are all interconnected. Bullying and mobbing attack all three and strike at the heart of who a person is.

EXCLUSION, SOCIAL PAIN, AND LOSS OF WORK FRIENDSHIPS AND RELATIONSHIPS

The psychological and emotional effects from bullying and mobbing also complicate family and social relationships (Duffy & Sperry, 2014). Targets who have become depressed or anxious frequently find it difficult to interact with family members and friends in their usual ways. Social distancing, isolation, and irritability are common responses to being bullied or mobbed, and these responses, needless to say, can negatively impact family and social relationships. (See chapter 8 for more information about the impact of bullying and mobbing on family relationships.) Similarly, if a target remains in the workplace, a sense of betrayal and confusion about whom to trust among coworkers renders workplace social relationships very difficult. Often, the safest emotional bet for a target is to isolate and distance from workplace interactions as much as possible. The result of workplace isolation and social distancing is the loss of social contact that was previously a source of familiarity and even satisfaction. In addition, workplace social contact is necessary in most situations to get the job done. Social isolation and distancing in the workplace lead to less communication, which leads to targets having fewer tools and resources with which to do their jobs effectively, thus aggravating trouble at work.

Work is a site of goal-oriented activity and a place in the world where, all going well, one can build an increasing sense of accomplishment and meaning in life. It is also the practical context within which most people earn a living and the means to support themselves and their family members. In most situations, work is also a social setting where friendships and important social relationships are formed and maintained. Work is a social group to which one contributes and from which one derives not only income but also the benefits of social relationships. Employees routinely talk about "my job," "my work group," "my department," "my company." People at work don't just have a job. They are connected to the group and to the social relationships that surround and contain their job. The kinds of connections that people form at work are basic and profoundly important to human well-being.

Social neuroscientists Eisenberger and Lieberman (2005) state that "along with the evolution of mammals, a species unique in their need for early nurturance and care, came a corresponding lifelong need for social connection. Indeed, this need has proved so essential to survival that social separation, like other unmet needs, is experienced as painful" (p. 110). Eisenberger and Lieberman (2005) explain that a significant portion of the same neural pathways in the brain and nervous system that are responsible for signaling pain after physical injury are also responsible for signaling pain after a social injury, such as exclusion from a group. Their work reveals that it is not just metaphorically or symbolically true to say that being left out or excluded hurts; it is literally and actually true.

From this and similar research, we now know that membership in a group is a basic survival need, like food and shelter, and that the removal or loss of that basic need comes with a high price. Ostracism is a kind of "social death," with consequences that can be both extreme and enduring (Wesselmann, Nairne, & Williams, 2012). Zadro (2004), in her study of chronic ostracism, cited feelings of alienation and isolation, learned helplessness, meaninglessness, depression, and low self-worth as typical outcomes. So, when a person's job is threatened or lost as a result of workplace bullying or mobbing, the threat of the loss of the job itself is a significant threat to survival. But so also is the loss of connection with the social group that is part of the job. Exclusion from the group is part and parcel of workplace bullying or mobbing, and it brings with it a social pain that is frequently underestimated in both its intensity and effects.

Nordgren, Banas, and MacDonald (2011) concluded that the experience of social pain impedes and distorts judgment in interpersonal relationships and can interfere with conflict resolution. Their research also found that people who are not experiencing social pain consistently underestimate the seriousness of the social pain of others and underempathize with those who are suffering from it. This underestimation of the seriousness of social pain has real-world implications in the workplace. Nordgren et al. (2011) reported that their ongoing research would examine how such underestimation of social pain affected organizational policy with respect to such issues as employee victimization (as occurs in bullying and mobbing) and bereavement and other relevant family medical leaves. When coworkers, other organizational members, family, and friends do not recognize the intensity of social pain experienced by bullying and mobbing targets and do not empathize with the targets, targets are set up for more loneliness, more isolation, and more social pain in a troubling vicious cycle.

Workplace bullying and mobbing represent a real and persistent threat to a person's job and to membership in the social group surrounding the job with all the associated severe losses just described. As bullying or mobbing progress in a workplace, they interfere with the flow of workplace banter and camaraderie. A bullied or mobbed worker, by definition, is someone who is branded as not worthy of full membership and participation in the workgroup. Workplace bullying and mobbing render the target as "different from," as "other," and, therefore, as untrustworthy as a conversational partner in the normal give and take of the office or factory floor. As an employee is targeted in bullying or mobbing, coworkers distance themselves, and, in response, the target also distances from coworkers. Bullying and mobbing result in a reciprocal and mutual dance of social distancing between the target and coworkers. The target ends up increasingly isolated and cut off from the communication flows that are both essential for the full functioning of a workplace and intrinsically enjoyable.

When people go to work every day, they develop relationships that become important to them, and the loss of those relationships as a result of workplace bullying and mobbing is another in a long list of losses suffered by targets. Workplace relationships run the gamut from casual to very important and meaningful to the worker. Sias (2009) describes workplace friendships as occurring in all types of organizations and between all types of employees at all levels of the organizational hierarchy. Her research underscores that workplace friendships provide crucial social support to workers while also facilitating both the flow of information within a company or organization and access to its sources of power and influence. Friendships connect an individual worker to the larger social group—the vital importance of which we have already examined. But workplace relationships are more than sources of social support and conduits for information flow within an organization; they are also intrinsically satisfying and rewarding. So, when workplace friendships are lost through bullying and mobbing, those losses can be very painful.

Sias, Heath, Perry, Silva, and Fix (2004) researched the deterioration of workplace friendships and found that workers whose workplace friendships had deteriorated were likely to feel isolated, frustrated, and unhappy and to characterize the whole experience as emotionally stressful or traumatic for them. Workplace friendships occur in just about every workplace, and they facilitate the accomplishment of work while also providing essential support and personal meaning to the workers involved. The workplaces also benefit because workers who are satisfied with their workplace relationships are more attached to their organizations (Venkataramani, Labianca, & Grosser, 2013). The loss of workplace friendships through bullying and mobbing reverberates through the organization, hurting both the workers involved and the organization itself.

AFTER BULLYING AND MOBBING: PROFESSIONAL REPUTATION AND REEMPLOYABILITY

The statistics about job stability and security once one has become a target of bullying and mobbing are sobering. It is bad enough that a target has to cope with workplace abuse and its effects while employed. The Workplace Bullying Institute (WBI), in its 2014 national survey of adults in the United States, reports that 61 percent of bullying and mobbing targets eventually lose their jobs (WBI/Zogby Analytics, 2014), adding insult to the injury of bullying and mobbing when considering the financial and reputational consequences attendant to job loss. The *2014 U.S. Workplace Bullying Survey* (WBI/Zogby Analytics, 2014) posed a question to survey respondents who had indicated that the abuse they had either experienced or witnessed had ended about what had made the workplace abuse stop. Twenty-nine percent of the targets had voluntarily quit their jobs to get away from the workplace mistreatment; 19 percent were constructively discharged or forced to quit when their working conditions were deliberately made worse; and 13 percent of the targets were fired. An additional 13 percent indicated that while the target did not actually lose his or her employment, he or she was transferred to a different department or unit. These are staggering figures. All told, 74 percent of the targets either lost their job through quitting, constructive discharge, termination, or through being transferred out of their department (WBI/Zogby Analytics, 2014). In practical terms, these statistics mean that a significant majority of targets of workplace bullying and mobbing are faced with the prospect of unemployment and having to look for and find new employment in the wake of the trauma of workplace abuse.

Finding a job when one is unemployed is challenging at the best of times. In the shadow of such an abusive experience as workplace bullying or mobbing, it is demonstratively more so. To appreciate the reemployment challenges for targets of workplace bullying and mobbing, it is helpful to understand what the concept of employability means and how it applies when looking for work. Understanding what employability means provides a window to the special challenges faced by bullying and mobbing targets in their efforts to find new jobs following job loss.

Employability is a psychosocial construct that refers to the packages of skills, attitudes, beliefs, flexibility, and openness to change that workers bring to actual and potential employment situations (Fugate, Kinicki, & Ashforth, 2004). The emphasis in current understandings of employability is on the individual's ability to change, to be resilient, and to approach new situations and challenges with both optimism and confidence (Fugate et al., 2004). Three elements of employability have been identified in the vocational and psychological literature: (1) career identity, (2) personal adaptability, and (3) social and human capital (Gowan, 2012). People have multiple identities in life corresponding to the activities, relationships, and roles that are important to them and that they rank order in their lives in terms of salience or importance (Hogg & Terry, 2000). Persons for whom career is the most important of their identities are likely to have more difficulty in adapting to unemployment following workplace bullying or mobbing than someone who, for example, prioritized family identity or religious or spiritual identity over work identity. When work is a person's primary or most salient identity, loss of work is devastating.

It is erroneous to believe that bullying and mobbing targets are happy to get out of their jobs or workplaces. There is a basic and important distinction between getting out of abusive circumstances and getting out of a job. While escaping abuse is unequivocally desirable, losing a job is not. For many, if not most targets, their jobs held meaning, provided at least some satisfaction, and were the focus of their conscientious attention and efforts. Their jobs became problematic as a result of abusive behavior directed toward them, not because of anything inherent in the nature of the work itself. In fact, after job loss, the more strongly that workers had been committed to their previous jobs, the more difficult their overall adjustment to job loss, and the more likely they were to experience negative and pessimistic psychological reactions (Leana & Feldman, 1990). For bullied and mobbed workers, loss of their jobs disrupts their networks of friendships and social relationships at work and results in the loss of opportunities to perform work for which they were trained and to which most were very dedicated.

What the research has found, then, is that the more strongly workers are attached to their jobs, the harder it is for them to adjust to ensuing job loss; in other words, they are less adaptable. Again, this adds insult to injury for bullied and mobbed workers who were attached to their jobs and who ultimately lost them as a result of workplace abuse. These targets had to suffer through abusive workplace behavior and face the pain of losing jobs to which they were strongly connected, making it doubly hard for such persons in the period following job loss, when resilience and adaptability are necessary parts of the recovery process. Optimism and confidence in the future are characteristics of personal adaptability—the second constituent of employability. With bullying and mobbing targets more prone to anxiety disorders and depression (Duffy & Sperry, 2012, 2014), targets start out at a disadvantage in terms of personal adaptability when considering others who have lost their jobs for different reasons and who do not have to contend with the layers of harm inherent in bullying and mobbing.

Social and human capital are the sum total of the knowledge, skills, experiences, and network of social relationships that a potential worker has to bring to bear on the search for new employment (Gowan, 2012). Social capital is particularly important for people who have lost jobs and are trying to find reemployment. Wolff and Moser (2009) describe social capital as the networks of social relationships and contacts that people have available to them.

For bullied and mobbed workers, social capital is almost always compromised. When targets have lost jobs due to bullying and mobbing, they are either pushed out or forced out or choose to leave to avoid more abuse. By virtue of having been bullied or mobbed, the trustworthiness of their former workplace relationships has been called into question, and targets are frequently unsure of whom they can trust and safely ask for both new job leads and references. Targets may feel betrayed by coworkers who did not stand up for them when they were subjected to abuse or who became active participants in the bullying or mobbing. Since reputational damage through gossip, slander, and the distribution of false information about a target are common negative acts in bullying and mobbing (Bultena & Whatcott, 2008), it is understandable that targets would be leery of risking the spread of personally and professionally detrimental information by asking people in their former network of work relationships to put in a good word for them with potential employers unless they were sure of the former coworkers' trustworthiness. If targets asked the wrong person, negative information about them could be disseminated to potential employers, thereby reducing their prospects of obtaining new employment. Bullying and mobbing can lay waste to the social capital of targets, leaving them underresourced in their attempts to find new employment after job loss. For targets, trust is a casualty of the experience of workplace abuse.

BELIEF IN A JUST WORLD: WHY IT IS IMPORTANT

Our underlying premises and beliefs about the world influence how we think about the world, how we view our place in it, and how we decide to act in it. One such underlying belief, frequently unexamined yet undeniably influential, is whether we believe the world to be a fair and just place. The basic assumption behind belief in a just world is that people get what they deserve in life: if they do good, good things happen to them. If they do bad, bad things happen. It does not take much looking around the world to figure out that the world can be a very harsh place where plenty of bad things happen to people who are good, innocent, or both. Even individuals who see unfairness and cruelty around them can still hold on to the belief that while the world in general is cruel and unfair, their personal world does not work that way and, in fact, is more fair and just than it is the opposite.

Most people hold on to a belief in the world as just, at least as it affects them personally, for reasons that have important psychological significance. Believing in a just world allows people to see the world as at least somewhat orderly and predictable, in which their actions will make a difference either for good or for bad. In other words, believing in a just world provides a basis for believing that individuals have a certain amount of control over events in their lives and that their actions will have consequences in relation to their intentions.

Research on just-world beliefs (Dalbert, 2001) has identified three primary functions of these beliefs: (1) just-world beliefs promote trust that people will be treated fairly by others; (2) just-world beliefs promote the assimilation of injustices (i.e., victims will try to make sense of injustices without having to give up their beliefs in a just world); and (3) just-world beliefs promote fair and just behavior toward others. The theory of just-world beliefs is complicated, especially with respect to the second function of just-world beliefs, the assimilation of injustice.

One of the ways in which people make sense of injustice toward others without having to give up their just-world beliefs is by assuming that the injustice or tragedy was somehow self-inflicted. He was killed in the boating tragedy because he was too tired, was out too late, and was going too fast. She got bullied at work because she had a personality disorder and was difficult to work with. Their house was destroyed in the brush fires because they had built in an area prone to wildfires. Victim blaming or victim derogation has been widely studied and documented with respect to just-world beliefs (Furnham, 2003; Hafer & Bègue, 2005).

Believing in a just world has been shown to be a powerful enough belief that when challenged by empirical evidence, that is, bad things happening to good people, observers will tend to view victims as somehow causing their misfortunes to hold on to their just-world beliefs rather than giving them up in the face of evidence to the contrary. Interestingly, with respect to school bullying, some research suggests that the victim blaming often associated with just-world beliefs does not apply in instances of bullying and that the opposite has been found to be the case; namely, strongly held just-world beliefs are associated with strong antibullying attitudes and reduced bullying behavior (Correia & Dalbert, 2008; Fox, Elder, Gater, & Johnson, 2010). More research is required to understand the relationship between just-world beliefs and attitudes toward victims of both workplace and school bullying.

Just-world beliefs are double-sided, with one side pointing to the tendency to blame victims as a way of protecting one's just-world beliefs and the other side pointing to the adaptive and coping benefits of believing in a just world and being disposed to treat others fairly. Both sides of just-world beliefs have important implications for understanding workplace bullying. On the one side, victim blaming has tremendous downside potential for victims of workplace bullying and mobbing. On the other side, the adaptive and coping benefits for mental health of believing in a just world have important upside significance for workplace bullying and mobbing victims who are attempting to recover from these devastating experiences.

On the positive side, believing in a just world brings with it, to a greater rather than lesser extent, the sense that the world is orderly and predictable and that fairness and justice will prevail over unfairness and chaos. Just-world beliefs support personal autonomy and self-efficacy in that the consequences of behavior are regarded as directly related to the intentions behind the behavior and to the quality of the efforts that people expend to do something. A body of research supports the benefits to personal mental health and well-being and overall psychological adjustment of holding just-world beliefs (Dalbert, 2007, 2009; Furnham, 2003; Maes & Schmitt, 2004; Otto, Boos, Dalbert, Schöps, & Hoyer, 2006). The mental health benefits of just-world beliefs are especially noted with respect to life satisfaction and to the experience of positive affect or mood (Correia, Batista, & Lima, 2009). Believing that one's personal world is fair and just is adaptive and helps people to carry on in the face of adversity and to believe that how they respond will make a difference.

The effects of workplace mobbing on just-world beliefs were researched in a study by Cubela Adoric and Kvartuc (2007). Their research investigated whether repeated and prolonged exposure to workplace mobbing had adverse effects on the just-world beliefs of employees and the relationship between just-world beliefs and psychological adjustment in the aftermath of such exposure. The study concluded that mobbing victims believed less in a personal just world than did their matched counterparts who had not been exposed to mobbing, suggesting that mobbing weakens personal beliefs in a just world. The study also found that mobbing victims believed more in the unfairness of the world and that they placed emphasis on the value of justice. With respect to psychological adjustment in the aftermath of exposure to workplace mobbing, Cubela Adoric and Kvartuc (2007) found that workplace mobbing victims were more depressed and pessimistic and were less trusting in the goodness of others than the control group members in the study. Overall, the study findings indicated that workplace mobbing exposure was marked by less-strong beliefs in a just world, less trust in the inherent goodness of others, and more depression and pessimism in comparison to persons not exposed to workplace mobbing. Mobbing victims experienced weaker belief in a personal just world and stronger belief in a general unjust world. These findings are concerning, and more research on the relationship between exposure to workplace bullying and mobbing and the effect on just-world beliefs and psychological adjustment is certainly needed.

The small cadre of clinical mental health practitioners in the United States who work with bullying and mobbing targets, this author among them, regularly note in informal communications the emphasis on obtaining justice that motivates so many targets of workplace bullying and mobbing. The experience of bullying and mobbing has violated their sense of justice and fair play, and their actions in response to having become a target of workplace bullying and mobbing are frequently motivated by an effort to restore their lost sense of justice in the world. At least at the outset, these targets who sought professional help are willing to expend any amount of emotional, financial, and personal resources to try and make right a situation they believe has profoundly violated their sense of justice. In her research on the remedial identity work of targets of workplace bullying and mobbing, Lutgen-Sandvik (2008) said, "Targeted workers feel compelled to justify themselves and their behaviour when confronted with accusations, threats and/or social ostracism" (p. 113).

Initially, the search for restoring justice outweighs practical concerns about the actual costs in money, time, and emotional resources that must be dedicated to fighting adverse workplace outcomes as a result of bullying and mobbing and the opportunity cost of allocating resources to such efforts. One of the responsibilities of practitioners who work with bullying and mobbing targets is to help them realistically assess both the actual and opportunity costs of a set of various responses to the workplace abuse and to help them determine a "best" course of action given their unique circumstances and preferences. The finding of Cubela Adoric and Kvartuc (2007) that workplace mobbing victims emphasize justice is borne out by this cadre of clinical practitioners who provide clinical support to them. Exposure to mobbing, based on both research and clinical practice, profoundly violates the organizing belief in a just world that is central to how people make sense of the world, and thrusts targets into a costly search for restoration of that lost sense of justice.

PSYCHOSOCIAL IMPACTS OF BULLYING AND MOBBING AND RECOVERY: A BRIEF NOTE

As discussed above, clinical experience in working with targets of workplace bullying and mobbing strongly supports the justice motivation of so many targets with respect to their responses to having been targeted. They are willing to fight back, often at huge costs to themselves, to restore their shattered sense of justice. Duffy and Sperry (2014) remind targets, their families, and their health care providers of what may be involved in fighting back:

> There is a huge asymmetry of power when an individual organizational member decides to take on the organization in whatever context. This power imbalance doesn't mean that you shouldn't fight back, but it does

mean that you need to know what you are getting yourself into. Therefore, it's essential that if you decide to fight back you set "fight" rules for yourself.

- You can't go this alone. Fighting back is stressful, and you need to know that you have support from family or friends that you can really count on. There are likely to be some dark days ahead.
- Set a limit on the amount of time and resources that you are willing and able to commit to fighting back. Adhere strictly to those limits. Know when to cut your losses and walk away.
- Don't make fighting the organization that mobbed you your next career. It isn't worth it. You can quickly use up all your financial and psychological resources trying to fight the organization in order to prove that you were not as they have portrayed you. (pp. 124–125)

As is fairly clear, there is more to recovery from bullying and mobbing than addressing the psychological consequences, such as anxiety and depression, and the physical consequences, such as gastrointestinal disturbances and cardiovascular problems, as critical as addressing these problems is. There are the myriad psychosocial effects of bullying and mobbing that also need to be addressed. These psychosocial effects that must be dealt with during the recovery process include the damage to personal and work identity, the social pain of exclusion, mistrust of others resulting from the actual or perceived betrayal by coworkers, loss of friendships and important social networks, difficulties with reemployability, obtaining references, obtaining leads for appropriate next jobs, and the implications of weakening or collapsed beliefs in a fair and just world. This is a tall order because so many life domains are involved.

Consequently, targets are likely to need the support of multiple providers over the course of their ongoing recovery from bullying and mobbing. The most likely service providers to whom targets will turn are physicians and other health care providers for their physical health problems; mental health providers for psychological, emotional, and many psychosocial problems; marriage and family therapists for family problems; career and occupational counselors for career and work problems; and life coaches for a number of psychosocial problems and for taking action and assuming responsibility for making positive changes in recovery. Ideally, all of these professional service providers who provide care and support to targets of bullying and mobbing would be informed and knowledgeable about bullying and mobbing, but that is not the case at the present time. So, again, the burden of protecting oneself and finding the best possible health care and other professional providers falls back on the targets themselves. To help targets choose the best possible professional service providers for help with their recovery from bullying and mobbing and recognizing that there are many providers who know very little about bullying and mobbing, two recommendations are offered here and expanded upon in chapters 13 and 14.

The first recommendation is for targets to choose a provider who is knowledgeable about and who has been trained in trauma-informed models of care (see chapters 13 and 14). The second recommendation is for targets to bring books, book chapters, and articles about workplace bullying and mobbing to their providers so that their providers can bridge some of the gaps in their knowledge about these severe workplace problems.

CONCLUSION

Harms and losses can pile up one on top of the other in the aftermath of workplace bullying and mobbing. The potential damage to the physical and psychological health of targets of bullying and mobbing is now well-established. What have been less considered are the psychosocial effects of bullying and mobbing and their implications, as discussed in this chapter, and the direct and vicarious harm to family members, as discussed in chapter 8. Personal and work identities are subverted by workplace bullying and mobbing, thrusting targets into the intense and difficult work of repair and revision of these identities. Personal and work identities matter because they shape who we believe ourselves to be and what we believe we can effectively do in the world. Damaged narratives of identity lead to less confident futures and to reduced engagement in the world. Less confidence and reduced engagement do not just impact targets; they also impact all those who depend on the targets.

The profound effects of social exclusion as a result of bullying and mobbing cannot be understated. Going from a valued member of such an important social group as a workplace to a demeaned, devalued, and isolated member represents a survival threat—not just to economic survival, although it is that, but more importantly to the sense of connection and belonging that is the basis of health, well-being, and productivity. The neuroscience of ostracism and exclusion has made it clear why targets are frequently so psychologically shattered by their experiences. Social exclusion is painful in precisely the same way as physical injuries are painful. From an evolutionary standpoint, the function that pain serves is a warning to the organism that a survival threat is underway (Eisenberger & Lieberman, 2005; MacDonald & Leary, 2005). Without having the words to explain why, perhaps targets have long read their own social pain of exclusion as a survival threat. Their sometimes intense reactions are best understood as a response to that survival threat and as a solution attempt to remain whole.

Bullying and mobbing can destabilize a target's sense of present and future financial security as worry and anxiety about job security increases. In situations where job loss is seen as a possible outcome of bullying and mobbing, a target may worry about financial obligations and the ability to meet them. A target's hopes and dreams for the future are then compromised by the threat of job loss. In American society, with its limited safety nets for people of working age, a threat to one's job can rapidly progress to becoming a survival threat. Withholding or denial of job references is a common negative act perpetrated against targets in bullying and mobbing situations, and the implications of that particular negative act for a target's future are significant, especially in such market economies as the United States. In terms of work commitment, targets who were most attached to their jobs and who lost them through bullying and mobbing are the very ones most likely to have difficult and complicated post–job loss adjustments. Couple that with the disruption of friendship and social networks as a result of bullying and mobbing and the corresponding loss of social support and of informal contacts through whom an unemployed worker is likely to hear about new opportunities and the bad news for targets just gets amplified.

Targets of bullying and mobbing see the world as less fair and less just than their counterparts who were not bullied or mobbed at work. While holding just-world beliefs can increase the likelihood that victims will be blamed for what happens to them—and that is never good news for workplace bullying and mobbing targets—the flip side is that for the targets themselves, holding such beliefs helps in recovery. People who believe the world is fair and just also believe that their personal decisions and actions will make a positive difference in their lives, thus promoting greater personal agency. However, bullying and mobbing targets have had the experience of being treated badly and unfairly at work, often while being fully committed to their jobs. For this group, how they act and what they do seems to make much less of a difference in their lives, and the outcome, for them, is an increased risk of disengagement and depression. Their solution attempts directed at restoring their lost sense of justice and fairness in the world are to engage in intensive efforts to challenge the workplace abuse and unfairness, often with insufficient attention to the personal and family costs of such efforts.

Bullying and mobbing should never have been understood as only affecting targets. The effects spiral out and encompass much wider relational networks, including family, friends, coworkers, and the organizations in which the bullying and mobbing have occurred. When workplace bullying or mobbing finally ends for a target, the psychosocial effects continue, and that is a critical fact for all stakeholders to know.

REFERENCES

Brown, A. D. (2015). Identities and identity work in organizations. *International Journal of Management Reviews, 17*(1), 20–40. doi:10.1111/ijmr.12035

Bultena, C. D., & Whatcott, R. B. (2008). Bushwhacked at work: A comparative analysis of mobbing and bullying at work. *Proceedings of the American Society of Business and Behavioral Sciences, 15*(1), 652–666.

Correia, I., Batista, M. T., & Lima, M. L. (2009). Does the belief in a just world bring happiness? Causal relationships among belief in a just world, life satisfaction and mood. *Australian Journal of Psychology, 61*(4), 220–227. doi:/10.1080/00049530802579515

Correia, I., & Dalbert, C. (2008). School bullying. *European Psychologist, 13*(4), 248–254.

Cubela Adoric, V., & Kvartuc, T. (2007). Effects of mobbing on justice beliefs and adjustment. *European Psychologist, 12*(4), 261–271.

Dalbert, C. (2001). *The justice motive as a personal resource: Dealing with challenges and critical life events.* New York: Kluwer/Plenum.

Dalbert, C. (2007). Introduction to the special section: Dealing with strain at the workplace: A just-world perspective. *European Psychologist, 12*(4), 250–252.

Dalbert, C. (2009). Belief in a just world. In M. R. Leary & R. H. Hoyle (Eds.), *Handbook of individual differences in social behavior* (pp. 288–297). New York: Guilford.

Duffy, M., & Sperry, L. (2012). *Mobbing: Causes, consequences, and solutions.* New York: Oxford University Press.

Duffy, M., & Sperry, L. (2014). *Overcoming mobbing: A recovery guide for workplace aggression and bullying.* New York: Oxford University Press.

Eisenberger, N. I. & Lieberman, M. D. (2005). Why it hurts to be left out: The neurocognitive overlap between physical and social pain. In K. D. Williams, J. P. Forgas, & W. von Hippel (Eds.), *The social outcast: Ostracism, social exclusion, rejection, and bullying* (pp. 109–127). New York: Cambridge University Press.

Fox, C. L., Elder, T., Gater, J., & Johnson, E. (2010). The association between adolescents' beliefs in a just world and their attitudes to victims of bullying. *British Journal of Educational Psychology, 80*(Pt 2), 183–198.

Fryers, T. (2006). Work, identity and health. *Clinical Practice and Epidemiology in Mental Health, 2*(12). http://doi.org/10.1186/1745-0179-2-12

Fugate, M., Kinicki, A. & Ashforth, B. (2004). Employability: A psycho-social construct, its dimensions, and applications. *Journal of Vocational Behavior, 65*(1), 14–38.

Furnham, A. (2003). Belief in a just world: Research progress over the past decade. *Personality and Individual Differences, 34*(5), 795–817.

Gowan, M. A. (2012). Employability, well-being and job satisfaction following a job loss. *Journal of Managerial Psychology, 27*(8), 780–798. doi:10.1108/02683941211280157

Hafer, C. L., & Bègue, L. (2005). Experimental research on just-world theory: Problems, development, and future challenges. *Psychological Bulletin, 131*(1), 128–167.

Hogg, M. A., & Terry, D. J. (2000). Social identity and self-categorization processes in organizational contexts. *Academy of Management Review, 25*(1), 121–140.

Leana, C. & Feldman, D. (1990). Individual responses to job loss: Empirical findings from two field studies. *Human Relations, 43*(11), 1155–1181.

Lutgen-Sandvik, P. (2008). Intensive remedial identity work: Responses to workplace bullying trauma and stigmatization. *Organization, 15*(1), 97–119.

MacDonald, G., & Leary, M. R. (2005). Why does social exclusion hurt? The relationship between social and physical pain. *Psychological Bulletin, 131*(2), 202–223.

Maes, J., & Schmitt, M. (2004). Transformation of the justice motive? Belief in a just world and its correlates in different age groups. In C. Dalbert & H. Sallay (Eds.), *The justice motive in adolescence and young adulthood: Origins and consequences* (pp. 64–82). London, England: Routledge.

Nordgren, L. F., Banas, K., & MacDonald, G. (2011). Empathy gaps for social pain: Why people underestimate the pain of social suffering. *Journal of Personality and Social Psychology, 100*(1), 120–128. doi:/10.1037/a0020938

Otto, K., Boos, A., Dalbert, C., Schöps, D., & Hoyer, J. (2006). Posttraumatic symptoms, depression, and anxiety of flood victims: The impact of the belief in a just world. *Personality and Individual Differences, 40*(5), 1075–1084.

Sias, P. M. (2009), *Organizing relationships: Traditional and emerging perspectives on workplace relationships*. Thousand Oaks, CA: Sage.

Sias, P. M., Heath, R. G., Perry, T., Silva, D., & Fix, B. (2004). Narratives of workplace friendship deterioration. *Journal of Social and Personal Relationships, 21*(3), 321–340. doi:10.1177/0265407504042835

Sveningsson, S., & Alvesson, M. (2003). Managing managerial identities: Organizational fragmentation, discourse and identity struggle. *Human Relations, 56*(10), 1163–1193.

Venkataramani, V., Labianca, G., & Grosser, T. (2013). Positive and negative workplace relationships, social satisfaction, and organizational attachment. *Journal of Applied Psychology, 98*(6), 1028–1039.

Walsh, K., & Gordon, J. R. (2008). Creating an individual work identity. *Human Resource Management Review, 18*(1), 46–61. doi:10.1016/j.hrmr.2007.09.001

Wesselmann, E. D., Nairne, J. S., & Williams, K. D. (2012). An evolutionary social psychological approach to studying the effects of ostracism. *Journal of Social, Evolutionary, and Cultural Psychology, 6*(3), 309–328.

Wolff, H., & Moser, K. (2009). Effects of networking on career success: A longitudinal study. *Journal of Applied Psychology, 94*(1), 196–206.

Woodward, K. (2015). *Psychosocial studies: An introduction*. New York: Routledge.

Workplace Bullying Institute (WBI)/Zogby Analytics. (2014). *2014 U.S. Workplace Bullying Survey*. Retrieved from http://www.workplacebullying.org/wbiresearch/wbi-2014-us-survey

Zadro, L. (2004). *Ostracism: Empirical studies inspired by real-world experiences of silence and exclusion* [Unpublished doctoral dissertation]. University of New South Wales, Sydney, Australia.

7

Workplace Bullying and Mobbing: A Neuropsychotherapeutic Perspective

Pieter J. Rossouw

Patterns of engagement are deeply rooted in the neural architecture of the human brain. These patterns form the unspoken rules of living, the way of interacting with each other, and eventually the norms within a society—our way of life. Who we are can ultimately only be studied in how we relate to each other, how we support and interact with each other, how we love and care for each other, and how we enhance the wellness of each other. To *be* is to be connected, and to be connected facilitates our capacity to thrive.

The principles of neuroscience developed over the past 150 years of modern science all point toward one overarching principle: the process of connectivity. All neural principles, from the ionic principle (the chemical actions in the neuron—acetylcholine and calcium releases), to the action potentials (the process of release of neurochemicals to activate the communication process), to releasing transmitters in specific synaptic spaces to communicate with connecting neurons (synaptic potentials), to establishing strong neural networks through ongoing activation of similar patterns, all point toward the overarching principle of neuroscience: the principle of connectivity.

Sadly, there is a flipside to the narrative of connectivity; *disconnection* has a profound affect on neural patterns. Moreover, *violations* of connectivity cause significant changes in the patterns of connectivity in the brain, and these can ultimately be seen not only in behaviors, thoughts, and feelings but also in the changes that occur in the activation of the brain—the chemicals, structures, and the neural networks. In this chapter, we will explore the effects of bullying and mobbing on the brain, why bullying and mobbing fall within the domain of *violation* of neural connectivity and thriving, and how such violations affect the function and structure of the brain.

The developing human brain is driven by a fairly large (in molecular terms) number of neuronal units whose sole purpose is to establish further connections (Kandel, Swartz, & Jessell, 2013). The molecular makeup of neurons is geared toward connections, and neuronal architecture allows for the capacity to develop up to 10,000 connections. The neuron has a close relationship with supportive units (glial cells) that ensure the strengthening of these connections, resulting in an ever-stronger developing network of connection highways within the neural system. These units (neurons) are capable of building the most delicate, intricate, and advanced communications networks in the universe. Approximately 100 billion neurons form a trillion connections to allow a highly complex communications system to exchange information, which we perceive as thinking, feeling, behaving, and being.

The complexity of the human brain increases in magnitude when we realize that the system is programmed to develop not in a set way, but in many ways; the communication networks are highly changeable. The brain is not a fixed entity at birth with a fixed set of connections. Nor is its development fixed or set to grow toward an unchanging, preprogrammed outcome. As the brain develops and matures, the external environment plays a role in this development. The ever-expanding science of epigenetics provides important insights into the role of the environment as a facilitating variable in the expression of the genetic footprint. The message is clear. The developing human brain consists of billions of ever-changing connecting units (neurons) and is constantly establishing (and strengthening) vast networks of communication, not just within itself, but also with others. The brain is part of a social system. I *am* because we *are*. Even when systems of connection discontinue, the connectivity that was has an ongoing effect. I *am* now because I *was* and we *were*.

Healthy neural connections and supportive environmental factors facilitate the ground rules for a proliferating neural network that forms the basis of thriving interactions and a healthy society. The wellness of a society can be measured by the level of thriving, supportive interactivity within it. These healthy neural connections can be scientifically measured by examining neurochemical processes in imaging pictures of neural connections in action, and scientifically demonstrated by looking at the strength of connecting structures in the brain. Neuroscience then effectively provides evidence of the day-to-day running of society—how we communicate, how we influence each other, and how we thrive together. What severely limits our propensity to thrive is to experience violation of our basic human needs, and this is the effect bullying and mobbing has on the victim—their psychological needs are violated.

BULLYING DEFINED AND THE ABSENCE OF REFERENCE TO NEUROSCIENCE AND THE BRAIN

The terms *bullying* and *mobbing* are widely used in literature, research, and day-to-day vernacular. Despite the common use of the terms, many countries (e.g., the United Kingdom and some states in the United States) do not have a legal definition of these terms. The term *mobbing* is often used to refer to bullying conducted by a group, and the words *abuse, peer abuse, harassment, rankism,* and *workplace harassment* are often used to refer to bullying in the workplace (Fuller, 2006).

Sugden et al. (2010) define bullying as "the act of intentionally and repeatedly causing harm to someone who has difficulty defending him or herself, and is a relatively wide-spread school phenomenon. Being a victim of bullying is associated with a broad spectrum of emotional problems; however, not all children who are bullied go on to develop such problems" (p. 2).

One of the classical definitions of bullying is from Batsche and Knoff (1994), who define bullying as a form of aggression in which one or more students physically and psychologically (and, more recently, sexually) repeatedly harass another student over a period of time. Another classical definition of bullying was described by Olweus (1994):

> I define bullying or victimization in the following general way: A student is being bullied or victimized when he or she is exposed, repeatedly and over time, to negative actions on the part of one or more other students. It is a negative action when someone intentionally inflicts or attempts to inflict, injury or discomfort upon another—basically what is implied in the definition of aggressive behaviour. Negative actions can be carried out by physical contact, by words, or in other ways, such as making faces or obscene gestures, and intentional exclusion from a group. To use the term bullying, there should also be an imbalance in strength (an asymmetric power relationship): the student who is exposed to the negative actions has difficulty in defending him/herself and is somewhat helpless against the student or students who harass. (p. 1173)

The Australian Human Rights Commission (2004) defines workplace bullying as "the repeated less favourable treatment of a person by another or others in the workplace, which may be considered unreasonable and inappropriate workplace practice. It includes behaviour that intimidates, offends, degrades or humiliates a worker."

These definitions (as is the case with almost all definitions) fall short because there is no reference to the neurological effects of bullying nor the long-term consequences for neural development and proliferation due to experiences that violate the basic needs of neural networks (thriving connectivity). In fact, current definitions of bullying and mobbing only refer to situational effects and descriptors, personal effects in terms of physical injury, emotional distress, and behavioral changes, but no definition focuses on the most fundamental components of the violation of wellness—that is, changes in neural architecture that in reality guide the cornerstone of the rule of law in society—the nature of connectedness. Connectedness that is facilitated through the principles of neuroscience (ensuring safety, attachment, control, and motivation to engage) will result in a thriving society of cognitive, emotional, and behavioral well-being. When these principles are violated, the essential cornerstones of well-being are compromised, resulting in patterns of disengagement with effects on cognition, emotion, and behavior and a deterioration of societal well-being. These violations can be identified on a neurobiological level.

NEURAL DEVELOPMENT AND CONNECTIVITY

The development of the brain from conception to maturity is of significant importance to this topic, as it provides insight into the hierarchy of communication links of neural networks as well as the interaction between the environment and the developing brain (bullying at different stages of neural development has different effects on the brain).

The brain develops from the "bottom to the top." This means that primitive systems develop first, and as they mature and increase in complexity, more advanced systems develop. Some systems are fully developed at birth, others are less developed, and some are completely undeveloped. When the first neural plates establish in the first few weeks after conception, they continue to develop into the brainstem (pons, medulla, and small parts of the cerebellum). This section (referred to as the *reptilian brain*) is responsible for regulating breathing, heart rate, and procreation (the progression of the species). This section of neural development (reptilian brain) is fully developed and fully functional at birth (MacLean, 1990). As the brain develops and matures in utero, a more advance section starts to develop. These areas, collectively referred to as the *limbic system* (thalamus, hypothalami, amygdalae, hippocampi, pituitary, basal ganglia, nucleus accumbens, etc.), are responsible for developing neural networks that regulate the person's interaction with the environment and as such are sometimes referred to as the *emotional brain*, the *downstairs brain* (Siegel, 2013), or the *impulsive brain* (Rossouw, 2014). This neural section is fully developed at birth but only partially functional. This neural cluster needs ongoing interaction with our environment to develop neural networks that facilitate effective connectedness with the external environment and to develop neural capacity (often referred to as *resilience*) to engage with day-to-day living. The development of the limbic system continues until the mid-twenties, when brain development reaches maturity.

Brain development (especially the limbic system) is dependent on the interaction with the environment to express its genetic footprint (genes express differently in different environments) as well as to develop neural networks to effectively engage with the environment. For maximal neural development, the brain needs an *enriched environment* so that healthy systems of connection from engaging with the environment develop into a thriving neural network. An enriched environment does not in any way imply a smooth, nonchallenging environment. In fact, research clearly shows there are detrimental effects of a completely nonchallenging environment (mollycoddling) on neural development. So an enriched environment is one that neuroscientists describe as satisfying the need for *controllable incongruence* (Grawe, 2007) as one of the cornerstones for healthy neural proliferation.

However, when the environment is significantly compromised (as is the case with bullying), then neural systems (especially in the limbic regions) not only respond to the compromised environment but also reorganize (regarding neural connections and physiological development) to enhance systems of protection. This reorganizing may be regarded as the onset of neural patterns of pathology. The symptoms we can observe are evident in changes in mood, cognition, and behavior. What directs these symptoms are changes in neurochemical production, neural structure and operation, and neural networking. These changes are the basic subjects of research into the effects of bullying and mobbing on the brain.

The concept of *neural plasticity* or *neuroplasticity* has been a hot topic both in neuroscience research as well as in the domains of psychological and physical well-being and recovery studies. The concept is rooted in the fundamental capacity of neurons to establish connections with other neurons and even change the course of neural connections. This capacity is an essential ingredient of neural growth and maturation—the establishment of more and more connections and eventually an extensive set of networks to maximize the interaction with the environment. Neural plasticity is inherent in the genetic makeup of the neural network. The process of maturation is integrally linked with the neural plastic capacity of brain cells. In enriched environments, neural plastic capacity activates on a daily basis to maximize neural proliferation.

However, in compromised environments (violations of basic needs, which is often experienced through bullying behavior), the same principle activates. Neural plasticity is the ability of the brain to establish new neural connections. In compromised environments, the brain also changes, and these changes occur with one single purpose—to ensure survival. Neuroscience researchers have found that in compromised environments, individuals establish stronger networks from the limbic system to the reptilian brain (which ensures breathing and controls heart rate, the basic survival responses). This process can be temporary. However, if such violations of basic needs activate at a very young age, or with great intensity or for prolonged periods, neurochemical changes and ultimately neural network changes occur, and the brain rewires itself at the cost of discontinuing patterns of engaging and thriving to enhancing neural patterns of protection and survival. This forms the basis of what scientists refer to as the *neurobiology of pathology*—a brain rewired to survive rather than to thrive.

Research is ongoing to identify specific changes and to what extent various experiences of violations of a safe environment (lacking needs fulfillment) cause neural changes in the brain. Research by molecular neuroscientists and Nobel Laureates Bert Sakmann (Betz & Sakmann, 1973) and Eric Kandel (1998, 2001, 2005, 2006) demonstrates an important principle of neural plasticity—that the brain changes its neural connectivity more quickly when pain and distress neural circuits are activated (compromised environments) than when wellness circuits are activated (enriched environments). In one case, a single experience of trauma was enough to facilitate new and permanent neural patterns of avoidance in comparison to 150 activations required to facilitate new neural patterns of engaging and thriving (Betz & Sakmann, 1973). The lesson from neuroscience research is clear: the neural architecture of the brain is geared toward engaging and thriving, but it only activates in this regard when the environment is enriched and not compromised. When compromised, research indicates that the neural system shifts its direction of connectivity to increase messages to the survival networks (connectivity to survive rather than connectivity to thrive). Among others, the severity of neural change is influenced by four key factors:

1. **Age:** When violation of safe, enriched environments is experienced at a young age (less mature, more vulnerable brain network activation)
2. **Intensity:** The level of intensity of violation of safe, enriched environments (severity of the incident(s))
3. **Duration:** The effect of ongoing violation of safe, enriched environments (time frame of the violation)
4. **Proximity:** The effect of the perpetrator(s) on the violation of safe, enriched environments (proximity of the person to the victim—a family member or caregiver, trusted friend, colleague, or religious leader)

THE DEVELOPING BRAIN AND GENETICS

A well-developing brain requires two key ingredients: a healthy genetic makeup as well as a safe, enriched environment. Traditionally, genes and the environment were seen as unrelated and in line with the Darwinian theory of natural selection. This theory holds that natural selection is the result of the evolution of the genetic material through the survival response (survival of the fittest). If this theory applied in the bullying and mobbing context, it can be viewed as the paradigm of "the weak will perish, and the strong will survive"—although the impact of the perpetrators on their victims might also fit the saying, *what does not kill you makes you stronger*.

In 1809, Jean-Baptiste Lamarck suggested another theory whereby an organism adopts traits as a result of the influence of the environment, and the offspring *inherit* those traits (changes in the gene pool). Today, Lamarck's work is viewed as the birth of the study of the interchange between genes and the environment: *epigenetics*. Bird (2007) describes this as "the structural adaptation of chromosomal regions so as to register, signal or perpetuate altered activity states" (p. 398).

Studies with genes that generate specific neurochemicals, such as dopamine and serotonin, show variables in genetic makeup that effect the production of these chemicals and as such may impact wellness and enhance risk (LeDoux, 2005; Rudy, 2008). This points to a strong genetic factor regarding risk (Sugden et al., 2010) and toward a deterministic approach (which is all about *nature*, with *nurture* playing a diminished role). However, a study by Phu and colleagues found the genetic footprint expressed very differently in different environments (Phu, Reddy, & Cameron, 2013).

BULLYING AND NEUROCHEMICALS

Understanding the effects of bullying on the brain has led to studies focusing on the role of neurochemicals and, in particular, changes in neurochemical production and activation as a result of experiencing bullying. One of the major challenges in studying biological data is the limitation of collecting neurochemical samples, and as a result, many animal studies with important indicators have been very difficult to replicate in human research. Advances in sample collection have led to saliva analysis, which provides a noninvasive window to access biological data. This procedure can be used to reliably collect data on such hormones as testosterone, cortisol, and dehydroepiandrosterone (DHEA; Hazler, Carney, & Granger 2006; Rossouw, 2013).

Elevated cortisol levels appear when the activity of the hypothalamus-pituitary-adrenal (HPA) axis is elevated. This indicates a state of fear in the individual, which then inhibits patterns of engaging and instead strengthens survival patterns of avoidance behavior. These patterns then become the default neural networks when stimulated and often have detrimental effects on well-being. Specifically, concerning bullying, significant differences in cortisol levels have been found in students who have experienced regular bullying. Students who were not bullied or experienced single or low levels of intimidation were found to have much lower levels of saliva cortisol production than students who experienced regular bullying or high-intensity bullying (Booth, Granger, & Shirtcliff, 2008). The researchers suggested that biological markers should be included in both assessments and intervention outcome measures for victims of bullying (Hazler et al., 2006; Rossouw, 2013).

The hormone DHEA is a protector chemical in the neural system and inhibits cortisol activity. It has a positive correlation with memory and cortical learning (thriving and learning behaviors—hippocampal and prefrontal cortical activation) in comparison with fear-based learning (protective systems of avoidance—amygdala and HPA activation). Researchers have found there is an inverse correlation between bullying and memory and learning (Vaillancourt et al., 2011).

BULLYING AND NEURAL STRUCTURES

The most significant contribution of modern neuroscience research is the shift it has facilitated in the paradigm of understanding of the operation and function of the brain. The classical approach views the brain like a bowl of soup, meaning that the brain consists of a large number of neurochemicals; the primary focus of doctors, therapists, and mental health workers is to enable a chemical balance, because those diagnosed with psychopathology have a *chemical imbalance* in the brain. Since the landmark publication of Erik Kandel's *New Intellectual Framework for Psychiatry* (1998), where he proclaimed the dawn of a remarkable scientific revolution that would change our perception of the brain, there were an impressive series of research papers published indicating how the brain consists of networks of neural connections and how the environment shapes these connections. This reconceptualized understanding of the brain opens new frontiers for research as well as our understanding of human wellness. This new paradigm of how the brain operates and functions also furthers the science of understanding the positive and negative effects of the environment on neural development and behavior (positive effects toward higher levels of thriving or detrimental effects, e.g., the results of bullying and mobbing).

This new paradigm has prompted researchers to look more closely at neural structures, how they communicate with each other, and how patterns of communication change as a result of enriched or compromised environments. As research has become more and more refined, detailed studies are being conducted into the short- and long-term effects of specific kinds of compromised environments (e.g., bullying and mobbing being linked with key variables, such as age, duration, intensity, and proximity) on neural networks and activation patterns.

Additionally, the role of key structures in the limbic region (emotional brain), that is, the amygdala, hippocampus, hypothalamus, basal ganglia, and pituitary gland, along with the anterior cingulate, orbitofrontal, and prefrontal regions (both left and right PFC), have been the source of many research projects—and there is much synergy in the research findings. The amygdala-hypothalamus-pituitary-adrenal system has been identified as the brain's early warning and fear response system. This response system plays a vital role in keeping us safe and protecting us from danger. It forms protective responses very early in life and becomes strongly wired at a young age to protect us from harm. However, researchers have found that these systems can become "overwired" when the environment is compromised, resulting in excessive fear-based responses that inhibit thriving responses and result in compromised neural networks. Bullying overexcites the fear system, resulting over time in increased amygdala volumes and lack of prefrontal decision making as well as an increase in racial stereotyping and patterns of avoidance (Phelps et al., 2000; Viding, McCrory, Blakemore, & Frederickson, 2011).

The hippocampus is the powerhouse in the limbic system responsible for short-term memory processing and the production of key neurochemicals (*brain-derived neurotrophic factor* (BDNF)), which enable neuroplasticity and neurogenesis. A well-functioning hippocampus has been directly correlated with inhibiting the risk of Alzheimer's disease and dementia and is the key to a happy, thriving life. Researchers found that exposure to acute psychological stress (like exposure to bullying) resulted in increased apoptosis (the death of neurons) and a reduction of hippocampal neurogenesis (Thomas, Hotsenpillar, & Peterson, 2007).

The corpus callosum provides the communication link between the two hemispheres and the deep brain structures (limbic system). Healthy neural networks are critical in the development of a well-integrated personality and ability to effectively navigate our interactions with the environment. A direct correlation has been found with the deterioration of the structural composition of the corpus callosum following verbal abuse (Teicher, Samson, Sheu, Polcari, & McGreenery, 2010). Social rejection and social pain caused structural impairment in the integrity of the anterior cingulate cortex and, in particular, the dorsal anterior cingulate cortical region (dACC) (Eisenberger, Lieberman, & Williams, 2003). These researchers found that bullying upregulates the more fear-based survival systems and compromises activity in the frontal (especially the right frontal) cortical regions. These regions are critical for the development of a sense of social connection and empathy and is the very reason why those who experience bullying (in the absence of supportive environmental role players) are at increased risk of developing antisocial personalities, psychopathy, and criminal behavior (Viding et al., 2011). An fMRI study conducted by Catherine Sebastian and colleagues found bullying increased activity in the orbitofrontal regions of victims, but not in the dACC region (Sebastian et al., 2010). They conceded that the marginal difference in regional activation might have been the result of slightly different methodologies and age-related changes.

The prefrontal cortical regions play a vital role in the development of executive functioning—social interactions, cognitions, mood, and behavior. Lesions or damage to these regions causes significant changes in mood, cognitions, and behavior, and even significant changes in personality. Probably one of the most cited cases of personality change is the case of a railway worker, Phineas Gage, who was severely injured when an iron rod pierced his skull and destroyed a significant portion of his right frontal lobe. He survived the ordeal but experienced a dramatic personality change (Adams, 2009). The case of patient EVR is also often cited as an example of major changes in social conduct and compromised decision making due to bilateral orbitofrontal meningioma (Saver & Damasio, 1991). In his research on the effects of aggressive behaviors, Giancola (1995) found significant detrimental effects on the dorsolateral and orbitofrontal cortical regions, and Ilie and colleagues (2014) found a direct correlation in suicidality, bullying, and mental health correlates of traumatic brain injury of adolescents (Ilie et al., 2014; Kumpulainen et al., 1998).

Research with *Aplysia californica* conducted by Eric Kandel (1998, 2005) has demonstrated this new paradigm in neuroscience. When environments are compromised, neural systems protect themselves; the thriving response shuts down, and the brain wires itself to survive. The result is decreased wellness, decreased longevity, and increased stress responses and pathology. And thus a new understanding has emerged. The traditional view of *what does not kill you makes you stronger* should read—in compromised environments—*what does not kill you makes you* WEAKER. And this deterioration in survival and functioning has profound effects on the strength and thriving of society as a whole.

FROM NEUROSCIENCE TO INTERVENTIONS

The principles of neuroscience research about the effects of bullying on the brain—for example, chemicals, structures, and networks—also provide important guidelines for interventions. The development of the brain (from the bottom to the top) indicates that interventions are likely to be more successful when the same pathways are followed.

Safety First

For example, a state of fear and unsafety compromises blood flow to cortical regions and, as a result, increases our survival responses. The implication here is that cognitive interventions are likely to be less successful when the victim experiences a sense of unsafety. When a person (neural system) experiences a sense of unsafety, changes in neural activation, as well as neurochemical production, take place. The HPA axis is activated, corticotrophin releasing factor (CRF) is activated in the hypothalamus, the adrenocorticotrophic hormone is released in the pituitary and norepinephrine, epinephrine and cortisol production are activated (adrenal glands), and the body is pushed into a state of hyperalertness. This state compromises serotonin flow, inhibits effective decision making, and lessens patterns of engaging. Unless the basic condition of safety is met, the likelihood of higher order neural activation will be compromised. So, a bottom-up approach is needed. This bottom-up approach or pathway is often (subconsciously) used because clinicians instinctively realize the importance of safety for their client before higher order strategies are implemented. Neuroscience highlights the reasons *why* ensuring a physical and psychological sense of safety needs to be the starting point of every intervention (Kaya & Rossouw, 2016; Rossouw, 2013, 2014).

The Basic Needs

Once the need for safety is facilitated and ensured, the three basic human needs must be addressed. From a neural perspective, these are the needs to connect (attachment need), to experience control (need for control), and the need to be motivated to engage (the dopamine-related need of avoiding pain and maximizing approach or pleasure). These needs are closely connected to the regulation of regional midbrain activity (involving the sensory activation centers—the thalamus, amygdala, hypothalamus, pituitary, hippocampus, and basal ganglia) and the downregulation of fear-based activation and upregulation of integrative activity (i.e., applying context—primarily hippocampal activation). These needs were elucidated by the brilliant neuroscientist Klaus Grawe (in close alignment with the research of Seymour Epstein) as

- The need for attachment,
- The need for orientation and control,
- The need for avoiding pain and maximizing pleasure, and
- The need for self-esteem and self-esteem enhancement (Grawe, 2007).

Further research has led to refinement of the activation of these needs (Rossouw, 2014) resulting in the identification of only three needs linked to the activation of the limbic system (the impulsive brain). These needs are

- The need for attachment (connection),
- The need for orientation and control, and
- The need for pain avoidance and pleasure maximization (motivation; Rossouw, 2014).

The need for the enhancement of self was identified to be aligned with the development of the prefrontal cortex and thus seen as a higher order need (the culmination of all the needs; Rossouw, 2014). The following paragraphs describe in more detail the three needs aligned with the function of the limbic system.

The need for attachment (connection)

It has been well established in research that healthy attachment relations are vital to the development of healthy brain function (Bowlby, 1969, 1973, 1980, 1988a, 1988b; Hart, 2010; Newman, Holden, & Delville, 2005; Sapolsky, 2000, 2004; Schore, 2012). Well-established patterns of attachment have been clearly linked to downregulation of the amygdala and upregulation of the hippocampus (Schore, 2012). The flipside—violation of attachment—has been linked to increased amygdala volume, decreased hippocampal volume, and increased presentation of patterns of pathology (Panksepp, 2005; Schore, 2012; Solomon & Siegel, 2013; Sporns, 2011).

Bullying violates the sense of attachment (connection). Research has demonstrated the variables that mediate the effect of bullying on the brain: age, duration, intensity, and proximity (Kaya & Rossouw, 2016; Rossouw, 2013). The need to connect (be part of the social construct—the fiber of society) is an integrated need for neural activation to flourish. Violation of this need not only results in changes in behavior; it also results in changes in neural activation patterns and creates patterns of avoidance that eventually result in pathological behavior. In short, bullying changes the brain. Research is now being conducting to investigate how genetic expression changes as a result of compromised environments. This research will not only provide an even more profound chapter in our understanding of the violations of basic needs but will also assist in devising guidelines for early intervention and developing resilience, thereby maximizing wellness.

The need for control

Epstein (1993) considered the need for control as the most fundamental of human needs. Flammer (as cited in Grawe, 2007, p. 212) describes this need as having the "maximum number of options available." This basic need describes the activation of limbic connectivity—hippocampal activation to enhance the development of frontal neural networks. This means the ability to proliferate, that is, to form strong, healthy neural connections, to enhance capacity (resilience) and having the strength to face the challenges of day-to-day life. When this need is compromised, the resulting neural networks develop into patterns of avoidance that enhance the survival response (strengthening primitive neural networks and, as a result, limiting the development of frontal neural networks—the "what does not kill you makes you weaker" principle). The effect of bullying and mobbing on the victim, therefore, frustrates the need for control and enhances patterns of avoidance, resulting in the risk of increased isolation, that is, a reluctance to engage or go back to school or work and increased resistance to engage in the day-to-day activities of society (Hunter & Boyle, 2010).

The need for motivation

The concept of motivation is often seen as a positive attribute to enhance outcomes. In neural terms, *motivation* is linked to the release of neurochemicals to enhance patterns of approach. These chemicals—endorphins and predominantly dopamine—are released when approach patterns are activated on a regular basis, and, as a result, they strengthen these patterns. In enriched environments (healthy, supportive contexts), dopamine is released when patterns of engagement occur. As a result, the development of rich prefrontal cortical networks is strengthened, resulting in a healthy sense of self, engaging activity, and patterns of thriving.

When the environments are compromised (as is the case with bullying and mobbing), patterns of avoidance activate, leading to less interaction and more avoidance; less contact and more disconnection; less social interaction and more social isolation; and less thriving and more focus on patterns of survival. When an ongoing violation of the motivation need is experienced, dopamine release is activated in association with the patterns of survival, the avoidance and isolation patterns. The result is that these neural activation patterns are then strengthened due to the dopamine release, and the protective patterns hold the networks "hostage"; victims will experience this as becoming "comfortable in their discomfort." This enhances the risk of disengaging and results in long-term patterns of social decline (Novick, Forster, Tejani-Butt, & Watt, 2011).

The implications for the violation of the motivation need indicate that early intervention is vitally important to ensure that the risk of getting stuck in patterns of avoidance is addressed as early as possible (Rossouw, 2013).

Bullying and Prefrontal Cortex Activation—The Integrated Sense of Self

Ultimately, violation of the primitive (safety) and basic needs (attachment, control, and motivation) inhibit the development of the integrated prefrontal cortical regions (the integrated social self). This has a highly detrimental effect on self-actualization and social interaction and severely inhibits the capacity to engage effectively in society. Apart from the enormous commercial cost that can be attributed to patterns of avoidance, the emotional loss in our ability to socialize and to share and care will have significant short-term (personal cost); medium-term (family, work, and interactions); and long-term (transgenerational effect on wellness) effects (Dulmus, Sowers, & Theriot, 2006; Esbensen & Carson, 2009; Mruk, 2006; Tanti, Stukas, Halloran, & Foddy, 2011).

Antibullying Interventions

Interventions for managing bullying and mobbing vary, from behavioral and psychoeducational to cognitive-behavioral and peer support interventions. Table 7.1 provides a snapshot summary of some of the intervention studies in the United States, Australia, and Finland. It is worth noting that these studies are all of school bullying, and although we can hypothesize that the psychological impact and change to brain activation and neural networks would appear almost identical in any scans or neurological assessment, it is acknowledged that there are some differences between school and workplace bullying. Perhaps the most obvious difference would be the greater physicality of schoolyard bullying and, conversely, the greater psychological character of workplace bullying.

It is interesting to note that from the range of interventions listed, no intervention strategies focus on dealing with bullying from a brain-based perspective. A neuroscience support program has recently been launched in Australia (Kaya & Rossouw, 2016). The focus of this project is to manage the effects of bullying by focusing on addressing the neural activation patterns. This intervention consists of a self-guided comic book exploring the bullying experience as well as talking through the effects of the experience on our basic human needs—safety, control, attachment, and motivation—and ultimately our sense of self. It is complemented by a clinician's manual to guide support workers (clinicians, teachers, or parents) to understand the effects of bullying on the brain; the changes in mood, cognition, and behaviors; and how to support young people to identify a sense of safety, reconnect, take control, and reintroduce a sense of motivation. Ultimately, the goal is to facilitate new neural pathways to enhance a sense of self and enhance resilience toward thriving and self-actualization. Comprehensive field testing will complement the project. Preliminary indications are that young people who have experienced bullying and who have used the brain-based workbook are shifting from patterns of avoidance toward patterns of engaging and activating new approach-oriented neural connections (in comparison to patterns of avoidance). These early results point toward higher levels of well-being and a reduction of pathology (reduced anxiety, depression, and avoidance behaviors; Kaya & Rossouw, 2016).

Table 7.1 Intervention Studies in the United States, Australia, and Finland

Study	Participants	Focus	Intervention Design	Main Outcomes
Cross, Pintabona, Hall, Hamilton, & Erceg (2004)	Primary school students ($N = 2,068$) in grades 4–5 from Western Australia Friendly Schools	Focus on social skills development	Intervention strategies target classroom curriculum work, promotion of peer support, and advice to families and teachers on intervention techniques.	There was no overall reduction in the frequency of bullying, but a significant reduction in specific indicators, such as "being ignored" or "being called names."
Olweus (2004)	Primary school students ($N = 21,000$) in grade 4–7 from >100 American schools	New national initiative against bullying	Olweus Intervention Program targets school-wide activities, classroom discussions and rules, and community awareness.	After eight months of intervention, engagement in bullying was reduced by 43% and being victimized reduced by 34%.
Bauer, Lozano, & Rivara (2007)	Middle school students from 10 American schools; 7 intervention schools ($N = 4,959$); and 3 control schools ($N = 1,559$)	The Olweus Intervention program was evaluated against a control group.	Olweus Intervention Program targets school-wide activities, classroom discussions and rules, and community awareness.	No overall effect was evident on rates of student victimization. There were significant reductions for subgroups (e.g., for white but not black students).
Slee & Mohyla (2007)	Primary school students ($N = 954$) aged 8–12 years, from Australian schools	Longitudinal evaluation of efficacy of PEACE Pack program in targeting school bullying	School-based application of the PEACE Pack encompasses education-based, practical resources for staff to create their own interventions.	After the yearlong intervention, 29% of boys and 20% of girls reported being bullied less. From pre- to postintervention, substantially more students reported feeling safe in school
Kärnä et al. (2011)	School students ($N = 150,000$) aged 8–16 years, from 888 Finish schools	Nonrandomized nationwide trial of the KiVA antibullying program	The KiVa program is a whole-school approach that includes elements of disciplinary methods, teacher training, classroom rules, parent information, videos, and cooperative group work.	After nine months of intervention, victimisation was reduced by 2.7% and bullying reduced by 1.9%. Estimated victims reduced by 3,900 and the number of bullies by 2,300.

One of the essential neurobiological indicators for wellness and neural capacity is the understanding of the neuroscience of resilience. Although the concept has been the focus of research for many decades, it is only recently that neuroscientists have begun investigating resilience from a neural perspective. The work of Richard Davidson explored the neural correlates of resilience and identified domains of resilience linked to neural networks (Davidson & Begley, 2012). These domains have been developed into a Predictive 6-Factor Resilience Scale (Rossouw & Rossouw, 2016), with a cell phone number and online applications available for clients and clinicians to work together to enhance resilience capacity.

SUMMARY

Bullying and mobbing is an ever-growing phenomenon in modern society. It is extensively addressed, yet much research is needed to understand the effects on the developing brain; the role of unaddressed bullying experiences on the economy; work-seeking practices (patterns of protection and avoidance); the roles (or lack thereof) of family, friends, and peer support; the countereffect of supervision; the key indicators of a well workplace (an antibullying culture); and the effects of resilience on strengthening neural networks, to name a few.

REFERENCES

Adams, R. (2009). The social brain: Neural basis of social knowledge. *Annual Review of Psychology, 60,* 693–716.
Australian Human Rights Commission. (2004). *What is workplace bullying?* Retrieved from http://www.humanrights.gov.au/info_for_employers/what.html
Batsche, G. M., & Knoff, H. M. (1994). Bullies and their victims: Understanding a pervasive problem in the schools. *School Psychology Review, 23,* 165–165.
Betz, W., & Sakmann, B. (1973). Effects of proteolytic enzymes on function and structure of frog neuromuscular junctions. *Journal of Physiology, 230*(3), 673–688.
Bird, A. (2007). Perceptions of epigenetics. *Nature, 447*(7143), 396–398.
Booth, A., Granger, D. A., & Shirtcliff, E. A. (2008). Gender- and age-related differences in the association between social relationship quality and trait-levels of salivary cortisol. *Journal of Research on Adolescence, 18*(2), 239–260. doi:10.1111 /j.1532-795.00559.x
Bowlby, J (1969). *Attachment and loss.* Vol. 1, *Attachment.* New York: Basic Books.
Bowlby, J. (1973). *Attachment and loss.* Vol. 2, *Separation, anxiety, and anger.* New York: Basic Books.
Bowlby, J. (1980). *Loss, sadness, and depression.* London, England: Hogarth.
Bowlby, J. (1988a). *A secure base: Clinical applications of attachment theory.* London, England: Routledge.
Bowlby, J. (1988b). *A secure base: Parent-child attachment and healthy human development.* New York: Basic Books.

Davidson, R. J., & Begley, S. (2012). *The emotional life of your brain: How its unique patterns affect the way you think, feel and live—and how you can change them.* New York: Hudson Street Press.

Dulmus, C. N., Sowers, K. M., & Theriot, M. T. (2006). Prevalence and bullying experiences of victims and victims who become bullies (bully-victims) at rural schools. *Taylor & Francis Group, 1*(1), 15–31. doi:10.1080/15564880500498945

Eisenberger, N. I., Lieberman, M. D. & Williams, K. D. (2003). Does rejection hurt? An fMRI study of social rejection. *Science, 302*(5643), 290–292.

Epstein, S. (1993). Implications of cognitive-experiential self-theory for personality and developmental psychology. In D. C. Funder, R. D. Parke, C. Tomlinson-Keasey, & K. Widaman (Eds.), *Studying lives through time: Personality and development* (pp. 399–438). Washington, D.C.: American Psychological Association.

Esbensen, F., & Carson, D. (2009). Consequences of being bullied: Results from a longitudinal assessment of bullying victimization in a multisite sample of American students. *Youth & Society, 41*(2), 209–233. doi:10.1177/0044118X09351067

Fuller, R. W. (2006). *All rise: Somebodies, nobodies, and the politics of dignity.* San Francisco, CA: Berrett-Koehler Publishers.

Giancola, P. (1995). Evidence for dorsolateral and orbital prefrontal cortical involvement in the expression of aggressive behavior. *Aggressive Behavior, 21*(6), 431–450.

Grawe, K. (2007). *Neuropsychotherapy: How the neurosciences inform effective psychotherapy.* New York: Taylor & Francis.

Hart, S. (2010). *The impact of attachment.* New York: W. W. Norton.

Hazler, R. J., Carney, J. V., & Granger, D. A. (2006). Integrating biological measures into the study of bullying. *Journal of Counselling and Development, 84*(3), 298–307.

Hunter, S. C., & Boyle, J. M. E. (2010). Perceptions of control in the victims of school bullying: The importance of early intervention. *Taylor & Francis, 44*(3), 323–336. doi:10.1080/0013188022000031614

Ilie, G., Mann, R. E., Boak, A., Adlaf, E. M., Hamilton, H., Asbridge, M., . . . Cusimano, M. D. (2014). Suicidality, bullying and other conduct and mental health correlates of traumatic brain injury in adolescents. *PLoS One, 9*(4), e94936.

Kandel, E. R. (1998). A new intellectual framework for psychiatry. *American Journal of Psychiatry, 155*(4), 457–469.

Kandel, E. R. (2001). The molecular biology of memory storage: A dialogue between genes and synapses. *Science, 294*(5544), 1030–1038.

Kandel, E. R. (2005). *Psychiatry, psychoanalysis and the new biology of mind.* Washington, D.C.: American Psychiatric Publishing.

Kandel, E. R. (2006). *In search of memory: The emergence of a new science of mind.* New York: W. W. Norton.

Kandel, E. R., Schwartz, J. H., & Jessell, T. M. (2013). *Principles of neural science* (5th ed.). New York: McGraw-Hill.

Kaya, M., & Rossouw, P. J. (2016). *Bullying: Taking control (manual).* Brisbane, Australia: Mediros.

Kumpulainen, K., Räsänen, E., Henttonen, I., Almqvist, F., Kresanov, K., Linna, S. L., . . . Tamminen, T. (1998). Bullying and psychiatric symptoms among elementary school-age children. *Child Abuse & Neglect, 22*(7), 705–717.

LeDoux, J. (2005). *Synaptic self: How our brains become who we are*. New York: Penguin.

MacLean, P. D. (1990). *The triune brain in evolution: Role in paleocerebral functions*. New York: Plenum Press.

Mruk, C. J. (2006). *Self-esteem research, theory and practice: Toward a positive psychology of self-esteem*. New York: Springer.

Newman, M. L., Holden, G. W., & Delville, Y. (2005). Isolation and the stress of being bullied. *Journal of Adolescence, 28*(3), 343–357. doi:0.1016/j.adolescence.2004.08.002

Novick, A. M., Forster, G. L., Tejani-Butt, S. M., & Watt, M. J. (2011). Adolescent social defeat alters markers of adult dopaminergic function. *Brain Research Bulletin, 86*(1/2), 123–128. doi:10.1016/j.brainresbull.2011.06.009

Olweus, D. (1994). Bullying at school: Basic facts and effects of a school-based intervention program. *Journal of Child Psychology and Psychiatry, 35*(7), 1171–1190.

Panksepp, J. (2005). *Affective neuroscience: The foundations of human and animal emotions*. New York: Oxford University Press.

Phelps, E. A., O'Connor, K. J., Cunningham, W. A. Funayama, E. S., Gatenby, J. C., Gore, J. C., & Banaji, M. R. (2000). Performance on indirect measures of race evaluation predicts amygdala activation. *Journal of Cognitive Neuroscience, 12*(5), 729–738.

Phu, C. L., Reddy, K. A. P., & Cameron, J. L. (2013). The effect of short-term stress on serotonin gene expression in high and low resilient macaques. *Progress in Neuropsychopharmacology & Biological Psychiatry, 44*, 143–153. doi:10.1016/j.pnpbp.2013.01.013

Rossouw, P. J. (2013). The effects of bullying on the developing brain: Strategies for effective interventions. In *Workplace, school, and cyberbullying* (pp. 102–122). Paper presented at No 2 Bullying Conference, Gold Coast, Australia. Nerang, Australia: Australian & New Zealand Mental Health Association.

Rossouw, P. J. (2014). Neuropsychotherapy: An integrated theoretical model. In P. J. Rossouw (Ed.), *Neuropsychotherapy: Theoretical underpinnings and clinical applications*. Sydney, Australia: Mediros.

Rossouw, P. J., & Rossouw, J. G. (2016). *The predictive 6 Factor resilience scale: Clinical guidelines and applications*. Sydney, Australia: RForce.

Rudy, J. W. (2008). *The neurobiology of learning and memory*. Boulder, CO: University of Colorado.

Sapolsky, R. M. (2000). Glucocorticoids and hippocampal atrophy in neuropsychiatric disorders. *Archives of General Psychiatry, 57*(10), 925–935.

Sapolsky, R. M. (2004). *Why zebras don't get ulcers: The acclaimed guide to stress, stress-related diseases, and coping*. New York: Griffin.

Saver, J. L., & Damasio, A. R. (1991). Preserved access and processing of social knowledge in a patient with acquired sociopathy due to ventromedial frontal damage. *Neuropsychologia, 29*(12), 1241–1249.

Schore, A. N. (2012). *The art of the science of psychotherapy*. New York: W. W. Norton.

Sebastian, C. L., Tan, G. C. Y., Roiser, J. P., Viding, E., Dumontheil, I., & Blakemore, S.-J. (2010). Developmental influences in the neural bases of responses to social rejection: Implications of social neuroscience for education. *Neuroimage, 57*(3), 686–694. doi:10.1016/j.neuroimage.2010.09.063

Siegel, D. (2013). *Brainstorm: The power and purpose of the teenage brain.* New York, NY: Penguin.

Solomon, M. F., & Siegel, D. J. (Eds.). (2003). *Healing trauma: Attachment, mind, body and brain.* New York: W. W. Norton.

Sporns, O. (2011). *Networks of the brain.* Cambridge, MA: MIT Press.

Sugden, K., Arseneault, L., Harrington, H., Moffitt, T. E., Williams, B., & Caspi, A. (2010). Serotonin transporter gene moderates the development of emotional problems among children following bullying victimization. *Journal of the American Academy of Child & Adolescent Psychiatry, 49*(8), 830–840.

Tanti, C., Stukas, A. A., Halloran, M. J., & Foddy, M. (2011). Social identity change: Shifts in social identity during adolescence. *Journal of Adolescence, 34*(3), 555–567. doi:10.1016/j.adolescence.2010.05.012

Teicher, M. H., Samson, J. A., Sheu, Y.-S., Polcari, A., & McGreenery, C. E. (2010) Hurtful words: Association of exposure to peer verbal abuse with elevated psychiatric symptom scores and corpus callosum abnormalities. *American Journal of Psychiatry, 167*(12), 1464–1471.

Thomas, R. M., Hotsenpiller, G., & Peterson, D. A. (2007). Acute psychosocial stress reduces cell survival in adult hippocampal neurogenesis without altering proliferation. *Journal of Neuroscience, 27*(11), 2734–2743. doi:10.1523/jneurosci.3849-06.2007

Vaillancourt, T., Duku, E., Becker, S., Schmidt, L. A., Nicol, J., Muir, C., & MacMillan, H. (2011). Peer victimization, depressive symptoms, and high salivary cortisol predict poorer memory in children. *Brain and Cognition, 77*(2), 191–199.

Viding, E., McCrory, E. J., Blakemore, S.-J., & Frederickson, N. (2011). Behavioural problems and bullying at school: Can cognitive neuroscience shed new light on an old problem? *Trends in Cognitive Science, 15*(7), 289–291.

8

Vicarious and Secondary Victimization in Adult Bullying and Mobbing: Coworkers, Target-Partners, Children, and Friends

Pamela Lutgen-Sandvik

> It is not enough to just understand the destructive impact [of] mobbing [on] the direct victim because that is only part of the story. Those who love the victim, those who depend on the victim, [and] those who have worked alongside the victim . . . pay a high price for workplace mobbing. (Duffy & Sperry, 2014, p. 95)

This chapter explores the harm to people in bullying targets' lives—coworkers, partners, children, and friends. Bullying (or mobbing) is persistent, harmful, and aggressive verbal, nonverbal, and symbolic behavior directed in a systematic way by one or more persons at work toward one or more others. Undeniably, targets suffer the most, and overwhelming evidence indicates that bullying distresses all aspects of targets' lives (Hogh, Mikkelsen, & Hansen, 2011); the experience is *crippling and devastating* (Adams & Crawford, 1992).

Targets suffer physical ailments, including gastrointestinal problems (e.g., irritable bowel syndrome), insomnia, weight gain or loss, and musculoskeletal problems (Vranceanu, Barsky, & Ring, 2009). Being mobbed and treated unjustly at work leads to chronic stress, high blood pressure, and increased risk of coronary heart disease (De Vogli, Ferrie, Chandola, Kivimäki, & Marmot, 2007; Kivimäki et al., 2005). Bullying and mobbing erodes targets' self-esteem, mental performance, and emotional strength (Brodsky, 1976; Einarsen & Mikkelsen, 2003; Keashly & Harvey, 2005). It often leads to depression (Namie, 2003); alcohol and drug abuse (Rospenda, 2002); symptoms of post-traumatic stress disorder (PTSD; Matthiesen & Einarsen, 2004); and even suicide (Leymann, 1990; Soares, 2012). Some targets are so damaged they cannot return to work once they have escaped the bullying, even when they go to different jobs where there is no bullying. Other targets can only return to their work lives after considerable counseling (Crawford, 1999; Leymann & Gustafsson, 1996).

The effects of adult bullying at work, however, are not limited to targets. The people around targets—intimate partners, family members, friends, and even children—experience tidal force changes in their lives (Lutgen-Sandvik, 2016). Coworkers often feel guilty when they fail to help, angry when management does little, and fearful of being the next target (Tye-Williams & Krone, 2015). Intimate partners feel overwhelmed by their targeted partners' abuse, unsupported by their targeted partner, and generally angry about the bullying situation (Sperry & Duffy, 2009). Parenting responsibilities and children's needs take a sideline as bullying continues to wear down relational connections and deteriorate communication quality (Lutgen-Sandvik & Namie, 2010). Friends can grow emotionally exhausted or irritated, or targets may avoid social contact as they struggle to deal with ongoing abuse (D'Cruz & Noronha, 2011).

The current chapter explores these issues; the chapter summarizes empirical research and applicable theory for understanding how adult bullying affects nonbullied others in the target's work and nonwork domains. Specifically, the chapter explores the dynamics around and effects of bullying on witnessing coworkers, target-partners, family, and friends.

PEOPLE AT WORK: COWORKERS AND BYSTANDERS

Workplace bystanders tend to respond similarly to the primary victim in terms of negative health and career effects, but not quite as intensely. (Duffy & Sperry, 2014, p. 95)

One of the tendencies, especially in U.S. organizations and popular culture, is to individualize the problem of workplace bullying. Supervisors, managers, and colleagues often blame targets for their own abuse or believe targets' reports of abuse are exaggerated and questionable. Thinking of bullying as simply dyadic, or between two people (i.e., a personality conflict), glosses over the communal character of workplace communication and impedes efforts toward resolving adult bullying. Because workplaces are sites of collective human interaction, what occurs between dyads or among members bleeds and buzzes throughout the workgroup and affects all in proximity (Namie & Lutgen-Sandvik, 2010). Because bullying is so volatile and aggressive, it typically spreads fear through entire workgroups and pushes members into one of three general bystander groups.

Workplace bullying is communal, a part of organizational culture and climate, not a personality clash or conflict between two equally positioned organizational members. As a communal phenomena, bullying affects coworkers who see or hear about bullying. Coworkers include anyone working with the target, regardless of position. In bullying situations, coworkers tend toward aligning with (a) those who gravitate toward or support aggressors (*aggressor allies*); (b) those who support or protect targets (*target allies*); and (c) those who attempt to distance themselves from the bullying conflict (*neutral* or *silent bystanders*).[1]

Witness Bystanders

Witness bystanders are employees who see targets bullied but who are not abused directly themselves, people whose "perceptions, fears, and expectations are changed as a result of being vicariously exposed to violence" (Barling, 1996, p. 35). Witness bystanders often report "significantly more general stress and mental stress reactions than employees from workplaces without bullying" (Hogh, Mikkelsen, & Hansen, 2011, p. 108) and often leave organizations after witnessing bullying (Lutgen-Sandvik, 2006). Whether aggressor ally, target ally, or silent audience member, witnessing coworkers suffer a number of negative effects from being exposed to or embroiled in bullying.

Aggressor Allies

Aggressor allies side with, or appear to side with, aggressors. Researchers call aggressor allies "passive bullies, followers, henchmen" (Olweus, 2003, p. 67); patrons; and pawns (Boddy, Ladyshewsky, & Galvin, 2010). Passive bullies and followers are those "who participate in bullying but do not usually take the initiative" (Olweus, 2003, p. 67). These "passive bullies can be equally troubling to the victim . . . where others are gathered willingly or unwillingly to participate in continuous malevolent actions" (Vickers, 2006, p. 271). Henchmen, on the other hand, actively take part in bullying conflicts. They loyally follow the aggressor's lead and work to undermine, remove, and sometimes even destroy the targets' reputations. Boddy and colleagues (Boddy, 2011; Boddy et al., 2010) argue that aggressors usually have two types of allies: patrons and pawns. Patrons help aggressors ascend to positions of power and are people to whom aggressors turn as third-party allies. Aggressors often choose these people as a support network. Pawns, who often emerge later as targets, are persons initially loyal to the aggressors, siding with them in bullying conflicts, but they later feel or discover they are being used or manipulated.

Because emotion is contagious and social, some bystanders will witness and then subsequently model aggressive communication and bullying. Whether bystanders mimic aggression depends in part on group cohesion, norms, and culture. If workgroup cohesion is high, bystanders' direct observations of bullying can increase their own use of aggression (Ferguson & Barry, 2011). Additionally, "norms of toughness . . . tend to reduce the likelihood that witnesses . . . will take action against it [i.e., bullying]. On the contrary, such norms tend to increase the odds that witnesses will join in and even applaud the action of workplace bullies" (Baron & Neuman, 2011, p. 217). The emergence of bullies is not as frequent as people becoming more rude and discourteous in everyday interactions, likely due to the reciprocal nature of communication (McCroskey & Richmonda, 2000). Some members become more uncivil over time, while others empathize with and try to help targets.

Target Allies

Target allies comprise the second witness or bystander group. In contrast to aggressor allies, these bystanders witness abusive interactions and side with the targets. They comprise a second, albeit smaller, group of bystanders—those who dislike the aggressors, who believe abuse is morally wrong, or who have relationships with targets. Ferguson and Barry (2011) suggest that directly witnessing another's abuse "affords the observer an opportunity to witness and, accordingly, vicariously experience the emotions of the target (or victim)[,] . . . [giving] the observer an opportunity to empathize with the victim, and perhaps to mentally place themselves in the victim's shoes" (p. 89). Other bystanders may eventually gravitate toward the target, especially if they shift from being aggressors' followers, patrons, or pawns to being targets.

Supporting targeted colleagues takes an incredible level of courage. Indeed, witnesses are pressured to distance themselves from targets, to shun targets, and to join in the aggressive or passive-aggressive attacks. Those who choose to support targets typically experience three primary negative effects: extreme negatively valenced emotion (anger, indignation, fear); workplace alienation; and damage to work-related identity. Feeling intense undesirable emotions is common for target allies. They often feel angry at their colleague's treatment, management's apparent lack of interest or effectiveness, and the aggressors and aggressor allies. Target allies often get involved because they believe bullying is immoral; their involvement and resistance is a moral imperative (Lutgen-Sandvik, 2006). They also experience fear, worrying that their support for targets might bring them to the aggressors' negative attention. Sadly, this is often the case; target supporters become targets after the original targets have been driven from the workplace (Lutgen-Sandvik & Tracy, 2012).

Alienation can also be an effect of supporting targets. Target allies often find themselves estranged from much of the workgroup. Target supporters can be accused of not being team players and called names such as "troublemaker" and "mentally ill" (Namie & Lutgen-Sandvik, 2010). Often, loss of reputation or damage to work-related identity also occurs with alienation. Supporting targets of bullying is, quite simply, an unpopular stance. When targets have support, bullying them is more challenging, so aggressors and aggressor allies usually deride target supporters (Lutgen-Sandvik & Fletcher, 2014). Suffering others' derision may be part of why high turnover rates are linked to witnessing abuse at work (Houshmand, O'Reilly, Robinson, & Wolff, 2012).

Silent Bystanders

Neutral or silent bystanders withhold their voice and allegiance, taking a Switzerland-type stance and striving to be uninvolved noncombatants. Members of this group side with no one. Silent bystanders typically want to stay out of the bullying processes that they witness happening to others, seeing targets being "undermined, disenfranchised, and emasculated" (Boddy et al., 2010, p. 124). Quite simply, they want to avoid becoming targets. Silent bystanders also want to maintain their privacy and personal freedom, which can be threatened if they become involved in the bullying situation. Additionally, by appearing neutral, silent bystanders may hope to avoid alienating aggressors, targets, or anyone allied with either side.

One might think silent bystanders are somewhat insulated from bullying's negative effects, but such is not the case. Silent bystanders, like other involved parties to workplace bullying, also suffer. If witnessing bystanders withdraw their support for targets, they can end up feeling quite guilty. "They may feel they stood by and did nothing, the organizational equivalent of watching a mugging on a daily basis" (Crawford, 2001, p. 26). If bullying continues, negative emotions spread; fear, anger, emotional exhaustion, and guilt plague bystanders and infect workgroups.

Bystanders most often remain silent, hoping they can avoid involvement. Silent bystanders may hope to avoid alienating aggressors, targets, or anyone allied with either side by appearing neutral. Sadly, this strategy rarely works because bullying conflicts are so emotionally charged—mainly because the stakes are high—that both target and aggressor groups negatively judge those who stand by silently (Lutgen-Sandvik, 2013). Like target allies, silent audience members have increased intentions to leave and exit rates compared to nonexposed workers and report higher rates of workplace negativity and stress and far less job satisfaction than nonexposed workers (Jennifer, Cowie, & Anaiadou, 2003).

Silent bystanders can experience dread and fear at work and practice hypervigilance to try and avoid being bullied. When these coworkers see and hear about others being bullied, they make the logical assumption that they could be next (Mulder, Pouwelse, Lodewijkx, & Bolman, 2014). Witnessing abuse can contribute to bystanders' reduced motivation, commitment, and efficiency in part due to waiting to be targeted or feeling unable to help targets.

Shifting Group Membership

Connection to bystander groups continuously varies and morphs (Lutgen-Sandvik, 2006). Targets' supporters may burn out; noninvolved persons can become targets or begin taking sides, and persons in the aggressors' circles of supporters are ousted. Persons safe from targeting can become targets when aggressors' alliances shift, which they commonly do. Aggressors often redirect aggression to persons who appear to be a threat or whose actions or words place aggressors in a negative light (Crawshaw, 2012). Past targets may stay silent to avoid further harm, but they slowly begin supporting targets when abuse escalates.

Common Negative Effects across Groups

Whether target ally, aggressor ally, or silent bystander, all witnesses to bullying experience some similar negative effects.[2] These include increased stress, greater intentions to leave one's job, lowered job satisfaction, negative ratings of job, and goal displacement. Nearly all workgroup members experience elevated stress when bullying is present (Lutgen-Sandvik, Tracy, & Alberts, 2007). Witnesses of bullying, regardless of their loyalties, exit organizations more frequently than employees who are not affected by bullying (Keashly, 2010). Witnesses are less satisfied with their jobs and rate their jobs lower overall than unaffected employees (Lutgen-Sandvik et al., 2007). In workgroups affected by persistent abuse, goal displacement occurs. The organizational goals for productivity or building a strong organizational culture take a backseat when bullying is left unaddressed. For involved workers, the primary goal shifts from work or relational tasks to hypervigilant self-protection (MacIntosh, 2005).

Aggressors

It bears noting that bullying likely also harms aggressors. With the exception of scholarship on school bullying (e.g., Smokowski & Kopasz, 2005), little research looks at the effects of bullying on the aggressors. However, the negative effects from aggressing against others can be extrapolated from research that focuses on the bullying perpetrators' perspective. Identified aggressors rarely see themselves as aggressors and often explicitly deny being aggressors (DeSanti, 2014), but their aggressive communication and symbolic behavior violate social norms and increase others' discomfort. As such, aggressors likely have difficulty developing and maintaining interpersonal workplace relationships (Lutgen-Sandvik & Fletcher, 2014) or may develop relatively superficial relationships because of others' fear, discomfort, or distrust (Jenkins, Zapf, Winefield, & Sarris, 2011). Aggressors may use aggressive behavior to get revenge or provoke someone (Neuman & Baron, 2005), which places aggressors in danger of retaliation and counterrevenge. Indeed, many aggressors say they feel bullied by others, which may simply be others' means of pushing back against the aggressors' aggression (Lutgen-Sandvik & Fletcher, 2014).

When organizational members begin to see someone as an aggressor, a number of unexpected and unpleasant outcomes emerge for aggressors. Bullying begins to have negative effects on their professional images, which can suffer irreparable harm (Lutgen-Sandvik, Dickinson, & Foss, 2012). If out of the fear of being perceived incompetent some organizational members develop a take-no-prisoners professional identity, others in the organization can begin to see the aggressors as interpersonally incompetent, regardless of technical competence. Aggressors can lose their jobs, suffer demotion, or experience transfers to less desirable positions (Lutgen-Sandvik, 2006), especially if their aggression seriously disrupts workgroup functioning.

PEOPLE AWAY FROM WORK: INTIMATE PARTNERS, CHILDREN, AND FRIENDS

When what happens at work is extreme—like being psychologically terrorized—targets experience intense, protracted negative emotions and moods that are quite likely to bleed into targets' private lives (Duffy & Sperry, 2014). Targets typically bring home the painful experiences and negative emotions from being harassed. Indeed, boundaries between work and nonwork domains can be quite permeable, especially when emotionally disturbing events occur (Riforgiate & Lutgen-Sandvik, 2014). The spillover of emotion and mood from work to nonwork can have destructive effects for people close to targets.

Work-life spillover theory helps explain some of the bleed over between domains that commonly occurs in bullying situations. Duffy and Sperry (2014) call this dynamic "isomorphism[,] . . . what happens in one domain of life is mirrored in another" (p. 100). Work-life spillover theory proposes that an employee's emotions and moods at work spread, inexorably burning into and damaging the employee's personal life (e.g., Ilies, Wilson, & Wagner, 2009; Krouse & Afifi, 2007; Staines, 1980). Bullying increases personal life stress, reduces personal life satisfaction, and negatively affects personal life relationships with friends, family members, and intimate partners (Lutgen-Sandvik, 2016).

Bullying-associated stress and increased personal life stress appear to occur in tandem, which is unsurprising. Targets worry about money, medical insurance, loss of standing, and character damage. They suffer self-doubt, eroded confidence, social ostracism, and harm to mental and physical health (Sperry & Duffy, 2009). In many different ways, these fears and resulting stress effect and involve much of targets' personal lives and the personal lives of their loved ones.

The following sections discuss the proven and potential effects of bullying on target-partners (spouses, significant others); children; and friends. The research reviewed casts a wide net to extend beyond bullying and mobbing research to explore parenting and friendship literatures. Research in these fields point to the potential harms associated with adult bullying.

Target-partners

Target-partners are adult intimate partners in long-term committed relationships with bullied employees (e.g., spouses, significant others, domestic partners). Ample research points to how marital partners' work lives affect one another, both negatively and positively (e.g., Demerouti, Bakker, & Schaufeli, 2005; Ilies et al., 2009; Poelmans et al., 2008; Thompson, Kirk, & Brown, 2005). When an aggressor at work targets one of the relational partners, the relationship can undergo pressures that profoundly test relational bonds, sometimes to the breaking point. As Duffy and Sperry (2014) note, "When both are hurting, it's much harder for each to know what to do to help and support the other" (p. 101).

Target-partner interviews suggest that relationships appear to toughen up, fall apart, or weather the storm when dealing with bullying at work (Lutgen-Sandvik & Namie, 2010).[3] About a third talked about how bullying strengthened their relationships. A female target-partner said, "We've really gotten stronger, . . . not in the way we would have chosen, but it [her partner being bullied] really did make us work together, stand together against it." In a similar vein, target-partners talked about bullying like a test they had successfully navigated.

Sadly, a third of the target-partners spoke of their partner's bullying as a shocking tragedy that decimated their relationships. "Mobbing gets in the way of intimacy" (Duffy & Sperry, 2014, p. 96), and targets and target-partners' emotional reactions can include "displaced anger, venting, and criticizing[,] . . . the kind of talk likely to inflame and make matters worse between partners" (p. 101). Targets' social withdrawal is also difficult for target-spouses. As a female target-partner explained, "He won't go out; he's afraid of seeing him[,] . . . running into him. He won't go to the movies . . . or anywhere really, even food shopping. At first, I tried to get him to go out, . . . but I gave up. Now I live my life, and he lives his. I'm just not ready to be a shut in." The final third were couples that simply "rode out the storm," as a male partner explained.

There seems little doubt that in addition to a host of harmful effects (e.g., PTSD, heart disease, high blood pressure, etc.), adult bullying is a serious threat to adult intimate relationships. The mechanisms linking adult bullying and relational degradation are varied, many of which are adaptive responses. Displaced aggression, emotional spillover and exhaustion, and reduced social capacity are discussed here.

Displaced aggression

Hoobler and Brass (2006) argue that displaced aggression can be the culprit. Displaced aggression occurs when bullied employees come home and vent work-related anger at their family members. In a meta-analysis of displaced aggression (Marcus-Newhall, Pedersen, Carlson, & Miller, 2000), authors invoke a kicking-the-dog metaphor: "a commonly used anecdote to illustrate displaced aggression [is as follows:] . . . A man's boss berates him but the man does not retaliate because he fears losing his job. Hours later, when he arrives home to the greeting barks of his dog, he responds by kicking it" (p. 670).

Because in the United States the primary perpetrators are usually highly placed people, targets are unlikely to fight back directly. Their bottled-up anger and resentment, however, can come out later in aggressive communication and interactions with adult intimate partners (Krahé, 2013). Displaced aggression at home often undermines the family (Hoobler & Brass, 2006). Family undermining is ongoing aggressive and passive-aggressive interactions among family members that directly undercut the family "and diminish the family member or partner's sense of self-worth" (Hoobler & Brass, 2006, p. 1187).

Emotional spillover and exhaustion

Emotional spillover occurs when the emotions evoked in one life domain (e.g., work) spillover into another life domain (e.g., family, friends). Targets beleaguered at work by unrelenting abuse, humiliation, or ostracism feel increasing levels of rage, terror, anxiety, and so forth. These emotions and the negative moods and emotions infect or taint interpersonal communication and relationships through a process of contagion (Sperry & Duffy, 2009). Work-life spillover theorists argue that the emotions and moods people feel in one life domain are similar emotions to what they feel in other life domains (e.g., Ilies et al., 2009; Krouse & Afifi, 2007; Staines, 1980). Additionally, spillover is most likely with elevated or extreme emotions (Staines, 1980), and being bullied at work elicits such emotion.

Target-partners can also experience emotional exhaustion from listening to, helping problem solve, providing support or defense, and so forth for bullied partners (Davenport, Schwartz, & Elliott, 2002). Over time, bullying colonizes targets' lives and becomes the central topic of conversation between intimate partners, often wearing down and emotionally exhausting target-partners (Lewis & Orford, 2005). When target-partners talked about the effects of bullying on their relationships, they said they felt "tired," "exhausted," "burned out," and "drained" from having to deal with their partners' ongoing abuse at work.

Reduced social capacity

When targets are under attack all day at work, they expend incredible levels of energy just to carry on at their jobs (Hogh, Mikkelsen, & Hansen, 2011). When they leave the abusive environment, they, unsurprisingly, often have little to give others, such as target-partners and children. In many cases, bullying reduces targets' capacity to respond socially to their intimate partners. Because of the unrelenting abuse at work, being supportive, listening empathetically, or maintaining a consistent level of warmth and affection can be exceedingly difficult (Duffy & Sperry, 2007; Sperry & Duffy, 2009). In many cases, targets talk incessantly (i.e., sensemaking) about their bullying experiences when away from work, which can wear out target-partners (Davenport et al., 2002). Of course, children are also affected by the home environment that adaptive responses to bullying cultivate.

Targets' negative emotion or mood at home can erode interpersonal social support that might help targets deal more constructively with aggressive workplace interactions. Without social support, targets might react at work with reciprocal aggression, which accelerates aggressive communication and negatively affects workgroups and organizations by association. In a kind of destructive feedback loop, the erosion of personal life destabilizes targets that become even less able to deal with the workplace bullying situations.

Children and Parenting

When a parent has been mobbed in the workplace, the effects don't just trickle down to the children, they pour down. (Duffy & Sperry, 2014, p. 103)

Successful parenting is labor intensive and requires consistently being present for children, both emotionally and physically. Parenting requires energy, attention, responsiveness, and awareness (Duffy & Sperry, 2014), and bullied adults simply do not have these resources available. Targeted parents have far less ability to attend and respond to children's needs because of the *acute preoccupation* with bullying or mobbing, which is characteristic of the phenomena.

Duffy and Sperry's (2014) clinical work with mobbed adults and target-spouse interviews (Lutgen-Sandvik & Namie, 2010) suggests that children can experience considerable harm when a parent is bullied at work. The effects of adult bullying on children is linked to targets' adaptive psychological and physiological responses to mobbing or bullying, "such as mental and physical health problems, symptoms of post-traumatic stress, burnout, increased intentions to leave [jobs], and reduced job satisfaction" (Nielsen & Einarsen, 2012, p. 309). Albeit inadvertently, these adaptive responses commonly lead to serious problems for children that are associated with undermined parenting.

Being the target of relentless abuse at work leaves targets drained of energy, anxious, inattentive, and depressed, a state in which they are far less likely to recognize and respond to their children's needs (Duffy & Sperry, 2014). Parenting involves helping children build new skills, solve problems, and so forth. Being bullied at work "robs a parent of the energy and motivation needed to keep pace with the daily demands that are part and parcel of helping children" (Duffy & Sperry, 2014, p. 105). Workplace bullying and mobbing typically interfere with parenting, so they have the potential to seriously affect children. Similar to bystanders who witness their coworkers' abuse, children of mobbed or bullied parents are secondary victims—people who are not directly bullied "but whose perceptions, fears and expectations are changed as a result of being vicariously exposed to violence" (Barling, 1996, p. 35).

In many cases, target-spouses try to compensate for the bullied partner's parental lapses or emotional distance, much in the way nondrinking parents compensate for drinking partners (Leonard & Eiden, 2007). In terms of parenting, target-partner interviews are telling. They talk of taking over the bullied partner's parenting responsibilities, becoming hypervigilant in their efforts to keep children from needing their other parent, and buffering interactions between the children and the bullied parent (Lutgen-Sandvik & Namie, 2010).

For children, "multiple risk factor exposure is more harmful than singular risk exposure" (Evans, Li, & Whipple, 2013, p. 1342), and adult bullying can pose multiple risks to children. Workplace bullying is linked to various adaptive responses, which bullied parents are likely to experience. Extrapolating from associated research on parental behavior, parenting, and children, the following explores the potential impact on children of several parental adaptive responses to bullying: job insecurity or loss, destructive marital conflict, alcohol or drug abuse, mental health issues, excessive demands at work, child neglect, and divorce.

Job insecurity or loss

When parents talk about job insecurity in front of children or lose their jobs, which is common in bullying, children can internalize negative beliefs and attitudes about work. "What may then get modeled for children is lack of faith and trust in work and, to an extent, lack of faith and trust in other people" (Duffy & Sperry, 2014, p. 106). Indeed, Barling, Dupre, and Hepburn (1998) found that parents' job insecurity affected children's perceptions of work life more than the number of actual layoffs. Targets of bullying typically experience extreme fear about their jobs; and many lose their jobs, so the fears are warranted (Hogh, Hoel, & Carneiro, 2011). Children, however, see their parents' loss of fundamental beliefs (e.g., hard work is rewarded; respect is a human right) and may begin to internalize those beliefs (Barling et al., 1998).

Destructive marital conflict

When a parent is bullied or mobbed at work, destructive marital conflict commonly follows, which often has a negative effect on family functioning and parenting and has been linked to a variety of risks for childhood disorders, including effects on psychological, physiological, social, and academic functioning (Cummings & Davies, 2002). Destructive marital conflict affects the quality of parental relationships, which in turn affects parent-child relationships, suggesting that when parent-parent relationships are negative, parent-child relationships can also be negative (Erel & Burman, 1995). Even furtive forms of anger, such as nonverbal cues indicating annoyance, irritation, resentment, emotional withdrawal, and the like, although indirect expressions of conflict, significantly contribute to children's distress (Cummings & Davies, 2002).

Alcohol or drug abuse

Research suggests that adult bullying and mistreatment contribute to targets' alcohol and drug abuse (Bartlett & Bartlett, 2011; Richman, Rospenda, Flaherty, & Freels, 2001; Yildirim & Yildirim, 2007). Parents who abuse alcohol show less positive involvement and express more emotion that is negative with their children than nonusing parents do. For these reasons and others, parental alcohol or drug abuse can have devastating effects on children. Children can develop more aggressive ways of interacting, have lower social competence, experience early-onset alcohol or drug use, and display antisocial behavior (Leonard & Eiden, 2007). Parental alcohol abuse often leads to increased marital conflict, which reduces effective parenting, and contributes to a higher incidence of child behavior problems (Leonard & Eiden, 2007). For example, boys may exhibit increased anger and girls increased sadness (El-Sheikh, 2005).

Children who witness a bullied parent abusing alcohol are likely to experience many of the same things other children experience when parents abuse alcohol—sadness and depression, reduced social engagement with peers, or shifts in their peer group toward risky behavior (Leonard & Eiden, 2007). For bullied parents who turn to alcohol, children can emerge as a major stressor. Research points to a negative spiral between parental drinking and children's behavior problems: parents who abuse alcohol "are at higher risk for having children with behavior problems, and children's behavior problems may increase parental stress and lead to more drinking" (El-Sheikh, 2005, p. 14).

Mental health issues

Targets are not abused because they have mental health issues, but research consistently points to being bullied or mobbed as antecedents to mental health issues (Hogh, Mikkelsen, & Hansen, 2011; Matthiesen & Einarsen, 2004; see also chapter 13). Bullied adults can, for example, become profoundly afraid or even terrified (Malinauskiene, Obelenis, & Sopagiene, 2005). Children living with a bullied parent may experience some of the effects associated with living with a mentally ill person. Some of the risks of living with someone with a mental illness include poorer physical health, more frequent doctor visits, and limited social activities (Gallagher & Mechanic, 1996).

One of the effects of chronic bullying and mobbing is acute depression, especially when targets have to remain in the work environment. Bullying drives targets to question everything about themselves, where they fit in the world, and the people they always thought themselves to be (Hogh, Mikkelsen, & Hansen, 2011; Lutgen-Sandvik, 2008). Answers to these questions are not forthcoming for targeted adults and contribute to depression. Parental depression, in turn, is linked to undesirable outcomes for children, such as becoming depressed themselves or developing decreased self-esteem (Weissman, Warner, Wickramaratne, Moreau, & Olfson, 1997).

Excessive work demands

Work demands typically increase exponentially for bullied or mobbed adults (Lutgen-Sandvik, 2013), which can undermine parenting activities (Bass, Butler, Grzywacz, & Linney, 2009). Job-related stress from excessive work demands can have terrible effects on parent-child relationships, usually leading to withdrawal from family interaction (Bumpus, Crouter, & McHale, 1999) and a lower frequency of child-related activities (Roeters, Van Der Lippe, & Kluwer, 2009).

Bullied or mobbed parents can find they have little energy left for interactions with their partners or children. In some cases, the parent with fewer work demands compensates for the overtaxed parent (Bass et al., 2009), drawing attention away from what the overtaxed parent is or is not doing at home (Lutgen-Sandvik & Namie, 2010). Bass et al. (2009) found that excessive work demands usually mean "less time spent on child care and less time spent on leisure [time] with children" (p. 201). They also found evidence of *parental compensation*; when one parent had excessive demands at work, the other parent took over more of the parenting responsibilities. In a study of target-spouses, the same parenting compensation was apparent; target-spouses often felt they compensated for the bullied parents' lack of involvement with children (Lutgen-Sandvik & Namie, 2010).

Child neglect

Workplace bullying appropriates nearly all of the targeted parents' energy and attention: "[Acute] preoccupation with key players and events in the chronology of mobbing is a typical response to workplace mobbing and doesn't begin to encompass the acute preoccupation, withdrawal, and impaired focus and concentration that occur in more severe mobbing injuries like depression and PTSD" (Duffy & Sperry, 2014, p. 104). Because of the acute preoccupation, bullied parents often lose interest and lack involvement in children's activities, show less concern about children's issues, and focus less on children than prior to the bullying situation (Lutgen-Sandvik & Namie, 2010). This and other forms of social withdrawal or distancing reduce parental functioning and leave children at risk of neglect.

Interviews with targets and target-spouses point to the risk of child neglect when one parent is bullied at work (Lutgen-Sandvik, 2013; Lutgen-Sandvik & Namie, 2010). Neglect, in turn, has a number of long-term negative effects on children and adolescents, including depression, anxiety, high-risk peer friendships, a reduced sense of belonging, and poor self-esteem (Sperry & Widom, 2013). Emotional information processing involves people's ability to recognize, process, and empathize with others' emotional expressions, such as joy, sadness, and anger. This ability can be less developed in people who experienced neglect as children (Young & Widom, 2014).

Divorce

In my interviews with target-partners, roughly a third talked about divorcing or separating from their spouses because workplace bullying had changed their partners so much, and some were divorced or going through divorce at the time of the study (Lutgen-Sandvik & Namie, 2010). To assume then that workplace bullying or mobbing can lead to divorce for some couples is not a great stretch, and when marriages or long-term adult relationships dissolve, the dissolution can create considerable turmoil in children's lives (Amato, 2000; Kim, 2011). Developmental harms associated with divorce include increased likelihood of dropping out of high school, deficits in cognitive skills, losses to psychosocial well-being, and degraded social relations (Kim, 2011). A study of marital instability and its effect on childhood adjustment found that children of divorce were at risk of "earlier initiation of sexual intercourse and emotional difficulties, . . . depressed mood, and suicidal ideation" (D'Onofrio et al., 2006).

Friendships

Friendship is the deliberate interdependence between people involving the experience and satisfaction of "companionship, emotional security, support, and self-validation" (Demir & Davidson, 2013, p. 527). Friends are crucial to adult well-being, and people with friends usually have a greater sense of well-being than those without (Hartup & Stevens, 1999). Basic values underlie most adult friendships: trust, honesty, respect, nonjudgment, being there, and similar life experiences and values (Blieszner & Adams, 1992; Galupo & Gonzalez, 2013). Friends feel satisfied when friendships include such experiences as working together toward a shared goal, respecting each other's privacy, offering advice, and so forth. Emotional support and shared interests are particularly significant in adult friendships (Blieszner & Adams, 1992).

Adult friendships usually center on support and companionship and are marked by in-depth disclosure, being more directive and authoritative, and symmetrical problem-solving interactions (Hartup & Stevens, 1999). These connections and the emotional support people receive through them are especially crucial during life crises, especially something as shocking and world changing as workplace bullying. Friends can help targets analyze the situation and reframe or rethink the situation in new ways (Blieszner & Adams, 1992). A friend's analysis and reframing may reduce the target's negative thinking and emotion and point toward better ways of handling the issue.

In addition to analyzing and reframing problems, friends help friends manage emotion and emotional displays (Kramer & Hess, 2002). Indeed, targeted adults typically find an empathetic ear with friends, a safe space in which to express volatile emotions, which can diffuse otherwise suppressed emotion in a benign and effective way. Friends help manage emotional reactions by recognizing and confirming targets' feelings, which reduces stress (Blieszner & Adams, 1992). Friendships satisfy a number of human needs; yet, like all relationships, they require an energy and time investment (Demir & Davidson, 2013).

Workplace friends

Friendships can be with work and nonwork people; whichever type, friends can suffer considerably when a friend is targeted (D'Cruz & Noronha, 2011). These people have special relationships with targets in which they share personal and work information (Sias, Gallagher, Kopaneva, & Pedersen, 2012). In situations of bullying, workplace friends can play important roles.

In D'Cruz and Noronha's (2011) research, when workplace friends became involved in the bullying situation, initially they completely protected the targets. Over time, however, workplace friends who had initially protected and defended targets significantly curtailed their efforts when supervisors and other coworkers communicated negative reactions. Bullying can cement workplace friendships and loyalties (Lutgen-Sandvik, 2006) and drastically challenges those relationships (D'Cruz & Noronha, 2011).

Being friends with targets at work has its risks. Workplace friends, more than other bystanders, are likely to leave their jobs when (or if) their target-friends are fired or quit (D'Cruz & Noronha, 2011; Lutgen-Sandvik, 2006; Vartia, 2001). So being a friend at work carries risks for bystanders, as noted in the earlier section. Being friends with a target can be a heartbreaking experience. Even when workplace friends do everything they can, they may still experience "regret over their limited effectiveness and struggle with confusion, guilt and remorse" (D'Cruz & Noronha, 2011, p. 272). Workplace friends, like targets in past research (Cowan, 2011), may find that HR's practices constrain efforts to help target-friends (Cowan, 2012).

Friends (nonwork)

Like parenting or being a marital partner, sustaining friendship takes energy and effort that targeted adults are unlikely to have. Maintaining friendships is crucial, but the processes associated with satisfying friendships can be difficult for targeted adults to sustain, especially with nonwork friends who take added effort to see. Workplace bullying strips the energy targets need to engage in these interactions with friends.

When targeted adults need their friends the most, those friendships are at considerable risk because of colonization (i.e., acute preoccupation) leading to vitality loss and social distancing (Duffy & Sperry, 2012, 2014). Targets have their lives colonized or taken over by being bullied at work; they respond by becoming acutely preoccupied with the experience as they attempt to make sense of and resolve or end the abuse. Thinking and talking about shocking workplace events and what to do requires a staggering amount of mental and physical energy (Qureshi et al., 2015). Social distancing is a common response and adaptation to being mobbed that affects friendships both at work and outside of work.

Ongoing attacks at work and defending against them come to *colonize*, or take over, nearly all aspects of targets' lives. Colonization occurs in part because bullying continues for so long; the average duration in the United States is 18 (Lutgen-Sandvik et al., 2007) to 23 (Namie, 2007) months. Targeted adults become *acutely preoccupied* with the workplace horrors—professional lives crumbling, excruciating loneliness, terror, loss of basic beliefs about life and work (Duffy & Sperry, 2014; Lutgen-Sandvik, 2008)—and far more.

The experience leaves little or no energy to invest in friendships with the mutuality so necessary to maintaining adult friendships. Because of the ways bullying colonizes targets' lives, bullying can lead to the immediate or eventual loss of friendship mutuality that is key to developing and sustaining friendships (Hartup & Stevens, 1999). Because bullying can continue for years, friendship communication can become strained because of the loss of mutuality. When target-friends feel as if they must always hear about the bullying situation or when targets fail to take target-friends' directive advice, friendships become strained. Friends can become emotionally exhausted and begin to distance themselves from target-friends as a means of self-defense. Friends who earlier listened and tried to help can begin to feel exhausted and irritated (Davenport et al., 2002). They may feel like they are receiving little in return or come to feel irritated because targets appear to ignore their requested and unrequested advice.

Part of how bullying colonizes targets' lives involves ceaseless sensemaking (e.g., talking incessantly about the workplace; Lutgen-Sandvik & McDermott, 2011). The acute preoccupation with identity work and repair (e.g., self-defense to others, fitting abuse into self-image) is another aspect of colonization (Lutgen-Sandvik, 2008). Both of these colonizing dynamics mark targets' conversations. Targets make sense of bullying by talking about the experience to work and nonwork friends and others (Lutgen-Sandvik, Alberts, & Tracy, 2008).

Sensemaking is a feature of adult bullying and mobbing from the beginning to the end and beyond. Targets continually try to figure out what happened and why, what they could have done differently, what they should do, what others think of them and the bully, whether others have been bullied, and on and on and on. Rumination runs rampant in these phenomena. Targets' acute preoccupation with abuse typically includes co-rumination or *excessive problem talk* with friends (Boren, 2013). Targets and their friends can feel worn down by chronic co-rumination. Even with very supportive friends, excessive problem talk strains relationships, and research suggests it is less than effective at solving problems (Boren, 2013).

Taken together, excessive rumination, sensemaking, identity work, and other colonizing processes and experiences deplete target energy. Like parenting or being a vital part of an adult relationship, maintaining friendships takes energy that targets simply do not have because they are dealing with chronic abuse at work. What energy targets do have is expended in excessive problem talk, self-defense claims, and so forth, which can come to wear out friends. They may come to feel as if they are always on the "giving" side of the friendship because targets are in extreme psychological pain.

DISCUSSION AND DIRECTIONS OF FUTURE RESEARCH

Research on bullying, mobbing, workplace aggression, and the like is impressive and expansive (e.g., Duffy & Sperry, 2012; Einarsen, Hoel, Zapf, & Cooper, 2011; Fox & Spector, 2005; Lutgen-Sandvik & Sypher, 2009). Some considerable gaps exist in our knowledge about the widespread risks bullying poses for targets' social and work circles. Much of what is discussed here is extrapolated from related research on marriage, children, and friendship, not specifically about how bullying or mobbing affects these relationships. More research is needed into the cohort groups and relationships workplace bullying harms, beyond target-focused research.

Target-focused research is rich and abundant; thousands of empirical studies and theoretical reviews comprise this body of work. Bystander-focused research is an emerging field with some great ideas about bystander training (Scully & Rowe, 2009; van Heugten, 2010) and other empirical evidence of harm to people who witness others' abuse (D'Cruz & Noronha, 2011; Lutgen-Sandvik et al., 2007; Vartia, 2001). Work in this area is still the exception in the field, given the number of works published each year on bullying and mobbing. Some ideas follow for extending our knowledge of workplace bullying's effects on bystanders:

- What mental, physical, or psychological harms are associated with witnessing workplace bullying?
- What, if any, effect does witnessing workplace bullying have on witnesses' work productivity?
  - Does workplace bullying affect organizational commitment, citizenship behavior, loyalty, and so forth?
- How do witnesses come to know about workplace bullying?
  - To whom do witnesses talk, when, and where in terms of others being bullied at their jobs?
- How do witnesses respond to bullying?
  - Are the responses to bullying more or less effective (e.g., in terms of helping the target feel better, ending bullying, protecting others, etc.)?
- How likely are witnesses to become targets?
  - Does moving from witness to target vary depending on the bystander group to which the witness belongs?

Bystander research is essential if we are to fully understand the ramifications of workplace bullying and mobbing, and bystanders are the second most frequently examined cohort involved in the phenomenon. Research on targets and bystanders, organizationally situated cohorts, is the foundation on which future scholars can build to understand the phenomena's effects outside the organization.

In terms of nonwork cohorts (target-partners, children, friends, family), extraorganizational research on bullying and mobbing is exceedingly rare (Duffy & Sperry, 2012, 2014; Hoobler & Brass, 2006; Lutgen-Sandvik & Namie, 2010). Some ideas follow for extending our knowledge of workplace bullying's effects on target-partners:

- What are the effects of workplace bullying on marital functioning and communication?
  - Does workplace bullying increase the likelihood of divorce or separation?
- How do target-partners deal with their partners' abuse?
  - Which ways are most or least effective at helping or supporting targets?
- What types of target-partner social support are most effective at helping or supporting targets?
- How do target-partners involve themselves in the bullying situation?
  - Do they avoid getting involved or get overinvolved?

In addition to target-partners, workplace bullying places children at risk, as bullying erodes parenting, yet we know very little beyond Duffy and Sperry's (2014) provocative and alarming work. Considerably more work is needed. Some ideas follow for extending our knowledge of workplace bullying's effects on parenting and children:

- What is the process through which children progress when one of their parents is bullied at work?
  - How does the child find out? How does either parent speak to the child about it? Does the child notice tension between parents or other cues that something is amiss?
- How does workplace bullying change children's family lives?
- In what ways has workplace bullying changed how children talk to parents?
  - Do children defer to the nonbullied parent or avoid certain subjects or times of the day?
- What ill effects has workplace bullying caused for children in the bullied parent's household?
- In what ways does workplace bullying affect children's school performance?
  - Does a parent's bullying affect children's academic work or after-school activity involvement?

When it comes to friends and workplace bullying, we know a little about what occurs between workplace friends (D'Cruz & Noronha, 2011), but almost nothing about nonwork friendships. Davenport et al. (2002) anecdotally mention the emotional exhaustion friends experience, likely because targets talk excessively about the problem. Duffy and Sperry (2014) explain that targets also socially withdraw when mobbed, so friendships can suffer at a time when targets need friendships the most. Possibly, the risks to friendship are neglect and exhaustion, but we simply do not know. Empirical research is practically nonexistent in this area. Some ideas follow for extending our knowledge of workplace bullying's effects on friends and friendships:

- How do targets bring up the subject of workplace bullying with their friends?
  - Does the friend have to "pull" information out of the target?
  - Does the target go to the friend and ask to talk?
- How does workplace bullying affect friendships?
  - Is there evidence of social withdrawal from friendships?
  - Is there evidence of emotional exhaustion?
- How do friends deal with and respond to a friend's abuse?
  - Which ways are most or least effective at helping or supporting targets?
- What types of social support are most effective for friends helping or supporting targets?

Aggressor-focused and family-focused workplace bullying research are two other areas that have received little or no research attention. Aggressor-focused studies are rare (e.g., Bloch, 2012; DeSanti, 2014), and family-focused work (aside from target-partner focused) is nonexistent. Some ideas follow for extending our knowledge of workplace bullying's effects on family members:

- How has a family member's bullying at work affected other family members?
  - Does one member's abuse at work affect family traditions, events, and so forth?
- How does the family talk about bullying at work?
  - Does blame-the-victim language or advice giving preside?
- How has workplace bullying affected family conversation?
- How has workplace bullying affected family relationships and connections?

Because workplace bullying research has a predominant target-focus, most of it has a pro-target stance, implied or otherwise. Aggressors, although sometimes demonized in the popular press, and sidelined in adult bullying scholarship, are likely harmed when they bully others (Lutgen-Sandvik et al., 2012). Aggressors are the people we love to hate, if only implied. Some may think, "Don't they deserve to be harmed for hurting others?" People working with aggressors argue that aggressors at work attack others out of fear and ignorance (Crawshaw, 2012). Whatever the reason, aggressors are troubled people who do themselves no good by abusing others at work. Aggressors lose others' respect; people at work ridicule and avoid them, and continued bullying leads to many being fired or demoted (DeSanti, 2014; Lutgen-Sandvik, 2006; Lutgen-Sandvik et al., 2012). Some ideas follow for extending our knowledge of workplace bullying's effects on aggressors:

- What happens to aggressors over time in their career trajectories?
  - Are they fired, promoted, or transferred repeatedly?
  - Are they rewarded for bullying?
- Do guilt and remorse play a part in aggressors' experiences?
  - How do they deal with guilt, remorse, or other involved emotions?
- What work-related ramifications have aggressors experienced because of bullying others?
- What personal-life ramifications have aggressors experienced because of bullying others?

CONCLUSION

Damage from dysfunctional working cultures reaches far beyond the workplace; adult bullying strains marriages, burdens friendships, and hurts children. Clearly, the harm from adult bullying at work is not limited to targets. Intimate partners, family members, friends, and even children are at risk when someone close to them is targeted. Coworkers often feel remorseful when they do not help targets, incensed when managers take no or ineffective action, and are afraid of being targeted themselves. Target-partners feel overwhelmed, unsupported, and angry as marriages are strained, some to the breaking point. Parenting and children become less important as persistent abuse at work degrades relational connections and undermines parental communication. Friends become exhausted from hearing about abuse for months and even years or grow irritated. Targets may come to avoid social contact, so friendships may wane from neglect. The current chapter explored these issues; the chapter summarized empirical research and applicable theory for understanding how adult bullying affected people in the targets' work and nonwork domains—witnessing coworkers, target-partners, children, and friends.

Target-adaptive responses to bullying create problems for the people in the targets' lives, and the number of people bullying and mobbing harms is astronomical. Conservatively, 1 in 10 people are bullied in the United States each year (Lutgen-Sandvik et al., 2007), which means approximately 15 million U.S. workers are bullied each year (Bureau of Labor Statistics, 2016). Hypothetically, if each target has one friend, one partner, and one child, adult bullying can devastate an *additional* 45 million people's lives. These numbers and the sheer volume of human pain linked to workplace bullying and mobbing call us as researchers to do all we can to restore respect, dignity, and civility to the workplace.

NOTES

1. Twemlow, Fonagy, and Sacco (2004) categorize bystanders as *bully bystanders* (become involved in bullying); *avoidant bystanders* (deny all responsibility); *victim bystanders* (become victimized in the process); and *helpful bystanders* (attempt to defuse situation).

2. Aggressors were omitted from the list due to limited research.

3. Except in the rare cases where targets suppress workplace experiences, relationships are rarely untouched by a partner being bullied at work.

REFERENCES

Adams, A., & Crawford, N. (1992). *Bullying at work: How to confront and overcome it*. London, England: Virago Press.

Amato, P. R. (2000). The consequences of divorce for adults and children. *Journal of Marriage and Family, 62*(4), 1269–1287. doi:10.1111/j.1741-3737.2000.01269.x

Barling, J. (1996). The prediction, experience and consequences of workplace violence. In G. R. VanderBos & E. Q. Bulatoao (Eds.), *Violence on the job* (pp. 29–50). Washington, D.C.: American Psychological Association.

Barling, J., Dupre, K. E., & Hepburn, C. G. (1998). Effects of parents' job insecurity on children's work beliefs and attitudes. *Journal of Applied Psychology, 83*(1), 112. doi:10.1037/0021-9010.83.1.112

Baron, R. A., & Neuman, J. H. (2011). Social antecedents to bullying: A social interactionist perspective. In S. Einarsen, H. Hoel, D. Zapf & C. Cooper (Eds.), *Bullying and harassment in the workplace: Developments in theory, research, and practice* (2nd ed., pp. 201–226). Boca Raton, FL: CRC Press/Taylor & Francis Group.

Bartlett, J. E., & Bartlett, M. E. (2011). Workplace bullying: An integrative literature review. *Advances in Developing Human Resources, 13*(1), 69–84. doi:10.1177/1523422311410651

Bass, B. L., Butler, A. B., Grzywacz, J. G., & Linney, K. D. (2009). Do job demands undermine parenting?: A daily analysis of spillover and crossover effects. *Family Relations, 58*(2), 201–215. doi:10.1111/j.1741-3729.2008.00547.x

Blieszner, R. M., & Adams, R. G. (1992). *Adult friendship*. Thousand Oaks, CA: SAGE Publications, Inc.

Bloch, C. (2012). How do perpetrators experience bullying at the workplace? *International Journal of Work Organisation and Emotion, 5*(2), 159–177. doi:10.1504/IJWOE.2012.049519

Boddy, C. R. P. (2011). Corporate psychopaths, bullying, and unfair supervision in the workplace. *Journal of Business Ethics, 100*(3), 367–379. doi:10.1007/s10551-010-0689-5

Boddy, C. R. P., Ladyshewsky, R., & Galvin, P. (2010). Leaders without ethics in global business: Corporate psychopaths. *Journal of Public Affairs, 10*(3), 121–138. doi:10.1002/pa.352

Boren, J. P. (2013). The relationships between co-rumination, social support, stress, and burnout among working adults. *Management Communication Quarterly, 28*(1), 3–25. doi:10.1177/0893318913509283

Brodsky, C. (1976). *The harassed worker*. Lexington, MA: D.C. Health and Company.

Bumpus, M. F., Crouter, A. C., & McHale, S. M. (1999). Work demands of dual-earner couples: Implications for parents' knowledge about children's daily lives in middle childhood. *Journal of Marriage and the Family, 61*(2), 465–475. doi:10.2307/353762

Bureau of Labor Statistics. (2016). *The employment situation—June 2016*. Retrieved from http://www.bls.gov/news.release/pdf/empsit.pdf

Cowan, R. L. (2011). "Yes, we have an anti-bullying policy, but . . .": HR professionals' understandings and experiences with workplace bullying policy. *Communication Studies, 62*(3), 307–327. doi:10.1080/10510974.2011.553763

Cowan, R. L. (2012). It's complicated: Defining workplace bullying from the human resource professional's perspective. *Management Communication Quarterly, 26*(3), 377–403. doi:10.1177/0893318912439474

Crawford, N. (1999). Conundrums and confusion in organisations: The etymology of the word "bully." *International Journal of Manpower, 20*(1/2), 86–93. doi:10.1108/01437729910268678

Crawford, N. (2001). Organisational responses to workplace bullying. In N. Tehrani (Ed.), *Building a culture of respect: Managing bullying at work* (pp. 21–31). London, England: Taylor & Francis.

Crawshaw, L. (2012). Coaching abrasive leaders: Contradictory tales of the Big Bad Wolf. In N. Tehrani (Ed.), *Workplace bullying: Symptoms and solutions* (pp. 132–148). London, England: Routledge.

Cummings, E. M., & Davies, P. T. (2002). Effects of marital conflict on children: Recent advances and emerging themes in process-oriented research. *Journal of Child Psychology and Psychiatry, 43*(1), 31–63. doi:10.1111/1469-7610.00003

Davenport, N., Schwartz, R. D., & Elliott, G. P. (2002). *Mobbing: Emotional abuse in the American workplace* (2nd ed.). Ames, IA: Civil Society Publishing.

D'Cruz, P., & Noronha, E. (2011). The limits to workplace friendship: Managerialist HRM and bystander behaviour in the context of workplace bullying. *Employee Relations, 33*(3), 269–288. doi:10.1108/01425451111121777

Demerouti, E., Bakker, A. B., & Schaufeli, W. B. (2005). Spillover and crossover of exhaustion and life satisfaction among dual-earner parents. *Journal of Vocational Behavior, 67*(2), 266–289.

Demir, M., & Davidson, I. (2013). Toward a better understanding of the relationship between friendship and happiness: Perceived responses to capitalization attempts, feelings of mattering, and satisfaction of basic psychological needs in same-sex best friendships as predictors of happiness. *Journal of Happiness Studies, 14*(2), 525–550. doi:10.1007/s10902-012-9341-7

DeSanti, L. (2014). *Workplace bullying, cognitive dissonance & dissonance reduction: Exploring the alleged perpetrator's experience & coping* [Unpublished masters thesis], Fielding Graduate University, Santa Barbara, CA.

De Vogli, R., Ferrie, J. E., Chandola, T., Kivimäki, M., & Marmot, M. G. (2007). Unfairness and health: Evidence from the Whitehall II study. *Journal of Epidemiology and Community Health, 61*(6), 513–518. doi:10.1136/jech.2006.052563

D'Onofrio, B. M., Turkheimer, E., Emery, R. E., Slutske, W. S., Heath, A. C., Madden, P. A., & Martin, N. G. (2006). A genetically informed study of the processes underlying the association between parental marital instability and offspring adjustment. *Developmental Psychology, 42*(3), 486–499. doi:10.1037/0012-1649.42.3.486

Duffy, M., & Sperry, L. (2007). Workplace mobbing: Individual and family health consequences. *The Family Journal, 15*(4), 398–404. doi: 10.1177/1066480707305069

Duffy, M., & Sperry, L. (2012). *Mobbing: Causes, consequences, and solutions*. New York: Oxford University Press.

Duffy, M., & Sperry, L. (2014). *Overcoming mobbing: A recovery guide for workplace aggression and bullying*. New York: Oxford University Press.

Einarsen, S., Hoel, H., Zapf, D., & Cooper, C. (Eds.). (2011). *Bullying and harassment in the workplace: Developments in theory, research, and practice*. Boca Raton, FL: CRC Press/Taylor & Francis Group.

Einarsen, S., & Mikkelsen, E. G. (2003). Individual effects of exposure to bullying at work. In S. Einarsen, H. Hoel, D. Zapf, & C. L. Cooper (Eds.), *Bullying and emotional abuse in the workplace: International perspectives in research and practice* (pp. 127–144). London, England: Taylor & Francis.

El-Sheikh, M. (2005). The role of emotional responses and physiological reactivity in the marital conflict–child functioning link. *Journal of Child Psychology and Psychiatry, 46*(11), 1191–1199. doi:10.1111/j.1469-7610.2005.00418.x

Erel, O., & Burman, B. (1995). Interrelatedness of marital relations and parent-child relations: A meta-analytic review. *Psychological Bulletin, 118*(1), 108–132. doi:10.1037/0033-2909.118.1.108

Evans, G. W., Li, D., & Whipple, S. S. (2013). Cumulative risk and child development. *Psychological Bulletin, 139*(6), 1342–1396. doi:10.1037/a0031808

Ferguson, M., & Barry, B. (2011). I know what you did: The effects of interpersonal deviance on bystanders. *Journal of Occupational Health Psychology, 16*(1), 80–94. doi:10.1037/a0021708

Fox, S., & Spector, P. E. (Eds.). (2005). *Counterproductive work behavior*. Washington, D.C.: American Psychological Association.

Gallagher, S. K., & Mechanic, D. (1996). Living with the mentally ill: Effects on the health and functioning of other household members. *Social Science & Medicine, 42*(12), 1691–1701. doi:10.1016/0277-9536(95)00296-0

Galupo, M. P., & Gonzalez, K. A. (2013). Friendship values and cross-category friendships: Understanding adult friendship patterns across gender, sexual orientation and race. *Sex Roles, 68*(11–12), 779–790. doi:10.1007/s11199-012-0211-x

Hartup, W. W., & Stevens, N. (1999). Friendships and adaptation across the life span. *Current Directions in Psychological Science, 8*(3), 76–79. doi:http://cdp.sagepub.com/content/8/3/76.shorthttp://cdp.sagepub.com/content/8/3/76.short

Hogh, A., Hoel, H., & Carneiro, I. G. (2011). Bullying and employee turnover among healthcare workers: A three-wave prospective study. *Journal of Nursing Management*, 19(6), 742–751. doi:10.1111/j.1365-2834.2011.01264.x

Hogh, A., Mikkelsen, E. G., & Hansen, A. M. (2011). Individual consequences of workplace bullying/mobbing. In S. Einarsen, H. Hoel, D. Zapf, & C. L. Cooper (Eds.), *Bullying and harassment in the workplace: Developments in theory, research, and practice* (2nd ed., pp. 107–128). Boca Raton, FL: CRC Press/Taylor & Francis Group.

Hoobler, J. H., & Brass, D. J. (2006). Abusive supervision and family undermining as displaced aggression. *Journal of Applied Psychology*, 91(5), 1125–1133. doi:10.1037/0021-9010.91.5.1125

Houshmand, M., O'Reilly, J., Robinson, S., & Wolff, A. (2012). Escaping bullying: The simultaneous impact of individual and unit-level bullying on turnover intentions. *Human Relations*, 65(7), 901–918. doi:10.1177/0018726712445100

Ilies, R., Wilson, K. S., & Wagner, D. T. (2009). The spillover of daily job satisfaction onto employees' family lives: The facilitating role of work-family integration. *Academy of Management Journal*, 52(1), 87–102. doi:10.5465/AMJ.2009.36461938

Jenkins, M. F., Zapf, D., Winefield, H., & Sarris, A. (2011). Bullying allegations from the accused bully's perspective. *British Journal of Management*, 23(4), 489–501. doi:10.1111/j.1467-8551.2011.00778.x

Jennifer, D., Cowie, H., & Anaiadou, K. (2003). Perceptions and experience of workplace bullying in five different working populations. *Aggressive Behavior*, 29(6), 489–496. doi:10.1002/ab.10055

Keashly, L. (2010, November 14–17). *From observation to engagement: Building coworker efficacy to address bullying*. Paper presented at the National Communication Association 96th Annual Convention, Chicago, Illinois.

Keashly, L., & Harvey, S. (2005). Emotional abuse in the workplace. In S. Fox & P. Spector (Eds.), *Counterproductive work behaviors* (pp. 201–236). Washington, D.C.: American Psychological Association.

Kim, H. S. (2011). Consequences of parental divorce for child development. *American Sociological Review*, 76(3), 487–511. doi:10.1177/0003122411407748

Kivimäki, M., Ferrie, J. E., Brunner, E., Head, J., Shipley, M. J., Vahtera, J., & Marmot, M. G. (2005). Justice at work and reduced risk of coronary heart disease among employees. *Archives of Internal Medicine*, 165(19), 2245–2251. doi:10.1001/archinte.165.19.2245

Krahé, B. (2013). *The social psychology of aggression* (2nd ed.). New York: Psychology Press.

Kramer, M. W., & Hess, J. A. (2002). Communication rules for the display of emotions in organizational settings. *Management Communication Quarterly*, 16(1), 66–80. doi:10.1177/0893318902161003

Krouse, S. S., & Afifi, T. D. (2007). Family-to-work spillover stress: Coping communicatively in the workplace. *Journal of Family Communication*, 7(2), 85–122. doi:10.1080/15267430701221537

Leonard, K. E., & Eiden, R. D. (2007). Marital and family processes in the context of alcohol use and alcohol disorders. *Annual Review of Clinical Psychology*, 3, 285. doi:10.1146/annurev.clinpsy.3.022806.091424

Lewis, S. E., & Orford, J. (2005). Women's experiences of workplace bullying: Changes in social relations. *Journal of Community and Applied Social Psychology*, 15(1), 29–47. doi:10.1002/casp.807

Leymann, H. (1990). Mobbing and psychological terror at workplaces. *Violence and Victims*, 5(2), 119–126.

Leymann, H., & Gustafsson, A. (1996). Mobbing at work and the development of post-traumatic stress disorders. *European Journal of Work and Organizational Psychology*, 5(2), 251–275.

Lutgen-Sandvik, P. (2006). Take this job and . . . : Quitting and other forms of resistance to workplace bullying. *Communication Monographs*, 73(4), 406–433. doi:10.1080/03637750601024156

Lutgen-Sandvik, P. (2008). Intensive remedial identity work: Responses to workplace bullying trauma and stigmatization. *Organization*, 15(1), 97–119. doi:10.1177/1350508407084487

Lutgen-Sandvik, P. (2013). *Adult bullying—A nasty piece of work: A decade of research on non-sexual harassment, psychological terror, and emotional abuse on the job*. St. Louis, MO: ORCM Press.

Lutgen-Sandvik, P. (2016). *Burned at work and at home: Adult bullying prevalence, features, and effects on personal life*. Unpublished manuscript, North Dakota State University. Fargo, ND.

Lutgen-Sandvik, P., Alberts, J. K., & Tracy, S. J. (2008, February 15–19). *The communicative character of workplace bullying and responses to bullying*. Paper presented at the Western States Communication Association Annual Convention, Denver/Boulder, Colorado.

Lutgen-Sandvik, P., Dickinson, E., & Foss, K. A. (2012). Painting, priming, peeling, and polishing: Constructing and deconstructing the woman-bullying-woman identity at work. In S. Fox & T. R. Lituchy (Eds.), *Gender and the dysfunctional workplace* (pp. 61–77). Northampton, MA: Edward Elgar Publishing.

Lutgen-Sandvik, P., & Fletcher, C. V. (2014). Conflict motivations and tactics of targets, bystanders, and bullies: A thrice-told tale of workplace bullying In J. G. Oetzel & S. Ting-Toomey (Eds.), *Sage handbook of conflict communication* (2nd ed., pp. 349–376). Thousand Oaks, CA: Sage.

Lutgen-Sandvik, P., & McDermott, V. (2011). Making sense of supervisory bullying: Perceived powerlessness, empowered possibilities. *Southern Communication Journal*, 76(4), 342–368. doi:10.1080/10417941003725307

Lutgen-Sandvik, P., & Namie, R. (2010, June 2–4). *Effects of bullying on interpersonal relationships: Tales from non-bullied partners*. Paper prepared for the 7th International Conference on Workplace Bullying and Harassment, Cardiff, Wales.

Lutgen-Sandvik, P., & Sypher, B. D. (Eds.). (2009). *Destructive organizational communication: Processes, consequences, and constructive ways of organizing*. New York: Routledge/Taylor & Francis.

Lutgen-Sandvik, P., & Tracy, S. J. (2012). Answering five key questions about workplace bullying: How communication scholarship provides thought leadership for transforming abuse at work. *Management Communication Quarterly*, 26(1), 3–47. doi:10.1177/0893318911414400

Lutgen-Sandvik, P., Tracy, S. J., & Alberts, J. K. (2007). Burned by bullying in the American workplace: Prevalence, perception, degree and impact. *Journal of Management Studies, 44*(6), 837–862. doi:10.1111/j.1467-6486.2007.00715.x

MacIntosh, J. (2005). Experiences of workplace bullying in a rural area. *Issues in Mental Health Nursing, 26*(9), 893–910. doi:10.1080/01612840500248189

Malinauskiene, V., Obelenis, V., & Sopagiene, D. (2005). Psychological terror at work and cardiovascular diseases among teachers. *Acta Medica Lituanica, 12*(2), 20–25.

Marcus-Newhall, A., Pedersen, W. C., Carlson, M., & Miller, N. (2000). Displaced aggression is alive and well: A meta-analytic review. *Journal of Personality and Social Psychology, 78*(4), 670–689. doi:10.1037/0022-3514.78.4.670

Matthiesen, S. B., & Einarsen, S. (2004). Psychiatric distress and symptoms of PTSD among victims of bullying at work. *British Journal of Guidance and Counseling, 32*(3), 335–356. doi:10.1080/03069880410001723558

McCroskey, J. C., & Richmonda, V. P. (2000). Applying reciprocity and accommodation theories to supervisor/subordinate communication. *Journal of Applied Communication Research, 28*(3), 278–289.

Mulder, R., Pouwelse, M., Lodewijkx, H., & Bolman, C. (2014). Workplace mobbing and bystanders' helping behaviour towards victims: The role of gender, perceived responsibility and anticipated stigma by association. *International Journal of Psychology, 49*(4), 304–312. doi:10.1002/ijop.12018

Namie, G. (2003). *The WBI 2003 report on abusive workplaces*. Retrieved October 19, 2003, from http://www.bullyinginstitute.org

Namie, G. (2007). *The WBTI 2007 U.S. Workplace Bullying Survey*. Retrieved March 4, 2012, from http://bullyinginstitute.org/wbi-zogby2.html

Namie, G., & Lutgen-Sandvik, P. (2010). Active and passive accomplices: The communal character of workplace bullying. *International Journal of Communication, 4*, 343–373.

Neuman, J. H., & Baron, R. A. (2005). Aggression in the workplace: A social-psychological perspective. In S. Fox & P. Spector (Eds.), *Counterproductive work behaviors* (pp. 13–40). Washington, D.C.: American Psychological Association.

Nielsen, M. B., & Einarsen, S. (2012). Outcomes of exposure to workplace bullying: A meta-analytic review. *Work & Stress, 26*(4), 309–332. doi:10.1080/02678373.2012.734709

Olweus, D. (2003). Bully/victim problems in school: Basic facts and an effective intervention programme. In S. Einarsen, H. Hoel, D. Zapf, & C. L. Cooper (Eds.), *Bullying and emotional abuse in the workplace: International perspectives in research and practice* (pp. 62–78). London, England: Francis & Taylor.

Poelmans, S., Stepanova, O., Masuda, A., Korabik, K., Lero, D., & Whitehead, D. (2008). Spillover between personal and professional life: Definitions, antecedents, consequences, and strategies. In K. Korabik, D. S. Lero, & D. L. Whitehead (Eds.), *The handbook of work-family integration: Research, theory, and best practices* (pp. 141–156). London, England: Elsevier.

Qureshi, M. I., Iftikhar, M., Janjua, S. Y., Zaman, K., Raja, U. M., & Javed, Y. (2015). Empirical investigation of mobbing, stress and employees' behavior at work place:

Quantitatively refining a qualitative model. *Quality & Quantity, 49*(1), 93–113. doi:10.1007/s11135-013-9976-4

Richman, J. A., Rospenda, K. M., Flaherty, J. A., & Freels, S. (2001). Workplace harassment, active coping, and alcohol-related outcomes. *Journal of Substance Abuse, 13*(3), 347–366. doi:10.1016/S0899-3289(01)00079-7

Riforgiate, S. E., & Lutgen-Sandvik, P. (2014, June 19–21). *Integrating and separating: Exploring perceptions and emotions associated with work-life boundary strength and spillover.* Paper presented at the Work and Family Researchers Network Annual Convention, New York.

Roeters, A., Van Der Lippe, T., & Kluwer, E. S. (2009). Parental work demands and the frequency of child-related routine and interactive activities. *Journal of Marriage and Family, 71*(5), 1193–1204. doi:10.1111/j.1741-3737.2009.00663.x

Rospenda, K. M. (2002). Workplace harassment, service utilization, and drinking outcomes. *Journal of Occupational Health Psychology, 7*(2), 141–155.

Scully, M., & Rowe, M. (2009). Bystander training within organizations. *Journal of the International Ombudsman Association, 2*(1), 89–95.

Sias, P. M., Gallagher, E. B., Kopaneva, I., & Pedersen, H. (2012). Maintaining workplace friendships: Perceived politeness and predictors of maintenance tactic choice. *Communication Research, 39*(2), 239–268. doi:10.1177/0093650210396869

Smokowski, P. R., & Kopasz, K. H. (2005). Bullying in school: An overview of types, effects, family characteristics, and intervention strategies. *Children & Schools, 27*(2), 101–110. doi:10.1093/cs/27.2.101

Soares, A. (2012). When darkness comes: Workplace bullying and suicidal ideation. In N. Tehrani (Ed.), *Workplace bullying: Symptoms and solutions* (pp. 67–80). London, England: Routledge.

Sperry, D. M., & Widom, C. S. (2013). Child abuse and neglect, social support, and psychopathology in adulthood: A prospective investigation. *Child Abuse & Neglect, 37*(6), 415–425. doi:10.1016/j.chiabu.2013.02.006

Sperry, L., & Duffy, M. (2009). Workplace mobbing: Family dynamics and therapeutic considerations. *American Journal of Family Therapy, 37*(5), 433–442. doi:10.1080/01926180902945756

Staines, G. L. (1980). Spillover versus compensation: A review of the literature on the relationship between work and nonwork. *Human Relations, 33*(2), 111–129. doi:10.1177/001872678003300203

Thompson, B. M., Kirk, A., & Brown, D. F. (2005). Work based support, emotional exhaustion, and spillover of work stress to the family environment: A study of policewomen. *Stress and Health, 21*(3), 199–207. doi:10.1002/smi.1056

Twemlow, S. W., Fonagy, P., & Sacco, F. C. (2004). The role of the bystander in the social architecture of bullying and violence in schools and communities. *Annals of the New York Academy of Science, 1036*(1), 215–232. doi:10.1196/annals.1330.014

Tye-Williams, S., & Krone, K. J. (2015). Chaos, reports, and quests: Narrative agency and co-workers in stories of workplace bullying. *Management Communication Quarterly, 29*(1), 3–27. doi:10.1177/0893318914552029

van Heugten, K. (2010, June 2–4). *Engaging bystanders as change agents in workplace bullying.* Paper presented at the 7th International Conference on Workplace Bullying and Harassment, Cardiff, Wales.

Vartia, M. (2001). Consequences of workplace bullying with respect to the well-being of its targets and the observers of bullying. *Scandinavian Journal of Work Environment and Health*, 27(1), 63–69.

Vickers, M. H. (2006). Toward employee wellness: Rethinking bullying paradoxes and masks. *Employee Responsibilities and Rights Journal*, 18(4), 267–281.

Vranceanu, A.-M., Barsky, A., & Ring, D. (2009). Psychosocial aspects of disabling musculoskeletal pain. *Journal of Bone & Joint Surgery*, 91(8), 2014–2018. doi:10.2106/JBJS.H.01512

Weissman, M. M., Warner, V., Wickramaratne, P., Moreau, D., & Olfson, M. (1997). Offspring of depressed parents: 10 years later. *Archives of General Psychiatry*, 54(10), 932–940. doi:10.1001/archpsyc.1997.01830220054009

Yildirim, A., & Yildirim, D. (2007). Mobbing in the workplace by peers and managers: Mobbing experienced by nurses working in healthcare facilities in Turkey and its effect on nurses. *Journal of Clinical Nursing*, 16(8), 1444–1453. doi:10.1111/j.1365-2702.2006.01814.x

Young, J. C., & Widom, C. S. (2014). Long-term effects of child abuse and neglect on emotion processing in adulthood. *Child Abuse & Neglect*, 38(8), 1369–1381. doi:10.1016/j.chiabu.2014.03.008

9

When Workplace Bullying and Mobbing Occur: The Impact on Organizations

Renee L. Cowan

A recent *New York Times* article (Kantor & Streitfeld, 2015) highlighting Amazon.com's negative and often abusive workplace culture and practices has brought to the fore an example of the effects aggressive, uncivil, and bullying practices can have on an organization. The article highlights such examples as rampant sabotaging of fellow coworkers, high turnover, employees regularly crying after grueling meetings, and shunning of those who cannot or will not work excessive hours. The article argues these practices are reflective of the Amazon culture. One former employee commented, "I would see people practically combust" (Kantor & Streitfeld, 2015, p. 2), and another told the authors, "Nearly every person I worked with, I saw cry at their desk" (p. 7).

It is clear bullying can be detrimental to perceptions of an organization's culture, resulting in trouble finding and retaining valuable talent. The focus of this chapter is the negative impact bullying and mobbing have on organizations. In the United States, it is clear bullying has negative effects on employees, groups, and the organizations. This chapter will specifically concentrate on the negative consequences to organizations at the individual, group, and organizational levels.

INDIVIDUAL-LEVEL AFFECTIVE ATTITUDINAL AND BEHAVIORAL CONSEQUENCES

U.S. researchers Neuman and Baron's (2005) *general affective aggression model* demonstrates that engaging in aggressive behavior can be attributed to a complex of cognitive, attitudinal, and physiological processes as well as past experiences and culture. Some of these aggressive and bullying behaviors include isolation, insults, threats, physically aggressive gestures, yelling and verbal abuse, and others (Fox & Cowan, 2014). Bullying behaviors and characteristics are discussed in detail in chapter 1. The effects of the negative behaviors associated with bullying and mobbing and the repetition of these behaviors can lead targets to be insecure, reduce communication, lack initiative, become depressed, and suffer from myriad stress-induced health issues, to name just a few (Davenport, Schwartz, & Elliott, 2005; Duffy & Sperry, 2014; Namie & Namie, 2011; Nielsen & Einarsen, 2012). The effects on targets are discussed in detail in chapters 5 and 6. U.S. researcher Lutgen-Sandvik (2008), in her work with American employees, found that the bullying experience resulted in a deep rupture to the targets' sense of who they were or their identity.

Likewise, Duffy & Sperry (2014), also U.S. researchers, discuss the severe impacts to the employee, their families, coworkers, and the organization when mobbing occurs. It has been argued that when systematic abuse such as bullying occurs, this moves targets to believe that the organization is also responsible for the abuse and not protecting them (Namie, Christensen, & Phillips, 2014; Rose, Shuck, Twyford, & Bergman, 2015). The Workplace Bullying Institute (Namie et al., 2014) found that 28 percent of targets believe the organization is responsible or to blame for the bullying. And Hollis (2015), who surveyed those in U.S. higher education administration (student affairs, human resources, executives, academic faculty, and others), found that 47 percent of administrators reported the organization did nothing in bullying situations or supported the bully. These effects and negative perceptions have real consequences for organizations, including lower job satisfaction, less organizational commitment, workplace disengagement, lower productivity and performance, increased intentions to leave, and actual turnover. The attitudinal, affective, and behavioral consequences of bullying for organizations will be the focus of this section; consequences will be discussed, and U.S. research will specifically be highlighted.

Attitudinal and Affective Consequences of Bullying

Recent research has made it quite clear that contemporary U.S. employees react negatively when subjected to abusive supervisors who bully or are caught working in organizations that condone this type of behavior. From decreased job satisfaction and workplace engagement to lowered overall organizational commitment, there are a host of negative attitudinal and affective consequences of bullying (Rose et al., 2015). Tepper (2000) demonstrated that abusive supervision or working under a bully boss results in less job satisfaction and less normative and affective commitment to the organization for U.S employees. These consequences were even more pronounced for those who felt they could not escape the situation and had less mobility. These findings have been echoed across the world, as evidenced in Nielsen and

Einarsen's (2012) meta-analysis of over 60 studies on bullying. Their subsequent model and findings demonstrate several negative organizational consequences of bullying, particularly reduced job satisfaction and organizational commitment.

Furthermore, Hershcovis and Barling (2010) also conducted a meta-analysis using 66 studies and demonstrated workplace aggression, including bullying, results in a host of negative consequences (e.g., turnover intent, interpersonal and organizational deviance, depression, emotional exhaustion), and these outcomes differ in magnitude depending on the perpetrator. Aggression and bullying enacted by supervisors resulted in the strongest negative relationships with satisfaction and organizational commitment; however, coworker aggression also resulted in significant negative relationships with these variables as well. It is clear that when bullying is present in organizations, those who are targeted feel less satisfied and committed to the organization. In many of these studies, the link is also made with lower productivity and intentions to leave as well as actual turnover (Hershcovis & Barling, 2010; Nielsen & Einarsen, 2012; Rose et al., 2015). Effects on productivity and intention to leave will be discussed in a subsequent section.

Beyond job satisfaction and organizational commitment, U.S. researchers Rose, Shuck, Twyford, and Bergman (2015) recently demonstrated dysfunctional and abusive leadership, seen in some bullying cases, results in negative effects such as lower motivation and less organizational citizenship behaviors (or behaviors that promote effective organizational functioning and are done simply for the good of the organization). Another related affective response to bullying is workplace disengagement (Hollis, 2015). U.S. researcher Hollis (2015) recently found bullying has a significant impact on how employees spend their time at work. In her study with higher education administrators, she found that 62 percent of respondents reported they had been the target of or had witnessed bullying, and this translated to 3.9 hours a day spent avoiding the workplace bully, or, put another way, disengaged from work.

Law, Dollard, Tuckey, and Dormann (2011) investigated the effect of workplace bullying on employee engagement more directly. For Australian employees, they found workplace engagement suffered when bullying occurred. *Workplace engagement* refers to "an individual employee's cognitive, emotional and behavioral state directed toward desired organization outcomes" (Shuck & Wollard, 2010, p. 103). Although workplace engagement has not been directly studied in U.S. bullying situations, Reio and Sanders-Reio (2011), U.S. researchers, found that workplace incivility (a milder form of workplace aggression) results in negative effects on workplace engagement. It is likely U.S. employees would also report less workplace engagement if being targeted by an office bully or stuck in an organization with a culture of bullying; however, this is an area that still needs to be empirically explored in the United States. Taken together, when bullying is present in organizations, targets and others feel less satisfied with their jobs, they are less motivated to work, they feel less valued, and they spend their time avoiding the bullying and disengaged from their job and workplace. With consequences such as these, it is clear there will be behavioral consequences; employees are likely to try to spend less time in this toxic environment, be less productive, and even exit the organization.

Negative Behavioral Consequences of Bullying

Absenteeism

A significant behavioral consequence of workplace bullying is increased absenteeism (taking sick time to stay away from work). There is much evidence that demonstrates bullying and mobbing are associated with increased absenteeism (Duffy & Sperry, 2014; Hoel, Sheehan, Cooper & Einarsen, 2011; Nielsen & Einarsen, 2012). Research in the United States and other countries has found that absence can be attributed to the degrading health status of the targeted employee as well as a lack of motivation to be in the abusive environment (Duffy & Sperry, 2014; Hoel et al., 2011). And recently it was found that long-term sickness absence was more prevalent for those who were frequently bullied (Ortega, Christensen, Hogh, Rugulies, & Borg, 2011). The cost of target illness, long-term sickness leave, and associated medical costs will be the focus of a subsequent section. In the United States, research conducted by the Workplace Bullying Institute (WBI; 2013) found that when targets take leave, they report using the Family Medical Leave Act (FMLA) and workers' compensation (WC). Bullying and mobbing can also result in presenteeism.

Presenteeism

Another significant behavioral consequence of workplace bullying is increased *presenteeism*, or going to work while sick. According to the same WBI report (2013), 51 percent of workplace bullied targets reported taking no leave and likely went to work sick. Johns (2010) describes presenteeism as "at work, but not working" because of health problems and illness (p. 520). Presenteeism, as a consequence of bullying, could be attributed to the fact that there is no paid sick leave law requiring organizations in the United States to provide paid sick leave to employees (Namie & Namie, 2011; WBI, 2013). This leaves many targets with no choice but to continue to go to work sick and endure the bullying environment. Johns (2010) reports that depression and "mental and nervous" (p. 529) problems resulted in more days lost to presenteeism. These are often health conditions associated with frequent bullying (Namie & Namie, 2011). In the United States, researchers have concentrated on the productivity consequences of presenteeism and found that presenteeism actually accounts for more productivity loss than absenteeism (Johns, 2010).

Performance and productivity

Aggression, such as that experienced in bullying situations, has been associated with lower performance and productivity. Hershcovis and Barling (2010) argue that when employees (targets and bystanders) are subjected to an extreme stressor, such as workplace bullying, they exhaust their cognitive and emotional energy dealing with the stressor and therefore have less energy to focus on performance and productivity. U.S. researcher Lutgen-Sandvik (2003) similarly argues that when workers experience emotional abuse at the hands of their supervisors or bully bosses, their focus shifts from their jobs and being productive to self-protection.

Also, Davenport and colleagues (2005) point to a reduction in the quality and quantity of work when dealing with mobbing. European researchers have found that bullying can lead to insecurity and a lack of concentration that leads to mistakes (Hoel, Sparks, & Cooper, 2001) Similarly, job strain and bullying have been found to result in depression-related productivity loss in Australia (McTernan, Dollard, & LaMontagne, 2013). In the United States, there is empirical evidence that low job satisfaction and organizational commitment are related to lower productivity (Judge, Thoerson, Bono, & Patton, 2001), but clearer links to bullying still need to be explored. Samnani and Singh (2014) argue that performance-enhancing compensation strategies (popular in U.S. organizations) that are supposed to encourage productivity likely have the opposite effect: encouraging bullying and less productivity. Taken together, the negative effects on employees' attitudes toward and affect for the organization as well as their resulting behaviors (more absenteeism, presenteeism, and lower productivity), it is not surprising many employees exit these organizations.

Intent to leave and turnover

Bullying and mobbing have been associated with increased turnover in organizations as well as higher intentions to leave the organization (Namie & Namie, 2011; Nielsen & Einarsen, 2012). Escaping the organization and the abuse is often reported as the only action that fully stops the situation (Namie & Namie, 2011; Lutgen-Sandvik, 2006) and is an effect of experiencing and acting to escape severe stress. Glambek, Matthisen, Hetland, and Einarsen (2014) found in their longitudinal study that workplace bullying was an antecedent to job insecurity and intention to leave. Turnover costs organizations money and possibly knowledge loss when the target leaves (Namie & Namie, 2011; Hoel et al., 2011). Turnover could hurt the organization's reputation if talent continues to leave and if employees are considering leaving because of abuse or witnessing abuse (Namie & Namie, 2011). Leading U.S. scholars on bullying and mobbing even advise employees to seek out "healthy" organizations and determine the organization's health status not only on the traditional dimension of profitability and overall performance but also on the well-being of their employees (Duffy & Sperry, 2014). If sought-after employees attend to organizational health preemployment, those organizations not deemed "healthy" will clearly have a harder time recruiting and retaining talent.

As the Amazon.com situation reported in the *New York Times* (Kantor & Streitfeld, 2015) demonstrates, U.S. targets leave or intend to leave organizations where abuse such as mobbing and bullying occur. A 2010 WBI research study demonstrates 41 percent of women and 36 percent of men who were bullied quit because of the bullying (as cited in Namie & Namie, 2011). However, WBI (2013) research also found it is hard for bullied U.S. employees to leave their jobs, which, in turn, increases presenteeism. They report that the effect of income loss was reported as the hardest reason to leave, followed by personal pride (or the idea that leaving is losing and the bully wins). Johnson and Rea (2009) found bullying was linked with an intent to leave the organization among nurses in Washington State. Lutgen-Sandvik (2006) found targets threatened to quit, encouraged others to quit, celebrated those who left, and actually left the organization in reaction to bullying.

Lutgen-Sandvik (2003) also theorized a *cycle of employee emotional abuse*, building on Swedish researcher Leymann's (1990) ideas on what actually happens in workplace emotional abuse situations. Lutgen-Sandvik (2003) theorized that not only do targets typically leave, get fired, or get pushed out of organizations, but this cycle regenerates and begins again with a new target after the previous target exits the organization. This theory points to a seemingly endless exit and turnover of bullied employees, which, if not arrested, will likely have negative effects on those who remain in the organization as well as on the organization's reputation.

Similarly, Keashly (2001) found when targets do not feel satisfied with an organization's actions and responses to bullying situations, this could also lead to intentions to leave. As Namie and Namie (2011) contend, responsibly dealing with bullying greatly benefits organizations, and left unchecked, bullying "kills good organizations" (p. 31). One way it begins to kill good organizations is through social influence and the infecting of those in and around the bullying situation.

GROUP-LEVEL NEGATIVE CONSEQUENCES FOR ORGANIZATIONS

It is clear that bullying and mobbing not only affect the targets of the abuse but others in the organization or work group who witness the abuse. The impact of bullying and mobbing on bystanders and witnesses is the focus of chapter 8, authored by Lutgen-Sandvik. However, because bullying can have a ripple effect on those witnessing the behavior and an impact on the social relationships in the organization (D'Cruz & Noronha, 2011; Namie & Namie, 2011, Rose et al., 2015), it can thus have an impact on the organization and its functioning, as it is very difficult to remain neutral in bullying cases (Namie & Namie, 2011; Namie & Lutgen-Sandvik, 2010). Therefore, I will also briefly discuss this issue.

U.S. researchers Namie and Lutgen-Sandvik (2010) talk about bullying as having a "communal character," where bullies often have active and passive accomplices. U.S. researchers Rose and colleagues (2015) report there is a spillover effect to groups, teams, and other units when dysfunctional leaders enact abuse. When employees believe that the organization could and should do something about the abuse, they report reducing their productivity in response, which can obviously have detrimental effects on overall organizational functioning and productivity (Davenport et al., 2005).

U.S. researchers Andersson and Pearson (1999) point to an almost multiplier effect where incivility escalates and multiplies, spreading and infecting work units and groups and even the organization's culture. Hoel, Sparks, and Cooper (2001) report bullying often results in a "climate of fear" (p. 4) that produces similar mental and physical health problems for witnesses and bystanders. Davenport and colleagues (2005) suggest mobbing can damage teamwork and cohesiveness in work groups. Other effects include a poor psychological environment (Vartia, 2001), a poor work environment, poor attitudes, and poor individual well-being (Cooper-Thomas et al., 2014) and persistent negativity in the workplace (Lutgen-Sandvik, Tracy, & Alberts, 2007). And employees report bullying hurts workplace relationships as well as adds to feelings of work overload and workplace negativity (Jennifer, Cowie, & Ananiadou, 2003).

Clearly, these effects can hurt the organization in terms of productivity, morale, and functioning as well as lead to a negative reputation of the company as one that is not healthy to work in (Davenport et al., 2005; Duffy & Sperry, 2014). However, in the United States, issues such as how witnesses and bystanders respond to bullying, how it affects them, what they do and do not do, and how this all ultimately affects the organization as a whole are only beginning to be explored. Research on how the group-level consequences of bullying and mobbing affect the organization, its reputation, and functioning should all be subjects of future bullying research.

ORGANIZATION-LEVEL NEGATIVE CONSEQUENCES

As discussed in the previous section, bullying and mobbing can hurt organizational culture and a positive working environment (Duffy & Sperry, 2014). Decreased employee satisfaction and commitment, increased presenteeism and absenteeism, higher intentions to leave and turnover, the spillover effect of increased aggression and negativity, and damaged workplace relationships all work to harm the organization and its reputation. These negative consequences also distract from the organization's mission and work to be done. Even the rumor that the organization might suffer from a negative culture or be led by an aggressive and uncaring leader can result in negative perceptions of the organization and repercussions in attracting good talent. (Consider the negative attention Amazon.com garnered after the scathing *New York Times* article (Kantor & Streitfeld, 2015) exposed a "bruising workplace" (see Liacas, 2015; Wemple, 2015).)

In this section, I will discuss how bullying and mobbing result in both intangible and tangible costs to organizations (Namie & Namie, 2011). Bullying and mobbing result in negative organizational-level consequences, such as damage to reputation and work culture, as well as increased monetary costs in several areas, including legal costs, threat of litigation, and increased disability and health costs.

Intangible Costs: Negative Organizational Culture and Loss of Reputation

A negative, aggressive, and dysfunctional organizational culture is often discussed as an antecedent to bullying situations in organizations (Cowan, 2014; Goodboy, Martin, Knight, & Long, 2015; Keashly & Jagatic, 2011; Salin, 2003). Organizational risk factors that encourage bullying are the focus of chapter 4. Here I will explore how a negative organizational culture and dysfunctional climate can also be an outcome or a consequence of bullying activity left unaddressed. Recent WBI (2013) research demonstrates that many U.S. organizations do nothing about bullying and mobbing when they learn it is occurring. Namie and Lutgen-Sandvik (2010) found that targets and witnesses overwhelmingly believe organizations are also responsible for bullying and do nothing in these situations. Namie, Christensen, and Phillips (2014) also found that U.S. organizations most often react to reports of bullying in a negative way, including denying that it is happening (25%), discounting the situation as not being serious (16%), and rationalizing it as a way of doing business (15%).

In the United States, most targets report bullying continues unabated even when the target seeks help from human resources (HR) and other leaders in the organizations (Lutgen-Sandvik, 2003; WBI, 2012b). Targets report that when they went to HR to seek help, HR actions were not helpful and retaliation followed (37%), or HR did nothing and took no action (30%). Targets report their organizations do not have specific antiharassment policies that specifically address bullying (61%), and if they do, these are not applied fairly

(17%). I found when interviewing U.S. HR representatives that most do not have a policy that addresses bullying, and others have a policy that they feel could be used in bullying situations, even though it is not a specific antibullying policy (Cowan, 2011). However, when the latter were analyzed, it was clear they would provide little tangible help for targets in bullying situations.

I speculate in this work that the absence of clear and specific antibullying policies communicates to employees that the organization does not care about these situations and will not act to stop them (Cowan, 2011). Even when organizations have policies that directly address bullying, they do no good unless they are implemented fairly and consistently (Woodrow & Guest, 2014). Mishandling of bullying by HR (especially when leaders or managers are accused) serves to erode trust, which can have detrimental effects and hurt the work environment (Harrington, Rayner, & Warren, 2012).

When leadership does nothing to stop bullying and HR does not have a policy that will actually address the situation, bullying becomes the "way things are done" and can result in negative organizational cultures and climates. U.S. researchers Pearson and Porath (2005) argue that incivility (a mild form of workplace aggression) left unchecked erodes organizational values and is too costly to be ignored. Taking this research into consideration, bullying—a more severe form of workplace aggression—likely does even more damage to an organization's mission, culture, working environment, and productivity (Davenport et al., 2005; Hoel et al., 2011). All of these issues affect reputation and the ability to attract and retain talent (Duffy & Sperry, 2014; Giga, Hoel, & Lewis, 2008; Pearson & Porath, 2005). Bullying and mobbing not only result in intangible costs for organizations but also tangible costs to the bottom line.

Tangible Costs: Leaves, Turnover, and Insurance Claims

How much does bullying and mobbing cost U.S. organizations? What is the monetary cost of not addressing this aggression or mishandling complaints and reports of bullying? The answers to these questions will be the focus of this section. The emotional, physical, and psychological impacts of bullying and mobbing are the focus of previous chapters in this book set. The research reported in these chapters demonstrates that in the United States, severe and traumatic health-related consequences are experienced as an effect of bullying and mobbing. Severe anxiety, loss of concentration, depression, mood swings, and post-traumatic stress disorder (PTSD) are all reported as symptoms associated with prolonged bullying and mobbing (Davenport et al., 2005; Duffy & Sperry, 2014; WBI, 2012a).

Severe physical effects of bullying and mobbing are also reported, including headaches, sleep problems, fatigue, and exhaustion (Duffy & Sperry,

2014; WBI, 2012a). WBI (2012a) also found in its survey of targets that 71 percent seek help from a physician and 63 percent saw a mental health professional. Another WBI (2013) poll found that 49 percent of targets surveyed take a voluntary or forced leave of absence, and 17 percent used short- or long-term disability leave. While it is a good sign that targets are seeking the medical attention they need, at the same time, this results in increased health care costs and risk to organizations. The significant impact on the health of targets and others in the abusive environment leads to increased leaves of absence (medical, disability, and others); turnover and replacement costs; and increased insurance claims (Namie & Namie, 2011).

Unchecked bullying and mobbing hits organizations straight in the pocketbook. Some cost estimates can range from $16,000 to $1 million per employee affected by the abuse (Hoel et al., 2011). Disability and medical leaves of absence, turnover, and increased insurance claims are all consequences of bullying and mobbing that cost the organization (Davenport et al., 2005; Namie & Namie, 2011). A recent study conducted by the Integrated Benefits Institute found poor health costs U.S. businesses $576 billion a year (Japson, 2012). This estimate accounts for many of the consequences associated with bullying, including wage replacement costs, medical and disability leaves ($117 billion), and productivity loss from absenteeism and presenteeism ($227 billion; Japson, 2012). We know that targets and others in the toxic culture eventually move to escape it, and one of the ways they do this is by taking sick leave, disability leave, and medical leave (WBI, 2013). One source estimated targets missed an average of 159 days of work on leave due to the psychological stress of bullying (Namie & Namie, 2011). Before these leaves are taken, we know affected workers come to work sick, as previously discussed, which also costs organizations. The Integrated Benefits Institute report (Japson, 2012) argues these costs are due in large part to prolonged illnesses such as depression and heart issues, which are health conditions associated with bullying and mobbing (Davenport et al., 2005; Duffy & Sperry, 2014; McTernan et al., 2013).

Hollis (2015) estimated the average cost of turnover associated with bullying for higher education personnel was $100,500. Focusing more specifically on the costs of turnover to organizations, in the United States, it is argued that those who are exemplary workers are those who are often bullied or mobbed, and they exit the organization because of the abuse (Duffy & Sperry, 2014; Lutgen-Sandvik, 2006; Namie & Namie, 2011). Organizations lose the value these exemplary workers create (WBI, 2016). This means replacement costs for these workers are high, as loss of knowledge and productivity suffer when exemplary employees have to be replaced. These are general cost estimates. The extent to which a particular organization is monetarily affected by bullying and mobbing will differ and will likely be more expensive for some organizations than others.

The WBI (2016) Web site gives employees in the United States a way to calculate the actual cost of bullying and mobbing on their particular organization and work unit based on individual employee counts. They suggest that time and number of employees affected estimates should be calculated first. How long was the bully allowed to operate without the issue being addressed? How many employees were affected? They argue, "Individually-based cost estimates calculated should pertain to all the people directly targeted for bullying AND those who were aware of it and indicated a desire to quit, transfer or took time off to repair their health. Research clearly indicates that witnesses are affected almost as strongly as the bullied" (WBI, 2016, para. 2). Witnesses and bystanders should be included in these individual estimates to determine a realistic estimate of how much bullying actually costs a particular organization.

WBI suggests several factors should be estimated and added together to determine the actual cost of bullying per individual (turnover, opportunity lost, absenteeism, presenteeism, legal defense cost, dispute resolution, trial costs, dispute resolution, settlements, workers' compensation, and disability claims). For conservative turnover estimates, they suggest multiplying the combined salaries of those employees who left by 1.5 (e.g., $50k salary would result in $75k to recruit and replace just this one employee; WBI, 2016). Absenteeism cost estimates can be calculated by dividing a salaried worker's annual salary by 2020 and getting an hourly rate (for nonsalaried, just use the hourly pay rate) and multiply this by hours off the job (e.g., $10 an hour multiplied by 1,272 (159 × 8 hours) – 159 is the average number of days missed according to Namie and Namie (2011), which results in $12,720 absentee cost). The tangible costs of litigation, dispute resolution, legal defense and settlements, and consultant costs will be discussed in the next section.

Tangible Costs: Litigation, Legal, and Consultant Costs

How much does it cost U.S. organizations to deal with the aftermath of bullying and mobbing in terms of litigation, increased legal costs, and trained consultants? The answer to this question will be the focus of this section. First, when organizations begin to address the toxic work environment and damaged relationships that result from bullying and mobbing, often costly professional consultants need to be retained to make a difference in the situation (Davenport et al., 2005; Lutgen-Sandvik, 2003; Namie & Namie, 2011). The cost of hiring professional consultants to lead mediation and dispute resolution efforts is staggering. Workplace health and safety consultants can cost up to $1,000 a day (this does not include travel and materials costs; United Alliance Services, 2016), and professional mediation services can cost upward of $200 an hour.

Remember, this is a likely scenario, as those who might normally engage in mediation and dispute resolution in an organization (human resources) are often not trusted by bullied targets (Harrington et al., 2012). It is argued that mediation and dispute resolution conducted by organizations, using their own employees who are often complicit in the situation, are not seen as fair and impartial procedures by targets (WBI, 2011). In many of these situations, it is reported that the bully faced no consequences (52%) or the target was terminated (18%) or quit (14%) (WBI, 2011). If the organization truly wants to deal with the issue in a fair manner and repair the workplace climate, avoiding a conflict of interest or perception of a conflict of interest is a necessity. Clearly, seeking the help of consultants can add up very quickly, costing organizations thousands of dollars. Bullying and mobbing also present costly litigation and legal risks to U.S. organizations (Namie & Namie, 2011).

Even though the United States has yet to pass a comprehensive law to address bullying and mobbing in the workplace, employees do still have avenues for legal redress if the situation also includes illegal harassment protected by Title VII (Paetzold, O'Leary-Kelly, & Griffin, 2007; WBI, 2016). A 2007 WBI report found that 20 percent of bullying situations also include illegal conduct related to a protected category (Namie & Namie, 2011). However, it is clear that the majority of bullying cases have little legal recourse. Legal avenues in bullying cases are the subject of chapters 18 and 19. Briefly, the tort of Intentional Infliction of Emotional Distress is a legal avenue for some, but these cases are rarely successful for a variety of reasons (Yamada, 2010, 2013). It is difficult to determine how much bullying costs organizations in terms of monetary awards through legal action because there is no law speaking to this issue; however, Namie and Namie (2011) discuss two cases where bullying cost the offending organization $325,000 and $1.4 million, so clearly this is a potential cost.

Although bullied employees at this point have little tangible legal redress (Yamada, 2013), even the threat of lawsuits is costly to organizations. When threatened with lawsuits, organizations have to retain costly legal teams, and although larger organizations might already employ in-house counsel, small and medium-sized companies may not. The WBI (2016) estimates this costs organizations upward of $30,000 for each threat and $60,000 or more if the lawsuit goes forward. Litigation and legal costs of bullying in countries with developed antibullying laws should prove instructive for the United States. In Norway, a court awarded a bullied target $383,000; in Spain, payouts have been as much as 30,000 euros (Dunn, 2003), and as much as 800,000 euros in the United Kingdom (Yamada, 2010). U.S. organizations should be paying attention, as there is overwhelming support by employees for a law addressing bullying and mobbing in the United States (Namie et al., 2014). And Namie and colleagues' (2014) research poll found that 93 percent of respondents support a new law that would protect workers from repeated abusive treatment over and above existing laws.

The response to these calls for a new law are, in part, being answered by the Healthy Workplace Bill, antibullying legislation authored by David Yamada that has served as the template for legal reform efforts in the United States (see Yamada, 2013). The Healthy Workplace Bill will be discussed in detail in chapter 18. Healthy Workplace Bill advocates urge supporters of antibullying legislation to contact their state legislators and let them know of their support for the bill (The Healthy Workplace Bill, n.d.). U.S. researchers Bergen and Cole (2015) found that if constituents contact their legislator about their views on antibullying bills, the probability the legislator will support the bill increases by 12 percent. This is an encouraging sign for the Healthy Workplace Bill and targets of bullying and mobbing.

In sum, workplace bullying and mobbing have significant impacts on an organization's bottom line. From intangible costs such as a negative organizational culture and working climate and damage to reputation, to the tangible costs of leaves, turnover, insurance claims, litigation, and threats of litigation, workplace bullying and mobbing are too costly for organizations to ignore.

CONCLUSION

In this chapter, I have demonstrated the devastating impact workplace bullying and mobbing can have on organizations by discussing the myriad consequences this abuse can have at the individual, group, and organizational levels. To save organizations from the extreme detrimental effects of bullying, U.S. researchers present many prescriptions and solutions for organizational leaders. Lutgen-Sandvik and Tracy (2012) suggest attending to the micro, meso, and macro factors that encourage bullying and mobbing. Cowan (2011) and others suggest a clear and comprehensive antibullying policy. Namie and Namie (2011) suggest leaders need to mobilize their organizations by recognizing when bullying and mobbing are taking place, trusting reports from their employees, and working to stop the abuse. They can do this by instituting an antibullying program in the organization and attending to factors that encourage abusive behavior.

Specifically addressing mobbing, Duffy and Sperry (2014) suggest a type of restorative justice is needed to help the mobbed individual to recover and try to become whole again. This includes acknowledgment of the abuse, an apology for the abuse, reparation or a repairing of the environment that led to the abuse, and monetary and other resource compensation. Also, Davenport and colleagues (2005) suggest that prevention is key, and this happens when organizations create awareness of mobbing, employees are educated on this type of abuse, and training is provided. They also suggest antimobbing policy, proactive risk assessments by the organization, and clear, fair paths to conflict resolution. The costs and impact of doing nothing in workplace bullying and mobbing situations is too high for any organization, but with action, these negative impacts could be mitigated to the benefit of employees and organizations.

REFERENCES

Andersson, L. M., & Pearson, C. M. (1999). Tit for tat? The spiraling effect of incivility in the workplace. *Academy of Management Review, 24*(3), 352–471. doi:10.5465/AMR.1999.2202131

Bergen, D. E., & Cole, R. T. (2015). Call your legislator: A field experimental study of the impact of a constituency mobilization campaign on legislative voting. *Political Behavior, 37*(1), 27–42. doi:10.1007/s11109-014-9277-1

Cooper-Thomas, H., Bentley, T., Catley, B., Gardner, D., O'Driscoll, M., & Trenberth, L. (2014). The impact of bullying on observers and targets. *New Zealand Journal of Human Resource Management, 14,* 82–95.

Cowan, R. L. (2011). "Yes we have an anti-bullying policy, but . . .": HR professionals' understandings and experiences with workplace bullying policy. *Communication Studies, 62*(3), 307–327. doi:10.1080/10510974.2011.553763

Cowan, R. L. (2014). "**it" rolls down hill and other attributions for why adult bullying happens in organizations from the human resource professional's perspective. *Qualitative Research Reports in Communication, 14,* 97–104. doi:10.1080/17459435.2013.835347

Davenport, N., Schwartz, R. D., & Elliott, G. P. (2005). *Mobbing and emotional abuse in the American workplace.* Collins, IA: Civil Society Publishing.

D'Cruz, P., & Noronha, E. (2011). The limits to workplace friendship: Managerialist and HRM and bystander behavior in the context of workplace bullying. *Employee Relations, 33,* 269–288. doi:10.1108/01425451111121777

Duffy, M., & Sperry, L. (2014). *Overcoming mobbing: A recovery guide for workplace aggression and bullying.* New York: Oxford University Press.

Dunn, S. (2003). What's going on with workplace bullying, mobbing and harassment internationally. Retrieved from http://workplacebullying.org/press/webpronews.html

Fox, S., & Cowan, R. L. (2014). Revision of the workplace bullying checklist: The importance of human resource management's role in defining and addressing workplace bullying. *Human Resource Management Journal, 1,* 116–130. doi:10.1111/1748-8583.12049

Giga, S. I., Hoel, H., & Lewis, D. (2008). The costs of workplace bullying. *Dignity at Work Partnership.* Retrieved from http://www.workplaceviolence.ca/sites/default/files/Giga%20et%20al.%20(2008)-The%20costs%20of%20workplace%20bullying_0.pdf

Glambek, M., Matthiesen, S. B., Hetland, J., and Einarsen, S. (2014). Workplace bullying as an antecedent to job insecurity and intention to leave: A six-month perspective study. *Human Resource Management Journal, 24*(3), 255–268. doi:10.1111/1748-8583.12035

Goodboy, A. K., Martin, M., Knight, J. M., & Long, Z. (2015). Creating the boiler room environment: The job demand-control-support model as an explanation of workplace bullying. *Communication Research* [Advance online publication]. doi:10.1177/0093650215614365

Harrington, S., Rayner, C., & Warren, S. (2012). Too hot to handle? Trust and human resource practitioners' implementation of anti-bullying policy. *Human Resource Management Journal, 22*(4), 392–408. doi:10.1111/1748-8583.12004

The Healthy Workplace Bill. (n.d.). Retrieved from healthyworkplacebill.org

Hershcovis, M. S., & Barling, J. (2010). Towards a multi-foci approach to workplace aggression: A meta-analytic review of outcomes from different perpetrators. *Journal of Organizational Behavior, 31*(1), 24–44. doi:10.1002/job.621

Hoel, H., Sheenan, M. J., Cooper, C. L., & Einarsen, S. (2011). Organizational effects of workplace bullying. In S. Einarsen, H. Hoel, D. Zapf, & C. L. Cooper (Eds.), *Bullying and harassment in the workplace: Developments in theory, research and practice* (pp.129–148). Boca Raton, FL: CRC Press, Taylor & Francis Group.

Hoel, H., Sparks, K., & Cooper, C. L. (2001). *The cost of violence/stress at work and the benefits of a violence/stress-free working environment.* Geneva, Switzerland: International Labour Organisation.

Hollis, L. P. (2015). Bully university?: The cost of workplace bullying and employee disengagement in American higher education. *SAGE Open, 5*(2). doi:10.1177/2158244015589997

Japson, B. (2012). U.S. workforce illness costs $576b annually from sick days to workers' compensation. Retrieved from http://www.forbes.com/sites/brucejapsen/2012/09/12/u-s-workforce-illness-costs-576b-annually-from-sick-days-to-workers-compensation/#989b21c7256f

Jennifer, D., Cowie, H., & Anaiadou, K. (2003). Perceptions and experience of workplace bullying in five different working populations. *Aggressive Behavior, 29*(4), 489–496.

Johns, G. (2010). Presenteeism in the workplace: A review and research agenda. *Journal of Organizational Behavior, 31*(4), 519–542.

Johnson, S. L., & Rea, R. E. (2009). Workplace bullying: Concerns for nurse leaders. *Journal of Nursing of Administration, 39*, 84–90.

Judge, T. A., Thoersen, C. J., Bono, J. E., & Patton, G. K. (2001). The job satisfaction–job performance relationship: A qualitative and quantitative review. *Psychological Bulletin, 127*(3), 376–407. doi:10.1037/0033-2909.127.3.376

Kantor, J., & Streitfeld, D. (2015, August 15). Inside Amazon: Wrestling big ideas in a bruising workplace. *New York Times.* Retrieved from http://www.nytimes.com/2015/08/16/technology/inside-amazon-wrestling-big-ideas-in-a-bruising-workplace.html?_r=0

Keashly. L. (2001). Interpersonal and systemic aspects of emotional abuse at work: The target's perspective. *Violence and Victims, 16*(3), 233–268.

Keashly, L., & Jagatic, K. (2011). North American perspectives on hostile behaviors and bullying at work. In S. Einarsen, H. Hoel, D. Zapf, & C. L. Cooper (Eds.), *Bullying and harassment in the workplace: Developments in theory, research and practice* (pp. 41–74). Boca Raton, FL: CRC Press, Taylor & Francis Group.

Law, R., Dollard, M. F., Tuckey, M. R., & Dormann, C. (2011). Psychosocial safety climate as a lead indicator of workplace bullying and harassment, job resources, psychological health and workplace engagement. *Accident Analysis and Prevention*, 43(5), 1782–1793. doi:10.1016/j.aap.2011.04.010

Leymann, H. (1990). Mobbing and psychological terror at workplaces. *Violence and Victims*, 5(2), 119–126.

Liacas, T. (2015, August 19). What will it take to make Amazon a great place to work? *The Guardian*. Retrieved from http://www.theguardian.com/sustainable-business/2015/aug/19/amazon-employee-abuse-rights-wages-walmart

Lutgen-Sandvik, P. (2003). The communicative cycle of employee emotional abuse: Generation and regeneration of workplace mistreatment. *Management Communication Quarterly*, 16, 471–501. doi:10.1177/0893318903251627

Lutgen-Sandvik, P. (2006). Take this job and . . . : Quitting and other forms of resistance to workplace bullying. *Communication Monographs*, 73, 406–433. doi:10.1080/03637750601024156

Lutgen-Sandvik, P. (2008). Intensive remedial identity work: Responses to workplace bullying trauma and stigmatization. *Organization*, 15(1), 97–119. doi:10.1177/1350508407084487

Lutgen-Sandvik, P., & Tracy, S. J. (2012). Answering five key questions about workplace bullying: How communication scholarship provides thought leadership for transforming abuse at work. *Management Communication Quarterly*, 26, 3–47. doi:10.1177/0893318911414400

Lutgen-Sandvik, P., Tracy, S. J., & Alberts, J. K. (2007). Burned by bullying in the American workplace: Prevalence, perception, degree and impact. *Journal of Management Studies*, 44(6), 837–862. doi:10.1111/j.1467-6486.2007.00715.x

McTernan, W. P., Dollard, M. F., & LaMontagne, A. D. (2013). Depression in the workplace: An economic cost analysis of depression-related productivity loss attributable to job strain and bullying. *Work & Stress*, 27(4), 321–338. doi:0.1080/02678373.2013.846948

Namie, G., Christensen, D., & Phillips. D. (2014). *2014 WBI U.S. workplace bullying survey*. Retrieved from http://www.workplacebullying.org/wbiresearch/wbi-2014-us-survey

Namie, G., & Lutgen-Sandvik, P. (2010). Active and passive accomplices: The communal character of workplace bullying. *International Journal of Communication*, 4, 343–373. doi:1932-8036/20100343

Namie, G. & Namie, R. F. (2011). *The bully-free workplace: Stop jerks, weasels, and snakes from killing your organization*. Hoboken, NJ: Wiley & Sons.

Neuman, J. H., & Baron, R. A. (2005). Aggression in the workplace: A social-psychological perspective. In S. Fox & P. Spector (Eds.), *Counterproductive workplace behavior* (pp. 13–40). Washington, D.C.: American Psychological Association. doi:10.1037/10893-001

Nielsen, M. B., & Einarsen, S. (2012). Outcomes of exposure to workplace bullying: A meta-analytic review. *Work & Stress*, 26(4), 309–332. doi:10.1080/02678373.2012.734709

Ortega, A., Christensen, K. B., Hogh, A., Rugulies, R., & Borg, V. (2011). One year prospective study on the effect of workplace bullying on long term sickness absence. *Journal of Nursing Management, 19*(6), 752–759. doi:10.1111/j.1365-2834.2010.01179.x

Paetzold, R., O'Leary-Kelly, A., & Griffin, R. (2007). Workplace violence, employer liability, and implications for organizational research. *Journal of Managerial Inquiry, 16*(4), 362–370. doi:10.1177/1056492606294521

Pearson, C. M., & Porath, C. L. (2005). On the nature, consequences and remedies of workplace incivility: No time for "nice"? Think again. *Academy of Management Perspectives, 19*(1), 7–18. doi:10.5465/AME.2005.15841946

Reio, T. G., Jr., & Sanders-Reio, J. (2011). Thinking about workplace engagement: Does supervisor and coworker incivility really matter? *Advances in Developing Human Resources, 13*, 462–478. doi:10.1177/1523422311430784

Rose, K., Shuck, B., Twyford, D., & Bergman, M. (2015). Skunked: An integrative review exploring the consequences of the dysfunctional leader and implications for those employees who work for them. *Human Resources Development Review, 14*, 64–90. doi:10.1177/1534484314552437

Salin, D. (2003). Ways of explaining workplace bullying: A review of enabling, motivating, and precipitating structures and processes in the work environment. *Human Relations, 56*(10), 1213–1232. doi:10.1177/00187267035610003

Samnani, A., & Singh, P. (2014). Performance enhancing compensation practices and employee productivity: The role of workplace bullying. *Human Resource Management Review, 24*(1), 5–16. doi:10.1016/j.hrmr.2013.08.013

Shuck, B., & Wollard, K. (2010). Employee engagement and HRD: A seminal review of the foundations. *Human Resource Development Review, 9*(1), 89–110. doi:10.1177/1534484309353560

Tepper, B. J. (2000). Consequences of abusive supervision. *Academy of Management Journal, 43*(2), 178–190. doi:10.2307/1556375

United Alliance Services. (2016). *Price estimates from workplace health and safety consultants*. Retrieved from http://www.unitedallianceservices.com/price-estimates-workplace-health-and-safety-consulting-services

Vartia, M. (2001). Consequences of workplace bullying with respect to the well-being of its targets and the observers of bullying. *Scandinavian Journal of Work, Environment and Health, 27*(1), 63–69.

Wemple, E. (2015, October 19). Amazon's weak attack on the *New York Times*. *Washington Post*. Retrieved from https://www.washingtonpost.com/blogs/erik-wemple/wp/2015/10/19/amazons-weak-attack-on-the-new-york-times

Woodrow, C., & Guest, D. E. (2014). When good HR gets bad results: Exploring the challenge of HR implementation in the case of workplace bullying. *Human Resource Management Journal, 24*(1), 38–56. doi:10.1111/1748-8583.12021

Workplace Bullying Institute (WBI). (2011). *The WBI website 2011 instant poll-D: Mediation, arbitration and workplace bullying*. Retrieved from http://www.workplacebullying.org/multi/pdf/2011-IP-D.pdf

Workplace Bullying Institute (WBI). (2012a). *WBI survey: Workplace bullying health impact*. Retrieved from http://www.workplacebullying.org/2012-d

Workplace Bullying Institute (WBI). (2012b). *The WBI website 2012 instant poll-C: Aftermath of requesting help from human resources*. Retrieved from http://www.workplacebullying.org/multi/pdf/WBI-2012-IP-C.pdf

Workplace Bullying Institute (WBI). (2013). *The WBI website 2013 instant poll-A: Workplace bullied targets forgo taking leave*. Retrieved from http://www.workplacebullying.org/multi/pdf/WBI-2013-IP-A.pdf

Workplace Bullying Institute (WBI). (2016). *Estimating the cost of bullying*. Retrieved from http://www.workplacebullying.org/individuals/solutions/costs

Yamada, D. C. (2010). Workplace bullying and the law: Emerging global perspectives. In S. Einarsen, H. Hoel, D. Zapf, & C. L. Cooper (Eds.), *Bullying and harassment in the workplace: Developments in theory, research and practice* (pp. 469–484). Boca Raton, FL: CRC Press, Taylor & Francis Group.

Yamada, D. C. (2013). Emerging American legal responses to workplace bullying. *Temple Political & Civil Rights Law Review, 22*(2), 329–354.

PART III

Prevention of Workplace Bullying and Mobbing

10

How Awareness and Education Can Help with Recognition of Workplace Bullying and Mobbing

Gary Namie, Ruth Namie, and Carol Fehner

This chapter examines a foundational element of the social justice movement to end workplace bullying and mobbing in the United States: public education, understanding, and awareness. Many audiences comprise this public. Targeted individuals are the primary group to educate about the benefits of recognition. Only after recognizing and naming what is happening to them will they take action to ameliorate the harmful effects. With recognition, health and mental health professionals can more quickly reverse the stress-related consequences for patients and clients. The success of convincing employers their best interests are served by addressing bullying depends on awareness and outrage that employees bring to challenge indifference and inactivity. Lawmakers responsible for advancing legislation to compel employer action are an important audience. They, too, are members of the broader public that has to be educated.

In chapter 16, we describe the benefits and shortcomings of raising awareness about workplace bullying in organizations. The focus here is on educating the public, drawing heavily upon over 20 years of work in this arena. Gary and Ruth Namie have been doing so mainly through the Workplace Bullying Institute, while Carol Fehner has engaged in this work as a labor educator.

Imagine one knows nothing about bullying. There are several ways to become aware. We first explore the indirect means by which that education can occur. A great deal of education is the accidental or inadvertent discovery of bullying and its potential effects on its targets. Next, we turn to directed activities designed to deliberately raise awareness of bullying and what could be done by different audiences to stop it. We claim modest successes after a 20-year campaign. We end with the emerging societal context—the new zeitgeist—that threatens to reverse all progress in educating the public to date.

INDIRECT PUBLIC EDUCATION

School-Age Bullying

Much is owed to workplace bullying's forerunner—school-age bullying. Dan Olweus launched the bullying-in-schools movement with foundational research in Norway, moving to America five years later (Olweus, 1978). His school training program intervention was the first one introduced in the United States and gained a dominant market position. Over the years, other programs followed. This increase in school antibullying programming meant that some teachers, students, parents, and administrators were aware of bullying and its harmful effects. Several years of continuing media coverage of school bullying has prepared the public to reject taunting, shaming, and ostracism of targeted children as acceptable, routine behavior. Previously, it was considered an inevitable rite of passage. It took a steady bombardment of print and broadcast media coverage to break the silence and reverse its valence from positive or neutral to negative conduct.

A spate of student suicides captures media attention like few other aspects of bullying. The vividness of the incidents makes them memorable. The cases highlight, and often hold responsible, social media's role in the taking of a life. Behind the headline was a child tormented by her or his peers—mocked, shamed, ridiculed, stalked—eventually driven to a decision for which there was no perceived alternative. For many observers, the causal connection is made and accepted that bullying triggered the suicide.

For adult bullying, the link between bullying and suicide was established only recently (Nielsen, Nielsen, Notelaers, & Einarsen, 2015). In that longitudinal study, researchers documented the perseverance of workplace bullying's effect on suicidal ideation over a five-year period. When adults take their lives after being exposed to workplace bullying, the media do not give these cases the same attention as they do to the cases of school-age children. It seems sufficient to discount the victims as troubled souls with myriad reasons to shorten their lives.

In many cases, this may be true. However, we have seen the unraveling of strong individuals triggered solely by bullying at work. Their sad trajectories started with workplace bullying, destroyed their relationships with partners and children, and led to abandonment by friends, and all of this was coupled with economic devastation. Over time, the origin of the destructive spiral in the workplace gets lost. One dramatic case for which the author served as expert witness made clear what it takes to link suicide to the workplace. The woman wrote three suicide letters explicitly documenting the record of her abuse by senior managers over the years. She took the letters to her office, where she took her life. Tragically, she made the link undeniable in a rare demonstration of clarity.

Media Coverage

As advocates for targets of workplace bullying, we have generally avoided prominent media suicide stories as a way to advance the cause. We have taken the same tack with reporting of workplace murders. Workplace massacres are cavalierly referred to as "going postal" by American media. Sadly, there was a string of major episodes involving postal workers in the 1990s in which several people were murdered by coworkers or former coworkers with guns (see the documentary *Murder by Proxy*; Chiaberi, Moll, & Rosen, 2010). A small, unknown number of massacres may have originated from long histories of workplace bullying. In these homicide cases where the murder victims were limited to supervisors or human resources or labor relations union representatives, long-term bullying may have been a potential contributing factor that needed to be ruled out. To be accurate, the media reporting would necessarily have to be as nuanced and complicated as were the origins of the massacre. The experience of the authors of this chapter is that contemporary reporters either cannot, or are not permitted by editors to, produce such reporting.

The U.S. antibullying movement has been blessed with years of positive media attention. The Workplace Bullying Institute (WBI) and affiliated professionals have been featured in print stories or in studio TV segments in well over 1,200 appearances. The outlets have ranged from the *New York Times*, the *Washington Post*, *The Economist*, *Bloomberg Business Week*, NPR, CBC, CNN, *The Today Show*, *Good Morning America*, *Dateline NBC*, *Oprah*, *The Howard Stern Show*, and a host of local radio and TV stations. The focus of press coverage has evolved.

In the beginning, circa 1998, the human-interest angle dominated. Tales of bullied targets were featured. Sympathy for targets was strong. Then, with the first of WBI's national scientific prevalence surveys in 2007, coverage emphases shifted to descriptive statistics about prevalence. Next came coverage of the legislative advances of the antibullying Healthy Workplace Bill (HWB). Reporters have repeatedly asked when America will have its first law against workplace bullying. Sadly, interest in the anecdotal—the human toll bullying takes on individuals—seems to have waned. Stories of American workplace bullying have shifted from the human interest to business to the political media sectors. Ideally, the final step in the press's journey will be to assign responsibility for bullying on employers and institutions. This is a hard sell to media owned by large corporations. Regardless of media placement, stories about bullying have provided the movement with free public exposure comparable to an unaffordable publicity campaign.

The value of media coverage for workplace bullying and mobbing to bullied targets is the increased likelihood that targets stumble upon these stories online, in print, or on broadcast media. When targets hear the terms "workplace bullying" or "mobbing," they have a name for their experiences.

Naming is powerful. Being bullied is nebulous. Targets are prone to blame themselves for their misery. Media accounts can lead to "aha" moments of clarity and discovery. Often, for the first time, upon hearing or reading a media story on bullying, (1) targets are able to know they are not the only ones to whom this happens, and (2) with the name and depictions reported, they know the problem is not of their making and affects many people in many workplaces. However, it is pure chance, an unknown likelihood that bullied targets will hear, watch, or read the accounts when they need it most.

Academics and Lawmakers

When the movement started, there were few American academics conducting bullying research. The numbers have grown exponentially. More graduate students choose to conduct their doctoral research on bullying. In turn, they become the new generation of faculty capable of raising student awareness about adult bullying. Generating research for publishing articles in low-circulation academic peer-reviewed journals is the path to job stability in the academy. It does little to educate the public. However, universities have learned to popularize the work of their faculty and staff. They tell media about the latest campus research. Bullying and mobbing research is instantly identifiable. It grabs headlines. In this way, academics contribute to public education.

Attendees at scientific and legal academic conferences are also an audience for messaging about workplace bullying and mobbing. Here are a few disciplines in which national and international themed conference presentations educate academics and practicing professionals: bullying (the longest running group is the International Association on Workplace Bullying and Harassment); management (American Management Association); psychology (American Psychological Association); public health (American Public Health Association); law (American Bar Association); law and mental health (International Academy of Law and Mental Health); law and labor (Oregon Labor Law Conference); arbitrators (National Academy of Arbitrators); social work (National Association of Social Workers); and work, stress, and health (APA, National Institute of Occupational Safety and Health, and Society of Occupational Health Psychology). Academics talking to academics is useful to the public when conference attendees disseminate the findings widely back home. Some professors are adept at social media (see Professor Yamada's *Minding the Workplace* blog, https://newworkplace.wordpress.com) and have public platforms to translate academic-speak into usable language for a mass audience.

Lawmakers are another limited audience. After the HWB or some legislative variant is introduced in a state's legislature, it must next be given a public hearing by the committee to which it was referred. At that hearing, the public is invited to attend and briefly comment. Advocates mobilize and prepare people to testify. Some statehouses broadcast committee hearings live and archive them as audio or video recordings. Technically, the audience for such hearings is the limited number of committee members, typically 5 to 15; the ability to publicize these hearings and replay testimony from them greatly expands the audiences. Local press coverage amplifies the message. Legislation can inform the public, even when the bill's progress on its way to becoming law stops in committee. Perhaps a bullied target, bullying manager, executive, or HR representative catches the story.

DIRECT PUBLIC EDUCATION

To reach the public, education about bullying and mobbing should not be left to chance. Therefore, advocates strive to provide more direct and permanent forms of education.

The Internet

Hosting Web sites is one of the earliest Internet-based activities used by those promoting antibullying awareness. Sites can house an unlimited number of pages and documents to educate any audience. The Internet was in its infancy when WBI began its work. The information related to workplace bullying was in a section devoted to bullied targets embedded in a Web site tailored for employers and general consulting. On New Year's Day 1998, we launched the first dedicated American site to help workplace bullied individuals at the domain www.bullybusters.org. The message was clear; bullied targets had a place to go and a phone number to call to share their stories.

That humble Web site has grown into a one-stop service site (www.workplacebullying.org) where targets find self-help information on static pages, a set of audio podcasts, and long-form webinars (e.g., impact on the family, preparing for the 1:1 bullying meeting). The WBI Web site unilaterally educates visitors who stumble upon it seeking a name for their experiences and solutions. It is passive. It requires an active visitor willing to search the site (a search engine is provided) for answers. For an emotionally fragile target in the early throes of bullying, the energy and focus to navigate a big Web site can be elusive.

Web sites are extended by newer social media—Facebook and Twitter. They allow sharing of experiences by bullied targets and a dialogue among users. The multiway communication enables exchanges of strategies, warnings, and success stories. There are many positives; caution is warranted, too. Targets may find social media easier than finding information through Web sites. Social media, as we have seen with young people, can turn perilously destructive and angry. Individuals feel disinhibited and make emotional entries, often without censoring themselves or anticipating the consequences of their words or expressions on vulnerable people. All told, however, in the adult world of bullying, the benefits of social media appear to outweigh the negative risks.

Another useful educational tool on the internet is YouTube. WBI has its own channel with over 200 videos. The channel is divided into sections. Television news segments covering workplace bullying cases illustrate the phenomenon with interviews with actual targets. Videotaped legislative committee hearings reside on the playlist for making U.S. antibullying law. Especially useful in those hearings are the arguments opposing any law to combat workplace bullying. There is a section about the engagement of unions in the antibullying movement. A set of videos related to "Freedom from Workplace Bullies Week" is also included.

Freedom from Workplace Bullies Week

WBI designated the third week in October each year as Freedom Week. It is held during Domestic Violence Awareness Month in the United States. Freedom Week is described as a chance to break through the shame and silence surrounding workplace bullying. It is a call to be daring and bold whether you are a target, family member, coworker, employer, union, mental health professional, medical professional, or legislator. The tradition is 10 years old. Many cities and counties proclaim Freedom Week. It was created solely to raise awareness about workplace bullying and mobbing.

Books

Books are the most traditional mode of education for any topic. The fields of workplace bullying and mobbing are no exception. Books range from the academic to employer-focused to self-help for bullied targets. At the risk of offending many by exclusion, we have included a nonexhaustive list of some of the titles written by Americans (or collections with many American authors) in a short appendix to this chapter.

Speeches: Public and Association Meetings

Whenever an advocate gives a speech, seminar, or workshop on the topic of workplace bullying and mobbing, it is direct in-person education. If the event is open to the public, the presenter is guaranteed a room full of bullied targets and their loved ones. Depending on the presenter's resources, rooms can be large or small. It is always important to remember the personal shame associated with being a bullied target. Shame attenuates attendance. Bullies do not attend voluntary events on the topic. Speeches are opportunities for presenters to show empathy for targets. It is validating for targets. During breaks and at the event's end, presenters face a line of targets desperate for coaching and counseling. In-person speeches personalize the Web sites, the blogs, the books, and media appearances.

Consultants and speakers can encourage employer and union clients to host a two-hour seminar free to the public at the end of a day of paid speaking or consulting. It is good community relations for the host, needed by targets in the town, and a way for advocates to reach the most critical subgroup of the public.

Above, we discussed reaching academic and professional audiences through conferences. In a similar way, speaking at trade association meetings allows advocates to reach key constituent groups who either affect, or are affected by, bullying and mobbing. At chamber of commerce gatherings, large and small employers can hear the message that they should prohibit bullying for their own self-interest, if not to ensure employee health and safety. At annual conferences of corporate defense lawyers, insurers, risk managers, HR, and executives, advocate speakers can foster positive attitudes toward targets and increase understanding of the entire workplace bullying phenomenon. An association meeting presentation is tailored mass education and a chance to directly recruit allies for the movement to stop bullying.

Union Education

Coauthor Carol Fehner has engaged in remediation of workplace bullying situations starting in 1992, five years before the start of WBI. As a union representative for a federal employee labor union, she used her leverage to compel management to stop bullying in a large federal agency. Besides fighting in the trenches, she worked tirelessly to have her union insert antibullying language in the national bargaining agreement.

Unions are membership organizations with employees. Nonelected administrative staff are typically members of a separate union. Therefore, the benefits from bullying education in union settings are twofold. The union, as employer, learns to act more responsibly and prevent its occurrence. As advocates for its members, unions learn how to minimize the emotional and health damage suffered by members who have endured bullying and mobbing.

This chapter's authors have all participated in training unions in how to recognize bullying. Some unions have taken extraordinary steps to train an internal team of workplace experts to assist colleagues in profound ways. They take calls from distressed members. The most emotionally fragile callers are triaged to counseling. Others have their experiences clarified to minimize harm. The experts partner with bullied members to make their workplaces safe from psychological threats. It is critical that union leaders understand bullying. When union leaders resist antibullying initiatives within their unions, they foster resentment and anger against the unions. Smart leaders know how to leverage antibullying services for members into an organizing edge.

Training for Professionals

There is a set of professionals whose roles in various industries touch workplace bullying and mobbing. They are mental health and medical professionals, attorneys, union stewards and representatives, human resources personnel, labor relations personnel, investigators, mediators, arbitrators, consultants, and corporate trainers. For this wide range of people, in 2008, WBI created a three-day education program called Workplace Bullying University (WBU).

WBU is an intensive, interactive graduate-level seminar. It includes multimedia instruction, group interaction, and all the resources required to launch an antibullying initiative at the participants' home organization. The instruction applies to corporations and unions, for-profit and nonprofit organizations, in the public and private sectors. The curriculum covers all aspects of workplace bullying—from profiles of perpetrators, targets, witnesses, enabling managers, and destructive leaders. Solutions are systemic and focus on changes to the work environment rather than reliance on personality change. Union strategies are shared. Finally, the state of U.S. public policy change is reviewed in the context of international precedents.

The small group sessions are clearly not education for the masses. However, by training established and emerging specialists, thought leaders, and subject matter experts, the program creators hope graduates will have access to several constituent groups in the future, thereby disseminating the message about bullying and its harmful effects more broadly than the creators alone could have done.

MODEST SUCCESSES

The U.S. movement to end workplace bullying and mobbing turned 20 years old in 2017. When we reflect on efforts to date, we observe and claim only modest successes. The greatest progress is symbolic rather than tangible—the societal use of the term *workplace bullying*. We infer acceptance of the problem from its use. At the start, we were met with giggles. We were asked by everyone, "Isn't this something about schools? Surely adults don't do that." Smirks gave way to acknowledgment. Certainly, targets appreciated the term that externalized and helped explain the experiences they were enduring. Once the hosts on the most popular TV shows uttered the phrase, workplace bullying was mainstreamed.

Raess v. Doescher (2008), an Indiana Supreme Court decision, also helped normalize workplace bullying. In trial court, the plaintiff, the operator of a heart-lung machine at a hospital, won a judgment against a cardiovascular surgeon defendant who had subjected him to an angry exchange that included physical aggression. The issue of workplace bullying had been introduced in the trial, in part through expert testimony by Gary Namie. The Indiana Supreme Court rejected a challenge to the admissibility of the expert testimony about workplace bullying, finding there was nothing in the record to suggest that the testimony was inadmissible. This case received considerable media attention because of how evidence of workplace bullying had been expressly introduced at trial.

The antibullying Healthy Workplace Bill was first introduced in 2003 in California. The bill, authored by Suffolk University law professor David Yamada, does not use the phrase "workplace bullying" in its key terms. Instead, it refers to subjecting an employee to "abusive conduct" (Yamada, 2013, p. 351). As attention to the HWB grew, WBI advocates began to replace "bullying" with "abusive conduct" in all writing and presentations. The transformation was complete when we inserted "abusive conduct" into the definition of bullying in the WBI *2014 U.S. Workplace Bullying Survey*, our scientific national prevalence study (Namie, 2014).

"Abusive conduct" raises the seriousness of the phenomenon above lingering associations or confusion with childhood bullying that the term may imply. By casting the circumstances as abusive, advocates are able to describe workplace abuse as the sole remaining form of abuse to not be considered taboo. Worse still, bullying is not yet close to being socially undesirable. It is still widely accepted and practiced. Abusive conduct belongs to the category of interpersonal abuses—child, partner, and elder—that have all been stigmatized and addressed by laws. It is no longer socially desirable to boast as a perpetrator of intimate partner violence. The uniqueness of abusive workplace conduct stands out. It is not yet frowned upon. It needs to become stigmatized and its practitioners portrayed more negatively than they now are. We consider the elevation of bullying to abusive conduct an indicator of progress toward the goal of making abusive conduct taboo.

A state workers' union, the Minnesota Association of Professional Employees (MAPE), achieved successes unimaginable when the U.S. movement began. Its story is described in chapter 16. In short, they discovered their members were suffering from exposure to bullying. Then, in three short years, MAPE created a system to rescue their members from bullying situations; nearly passed a law to prod the state, as employer, to collaboratively write the first state policy against bullying; and are training a large cadre of members to help their union brothers and sisters. Their committed work is ongoing. MAPE can inspire other unions to fully engage against workplace bullying.

Several companies, government agencies, and military organizations have crafted antibullying policies. This is a growing trend, even though no laws currently exist to compel employers to act against bullying. The State of Minnesota was pushed by one of its unions. Corporate defense attorneys regularly advise their clients to preclude litigation by proactively writing a policy to cover mistreatment beyond the boundaries of protected status group membership. Government agencies are making the greatest leap forward. The military is coupling bullying with *hazing*, a physical form of abusive conduct that the military academies are committed to eliminating completely. For these and other reasons, there has been steady progress in employers voluntarily adopting policies to address workplace bullying and mobbing.

There has also been some progress in the legislative arena. The reader is referred to chapter 18 of this volume for a thorough assessment of the status of the legislative advocacy work to enact state laws in the United States. Some bills have passed using the HWB definition of abusive conduct.

AMERICAN ZEITGEIST

Positive gains in the U.S. movement against workplace bullying and mobbing should not be assumed to be increasing in the direction of a smooth upward slope. There have been many ups and downs—all to be expected. The movement is not anticorporate, but its opponents have portrayed it as such. It is antiabuse. Defenders of abuse have a morally dubious task of defending its use. Yet defend they do. But advocates can claim the high ground while waiting for society to realize the indefensibility of employing abusive tactics in the workplace. The gains mentioned above have been achieved.

Workplace bullies are often regarded as narcissistic, Machiavellian, and subclinically psychopathic—a melding of personality traits called the *dark triad* (Paulhus & Jones, 2015). As such, they are grandiose thinkers and can become aggressive when challenged or threatened; they strategically manipulate others for personal gain, are callous, lack empathy, poorly control their own behavior, are pathological liars, are irresponsible, and mask it all under a charismatic cloak. Such perpetrators willingly destroy coworkers or subordinates who pose a threat, real or imagined, when the work environment encourages or fails to stop the psychological assaults. These individuals are the abusers we need to stop. The organizations in which such disturbing behavior is tolerated urgently need to transform their cultures.

The conduct and results of the 2016 presidential campaign and election present an external threat of enormous magnitude to this growing antibullying movement. Donald Trump's bullying style quickly became evident in the United States and worldwide. He insulted groups by race, color, gender, nationality, and disability. His presence as America's president may damage this movement, possibly reversing years of progress. His unlimited media exposure is likely to capture his unchecked propensity to insult, berate, and humiliate others. In this way, America has a bully as role model on constant display. Children and adults alike have mimicked him and likely will continue to do so.

Our principal concern is that watching Trump dominate challengers to his authority will embolden bullies in the workplace. In the immediate aftermath of Donald Trump's election, the Southern Poverty Law Center (2016) tracked a sharp increase in hate incidents in the United States, with the most prevalent forms being harassment apparently motivated by immigration status and race. The majority of incidents happened in K–12 schools, followed closely by businesses and then universities and colleges.

Executives and managers who were growing accustomed to conforming to new standards of conduct dictated by new no-bullying policies will be free to revert to old ways. Executives can easily cancel policies that make them feel uncomfortable as long as no law compels the policies. The abusers' rationale for reversion will be, "If the president can abuse, then why do I have to stop?" When prominent individuals are shown to behave with impunity in unacceptable and destructive ways, it increases the likelihood that a more antisocial norm will evolve.

We fear a mocking of the antibullying movement, tagging it as somehow honoring, or manufacturing, weak individuals who could not defend themselves. There will be a greater emphasis on celebrating strength, however manifested. In the more aggressive world, everyone needs to learn to fight. America risks becoming an even coarser society.

If we are ever to stop bullying and mobbing in the workplace, we need workplaces to operate in a more, not less, collective manner. We should value communal efforts with team members engaged in affiliative behaviors instead of interpersonal aggression. Unremitting exposure to a bully who must constantly "win" (a zero-sum game in which others must be obliterated as threatening competition) cannot be good for American society. The fight may be more uphill than ever, but we will prevail. Education can help us to overcome the darkness.

REFERENCES

Chiaberi, E. (Producer/Director), Moll, J. (Producer), & Rosen, M. (Producer). (2010). *Murder by proxy: How America went postal* [Motion picture]. United States: Aldamisa.

Namie, G. (2014). *2014 WBI U.S. workplace bullying survey*. Retrieved from http://workplacebullying.org/multi/pdf/WBI-2014-US-Survey.pdf

Nielsen, M. B., Nielsen, G. H., Notelaers, G., & Einarsen, S. (2015). Workplace bullying and suicidal ideation: A 3-wave longitudinal Norwegian study. *American Journal of Public Health, 105*(11), e23–e28.

Olweus, D. (1978). *Aggression in the schools: Bullies and whipping boys*. Hoboken, NJ: John Wiley & Sons.

Paulhus, D. L., & Jones, D. N. (2015). Measures of dark personalities. In G. J. Boyle, D. H. Saklofske, & G. Matthews (Eds.), *Measures of personality and social psychological constructs* (pp. 562–594). London, England: Academic Press.

Raess v. Doescher, 883 N.E. 2d 790 (Ind. 2008).

Southern Poverty Law Center. (2016). *Update: Incidents of hateful harassment since election day now number 701*. Retrieved from https://www.splcenter.org/hatewatch/2016/11/18/update-incidents-hateful-harassment-election-day-now-number-701

Yamada, D. C. (2013). Emerging American legal responses to workplace bullying. *Temple Political & Civil Rights Law Review, 22*(2), 329–354.

APPENDIX

The following is a partial listing of books that serve as useful introductions to workplace bullying, mobbing, and related behaviors written by American authors or containing chapters with many contributions from American authors. Along with the other chapters in these volumes, they provide readers with insightful, informative, and accessible information, analyses, and commentary on bullying and mobbing at work.

Babiak, P., & Hare, R. D. (2007). *Snakes in suits: When psychopaths go to work*. New York: Regan Books.

Balcerzak, J. (2015). *Workplace bullying: Recognizing, preventing, and treating emotional abuse in adult work environments*. Washington, D.C.: National Association of Social Workers.

Curry, L. (2016). *Beating the workplace bully: A tactical guide to taking charge*. New York: AMACOM.

Daniel, T. A., & Metcalf, G. S. (2016). *Stop bullying at work: Strategies and tools for HR, legal & risk management professionals* (2nd ed.). Alexandria, VA: SHRM Books.

Duffy, M., & Sperry, L. (2012). *Mobbing: Causes, consequences, and solutions*. New York: Oxford University Press.

Duffy, M., & Sperry, L. (2014). *Overcoming mobbing: A recovery guide for workplace aggression and bullying*. New York: Oxford University Press.

Einarsen, S., Hoel, H., Zapf, D., & Cooper, C. L. (Eds.). (2011). *Bullying and harassment in the workplace: Developments in theory, research and practice* (2nd ed.). Boca Raton, FL: CRC Press.

Hornstein, H. A. (1997). *Brutal bosses and their prey: How to overcome abuse in the workplace*. New York: Riverhead.

Lutgen-Sandvik, P. (2013). *Adult bullying—a nasty piece of work: A decade of research on non-sexual harassment, psychological terror, and emotional abuse on the job.* St. Louis, MO: ORCM Press.

Maltby, L. (2009). *Can they do that? Retaking our fundamental rights in the workplace.* New York: Portfolio.

Namie, G., & Namie, R. (2009). *The bully at work: What you can do to stop the hurt and reclaim your dignity on the job* (2nd ed.). Naperville, IL. Sourcebooks, Inc.

Namie, G. M., & Namie, R. (2011). *The bully-free workplace: Stop jerks, weasels and snakes from killing your organization.* Hoboken, NJ: John Wiley & Sons.

Pearson, C., & Porath, P. (2009). *The cost of bad behavior: How incivility is damaging your business and what to do about it.* New York: Portfolio.

Schnall, P. L., Dobson, M., & Rosskam, E. (Eds.). (2009). *Unhealthy work: Causes, consequences, cures.* Amityville, NY: Baywood.

Schnurr, P. P., & Green, B. L. (Eds.). (2004). *Trauma and health: Physical health consequences of exposure to extreme stress.* Washington, D.C.: American Psychological Association.

Sutton, R. I. (2007). *The no asshole rule: Building a civilized workplace and surviving one that isn't.* New York: Warner Business Books.

Twale, D. J., & DeLuca, B. M. (2008). *Faculty incivility: The rise of the academic bully culture.* San Francisco, CA: Jossey-Bass.

Zimbardo, P. (2008). *The Lucifer effect: Understanding how good people turn evil.* New York: Random House Trade Paperbacks.

11

The Role of Human Resources in Bullying and Mobbing Prevention Efforts

Teresa A. Daniel

> HR serves as a "serious buffer" for other employees in the organization—between management and employees. We are the "organizational shock absorbers." If HR professionals won't stand up to a bad manager, who will? But HR pays a heavy price for doing that. (Study participant in Daniel, 2012a)

The evidence is overwhelmingly clear that workplace bullying and mobbing can seriously damage the health and well-being of affected employees (Namie & Namie, 2003, 2011; Porath, 2016b). It can also poison an organization by undermining employee morale and by eroding any sense of loyalty, trust, or teamwork (McLaughlin, 2014; Pearson & Porath, 2009; Porath, 2016b; Society for Human Resource Management, 2012). Moreover, the "climate of fear" created by a bully-prone environment is likely to impact an organization through the loss of productivity as well as increased absences, disengagement, and higher turnover (Rayner, 1999). In a nutshell, bullying is bad management at its absolute worst, and it represents real risks to organizations if left unchecked.

In this chapter, we will examine the role of *human resources* (HR) in responding to and preventing—or at least minimizing—the occurrence of workplace bullying and mobbing, the complexities of managing these various responsibilities and organizational expectations, and some promising strategies that may be useful in HR's efforts to tackle this complex workplace problem on behalf of both employees and their organization.

ORGANIZATIONAL ROLE OF HR PROFESSIONALS

A review of the relevant management and practitioner literature suggests that HR professionals have at least five unique organizational roles when it comes to their involvement in bullying and mobbing prevention efforts.

These include corporate insider with primary responsibility for managing workplace conflicts, employee advocate, protector of management interests, and toxin handler. In addition, HR is sometimes personally the target of this type of management abuse. Each of these roles will be examined next.

Role as Corporate Insider with Responsibility to Help Manage Conflict

In addition to their myriad other responsibilities, HR professionals are integral actors in situations of workplace conflict and are widely viewed as the organizational insiders best suited to take a leading role in the prevention and elimination of bullying and mobbing in the workplace (Cowan, 2009; Curry, 2015; Daniel & Metcalf, 2016; Fox & Cowan, 2015a, 2015b; Harrington, Warren, & Rayner, 2015; Lewis & Rayner, 2003; Maxwell, 2015; Yamada, 2012, among others).

The results of the 2012 Society for Human Resource Management (SHRM) survey also confirm HR's central role in situations of bullying and mobbing (SHRM, 2012). Based on the responses of 401 HR managers, SHRM found that targets bring their bully-related complaints to HR in 89 percent of all situations. They also report that the HR department has the official responsibility for handling employee complaints in 87 percent of the companies represented in the study. These findings suggest that HR professionals in most organizations deal with the issue of workplace bullying from start to finish.

That HR tends to be a reflection and extension of the management philosophy and practices of the top organizational leaders is widely regarded as true (Yamada, 2009). As a result, senior leaders must lead and model respectful behaviors at work, as it is the tone set at the top that either allows bullying to flourish or prevents it (Equal Employment Opportunity Commission, 2016). HR cannot do the important job of preventing workplace bullying without support from the organization's senior leaders.

Role as Employee Advocate

Another key role for HR professionals is to serve as an employee advocate for those who are targets of bullying or mobbing (Grillo, 2014; SHRM, 2016d; Ulrich, 1997). This requires taking action to protect employees from abusive managers, while at the same time safeguarding the prerogative of managers to push employees to meet (or exceed) company performance goals, even though they may be perceived as a "tough" boss (Daniel, 2009a, 2009b, 2009c; Daniel & Metcalf, 2016). Striking that balance, though, is not an easy task due in large part to conflicts among multiple and competing HR roles, a lack of specific organizational policies and guidelines for dealing with bullying, and ambiguous definitions and criteria for determining when behavior rises to the level of bullying (Fox & Cowan, 2015b).

Role as Protector of Management and Organizational Interests

Senior leaders in a study by Daniel (2013a) suggest that HR practitioners possess considerable strength in four key areas that serve to benefit and protect the interests of both management and the organization: education and training of the workforce; mitigation of risk to the organization (e.g., minimizing the potential for lawsuits or regulatory violations); providing reliable basic HR services (e.g., policy development, strategies about human capital deployment, hiring, benefits, and communication); and protecting the interests of both employees and management (e.g., investigating and resolving workplace conflicts, coaching and challenging senior leaders about important people-related decisions).

In partnership with the company's legal counsel, HR is called upon to investigate employee complaints, including those related to workplace bullying and mobbing. If the allegations of misconduct are confirmed, HR generally first confers with legal counsel and then with senior leaders to determine the appropriate consequences for the bully and support for the target (Daniel, 2009a, 2009b, 2009c; Daniel & Metcalf, 2016). The investigative aspect of the role has often caused HR to be perceived as the "internal police" of the organization, a characterization to which most practitioners object and a role that they generally find to be uncomfortable (Daniel, 2011, 2012a; Fox & Cowan, 2015a).

Ulrich (1997) acknowledges the paradox inherent in the multiple roles that HR must navigate, especially when it comes to representing the interests of both the employee and the organization. He argues that HR professionals "can both represent employee needs *and* implement management agendas, be the voice of the employee *and* the voice of management, act as partner to both employees *and* managers" (p. 45)—but it clearly is not easy to straddle these often competing roles. It is not surprising, then, that more than half of the HR leaders responding to a recent survey by a global talent management firm about the complexity of the HR role reported feeling "overwhelmed," and 52 percent reported that they "did not have the ability to fully cope" with it (SHRM, 2013).

Unfortunately, HR is often perceived by employees as siding with management in some of the worst workplace bullying situations brought to their attention. There is all too often some truth to that perception. The uncomfortable dilemma commonly faced by HR practitioners is aptly stated by Yamada (2013a):

> In good and bad workplaces alike, HR answers to top management, not to individual employees. Too many well-meaning team players have learned that lesson painfully, thinking that a seemingly empathetic HR

manager is a sort of confidante or counselor. There are plenty of good, supportive HR people out there, but ultimately their job is to support the employer's hiring and personnel practices and interests. (para. 6)

Role as "Toxin Handler"

HR practitioners are regularly confronted by distressed employees who bring emotionally charged problems to them—issues such as layoffs, harassment complaints, substance abuse, and personality or work conflicts—based on their desire to ensure that the issues are properly addressed (Kulik, Cregan, Metz, & Brown, 2009). In responding to these situations, HR practitioners serve their organizations as "toxin handlers"—defined as empathetic managers willing to try to address the pain and suffering often experienced by employees at work (Frost, 2003, 2004; Frost & Robinson, 1999; Metz, Brown, Cregan, & Kulik, 2014). Fox and Cowan (2015b) use the term *emotional laborers* to describe the role HR plays in resolving conflict situations. Similarly, it has also been suggested by HR practitioners that they serve as "organizational shock absorbers," given their frequent involvement with the emotional stress and tension caused by the bully in their efforts to resolve the situation (Daniel, 2009a, 2009b, 2009c, 2011, 2012a, 2012b).

In a study conducted by Kulik, Cregan, Metz, and Brown (2009), HR managers reported that "almost 25% of their time, on average, is spent on emotionally charged problems" (p. 707). That practitioners assume this role is not unexpected given that "caring about people" has historically been a hallmark contribution of the HR profession (Falcone, 2002; Meisinger, 2005). However, what *is* unexpected (and somewhat startling) is the perception among HR professionals that about a quarter of the time they spend at work is spent on stressful issues and situations eliciting intense emotions.

Role as the Personal Target of Management Abuse

It may be somewhat surprising to learn that HR professionals are sometimes caught in the crossfire too. Recent studies suggest that between 27 percent (SHRM, 2012) and 31.4 percent (Daniel, 2011, 2012a) of HR practitioners have personally been the targets of bullying at work. Interestingly, most of the abuse is generated toward HR by members of the organization's senior leadership (SHRM, 2012) or their immediate supervisor (Daniel, 2012a).

How do HR professionals make sense of this mistreatment? In a study conducted by Daniel (2011, 2012a), HR practitioners suggest that it is the nature of the organizational role of HR itself that may substantially contribute to the dynamic. Study participants noted that HR practitioners are frequently required to coach or challenge business leaders to achieve the best decisions possible for the organization. At times, these discussions can get quite intense, triggering a negative or defensive response that subsequently results in backlash or retribution, including bullying. As a result, study participants posit that insecure managers may see competent HR managers as a professional threat. They also suggest that their organizational role is not fully appreciated or understood and that they are often perceived as lacking business knowledge, professional credentials, education, or organizational fit. Regardless of the justifications used by senior leaders for bullying HR practitioners, there is no doubt that personally being a target of bullying makes it exponentially harder for HR to protect other employees in the organization (D'Cruz & Noronha, 2010; Ferris, 2004; Griffith, 2013; Harrington, Rayner, & Warren, 2012; Namie & Namie, 2011; Lewis & Rayner, 2003).

PERCEPTIONS OF HR'S ROLE AND PERFORMANCE

There are vastly different views of HR's role and judgments about how their effectiveness in handling situations of bullying and mobbing that largely depend on one's organizational position. As a result, the perceptions of HR professionals, bullied targets, perpetrators of bullying or mobbing, senior organizational leaders, and the national SHRM organization will be examined next.

The View of HR Professionals

Cowan (2009) reports that HR professionals generally define and understand bullying much like targets do, but they have a difference of opinion about the elements required to cause a situation to be labeled "bullying." Concerns about how to define and identify the problem, management style, conflict skills, and personality clashes as well as their low power position within the organization were identified as causing a high level of complexity in terms of their response to target concerns—equating their role to "walking a tightrope" (p. 238). Importantly, they were strongly of the opinion that HR take complaints of bullying very seriously and that they act appropriately to address these types of situations.

Confirming Cowan's earlier research, a more recent study by Fox and Cowan (2015b) suggests that, as a profession, HR practitioners do not perceive themselves as failing to assist targets who come to them for help. Instead, they understand their roles in bullying situations as follows: *trusted listener*; an *objective, neutral third-party investigator*; a *management adviser*; and a *mediator, trainer, and coach*.

HR professionals are strongly of the opinion that it is incumbent upon them to intervene when they become aware of a conflict situation. In fact,

97 percent of the participating HR practitioners in SHRM's 2012 study indicated that they personally felt that it was their responsibility to step in (e.g., to investigate, document, discipline, etc.) when bullying is reported or suspected—with 77 percent agreeing "to a large degree" and 20 percent agreeing "to some degree" (SHRM, 2012).

In combination, these studies suggest that HR practitioners are of the opinion that it is their responsibility to try to resolve issues of workplace conflict. Moreover, they are of the general opinion that they take a balanced approach—looking out for the interests of both the employee *and* the organization when attempting to solve a complaint of workplace bullying. Interestingly, their understanding of the role of HR was often in conflict with how they believed bullied employees and senior management viewed their responsibilities, creating yet another paradox and adding further complexity to their role (Fox & Cowan, 2015a).

The View of Bullied Targets

Despite the fact that bullied employees are often publicly humiliated, viciously teased, called derogatory names, are the subjects of malicious rumors, stripped of their responsibilities, ostracized, denied promotional opportunities, and much more, research consistently confirms that HR often fails targets by not taking their issues seriously enough (Barrow, 2012; Namie & Namie, 2003, 2011; Workplace Bullying Institute, 2000, 2007, 2010, 2012, 2014b). Once a target files a complaint with HR, the bully often then takes steps to discredit, discipline, demote, and ultimately terminate the targeted employee for poor job performance—often labeling them as "incompetent" or as a "troublemaker" (e.g., Barrow, 2012; Curry, 2015; Namie, 2003, 2010a, 2010b; Namie & Namie, 2003, 2011; WBI, 2014a, 2014b, among others).

Porath (2016b) reports that more than 85 percent of individual targets who chose to avoid or confront perpetrators are unsatisfied with how the situation ended. Moreover, they report that relying on institutional remedies—like going to HR—rarely works either. A mere 15 percent of those who reported the incidents to their employers confirmed that they were satisfied with how their employers responded to their bullying complaints.

In a study designed to understand how HR professionals interpret and respond to claims of bullying in the United Kingdom, Harrington, Warren, and Rayner (2015) found that HR enacts "symbolic violence" on employees who raise claims of bullying against their managers. They do this by taking hard evidence of bullying behaviors and interpreting it to favor the manager. In so doing, HR determines such abusive misconduct to be a legitimate management practice, thereby protecting the interests of the organization at the expense of HR's employee advocacy role.

Similarly, Harrington, Rayner, and Warren (2012) report that the typical HR response is to take action favoring the bully. In their study, HR practitioners "rarely" determine that a situation rises to the level of bullying when a manager is accused. They conclude that HR practitioners prioritize their relationships with managers and automatically distrust bullying claims made by employees—leading to a reasonable conclusion that dealing with employee complaints of bullying may simply be "too hot to handle" for HR practitioners (Harrington, Rayner, & Warren, 2012).

D'Cruz and Noronha (2010) found that HR is viewed by targets as a "one-sided managerial function"—meaning that HR is viewed as being focused solely on the interests of the organization. Because of this, they concluded that, in most instances, the bullied employee is left with "nothing more than their own individual voice," rendering them "completely vulnerable, with no avenues for redressal" (p. 530).

Similarly, Lewis and Rayner (2003) found that the typical execution of human resource management in most organizations—as a management ideology that promises to put "people issues" at the center of strategic decision making—creates an environment in which bullying remains unchallenged, is allowed to thrive, or is actually encouraged in an indirect way. Paradoxically, they found that the prevalence of bullying incidents actually *increases* in such environments. This led them to descriptively refer to the HR function as it exists in many organizations as a "a wolf in sheep's clothing" (p. 370).

Given these dismal statistics and findings, most would conclude that seeking counsel and protection from HR is essentially a no-win situation for bullied targets (Namie, 2010a, 2010b, 2012). Sadly, the outcomes consistently reported by these empirical studies are the reason that many targets report feeling victimized by both the bully *and* the HR department (D'Cruz & Noronha, 2010; Ferris, 2004, 2009; Harrington et al., 2012; Lewis & Rayner, 2003).

The View of the Perpetrators

Curiously, bullies rarely suffer career setbacks because the bully's supervisor often protects the bully and ignores the evidence—particularly if the individual is viewed as a "high performer." Recent survey data supports this conclusion. The 2014 study by the Workplace Bullying Institute (WBI, 2014b) found that 72 percent of employers react in a way that either condones or explicitly sustains the behavior, while less than 20 percent take action to stop the abuse. According to the study, 25 percent of employers *denied and/or failed to investigate* allegations of bullying, 16 percent *dismissed the allegations* as not being serious, 15 percent of employers *rationalized* the abusive behaviors, and 11 percent actually *defended the actions* because executive-level officials and midlevel managers were being accused. Astoundingly, 5 percent actually *encouraged* the workplace abuse.

These results are not a fluke; they have been repeatedly confirmed in prior empirical studies as well (WBI, 2000, 2007, 2010, 2012). Accordingly, with little to no organizational accountability, bullies often feel fairly confident about using abusive tactics as a management technique, safe in the belief that HR will either take their side or do nothing at all—and the empirical evidence is on their side.

The View of Senior Organizational Leaders

Daniel (2013a) examined how senior leaders in organizations throughout North America perceive the effectiveness of HR professionals to identify the friction points that most commonly lead to incidents of bullying or increased conflict. Executives in this study expressed frustration with HR due to their widely shared perceptions that HR practitioners (1) lack an understanding of business fundamentals; (2) are so focused on administration, rules, and processes that they are impediments to progress; (3) frequently say "no" without suggesting alternative solutions; and (4) are slow to act—or simply fail to respond at all.

While much of the criticism is undoubtedly valid, it should be noted that there are also a number of contributing factors that may help to explain why HR professionals are not perceived by many in the organization to be strong advocates for the interests of bullied targets:

1. HR practitioners are often personally bullied by senior leaders (Daniel, 2009a, 2009b, 2009c, 2011, 2012a; SHRM, 2012). It is extremely difficult to be an employee advocate at the same time that one is also a victim (D'Cruz & Noronha, 2010; Ferris, 2004; Griffith, 2013; Harrington et al., 2012; Lewis & Rayner, 2003; Namie & Namie, 2011).
2. Senior organizational leaders often tie HR's hands by failing to hold perpetrators accountable for their abusive actions, particularly if the bully is a high performer (Daniel & Metcalf, 2013, 2014b; D'Cruz & Noronha, 2010; Ferris, 2004, 2009; Harrington et al., 2012; Lewis & Rayner, 2003, Namie & Namie, 2011).
3. There are concerns among HR practitioners that if they are perceived by senior management as too closely aligning with the interests of bullied targets, their own job security and personal advancement may be jeopardized (Daniel, 2011, 2012a; D'Cruz & Noronha, 2010; Ferris, 2004, 2009; Harrington et al., 2012; Lewis & Rayner, 2003).

Importantly, while there *is* evidence to support the view that bullies act with malice or intent to harm their targets (Daniel, 2009a, 2009b, 2009c;

Namie, 2014; WBI, 2014a), it should be noted that there is *no evidence* to suggest any malice or bad intent by HR professionals toward targets when they respond to their complaints of bullying or mobbing (Daniel, 2011, 2012a; Fox & Cowan, 2015a; Woodrow & Guest, 2014).

Instead, the actions and response of HR practitioners are often dictated by the policies and tone of their senior leadership, as noted by Yamada (2010):

> All too often, however, it boils down to these truths: In workplaces that adopt and *practice* strong ethical values, HR practitioners can play a significant role in advancing a positive mission. By contrast, in workplaces that regard employees as expendable commodities, HR practitioners frequently become willing executioners of bad employment practices. (para. 14)

The View of the Society for Human Resource Management (SHRM)

SHRM is the world's largest HR membership organization devoted to HR management, with more than 285,000 members in over 165 countries (SHRM, 2016a). SHRM provides resources to serve the needs of global HR professionals and advance the professional practice of HR management. To this end, this global organization recently issued the new *SHRM Body of Competency and Knowledge* (2016d) guidelines, which help to provide further clarity about expectations for HR's role when dealing with, among many other issues, the management of workplace conflict.

These guidelines are very explicit about the expectation that HR will help manage relationships in the workplace; in fact, this competency specifically includes "serving as an advocate when appropriate" (Behavioral Competency #4—Relationship Management). In addition, HR professionals are expected to supervise HR investigations (together with legal counsel), recognize excessive HR liabilities and provide proactive strategic guidance for remediation, and coach executives on people-management issues (Behavioral Competency #5—Consultation).

The expectations for HR professionals move from relatively basic transactional responsibilities at an early level (e.g., provide basic information for the resolution of conflicts); to more complex relationships at the senior level (e.g., mediate difficult employee relations or other interactions as a neutral party); to even more complex and strategic responsibilities at an executive HR level (e.g., create conflict resolution strategies and processes throughout the organization). Importantly, the guidelines specifically require HR professionals to interact in situations of workplace conflict "as a neutral party." Additional discussion about executive expectations for HR success can be found in the recommendations included in the *SHRM Survey Findings: Using Competencies to Achieve Business Unit Success—The Executive Perspective* (SHRM, 2016e).

This examination of HR's role confirms that there are a growing number of empirical studies that help to explain and illuminate HR's role in mobbing and bullying situations. Because it is a complex and nuanced issue, it is fair to conclude that there is still much to be learned (Salin, 2008). Deciding when (or even whether) to intervene in a workplace conflict is one of the areas with which HR professionals have struggled for some time, but for which there are now some guidelines. How to make this important call will be discussed next.

HR'S DECISION TO INTERVENE IN A WORKPLACE CONFLICT—IS IT BULLYING OR NOT?

Despite the perception that HR is frequently not an advocate for bullied employees, they are usually the first group to be notified about a complaint of bullying or mobbing (SHRM, 2012). As is often the case with other types of complaints made by employees, the facts of these types of situations are frequently in dispute. Because of this, it can be difficult for HR professionals to ascertain whether the problem described is actually bullying (and should be further investigated and addressed) or whether it is simply the complaint of an employee working for a tough boss with demanding performance standards (in which case it is not bullying and no organizational intervention is required).

This distinction is an important one. Why? Because once this identification is made, the HR practitioner can then make a more informed decision about whether to intervene by further investigating the situation—or not. For years, the argument was that it was simply not possible to deal with this type of conflict because there was no clear definition of bullying, making it a difficult problem to identify and correct. Fortunately, that is no longer the case, and we now have clear definitions to work with in the United States (Healthy Workplace Bill, 2016; Workplace Bullying Institute, n.d.). Moreover, there is now some general guidance to assist HR practitioners in identifying a workplace bully as opposed to someone who is simply a "tough boss" (Daniel, 2009a, 2009b, 2009c). These guidelines will be examined next.

Actions of a Workplace Bully

In a study of HR professionals, Daniel (2009a, 2009b, 2009c) found that workplace bullies can be identified by several common characteristics, including widespread perceptions that bullies

- frequently misuse their power and authority
- focus on their own personal self-interests, as opposed to the longer-term good of the organization

- are prone to emotional outbursts
- are often inconsistent and unfair in their treatment of employees

The actions of bullies are perceived as *overwhelmingly negative* and typically include these behaviors: a need for control, exploitation, intimidation, threats, humiliation and embarrassment, a failure to communicate, manipulation, engaging in a pattern of obstructive behavior over time, ostracizing and ignoring employees, and gossiping or spreading rumors about their targets. In their own words, participants in the study describe a workplace bully like this:

> "With a bully, there's no goal orientation. There's nothing to do with your job. There's nothing to do with the company. It's simply something that has irritated the individual." (Daniel, 2009c, p. 129)
> "It has maddened him to the point that [he] is driven to make a person's life miserable . . . either with verbal threats or actual actions against" the individual." (Daniel, 2009c, p. 187)
> "[Bullies] throw caution to the wind as far as feelings are concerned, and their agenda is simply 'I'm going to get you.'" (Daniel, 2009c, p. 130)

Actions of a Tough Boss

Conversely, the behaviors and tactics of tough bosses are described quite differently. They are widely perceived to be

- objective, fair, and professional
- self-controlled and unemotional
- performance-focused—insistent on meeting high standards and holding employees accountable for meeting those expectations
- organizationally oriented—consistently operating to achieve the best interests of their companies

The actions of a tough boss are perceived by their employees to be *overwhelmingly positive*. Tough bosses are perceived as possessing several common characteristics: they are typically highly interactive, frequently engage in two-way communication, and really listen to their employees. In addition, they also engage in the active mentoring of their subordinates through coaching, counseling, and frequent performance feedback.

Although groups led by tough bosses most certainly do experience conflict, the perception is that they work hard to quickly resolve problems by engaging in honest and respectful discussions. In addition, while their intense focus on results may create tension and stress, their employees do not take the situations personally, nor do they experience diminished feelings of self-worth or adverse personal or health effects. In their own words, participants in the study describe tough bosses like this:

> "Fairness and intent differentiate a workplace bully from other conflicts. . . . I didn't mind him saying 'That's bull' because he respected me." (Daniel, 2009c, p. 146)
> "People understand that the boss has the 'right intent' even when she is being tough on them. [They have] good intentions geared toward making the company better." (Daniel, 2009c, p. 147)
> "[There was] no intent to intimidate, threaten, or embarrass." (Daniel, 2009c, p. 146)

A Clear Distinction—The Presence of Malice

This study unequivocally suggests that bullying is an unambiguous and intentional form of abusive workplace behavior. It is the presence or absence of *malice* that determines whether a conflict at work is actually workplace bullying—with malice being defined as "the desire to cause pain, injury, or distress to another" ("Malice," n.d.), a finding that has also been confirmed by the Workplace Bullying Institute's *2014-B Instant Poll: Intent of Workplace Bullies* (WBI, 2014a) and which is also included in the definition of bullying included in the draft legislation of the *Healthy Workplace Bill* (2016).

Making the Call—To Intervene or Not?

If the facts *do suggest* that malice is present, this would serve as a signal that the next set of organizational protocols should be followed—moving from the target's subjective complaint to a more objective fact-finding investigation (much like what occurs after a sexual harassment complaint is filed with HR). This is clearly a huge responsibility and, in most situations, a fairly difficult assessment for HR practitioners to make.

Conversely, if the facts presented *do not suggest* that malice is present, it would be appropriate to have a discussion with the complaining employee about why the situation is not considered to be bullying (and not waste time and organizational resources investigating the matter further). At that time, it would also be prudent to discuss possible strategies that the target might consider to minimize the tension and improve the existing workplace situation as well as to discuss resources that are available to support and care for the employee who is experiencing the situation as highly stressful.

It is mission critical for HR to be able to identify and distinguish bullies from tough bosses so that an informed decision can be made about how to respond to the situation. However, rather than dealing with such conflicts after the fact, proactively taking action to prevent the abuse from occurring in the first place is the preferred approach. As a result, a wide array of promising strategies that may be considered by HR professionals and their organizations to respond to or prevent—or at least minimize—these types of workplace conflicts will be discussed next.

ORGANIZATIONAL STRATEGIES TO DEAL WITH WORKPLACE BULLYING AND MOBBING

Researchers and practitioners have suggested a fairly broad range of potential responses to prevent and manage bullying at work. Hubert (2003) proposes a systematic approach to addressing workplace bullying that includes five key phases: prevention, uncovering, support, intervention, and aftercare. Similarly, McCarthy, Henderson, Sheehan, and Barker (2002) suggest that any effective response to workplace bullying needs to include "prevention, redress/resolution, and support" (pp. 27–30).

As is the case with most organizational interventions, there is no one-size-fits-all approach when it comes to the prevention of bullying and mobbing; instead, companies should take a systemic and tailored approach, adopting strategies at multiple levels that fit their unique culture and individual needs—all of which will work together to mutually support and reinforce the company's changing expectations (D'Cruz, 2012; Daniel & Metcalf, 2016; Ferris, 2004; Harrison, 2015; Harrison & Daniel, 2014; Salin, 2008; Tehrani, 2012; Woodman & Cook, 2005, among others).

Building on earlier frameworks offered by McCarthy et al. (2002) and Frost (2003), four key approaches will be discussed next: *prevention* strategies, *intervention* strategies, *restoration and recovery* strategies, and *accountability* strategies. Each of these alternative approaches will be considered separately; however, organizations should proceed cautiously, as there is still relatively little known about the long-term effectiveness of any of these suggested ways to deal with the problem (Branch & Murray, 2008; Einarsen, 2000; Raver, 2005).

Prevention Strategies

Based on a growing body of evidence-based research, some recommended strategies are described next.

Develop a culture of respect

It is recommended that organizations take steps to move from a *culture of fear* to a *culture of respect* by establishing and maintaining a workplace culture that requires that both respect and dignity be afforded to all employees, that is, a workplace climate where employees feel valued and supported and where they are encouraged to do their best work (Daniel, 2003a, 2003b; Rayner, 1999). In research released by the Society for Human Resource Management Foundation (SHRM, 2016b, 2016c), the respectful treatment of employees at all levels is the single most important contributor to the overall job satisfaction of employees.

When employees perceive that their organization is fair, respectful, and committed to them, they tend to reciprocate by giving their best effort as well—a concept which has been referred to as *perceived organizational support* (Eisenberger, Huntington, Hutchison, & Sowa, 1986; Rego & Cunha, 2008). Moreover, there is research suggesting that organizations that create an ethical infrastructure to support a respectful culture (through the implementation of their policies, conflict management training, formal sanctions, communication, social norms, and conflict management climate) are perceived as more successful in their interventions against workplace bullying (SHRM, 2016b; Einarsen, Mykletun, Skogstad, Einarsen, & Salin, 2015).

Adopt new policies or update existing ones

Researchers and practitioners have recommended that antibullying policies should be adopted or updated to include language that specifically details the type of abusive misconduct that is prohibited (along with examples). In addition, the policy should assure that there will be no retaliation for raising an issue and detail the possible consequences for failing to observe these behavioral expectations (e.g., Cowan, 2011; Daniel, 2009a, 2009b, 2009c; Daniel & Metcalf, 2016; Deschenaux, 2007; Namie, 2016; Namie & Namie, 2003, 2011; Richards & Daley, 2003; SHRM, 2012, 2016a, just to name a few).

Including a provision requiring *all* employees to notify management if they see a fellow employee being mistreated will ensure that coworkers who witness a problem feel obligated to speak up and alert the company's management before the situation escalates further (American Bar Association, 2012; SHRM, 2016d). Given that policies and practices are considered to be contractually enforceable in most jurisdictions, it should be noted that HR typically works in close partnership with the company's legal counsel to navigate the myriad potential issues with legal implications.

Ensure periodic communication and training about conduct expectations

HR can implement and enforce the company's conduct expectations through periodic training and frequent internal communications (Branch, 2006). It may also be pragmatic—as well as both cost- and time-effective—to incorporate antibullying expectations into existing policies and programs rather than launching a brand-new antibullying initiative from scratch

(Daniel, 2009a; Daniel & Metcalf, 2016; Namie & Daniel, 2012; Richards & Daly, 2003; McCarthy et al., 2002).

Moreover, consistent with recommendations by the EEOC's (2016) *Select Task Force on the Study of Harassment in the Workplace*, it is a good idea for companies to offer workplace civility training that focuses on the promotion of respect and civility at work. In addition, teaching bystanders to recognize potentially problematic behaviors can improve the sense of collective responsibility that employees feel and provide the tools and resources that bystanders need to intervene when they witness bullying or mobbing behavior. When trained properly, witnesses to problematic behaviors (e.g., supervisors, colleagues, and managers) can be an organization's most important resource in preventing and stopping this form of workplace abuse.

Track key metrics and regularly audit key processes

Critical HR processes should be regularly audited, and metrics should be tracked in key areas (e.g., employee complaints, employee discipline, workers' compensation claims, absenteeism, and termination). Regular monitoring of this data can serve as an "early alert" to the organization about potential problems that may be developing (Daniel, 2003a, 2003b, 2009a; Daniel & Metcalf, 2016; McCarthy & Barker, 2000).

Conduct periodic climate surveys

Employee satisfaction surveys are typically used by organizations to assess the "climate" of the organization—how employees are feeling about key issues related to employee engagement. This data can also serve to alert the company about problems that may be developing; however, action should be taken quickly to address any problems identified by the survey data. Doing so will help to generate trust among employees because they will see that the organization is taking their feedback seriously (Van Rooy & Oehler, 2013).

Intervention Strategies

Other strategies focused at the individual level—but which are also likely to positively affect an organization's culture—include efforts to screen, hire, and promote individuals with high emotional intelligence and competency to lead or manage people. Some promising initiatives are discussed next.

Conduct extensive interviews and background investigations

Extensive interviews and background checks should be conducted on potential new hires with the goal of learning as much as possible about the quality of their communication and conflict resolution skills (Aamodt, 2015, 2016; McKee, 2016; Porath, 2016a, 2016b). It is also a good idea to review turnover statistics in departments or divisions under the candidate's control because a high departure rate can be a potential danger signal—or at least a reason to conduct more due diligence.

Hire, promote, and train leaders with high emotional intelligence

Truly effective leaders are distinguished by a high degree of emotional intelligence (widely referred to as *EQ*) that includes self-awareness, self-regulation, motivation, empathy, and social skill (Goleman, 2004, 2006; Mayer & Salovey, 1997). An emphasis on hiring, training, and promoting leaders with high EQ can help an organization move toward the creation of a more positive workplace environment (Arnold, 2016; Bradberry, Greaves, & Lencioni, 2009; Deloitte University Press, 2016; Huhman, 2014; Jordan, Murray, Ashkanasy, & Connor, 2005; Lynn, 2008; McKee, 2016; Millennial Branding, 2014; Murray & Jordan, 2006; Porath, 2016a, 2016b). Behavioral interviews, structured interviews, and role-playing exercises, while expensive, can also be effective screening measures to prevent a bad hire (Porath, 2016a; Wilkie, 2016).

Expand orientation programs to include conduct expectations

The on-boarding process for new hires is an ideal time to stress the organization's values and its desire to maintain an ethical and respectful culture. Asking senior leaders to make brief comments to new groups of employees about these issues can also send a strong message about cultural norms that may help to minimize the potential for future misconduct (Van Maanen & Schein, 1979).

Provide early coaching and management and leadership skills training

The literature supports the contention that actions taken to increase the competence of an organization's leaders in dealing with bullying is of critical importance (Dugan & O'Shea, 2014; Salin, 2008; Schramm, 2016). All too often, new managers are promoted into management roles without having been provided with the requisite training to actually prepare them for the new job (Frost, 2003; Lesko, 2015).

Mentoring and coaching as a part of professional development can be an important way to create strong leaders (DiGirolamo, 2015; Germain, 2011; SHRM, 2016e). In addition, leadership training that includes a focus on emotions and interpersonal skills can help individuals improve their emotional intelligence and better understand how their behavior impacts others, which may cause them to adopt a more positive and effective management style (Frost, 2003; Goleman, 2004, 2006; Jordan et al., 2005; Kets de Vries, 2010; Murray & Jordan, 2006).

Provide enhanced "soft skills" training

Hard skills are the technical expertise and knowledge needed to perform a job, while *soft skills* are interpersonal qualities and personal attributes that an individual possesses (also referred to as *people skills*). Soft skills training focuses on the issues related to the development of greater emotional intelligence, integrity, communication, courtesy, responsibility, social skills, positive attitude, professionalism, flexibility, teamwork, and work ethic (Feffer, 2016; Higginbottom, 2015; Robles, 2012; SHRM, 2015). These skills are vital to the development of strong managers but are often missing. Robles (2012) found that executives overwhelmingly indicate that integrity and communication are the top two soft skills needed by employees in today's workplace but are often in short supply.

Modify performance evaluation and reward systems

It is recommended that steps be taken to incorporate measures of civility, empathy, and kindness into performance evaluation and reward systems so that employees are evaluated and rewarded not only on the results that they achieve but also on *how* they accomplish those results (Daniel, 2013b; Daniel & Metcalf, 2013, 2014a, 2014b, 2015, 2016). Implementation of 360-degree performance reviews can also be an effective strategy so that leaders and managers regularly receive feedback from not only their immediate supervisors but also from their colleagues and subordinates; however, it is generally recommended that this type of feedback only be used for purposes of employee development—not for evaluation (McKee, 2016; Mueller-Hanson & Pulakos, 2015).

Restoration and Recovery Strategies

It is typically up to HR professionals to help targets strategize about how to handle the bully's negative behavior and guide him or her to available resources. This can include help with coping and stress management strategies, support via employee assistance programs, access to coaching and counseling, plus information about employee benefits (Duffy & Sperry, 2012, 2014; Griffith, 2013; McCarthy et al., 2002; Richards & Daley, 2003; Tehrani, 2003). There is clear evidence to suggest that the provision of support to those affected by bullying can reduce its negative impact on the target's ability to cope (Duffy & Sperry, 2012, 2014; Lewis & Orford, 2005; Leymann & Gustafsson, 1996; Quine, 1999).

Some of the most promising ways to provide this support and assistance for targets are discussed next.

Offer coping skills, conflict resolution and resilience training

The development of coping skills and resilience have been suggested as strong ways to help targets handle workplace bullying experiences (Duffy & Sperry, 2012, 2014; McCarthy et al., 2002). In an earlier study, McCarthy et al. (2002) found that training in interpersonal skills, conflict resolution, and stress management assisted targets to cope with workplace bullying and manage their emotions better. In addition, counseling and rehabilitation are appropriate interventions for targets (Duffy & Sperry, 2012, 2014; Tehrani, 2012; Vartia, Korppoo, Fallenius, & Mattila, 2003).

Establish restorative justice procedures

The implementation of restorative justice practices has also been deemed a helpful response to workplace bullying situations. With this process, targets and bullies are brought together to discuss the harm done to the target and to identify ways to make amends and repair the relationship, including an apology from the perpetrator to the target. The goal of a restorative justice process is to make the target "whole" again—to the maximum extent possible (e.g., Duffy & Sperry, 2012, 2014; Duncan, 2011; Namie & Namie, 2003, 2011; Yamada, 2013b; Zehr, 2001).

Accountability Strategies

It is also important to ensure that there is accountability for those who fail to observe behavioral norms at work (Namie & Namie, 2003, 2011; Posen as cited in Owens, 2014). To this end, some possible strategies are discussed next.

Provide early intervention and coaching for abrasive employees

If an individual displays abrasive characteristics (e.g., behaviors that do not rise to the level of bullying or mobbing but do create tension and friction between employees), it is important to intervene early. With the help of an experienced coach, it is possible for abrasive managers to overcome their personal limitations or blind spots—*if* they are personally willing to accept the fact that they need to change—by developing more self-awareness and learning more effective ways to interact with others (Harrison, 2015; Harrison & Daniel, 2014). However, when coaching and confronting the bully fail to change that person's behavior, it is up to HR to counsel targets and confer with managers to decide on the appropriate disciplinary action for the bully, up to and including termination (Daniel, 2009a, 2009b, 2009c; Daniel & Metcalf, 2016, Yamada, 2012).

Establish fair reporting and investigation processes

Internal processes designed to resolve conflict create an incentive for employees to try to resolve conflicts directly with their employer (rather than filing complaints with regulatory agencies or engaging in costly and time-consuming litigation). If established, these complaint procedures should be easily accessible, fair, and transparent and should include timely reporting and investigation processes as well as strong antiretaliation protections (Daniel, 2003a, 2003b, 2009a; Merchant & Hoel, 2003).

Ensure that the risks of bullying are greater than the rewards

Bullies are likely to assess the potential risks associated with using abusive tactics and the potential benefits to be gained from their use. If the likelihood of discipline is low and the potential payoff is high (e.g., higher bonuses, promotions, etc.), bullying is likely to continue to be a viable strategy for personal success. As a result, it is imperative that the cost of bullying (e.g., the risk of discipline or other sanctions) outweighs the potential to personally benefit from its use through increased pay, promotions, and other rewards (Daniel, 2009a; Daniel & Metcalf, 2013, 2014b, 2015, 2016; Ferris, 2004, 2009).

Engage in postproject after-action evaluations

The U.S. military is widely credited for creating the process of *after-action reviews*—a structured review or debrief process analyzing *what* happened, *why* it happened, and *how* it can be done better by the participants and leaders responsible for the project or event (Department of the Army, 1993). The implementation of a similar process within an organization can create greater self-awareness among those involved in a bullying situation, thus potentially creating a stronger impetus for personal behavioral change (Daniel & Metcalf, 2014a, 2015).

Impose real accountability and consequences

Harrison (2015) suggests that abrasive leaders should be put on notice and given a chance to correct their abusive behavior. After a reasonable period of coaching and training, though, the employment relationship should be terminated with those who are not able (or simply not willing) to change (Daniel & Metcalf, 2015, 2016; Harrison, 2015; SHRM, 2016d; Yamada, 2012). Organizations where interpersonal bullying is ignored or overlooked permit it (either directly or unwittingly) because bullying gets normalized—and subsequently reproduced—because it remains unaddressed and begins to be an accepted part of the organizational culture (Branch, Ramsay, & Barker, 2007; Daniel & Metcalf, 2013, 2014b, 2015, 2016; Lewis & Rayner, 2003; Owens, 2014; Salin & Hoel, 2011).

Many of these practices have been described in the HR literature as "high-performance work practices" (Huselid, 1995) or "sophisticated" HR practices (Heffernan & Flood, 2000) and are generally viewed as viable strategies for creating sustainable organizational change. Importantly, as outlined in the SHRM *Body of Competency and Knowledge* (2016d) guidelines, HR professionals are expected to possess the foundational competencies necessary to implement most, if not all, of these recommendations. While a more detailed examination of the competency guidelines is beyond the scope of this article, it should be noted that SHRM has provided important guidance about HR's expected organizational role and competencies with respect to numerous workplace matters. Accordingly, SHRM's competency and knowledge guidelines for HR professionals are highly recommended to the readers desiring additional information and clarity in this regard. In addition, an expanded discussion about the strategies and tools discussed in this chapter can be found in a newly released book by Daniel and Metcalf (2016) titled *Stop Bullying at Work: Strategies and Tools for HR, Legal, & Risk Management Professionals*.

CONCLUSIONS

As the information discussed in this chapter has shown, HR professionals are front and center in responding to and preventing situations of workplace bullying and mobbing—as they should be. Namie and Namie (2011, pp. 128–130) provide an important note of caution about HR's role, though, suggesting that the primary responsibility for antibullying initiatives should be retained by the organization's senior leaders and not simply delegated to HR to handle on its own. If senior leaders do not take an active and visible role in promoting antibullying efforts, employees can easily misinterpret their absence to suggest that they do not find the issue to be serious enough to warrant their time and attention.

Spearheading change is hard under the best of circumstances, and implementing changes to an organization's culture is an especially difficult undertaking. Those who currently benefit from the use of bullying tactics have much to lose if the changes are successful and bullying as a management strategy is no longer accepted by the organization (Daniel & Metcalf, 2013, 2014a, 2014b, 2015, 2016; D'Cruz & Noronha, 2010; Ferris, 2004, 2009; Tehrani, 2012;). As a result, HR professionals should prepare for the fact that these individuals will be vigilant in their efforts to sabotage any efforts to change the culture (Namie & Namie, 2011). It is no doubt a serious understatement to suggest that change is usually complex, messy, and often brings out the worst in people (Kotter, 1995).

Despite the organizational complexity that can reasonably be anticipated, new strategies should be implemented with the ultimate goal of impacting the culture of the organization, while at the same time strengthening and supporting the organization's leaders and managers, providing restoration and recovery measures for targets, and ensuring that there are accountability measures for those bullies who cannot—or will not—change. The essence of HR's unique (and often difficult) organizational role in managing conflict situations is to "walk the tightrope" to ensure that employees are protected from abusive and bullying managers *and* that managers retain the right to require performance excellence, even though they may be widely considered to be tough bosses (Daniel, 2009a, 2009b, 2009c; Cowan, 2009).

When it comes to bullying at work and HR's role, Yamada (2013a) succinctly nails it when he observes these common workplace relationships:

- *Good workplace + Good HR = Ideal combo.* Reports of bullying are likely to be treated fairly and workplace bullying is much less likely to occur in such organizations.
- *Good workplace + Bad HR = Bullying is still less likely to occur.* However, when it does, HR may impede a just response while keeping management out of the loop.
- *Bad workplace + Good HR = Lousy organization.* These types of companies are not good for the target or HR. In fact, HR may also be bullied if it rallies to help the target.
- *Bad workplace + Bad HR = Situation is very likely hopeless.*

Creating and sustaining a psychologically healthy workplace—built on mutual respect and dignity for all—benefits both employees and their organizations. The empirical evidence unequivocally confirms that a respectful workplace environment results in higher levels of employee morale and job satisfaction, lower turnover, reduced health costs, higher productivity, and greater profitability for the organization (Namie & Namie, 2003, 2011; Pearson & Porath, 2009; SHRM, 2012, 2016b, 2016c, and many others). Coincidentally, demonstrating the courage and leadership necessary to confront this destructive workplace issue is also likely to result in a more effective and admired HR department.

REFERENCES

Aamodt, M. G. (2015). Using background checks in the employee selection process. In C. Hanvey & K. Sady (Eds.), *Practitioner's guide to legal issues in organizations*. New York: Springer.

Aamodt, M. G. (2016). *Conducting background checks for employee selection*. Retrieved from https://www.shrm.org/Research/Documents/SHRM-SIOP%20Background%20Checks.pdf

American Bar Association. (2012). *Model anti-bullying policy*. Retrieved from http://www.americanbar.org/content/dam/aba/events/labor_law/2012/03/national_conference_on_equal_employment_opportunity_law/mw2012eeo_eisenberg2.authcheckdam.pdf.

Arnold, T. K. (2016, January 8). *Spotting the emotionally intelligent candidate*. Retrieved from https://www.shrm.org/hrdisciplines/employeerelations/articles/pages/emotionally-intelligent-leaders.aspx

Barrow, L. (2012, January 30). Workplace bullying and the role of HR management [Blog post]. Retrieved from http://www.hrvoice.org/workplace-bullying-and-the-role-of-human-resource-management

Bradberry, T., Greaves, J., & Lencioni, P. (2009). *Emotional intelligence 2.0*. San Diego, CA: Talent Smart.

Branch, S. (2006). *Upwards bullying: An exploratory study of power, dependency and the work environment for Australian managers* (Unpublished doctoral dissertation). Griffith University, Queensland, Australia. Retrieved from https://www120.secure.griffith.edu.au/rch/file/d681dc3b-64d8-9968-14d2-8089fcd1637d/1/02Main.pdf

Branch, S., & Murray, J. (2008, December 5). *Building relationships and resilience in the workplace: Construction of a workplace bullying training program*. Paper presented at the Australia and New Zealand Academy of Management Conference, Auckland, New Zealand. Retrieved from http://epublications.bond.edu.au/business_pubs/117

Branch, S., Ramsay, S., & Barker, M. (2007). Managers in the ring line: Contributing factors to workplace bullying by staff, an interview study. *Journal of Management and Organization, 13*(3), 264–281.

Cowan, R. (2009). *Walking the tightrope: Workplace bullying and the HR professional* (Unpublished doctoral dissertation). Texas A&M University, College Station, TX. Retrieved from http://oaktrust.library.tamu.edu/bitstream/handle/1969.1/ETD-TAMU-2009-12-7497/COWAN-DISSERTATION.pdf

Cowan, R. (2011). "Yes, we have an anti-bullying policy, but . . .": HR professionals' understandings and experiences with workplace bullying policy. *Communication Studies, 6*(3), 307–327.

Curry, L. (2015, September 26). *How HR can and should handle bullies*. Retrieved from http://www.workplacebullying.org/leaders1

Daniel, T. A. (2003a). Developing a "culture of compliance" to prevent sexual harassment. *Employment Relations Today, 30*(3), 33–42. doi:10.1002/ert.10096

Daniel, T. A. (2003b). Tools for building a positive employee relations environment. *Employment Relations Today, 30*(2), 51–64. doi:10.1002/ert.10086

Daniel, T. A. (2009a). *Stop bullying at work: Strategies and tools for HR & legal professionals*. Alexandria, VA: SHRM Books.

Daniel, T. A. (2009b, June 1). Tough boss or workplace bully? *HR Magazine, 54*(6). Retrieved from http://www.shrm.org/publications/hrmagazine/editorialcontent/pages/0609daniel.aspx

Daniel, T. A. (2009c). *"Tough boss" or workplace bully? A grounded theory study of insights from human resource professionals* (Doctoral dissertation). Retrieved from ProQuest. (Accession Number 3350585)

Daniel, T. A. (2011, May 1). When bullying hits home. *HR Magazine, 56*(5). Retrieved from http://www.shrm.org/publications/hrmagazine/editorialcontent/2011/0511/pages/0511brief.aspx

Daniel, T. A. (2012a). Caught in the crossfire: When HR practitioners become targets of bullying. *Employment Relations Today, 39*(1), 9–16.

Daniel, T. A. (2012b, April). *Managing difficult employees and disruptive behaviors.* Retrieved from https://www.shrm.org/templatestools/toolkits/pages/managingdifficultemployeesa.aspx

Daniel, T. A. (2013a). Executive perceptions about the effectiveness of human resources. *Employment Relations Today, 40*(2), 1–11. doi:10.1002/ert.21405

Daniel, T. A. (2013b). *Executive success and the increased potential for ethical failure.* Retrieved from http://www.shrm.org/LegalIssues/EmploymentLawAreas/Documents/Legalpercent20Report0713.pdf

Daniel, T. A., & Metcalf, G. S. (2013). Taming the beast: How American corporations unwittingly conspire to make bullying a rational choice. *Proceedings of the International Society for Systems Science, 57.*

Daniel, T. A., & Metcalf, G. S. (2014a, October 30–November 2). *A preliminary exploration into toxic leadership in the U.S. Army.* Paper presented at the 16th Annual International Leadership Association Global Conference, San Diego, California.

Daniel, T. A., & Metcalf, G. S. (2014b, June 17–20). *Taming the beast: How American corporations conspire to make workplace bullying a rational choice.* Paper presented at the 9th International Conference on Workplace Bullying and Harassment, Milan, Italy.

Daniel, T. A., & Metcalf, G. S. (2015). *Crossing the line: An examination of toxic leadership in the U.S. Army.* Retrieved from https://www.researchgate.net/publication/274252085_Crossing_the_Line_An_Examination_of_Toxic_Leadership_in_the_U.S._Army. doi:10:13140/RG.2.1.2700.4969

Daniel, T. A., & Metcalf, G. S. (2016). *Stop bullying at work: Strategies and tools for HR, legal & risk management professionals* (2nd ed.). Alexandria, VA: SHRM Books.

D'Cruz, P. (2012). *Workplace bullying in India.* New Delhi, India: Routledge.

D'Cruz, P., & Noronha, E. (2010). Protecting my interests: HRM and targets' coping with bullying. *The Qualitative Report, 15*(3), 507–534.

Deloitte University Press. (2016). *Global human capital trends 2016 report.* Retrieved from http://www2.deloitte.com/global/en/pages/human-capital/articles/introduction-human-capital-trends.html?id=us:2pm:3lp:dup3018:eng:cons:040616:hct16#

Department of the Army. (1993). *A leader's guide to after-action reviews* (TC 25-20). Retrieved from http://www.au.af.mil/au/awc/awcgate/army/tc_25-20/tc25-20.pdf

Deschenaux, J. (2007, September 20). *Experts: Anti-bullying policies increase productivity, add to bottom line.* Retrieved from http://workplacebullying.org/press/SHRM092007.html

DiGirolamo, J. (2015). *Coaching for professional development.* Retrieved from https://www.shrm.org/Research/Documents/SHRM-SIOP%20Coaching%20for%20Professional%20Development.pdf

Duffy, M., & Sperry, L. (2012). *Mobbing: Causes, consequences and solutions.* New York: Oxford University Press, Inc.

Duffy, M., & Sperry, L. (2014). *Overcoming mobbing: A recovery guide for workplace aggression.* New York: Oxford University Press.

Dugan, B. A., & O'Shea, P. G. (2014). *Leadership development: Growing talent strategically.* Retrieved from https://www.shrm.org/Research/Documents/SHRM-SIOP%20Leader%20Development.pdf

Duncan, S. (2011). Workplace bullying and the role restorative practices can play in preventing and addressing the problem. *Industrial Law Journal, 32,* 2331–2366.

Einarsen, S. (2000). Harassment and bullying at work: A review of the Scandinavian approach. *Aggression and Violent Behavior, 5*(4), 379–401.

Einarsen, K., Mykletun, R.J., Skogstad, A., Einarsen, S., & Salin, D. (2015, May 24). *Ethical infrastructure in combating unethical behavior in organizations: The case of workplace bullying.* Paper presented at EAWOP Conference, Oslo, Norway.

Eisenberger, R., Huntington, R., Hutchison, S., & Sowa, D. (1986). Perceived organizational support. *Journal of Applied Psychology, 71*(3), 500–507.

Equal Employment Opportunity Commission (EEOC). (2016). *Select task force on the study of harassment in the workplace.* Retrieved from https://www.eeoc.gov/eeoc/task_force/harassment

Falcone, P. (2002, October). Understanding the HR mind-set. *HR Magazine, 47*(10), 117–122.

Feffer, M. (2016, April 1). HR's hard challenge: When employees lack soft skills. *HR Magazine, 61*(3). Retrieved from https://www.shrm.org/publications/hrmagazine/editorialcontent/2016/0416/pages/0416-soft-skills.aspx

Ferris, P. A. (2004). A preliminary typology of organizational responses to allegations of workplace bullying: See no evil, hear no evil, speak no evil. *British Journal of Guidance & Counseling, 32*(3), 389–395.

Ferris, P. A. (2009). The role of the consulting psychologist in the prevention, correction of bullying and mobbing in the workplace. *Consulting Psychology Journal: Practice and Research, 61*(3), 169–189.

Fox, S., & Cowan, R. L. (2015b). Being pushed and pulled: A model of U.S. HR professionals' roles in bullying situations. *Personnel Review, 44*(1), 119–139.

Fox, S., & Cowan, R. L. (2015a). Revision of the workplace bullying checklist: The importance of human resource management's role in defining and addressing workplace bullying. *Human Resource Management Journal, 25*(1), 116–130.

Frost, P. J. (2003). *Toxic emotions at work: How compassionate managers handle pain and conflict.* Boston, MA: Harvard Business School Publishing.

Frost, P. J. (2004). Handling toxic emotions: New challenges for leaders and their organization. *Organizational Dynamics, 33*(2), 111–127.

Frost, P. J., & Robinson, S. (1999, July/August). The toxic handler: Organizational hero—and casualty. *Harvard Business Review.* Retrieved from https://hbr.org/1999/07/the-toxic-handler-organizational-hero-and-casualty

Germain, M. L. (2011). Formal mentoring relationships and attachment theory: Implications for human resource department. *Human Resource Development Review, 10*(123), 54–65.

Goleman, D. (2004, January). What makes a leader? *Harvard Business Review.* Retrieved from https://hbr.org/2004/01/what-makes-a-leader

Goleman, D. (2006). *Social intelligence: The new science of human relationships*. New York: Bantam.

Griffith, D. B. (2013, October 4). *Responding to workplace bullying, the role of HR*. Retrieved from https://www.higheredjobs.com/articles/articleDisplay.cfm?ID=461

Grillo, M. C. (2014, October 8). Straddling the line or embracing the dichotomy: HR's role as an employee advocate as necessary to remain (or become) a business partner [Blog post]. Retrieved from http://www.cornellhrreview.org/straddling-the-line-or-embracing-the-dichotomy-hrs-role-as-an-employee-advocate-as-necessary-to-remaining-or-becoming-a-business-partner

Harrington, S., Rayner, C., & Warren, S. (2012). "Too hot to handle?": Trust and human resource practitioners' implementation of anti-bullying policy. *Human Resource Management Journal, 22*(4), 392–408.

Harrington, S., Warren, S., & Rayner, C. (2015). Human resource management practitioners' responses to workplace bullying: Cycles of symbolic violence. *Organization, 22*(3), 368–389.

Harrison, L. (2015). *Bringing and organizational lens to the complex issue of abrasive leadership*. Retrieved from http://www.saybrook.edu/rethinkingcomplexity/rc-posts/bringing-organizational-lens-complex-issue-abrasive-leadership

Harrison, L., & Daniel, T. A. (2014, November 1). *A perfect storm: A systems view of the phenomenon of abrasive leadership*. 16th Annual International Leadership Association Global Conference, San Diego, California.

Healthy Workplace Bill. (2016). Retrieved from http://healthyworkplacebill.org

Heffernan, M., & Flood, P. (2000). An exploration of the relationships between the adoption of managerial competencies, organizational characteristics, human resource sophistication and performance in Irish organizations. *Journal of European Industrial Training, 24*(2–4), 128–136.

Higginbottom, K. (2015, May 21). Graduates with soft skills will become increasingly important. *Forbes*. Retrieved from http://www.forbes.com/sites/karenhigginbottom/2015/05/21/graduates-with-soft-skills-will-become-increasingly-important/#27f583872a20

Hubert, A. (2003). To prevent and overcome undesirable interactions: A systematic approach model. In S. Einarsen, H. Hoel, D. Zapf, & C. L. Cooper (Eds.), *Bullying and emotional abuse in the workplace: International perspectives in research and practice* (pp. 299–311). London, England: Taylor & Francis.

Huhman, H. R. (2014, June 18). The 10 unique soft skills employers desire in new hires. *Entrepreneur*. Retrieved from https://www.entrepreneur.com/article/234864

Huselid, M. (1995). The impact of human resource management practices on turnover, productivity, and corporate financial performance. *Academy of Management Journal, 38*(3), 635–672.

Jordan, P., Murray, J., Ashkansay, N., & Connors, P. (2005). *Examining the impact of relational and behavioral training interventions on individual emotional intelligence*. Paper presented at the Sixth Australian Industrial & Psychology Conference, Surfers Paradise, Queensland, Australia.

Kets de Vries, M. (2010). *Faculty & research working paper: Developing leaders and leadership development*. Retrieved from http://sites.insead.edu/facultyresearch/research/doc.cfm?did=45346

Kotter, J. P. (1995, May/June). Leading change: Why transformation efforts fail. *Harvard Business Review*. Retrieved from https://hbr.org/1995/05/leading-change-why-transformation-efforts-fail-2

Kulik, C. T., Cregan, C., Metz, I., & Brown, M. (2009, September/October). HR managers as toxic handlers: The buffering effect of formalizing toxic handling. *Human Resource Management, 48*(5), 695–716.

Lesko, A. (2015). *New manager influences: Probing the effects of career motivation on work engagement* (Doctoral dissertation). Retrieved from ProQuest. (Accession Number 3279207)

Lewis, S., & Orford, J. (2005). Women's experiences of workplace bullying: Changes in social relationships. *Journal of Community & Applied Social Psychology, 15*(1), 29–47.

Lewis, D., & Rayner, C. (2003). Bullying and human resource management: A wolf in sheep's clothing? In S. Einarsen, H. Hoel, D. Zapf, & C. L. Cooper (Eds.), *Bullying and emotional abuse in the workplace: International perspectives in research and practice* (pp. 370–382). London, England: Taylor & Francis.

Leymann, H., & Gustafsson, A. (1996). Mobbing at work and the development of post-traumatic stress disorders. *European Journal of Work and Organizational Psychology, 5*(2), 251–275.

Lynn, A. B. (2008). *The EQ interview: Finding employees with high emotional intelligence*. New York: AMACOM.

Malice. (n.d.). In *Merriam-Webster*. Retrieved from http://www.merriam-webster.com/dictionary/malice

Maxwell, S. M. (2015). *An exploration of human resource personnel and toxic leadership* (Doctoral dissertation). Retrieved from ScholarWorks. (Accession Number 548)

Mayer, J. D., & Salovey, P. (1997). What is emotional intelligence? In P. Salovey & D. J. Sluyter (Eds.), *Emotional development and emotional intelligence: Educational implications* (pp. 3–31). New York: Basic Books.

McCarthy, P., & Barker, M. (2000). Workplace bullying risk audit. *Journal of Occupational Health & Safety–Australia and New Zealand, 16*, 409–418.

McCarthy, P., Henderson, M., Sheehan, M., & Barker, M. (2002). Workplace bullying: Its management and prevention. In *Australian Master OHS and Environment Guide 2003* (pp. 519–549). Sydney, Australia: CCH Australia Limited.

McKee, A. (2016, February 5). How to hire for emotional intelligence. *Harvard Business Review*. Retrieved from https://hbr.org/2016/02/how-to-hire-for-emotional-intelligence?cm_sp=Article-_-Links-_-Top%20of%20Page%20Recirculation

McLaughlin, K. (2014, September 24). Workplace bullying: A silent epidemic. *HR Magazine, 59*(10). Retrieved from http://www.shrm.org/publications/hrmagazine/editorialcontent/2014/1014/pages/1014-viewpoint-workplace-bullying.aspx

Meisinger, S. R. (2005). The four Cs of the HR profession: Being competent, curious, courageous, and caring about people. *Human Resource Management, 44*(2), 189–194.

Merchant, V., & Hoel, H. (2003). Investigating complaints of bullying. In S. Einarsen, H. Hoel, D. Zapf, & C. L. Cooper (Eds.), *Bullying and emotional abuse* in the workplace: International perspectives in research and practice (pp. 259–269). London, England: Taylor & Francis.

Metz, I., Brown, M., Cregan, C., & Kulik, C. T. (2014). "Toxin handling" and well-being: The case of the human resource manager. *European Journal of Work & Organizational Psychology, 23*(2), 248–262.

Millennial Branding. (2014). *Multi-generational job search survey 2014*. Retrieved from http://millennialbranding.com/2014/multi-generational-job-search-study-2014

Mueller-Hanson & Pulakos, E. D. (2015). *Putting the "performance" back in performance management*. Retrieved from https://www.shrm.org/Research/Documents/SHRM-SIOP%20Performance%20Management.pdf

Murray, J. P., & Jordan, P. J. (2006, August 14). *Improving emotional intelligence and performance through emotions focused training interventions*. Paper presented at the Annual Meetings of the Academy of Management, Atlanta, Georgia.

Namie, G. (2003, November/December). Workplace bullying: Escalated incivility. *Ivey Business Journal*. Retrieved from http://iveybusinessjournal.com/publication/workplace-bullying-escalated-incivility

Namie, G. (2010a, August 5). *HR: Friend or foe of workplace bullying targets?* Retrieved from http://www.workplacebullying.org/hr-and-workplace-bullying

Namie, G. (2010b, August 13). *New research shows HR's negative role in workplace bullying*. Retrieved from http://www.workplacebullying.org/dcruz-study

Namie, G. (2012, May 25). *Search for HR heroes begins at WBI*. Retrieved from http://www.workplacebullying.org/hr-heroes

Namie, G. (2014, October 17). *About the bully's intent to harm*. Retrieved from http://www.workplacebullying.org/tag/malice

Namie, G. (2016, February 25). *C-suite rationale to address workplace bullying*. Retrieved from http://www.workplacebullying.org/tag/gary-namie

Namie, G., & Daniel, T. A. (2012). *Master's series for HR professionals: Workplace bullying* [DVD]. United States: Workplace Bullying Institute.

Namie, G., & Namie, R. (2003). *The bully at work: What you can do to stop the hurt and reclaim your dignity on the job*. Naperville, IL: Sourcebooks.

Namie, G., & Namie, R. (2011). *The bully-free workplace: Stop jerks, weasels, and snakes from killing your organization*. New York, NY: John Wiley & Sons.

Owens, D. M. (2014, March 1). Dr. David Posen's prescription for work stress. *HR Magazine, 59*(3). Retrieved from https://www.shrm.org/publications/hrmagazine/editorialcontent/2014/0314/pages/0314-workplace-stress.aspx

Pearson, C., & Porath, C. (2009). *The cost of bad behavior: How incivility is damaging your business and what to do about it*. New York: Portfolio.

Porath, C. (2016a, February 3). How to avoid hiring a toxic employee. *Harvard Business Review*. Retrieved from https://hbr.org/2016/02/how-to-avoid-hiring-a-toxic-employee

Porath, C. (2016b, April). Managing yourself: An antidote to incivility. *Harvard Business Review*, 108–111. Retrieved from https://hbr.org/2016/04/an-antidote-to-incivility

Quine, L. (1999). Workplace bullying in NHS community trust: Staff questionnaire survey. *British Medical Journal, 318*(7178), 228–232.

Raver, J. (2005, August 8). *Workplace bullying: International perspectives on moving from research to practice*. Symposium conducted at the Academy of Management meeting, Honolulu, Hawaii.

Rayner, C. (1999). From research to implementation: Finding leverage for prevention. *International Journal of Manpower, 20*(1/2), 28–38.

Rego, A., & Cunha, M. P. (2008). Workplace spirituality and organizational commitment: An empirical study. *Journal of Organizational Change Management, 21*(1), 53–75.

Richards, J., & Daley, H. (2003). Bullying policy: Development, implementation and monitoring. In S. Einarsen, H. Hoel, D. Zapf, & C. L. Cooper (Eds.), *Bullying and emotional abuse in the workplace: International perspectives in research and practice*. London, England: Taylor & Francis.

Robles, M. M. (2012). Executive perceptions of the top 10 soft skills needed in today's environment. *Business Communication Quarterly, 75*(4), 453–465.

Salin, D. (2008). The prevention of workplace bullying as a question of human resource management: Measures adopted and underlying organizational factors. *Scandinavian Journal of Management, 24*(5), 221–231.

Salin, D., & Hoel, H. (2011). Organizational causes of workplace bullying. In S. Einarsen, H. Hoel, D. Zapf, & C. L. Cooper (Eds.), *Bullying and emotional abuse in the workplace: International perspectives in research and practice*. London, England: Taylor & Francis.

Schramm, J. (2016, April 1). Survey: Employees lack critical competencies. *HR Magazine*. Retrieved from https://www.shrm.org/publications/hrmagazine/editorial content/2016/0416/pages/0416-competencies-leadership.aspx

Society for Human Resource Management (SHRM). (2012, February 28). *SHRM survey findings: Workplace bullying*. Retrieved from http://www.shrm.org/research /surveyfindings/articles/pages/workplacebullying.aspx

Society for Human Resource Management (SHRM). (2013, August 2). *Organizational complexity overwhelms many HR leaders*. Retrieved from https://www.shrm.org/hr disciplines/orgempdev/articles/pages/organizational-complexity-overwhelms-hr .aspx

Society for Human Resource Management (SHRM). (2015). *SHRM research: Workforce readiness and skills shortages*. Retrieved from https://www.shrm.org/Research /FutureWorkplaceTrends/Documents/Workforce%20Readiness%20and%20 Skills%20Shortages.pdf

Society for Human Resource Management (SHRM). (2016a). *About SHRM*. Retrieved from https://www.shrm.org/about/pages/default.aspx

Society for Human Resource Management (SHRM). (2016b). *Creating a more human workplace where employees and businesses thrive*. Retrieved from https://www.shrm.org/ about/foundation/products/documents/4-16%20human%20workplace-final.pdf

Society for Human Resource Management (SHRM). (2016c). *Employee satisfaction and engagement: Revitalizing a changing workforce*. Retrieved from https://www .shrm.org/Research/SurveyFindings/Articles/Documents/2016-Employee-Job -Satisfaction-and-Engagement-Report.pdf

Society for Human Resource Management (SHRM). (2016d). *The SHRM body of competency and knowledge*. Retrieved from https://www.shrm.org/Documents/SHRM -BoCK-FINAL.pdf

Society for Human Resource Management (SHRM). (2016e). *SHRM survey findings: Using competencies to achieve business unit success—the executive perspective*. Retrieved from https://www.shrm.org/hr-today/trends-and-forecasting/research-and-surveys/Documents/SHRM%20Survey%20Findings_Using%20Competencies%20to%20Achieve%20Business%20Unit%20Success_FINAL.pdf

Tehrani, N. (2003). Counseling and rehabilitating employees involved with bullying. In S. Einarsen, H. Hoel, D. Zapf, & C. L. Cooper (Eds.), *Bullying and emotional abuse in the workplace: International perspectives in research and practice* (pp. 270–284). London, England: Taylor and Francis.

Tehrani, N. (2012). *Workplace bullying: Symptoms and solutions*. New York: Routledge.

Ulrich, D. (1997). *HR champions: The next agenda for adding value and delivering results*. Cambridge, MA: HBR Press.

Van Maanen, J., & Schein, E. H. (1979). Toward a theory of organizational socialization. *Research in Organizational Behavior, 1,* 209–264.

Van Rooy, D. L., & Oehler, K. (2013). *The evolution of employee opinion surveys: The voice of employees as a strategic management tool*. SHRM-SIOP Science of HR White Paper Series. Retrieved from https://www.shrm.org/Research/Articles/Documents/SIOP%20-%20Employee%20Engagement%20final.pdf

Vartia, M., Korppoo, L., Fallenius, S., & Mattila, M. (2003). Workplace bullying: The role of occupational health services. In S. Einarsen, H. Hoel, D. Zapf, & C. L. Cooper (Eds.), *Bullying and emotional abuse in the workplace: International perspectives in research and practice* (pp. 285–298). London, England: Taylor and Francis.

Wilkie, D. (2016, March). Are you in a bully-prone industry: Why bad behavior is more prevalent in certain fields and what you can do about it. *HR Magazine*. Retrieved from https://www.shrm.org/publications/hrmagazine/editorialcontent/2016/0316/pages/0316-bully-prone-industries.aspx

Woodman, P., & Cook, P. (2005). *Bullying at work: The experience of managers*. London, England: Chartered Management Institute.

Woodrow, C., & Guest, D. D. (2014). When good HR gets bad results: Exploring the challenge of HR implementation in the case of workplace bullying. *Human Resource Management Journal, 24*(1), 38–56.

Workplace Bullying Institute (WBI). (n.d.). *Definition of workplace bullying*. Retrieved from http://www.workplacebullying.org/individuals/problem/definition

Workplace Bullying Institute (WBI). (2000). *2000 U.S. hostile workplace survey*. Retrieved from http://www.workplacebullying.org/multi/pdf/N-N-2000.pdf

Workplace Bullying Institute (WBI). (2007). *2007 U.S. workplace bullying survey*. Retrieved from http://www.workplacebullying.org/wbiresearch/wbi-2007

Workplace Bullying Institute (WBI). (2010). *2010 U.S. workplace bullying survey*. Retrieved from http://workplacebullying.org/multi/pdf/WBI_2010_Natl_Survey.pdf

Workplace Bullying Institute (WBI). (2012). *2012 instant poll C—aftermath of requesting help from human resources* Retrieved from http://www.workplacebullying.org/multi/pdf/WBI-2012-IP-C.pdf

Workplace Bullying Institute (WBI). (2014a). *2014-B instant poll: Intent of workplace bullies*. Retrieved from http://www.workplacebullying.org/wbi-2014-ip-b

Workplace Bullying Institute (WBI). (2014b). *2014 U.S. workplace bullying survey*. Retrieved from http://www.workplacebullying.org/wbiresearch/wbi-2014-us-survey

Yamada, D. (2009, January 4). "HR was useless" [Blog post]. Retrieved from https://newworkplace.wordpress.com/2009/01/04/hr-was-useless

Yamada, D. (2010, September 27). Can an ethical HR officer survive at a bad company? [Blog post]. Retrieved from https://newworkplace.wordpress.com/2010/09/27/can-an-ethical-hr-officer-survive-at-a-bad-company

Yamada, D. (2012, January 9). Workplace bullying is bad for business. [Blog post]. Retrieved from http://www.workplacebullying.org/yamada-2

Yamada, D. (2013a, October 28). HR, workplace bullying, and the abandoned target [Blog post]. Retrieved from https://newworkplace.wordpress.com/2013/10/28/hr-workplace-bullying-and-the-abandoned-target

Yamada, D. (2013b, January 14). Restorative justice and workplace bullying [Blog post]. Retrieved from https://newworkplace.wordpress.com/2013/01/14/restorative-justice-and-workplace-bullying

Zehr, H. (2001). *The little book of restorative justice*. Retrieved from http://www.unicef.org/tdad/littlebookrjpakaf.pdf

12

Innovative Practices in Workplace Conflict Resolution

John-Robert Curtin

Workplace bullying and mobbing situations call upon organizations to respond fairly, promptly, and thoughtfully. In this chapter, some innovative practices in organizational and workplace conflict resolution will be presented. These practices can be effective in working with stakeholders in bullying and mobbing scenarios. They include alternative dispute resolution, restorative justice, behavioral transition, and processes involved in creating empathic organizations. Selected existing programs designed to proactively address troublesome workplace behavior will also be reviewed, such as the Cup of Coffee Program at Vanderbilt University School of Medicine. How minimizing or denying the presence of conflict can actually intensify conflict in settings will also be discussed.

Thus, the importance of how conflict is managed relative to bullying and mobbing, rather than the existence of the situations themselves, is the primary focus of this chapter, which will also cover the following:

- Understanding conflict: both positive and negative conflict.
- The underlying causes of negative conflict: seven states of human beings.
- Bullying as a learned behavior.
- Treating bullying as a public health issue.
- Creating a three-part system for preventing and correcting workplace bullying, harassment, and other negative behaviors: stakeholder knowledge, safe reporting, and restorative practices.
- The value of an independent ombuds.
- Creating and empowering work unit trust leaders.
- Building workplace capacity for civility.

UNDERSTANDING BOTH POSITIVE AND NEGATIVE CONFLICT

Human conflict is normal and natural. How conflict is managed determines whether the outcome is positive or negative. Workplace conflicts that are civil, respectful, open, truthful, and discussed with active listening can lead to better organizational outcomes, better products, stronger and more cohesive teams, and positive overall outcomes. Conflicts left unmanaged or that hide below the organizational radar will fester and turn negative with wrongful assumptions by the parties involved, and, over time, they can undermine the core interpersonal relationships needed for successful teams.

Harassment, intimidation, bullying, mobbing, social exclusion and other negative power imbalances should have no place in the modern workplace, but just as in society as a whole, organizations often find they have more negative behavior than they would have expected, sometimes with tragic effect. A preferred workplace should transmit a common culture and common standards of citizenship and civility, but, unfortunately, common standards, much like common sense, are not that common.

UNDERSTANDING COMMON ROLES IN CONFLICTS

Successful outcomes necessitate successful strategies for identifying and managing conflicts, both positive and negative. Most negative conflicts, bullying, and harassment and many negative behaviors have three roles in common: offenders, targets, and bystanders. Offenders usually instigate the initial conflict, even if it is only mild disagreement or criticism. Targets tend to react with a real or perceived lack of power and tend to interpret the actions of the offenders as threatening personal attacks. Bystanders are an evolving constellation of interest and include witnesses to the event and those that learn of the conflict after the event. Bystanders include supporters of the offenders, supporters of the targets, supporters of justice, and supporters of drama (Curtin, 2016). Each of these groups of bystanders can continue to grow, evolve, and mutate, as is often the case if the conflict progresses into a typical drama triangle (Karpman, 1968).

The drama triangle is a psychological and social model of human interaction, based on the work of Eric Berne (1996). Typically, the drama triangle evolves and interchanges the roles of offender, target, and bystander multiple times, thereby becoming cyclical. For example, in bullying incidents, if some bystanders intervene and physically or electronically attack the bully, then the original bully becomes bullied, and therefore the new target. The bystanders become the bullies, and the original target becomes the new bystander. If the original target, now the new bystander, attempts to intervene with the bullying of the original offender, by the original bystanders, then the cycle is again reversed. If not interrupted or treated, the drama triangle can simply continue as a sick, damaging, and expanding game. This pattern can often be observed in organizations, and as even the bizarre becomes normal over time, the drama triangle becomes embedded in the culture as a never-ending game of corporate "gotcha." The drama triangle will provide continued drama to all three groups, unless interrupted through a restorative process.

EXPLAINING WORKPLACE BULLYING

Among youth, to be considered bullying (Massetti, Swearer, Potter, & Martin, 2011), behavior must be aggressive and include the following:

- *An imbalance of power:* Power imbalances, such as physical strength to control or harm others, can change over time and in different situations, even if they involve the same people.
- *Repetition:* Bullying behaviors happen more than once or have the potential to happen more than once.

Adult bullying is sometimes an extension of youth bullying behaviors and includes abuse of company position, denying information, hiding behind tough management perceptions, and intentional isolation. Bullying often includes such actions as making threats, spreading rumors, attacking or threatening someone physically or verbally, and excluding someone from a group or from needed information. It also includes both personal actions and electronic actions that are often referred to as cyberbullying.

Bullying as a Learned Behavior

Although there is not a single sociology theory that explains bullying, several theories combined can give some insight into the behavior. Over time, many organizations have failed to recognize the seriousness of bullying and its long-term effects on offenders, targets, and bystanders. Often, organizations fail to take positive corrective actions for all three groups, leaving everyone involved to the mercy of the consequences of unmanaged negative behavior (Belak, 2013). *Defiance theory* can explain some negative reinforcement, as youth and adult bullies sometimes feel a compelling need to express defiance of authority (Christensen & Dorn, 1997). If this behavior is rewarded by peer admiration or other consequences that the bully interprets as positive, defiance theory will have a continuing impact on the repetition of the negative behavior. Defiance theory also reinforces the learned nature of bullying whereby bullies will continue their damaging behavior due to peer admiration and other perceived rewards, such as reinforcement by senior management considering the bully's behavior as tough management.

Labeling Theory and Bullying

Some bullying can be explained under *labeling theory* (Lemert, 1951), where others label a person and the person often accepts and mimics the label. Labeling theory can be a form of stereotyping and, more often than not, becomes a self-fulfilling prophecy (Rosenthal & Jacobson, 1968). When told that they are a bully, some will rationalize this label as their tough management style and continue to act accordingly. The initial label and any secondary labels explain the reason some bullies continue with the behavior as they try to live up to the negative labels that have been assigned to them.

If labeling theory is considered with defiance theory, as mentioned above, as well as with social learning theory, it is possible to see how all three theories can be interconnected to somewhat explain bullying behavior. However, *strain theory* (Merton, 1957) may also play into bullying, where bullies see their actions as a way of getting what they want. In workplace situations, bullies often use their behavior to control peers or subordinates to achieve their own personal objectives. Strain theory may also help explain how friends and associates of the bully often join in the bullying so as not to become targets themselves or to be accepted in the group surrounding the bully. Strain theory shows that social structures within a society can pressure individuals to commit negative acts to obtain what they believe they need to function in the society. It can therefore explain the discrepancies between culturally defined goals and the desire to find any means to achieve those goals. Merton described five types of deviance: conformity, innovation, ritualism, retreatism, and rebellion.

Again, learned behavior plays an important role in continued bullying and demonstrates that bullying might best be explained though a combination of justice theories acting in concert. The most powerful arguments may be explained by bullying being seen as a learned behavior (Sutherland, 1947), and it is reinforced as the bully continues to use the bullying behavior to either self-medicate or to satisfy an underlying need.

States of Being and Bullying

Most offenders, whether they are violent, bullying, lying, promoting social exclusion, committing harassment, or practicing other negative behaviors, have the roots of their behavior in a problem that manifests itself in the offense committed. The offense is almost always a symptom of a deeper problem (Curtin, 2016). Therefore, when we simply punish the offender or conduct a corrective conference around the offense, we often correct that particular symptom but do little to address the underlying problem. That problem is almost always some form of reaction to one or more of the offender's *states of being*. People have seven states of being (Curtin, 2016; see table 12.1).

The amount of positive control one has with each of the seven states is a measure of positive stability. When one does not have positive control or stability over one or more of the seven states of being, there is a tendency to compensate for the lack of control, typically with negative thoughts, actions, and deeds. Control is then established through conscious or unconscious rationalization as justification for negative behavior (Curtin, 2016). This is the trap in which most offenders are caught as they continue to "medicate" themselves with the same negative behavior as a means of personal control. Consequently, as this form of "medication" often produces a desired outcome, the negative actions are rationalized, and the behavior becomes learned and is often repeated.

It logically follows that if we only treat actions or behaviors, the underlying problem may continue to manifest itself in other negative actions. It is often easier to see this phenomenon in adolescents who have been acting as bullies. If only the bullying behavior is addressed, without a restorative process, the problem may manifest itself in other areas. The new behavior is actually the underlying problem manifesting itself in a different action. Treating just the negative action will usually result in new negative actions until the real problem is addressed. If the bully is punished, without a restorative process, the bully may actually feel rewarded by receiving what he or she was looking for, that is, attention, status, and recognition.

Japanese automakers actually have a process that is useful to mention here. Their process involves thinking of every defect as an onion. They will continue to peel the layers of the onion/problem until they find and can document that they are at the original source. For example, they may find that a

Table 12.1 States of Being for Each Individual

1. Mental state of being (measure of stability, intelligence, competency)
2. Emotional state of being (emotional orientation, emotional control)
3. Physical state of being (health, mobility, fitness)
4. Transpersonal state of being (how we see others and how we perceive they see us (emotional intelligence))
5. Values state of being (one's concept of morality)
6. Ethical state of being (personal ethics, spiritual intelligence)
7. Historical and inherited state of being (ranges from a sense of entitlement to one of being repressed and discriminated against and can include levels of wealth, inherited traits, or learned inherited prejudices and hatred)

defect in a part is caused by another related part. Rather than stopping the analysis at this point, they ask why the other part is reacting that way. They may find that it meets their specifications, but the specifications were not exactly what the engineers had suggested, or purchasing or contracting may have amended the original specifications, or the quality control at the receiving and testing of the part was faulty. They will continue down all paths until they find the original source and correct it. They have learned over time that only correcting individual symptoms produces new and different symptoms. Negative behavior often has the same result; namely, when only the symptom is corrected, new symptoms will appear. They will look new and different, but they are still the result of not correcting the problem at its source.

RESTORATIVE PRACTICE: A PROMISING WORKPLACE INTERVENTION

Restorative practice coupled with safe reporting and stakeholder knowledge can provide organizations with the tools they need to reach root problems and correct negative behaviors in a positive reintegrative manner. *Restorative justice* is a process that focuses on the harm done to targets and the obligation that it creates for the offender and the society to rectify the harm and reintegrate the offender into society. Its adoption in workplace settings is just beginning to be utilized as a way of moving from progressive disciplinary intervention to interventions designed to reintegrate offenders back into productive and healthy roles within the workplace (Wachtel, O'Connell, & Wachtel, 2010). To understand how restorative practice can be beneficial to a workplace environment, it is important to understand restorative justice and restorative practice.

Restorative justice roots are ancient, dating back to a time when we existed in clans and tribes (Zehr, 2002). At that period in human history, small groups of people needed every member of their group for the group's survival. Because they needed everyone for the survival of the clan, they did not have the luxury of banning or disposing of members of the group simply because they broke one of the rules or offended another member of the clan. They did not use progressive discipline and human resources checklists to fire members of their group. In their simple sophistication, they knew that reintegrating offenders was the best way for the group to succeed. Many early tribes in North America, New Zealand, and Australia used what is now commonly referred to as restorative justice, through tribal councils or societal circles, to determine the harm caused by an offense, to rectify the harm, and to reform the offender to full functioning as part of the tribe (Zehr, 2002).

If we compare the ancient need to include all members of a clan for survival to modern organizations and businesses, it should be readily apparent that organizations, having spent precious resources recruiting and training personnel, should be reluctant to needlessly lose any employees. They should be reluctant to lose employees that have been targets of abuse who exit to avoid continued abuse. They should be reluctant to lose any offenders through disciplinary action that either results in dismissal or has them angry and quietly seeking revenge. They should also be reluctant to lose employees in place, those that stay but become increasingly disengaged and begin practicing presenteeism—*I will have my body at the workplace, but not my heart or mind.*

To fully understand restorative practice, it is helpful to examine its ancient roots and to understand how restorative practice is reemerging as a system counter to our present "blame and punishment" system. Modern-day restorative justice in North America grew out of an interesting experiment in Elmira, Ontario, Canada. Mark Yantzi, then a probation officer, was working with two juveniles who had vandalized several properties in Elmira in 1974. He wondered what would happen if the young men actually met the people who owned the properties the young men had vandalized. Would a face-to-face meeting with the people they had harmed change anything? The property owners agreed to meet. The success of the meeting and the subsequent healing that took place for the owners and the offenders was profound, as the property owners finally had answers to their questions of why, and the offenders learned that their bad choices had affected many more people than they had imagined (Butler, 2004).

Mark Yantzi was an active member of the Mennonite Church, and word quickly spread throughout the church of the remarkable success that he had achieved. The practice was adopted by other Mennonite churches and the Seventh-day Adventist Church, and modern-day restorative justice was born in North America.

New forms of restorative justice are beginning to gain acceptance in present Western societies, with New Zealand and Australia leading the way. In Australia and New Zealand, the civil and criminal justice systems began by adopting the family group conferencing patterned after the original people's tribal conferencing circles (Wachtel et al., 2010). New Zealand adopted the system based on the ancient traditions of the Maori people, and in 1989, its entire juvenile justice system was revised to make restorative justice the norm for virtually all of its juvenile cases (Zehr, 2002).

Workplace intervention personnel need to be trained in restorative justice practices to correctly address all three groups: targets, offenders, and bystanders (Braithwaite, 1989). First, they must restore all parties to a stable position that deals with the harm done and the obligations to rectify that harm (Wachtel et al., 2010). Second, they need to assist targets, offenders, and bystanders in moving in a positive direction and in setting goals, objectives, and necessary progressive steps to achieve these goals and objectives. The restorative process provides all three groups the opportunity to establish the foundation for their own personal growth and to begin the collective development of an environment of trust, respect, and dignity (Duncan, 2010).

The two standard forms of justice in the United States are the civil and criminal justice systems. As discussed below, the civil justice system compensates individuals for injuries to person and to property, primarily through monetary damages and other orders issued by the courts. The criminal justice system involves the state holding individuals responsible for harmful behavior, with the possibility of imprisonment and other forms of punishment.

The restorative justice system differs dramatically, in that it is victim-focused, in a way that involves the offender. It uses a process that is directed toward the harm that has been done to the victim and the responsibility and obligations the offender has to rectify the harm. The principle underlying restorative justice is dealing with the harm done to the victim, repairing the harm with the help of the offender, and then reintegrating the offender into society (Zehr, 2002). In the restorative justice process, the victim plays a central role in determining what will repair the harm and how the offender might agree to meet his or her obligations and responsibilities of restoration from that harm. The offender's agreement should not only repair the harm but also allow the offender to be reintegrated into society.

The criminal and civil justice systems are better known by most Americans and are based on the premise that offenses are either crimes against the state or violations against another person's or institution's property or ownership. The court system will determine who is to blame and decide what the correct penalty should be for the violation. In the criminal justice system, the prosecutor's role is to represent the people as a whole, which includes policy goals of punishment, deterrence, prevention, rehabilitation, and mercy, while exercising discretion on decisions to prosecute. The victim may play a role in providing statements and evidence, and, increasingly, victim's assistance and compensation programs operating out of a prosecutorial framework play a role too. Nevertheless, the focus tends to be on the alleged perpetrator's actions. In the civil justice system, notably tort and employment law, the policy goals may include compensation, prevention, and deterrence, plus occasionally punishment. Monetary damages and injunctive orders (such as reinstatement in wrongful discharge claims) are the main forms of relief.

Clearly, restorative justice is different from the criminal system; it is focused on victims, while the criminal justice system is focused on offenders. In fact, the entire criminal justice system is offender-focused. In the civil system, the focus is most often on damages. Damages are defined as an amount of money representing the solution to a problem or harm done. Money damages typically do not address the deep feelings of each of the parties to the complaint.

The practice of restorative justice addresses feelings and underlying interests and needs and can provide a more complete and lasting solution than either a court ruling or a settlement conference.

Steps in the Restorative Justice Process

The restorative justice process normally begins with an explanation of the process to the three main groups involved: the offender, the victim, and the bystanders or supporters. The initial meetings should be conducted independently to determine whether the parties understand the process and whether the victim is willing to go forward. The victim has the right to refuse to participate, and that right should be completely and totally honored without any pressure. Because the process focuses on the harm that has been caused and the damage done to a real person, the rights of the harmed supersede the rights of the offender and the bystanders. If the victim does not want to participate or is unable to participate, the restorative justice practitioner should still meet with the offender to begin the process of the offender confronting the harm that he or she has caused. Often, a bystander or supporter of the victim might agree to stand in as a surrogate and offer insight into the effect the offense has had on the victim. This storytelling can have almost the same effect as having the victim present (Harvey, 2010).

At this point in the process, the purpose is for the offender to begin to understand that the victim is a human being and has a real name, a family, a life interrupted, and a need to understand "why": "Why did you do what you did, and why to me?" It is also an important part of the process for the offender to hear from his or her own family and friends to understand the impact that the offense has had on them as well. After hearing from their supporters, offenders often feel what has been called *reintegrative shaming* (Braithwaite, 1989), and they begin to realize that their actions have affected not only the victims but also their own family and friends. Reintegrative shame centers on the act, not the person, and separates the act from the actor (Morrison, 2002).

There continues to be debate over the term *shame*, with many misunderstanding or confusing what Braithwaite (1989) meant by "reintegrative shame." *Personal embarrassment* might be a better term, without the negative connotations of *shame*, which is perhaps what Braithwaite meant when he coined the term *reintegrative shaming*. Offenders often feel embarrassed when they realize the harm they have caused to the victim as well as to their own colleagues, family, and friends. It can be a powerful moment in the process when offenders make this realization and feel this embarrassment. Only a small number of people, 1–3 percent, are estimated to be true psychopaths or sociopaths who cannot feel empathy (*Diagnostic and Statistical Manual of*

Mental Disorders, 4th ed., text revision, American Psychiatric Association, 2000). The rest of the population can develop and grow a sense of caring and empathy. Variations of this restorative process are beginning to be employed in the workplace, with some promising results. Some of the first attempts have taken place in school settings, where schools have adopted restorative practices for their students and then applied the same practice to staff incidents (Wachtel et al., 2010).

For the victim, the process toward understanding and forgiveness begins at this stage as well, especially if the victim understands that forgiveness does not mean forgetting, but understanding. It is an understanding of the "why," even if it does not make logical sense. It is the end of asking "why" and the beginning of understanding. This crucial step allows the victim to adopt forgiveness, not for the offender, but for himself or herself. For as long as victims hang on to the question "why," the offense continues to control their lives. The process of forgiveness is to free one's own life, not necessarily the life of the offender.

Once the offender and the victim have begun to move forward, it is important to address and seek the cooperation of the bystanders or support group. The bystander group includes persons occupying various positions with respect to the originating conflict, and it is important to recognize to which group each individual belongs. For example, some bystanders may have been witnesses to the offense, and others may have learned about it later from any one of the parties involved. There may be supporters of the offender, supporters of the victim, or supporters of justice. There will be bystanders who just enjoy the drama and would like it to continue (Karpman, 1968). All of these group members are involved in the process and can be invaluable, or they can destroy the process and any good work that has been done. Each must be either brought into the process for good or, if this is not possible, at least separated from the process.

The following are examples of restorative statements and questions that can be used in a restorative justice conference. "If you really want to help [*name of target*], then you will" is a good statement. A useful question can be, "What would you like to do to help [*name of target* or *name of the offender*] heal and move forward with [*his* or *her*] life?" The facilitator should listen carefully to the participants' answers and, if possible, have them commit them to writing to be utilized later in the process when creating a statement of agreement with all the parties involved (International Institute for Restorative Practices (IIRP), 2009).

At this point in the process, it may be possible for the offender, the victim, and the constructive bystanders or supporters to begin a facilitated discussion to help determine what corrective measures are possible. Again, the restorative justice facilitator must have the correct skills and questions to ensure that the meeting does not cause further harm. Questions must be asked and answers given to begin the restorative process. The process continues until the three groups—victim, offender, and bystanders—come to a shared bond and possible agreement. At this point, much like in a compassionate mediation settlement, the question becomes, "Where do you want to go from here? What would cure the harm done? What does justice look like in this case, and how can we achieve it" (Harvey, 2010)?

As the process unfolds, the restorative justice practitioner begins developing a written contract in sufficient detail so that each person signing will know the role that he or she has agreed to perform moving forward. The contract becomes a morally binding agreement, and in some cases, when the courts or criminal justice system are involved, the contract may become a legal document. Restorative justice is a true attempt at real justice, with both the victim and the offender being able to understand and move forward in positive directions. It can restore the faith of the victim and be the first step in changing a pattern of negative actions for the offender (IIRP, 2009).

Myths and Realities about Restorative Justice in the Workplace

There are some common myths about restorative justice that are important to address:

- *Myth:* Restorative justice/restorative practice does not fit the workplace environment. *Reality:* It can be a great fit if used wisely by a trained coach or facilitator. The healing process for all three groups—the target, the offenders, and the bystanders—can be transforming for a work team, thereby demonstrating that the organization cares about and values all of its employees and is willing to spend the necessary time to correct and improve workplace culture.
- *Myth:* Restorative justice is too time consuming, and there are not available resources to pay for it. *Reality:* It is important to consider the amount of time spent in continuing to address additional symptoms. Then there is the time and cost of continued interventions and progressive discipline. Often, after a confrontational intervention, none of the parties involved feel satisfied. It can be difficult for any of the parties to a trial, for example, to begin to move forward. Often the harm has neither been addressed nor repaired, and the parties continue to trade punches, at least mentally. It can be hard to see whether justice has truly been served, unless one only considers punishment as serving justice (IIRP, 2009).

    In workplace situations, too much time can be spent repeatedly correcting the same negative behaviors. Bullying and harassment are often a symptom of an underlying problem or a learned behavior that offenders perceive as a reward, so taking the time to help correct the underlying problem can have lifelong positive effects. Restorative justice can help the offenders to understand the harm that their underlying problem is causing them. They can also learn the harm that it has caused to the victims, their work communities, and the families and friends of the victims as well as to the offenders' own families and friends (Wachtel et al., 2010).

- *Myth:* Restorative justice is difficult for the victim and the victim's supporters. *Reality:* As restorative justice is victim-focused and the victim's safety and well-being are paramount, it is not nearly as difficult on the victim as being revictimized in court by both the prosecutor and the defense attorney or in a workplace with inadequately trained supervisors or human resource staffers controlling the meeting. In court, the victims rarely get to tell their own stories or fully understand what is destroying their self-confidence or self-esteem. The prosecutor and the defense attorney will both tell a story that may have only some reference to the victim's story. Victims almost never learn to understand the "why." Why did this happen? Why me? Victims are often trapped in the "why," some for the rest of their lives. Restorative justice can be the first step in escaping the "why" trap.

  In addition, because restorative justice is victim-focused, a victim can avoid the process, if it will be too traumatizing, by allowing a surrogate to stand in and explain the effect the offense has had on the victim. Once a conference has occurred, if the offender is ready to be part of the restoration process and has agreed to a designated plan, the victim can often reenter the process and begin healing (Harvey, 2010).
- *Myth:* Restorative justice does not hold the offender accountable. *Reality:* The process is designed to truly hold the offender accountable, because real accountability comes when the offender understands and accepts the harm that he or she has caused (Braithwaite, 1989). Restorative justice can be a powerful process to not only correct harms and reintegrate the offender into society, but also to help the victim and the society heal from the offense and build new positive relationships. When used correctly in the workplace, it can help reestablish trust, increase motivation, promote civility, and heal employees, supervisors, and managers.

COACHING WORKPLACE OFFENDERS

During the restorative process, if a coach is familiar with *behavioral transition* (a concept that this author has developed through coaching experience), it is easy to spot a condition that affects most offenders. It is what can be described as "being stuck in the what." Most offenders are "stuck in the what," and they are trapped in the "what." It is how people refer to them: "He is a bully" or "She is a liar." That is "what" they are. The label traps them, and they are equally trapped in the "what" because their underlying problem continues to guide them into bad decisions as they try to "medicate" for it. If that underlying problem remains untreated, then additional labels will usually be added to the original label as more symptoms manifest into other offenses. In the workplace, this labeling is often conducted through the grapevine and rumor mill within the rank and file.

Sometimes, if this negative behavior is from a supervisor, the behavior will be interpreted by senior management as tough management, causing those who suffer under the behavior to believe that management approves of the offender's management style. For the supervisor, this tacit acceptance reinforces their medicating actions and continues their rationalized learning.

Those that suffer under the behavior are left with few choices, and all of them are less than desirable. They can leave, and those who can leave usually do, thereby depriving the company of some of its best employees. Employees who cannot leave go into survival mode and protect themselves with one or more destructive behaviors, such as presenteeism, disengagement, or petty sabotage. They may also turn the pressure inward and suffer depression, stress, and other physical and debilitating illnesses. In such cases, the employee, his or her family, and the company all suffer. It is not only the direct targets of bullies who are affected, but the bystanders as well, and some bystanders will join in the bullying for acceptance, or decide to leave the company, or go into their personal survival mode as protection.

Understanding what it means for the offender to be trapped in the "what" allows for a desired behavioral transition. It starts with addressing the "what" and changing the "what" to a "why." Why does the offender make these bad choices? The best way to find out is with a trained coach working with offenders to help them talk about what they think is the "why."

Behavioral transition, my concept from coaching, allows the trained coach to work with an offender to help him or her establish a direction and develop a *transformative prescription* and immediately begin taking small steps in a positive direction. The facilitator should discuss the trap of the "what" and how to begin to move from the "what" to the "why." With coaching, offenders can begin to understand how to stop treating their problems with negative actions and begin to ameliorate them with positive actions, opening the door to liking their new selves and their new actions more. When offenders begin this kind of journey and follow their own transformative prescriptions, it empowers them to change their actions, their attitudes, and their lives.

WORKING WITH WORKPLACE TARGETS

Restorative justice treats the target as the focal point in restorative justice conferences. The target can decide if and how to participate. If targets, or targets' surrogates, choose to participate, their stories become a critical part of the restorative process, and their feelings, fears, and needs become central to the process. The process is designed to do "no further harm" to the target, and the target becomes an active participant in the restorative process and reintegration plan for the offender.

As previously discussed, the work of helping an offender move from the "what" to the "why" and a target move from the "why" to the "what" is critical to the healing process. Targets get stuck in the "why" the same way that offenders get stuck in the "what." Being stuck in the "why" begins a downward spiral that can ultimately lead to victim syndrome, depression, and all the associated negative health consequences.

One way that targets become victims is through their own difficulties in dealing with why the bullying or negative behavior has occurred. Ironically, targets bully themselves into becoming victims by getting stuck in the "why" and going round and round asking, "Why me? Why am I always the one? What could I have done differently? Did I bring this on myself?"—and on and on and on. There is often no logical answer to this "why" question, only a whirling around and around without any direction, except slipping down into depression.

Understanding the "why" is an important step in the process, and trained coaches can often present questions during the session that will help the target understand the "why." Behavioral transition can take this a step further in a private session with the target after the original restorative justice session has concluded to further help the target deal with any lingering "why" thoughts. The coach should also explain that they are not saying, "Get over it" or "Just forgive and forget." What has happened to the target is an affront to humanity, and targets did not bring it upon themselves. Targets can be helped to understand that they were in the wrong place at the wrong time and henceforth a "target" that was part of another person's life-problem drama.

Being a target is no different than if while walking through a shopping mall, one was knocked down by a chandelier that fell from the ceiling. If that happened, should the target spend a lifetime asking whether that chandelier was just waiting for them to walk underneath so it could attack? Was it because the target was wearing the wrong clothes? Was the target asking for it? Of course not. It was an accident that happened when the target was in the wrong place at the wrong time. Of course, not all bullying is merely an accident, but understanding the concept of target is important to help the target avoid taking on the destructive role of victim. If targets did have some complicity in the cause of the offense, they need to address it, take some responsibility, and begin changing their behavior to amend their actions going forward.

Once targets can understand that they are in fact targets and not victims, they can begin taking small steps toward the renewed goals they have identified. They may begin to see that the negative behavior they have endured would probably have happened to another employee if they had not been available. At this point, targets begin to understand that what happened to them was an accident of time and place, a "what," and that there are no real answers to the "why," only huge amounts of negative energy that have been holding them back. Changing the "why" to a "what" will allow targets to proceed with their transformative prescription and their lives by converting the previous negative energy to positive energy empowering their small forward steps.

WORKING WITH WORKPLACE BYSTANDERS AND SUPPORTERS

Bystanders and supporters are critical to the success of the process. It is important for bystanders to be part of the story and the solution; their active involvement and subsequent role in the behavioral transition process is essential. Unless bystanders and supporters are helping the offenders or the victims move forward, they will help keep them trapped in place. It is therefore equally important to work with the various bystander members to help them understand their roles within the healing process. Bystanders need to learn the difference between giving support versus enabling. They need to understand how they can give small bits of encouragement to help the offender or the target take the next small step. Sometimes comments like, "Maybe you can just finish this small piece and then decide what you want to do next," can be helpful. Each time a person takes that next small step, he or she will feel a sense of accomplishment and like himself or herself for it. Each time a person feels that sense of accomplishment, no matter how small, it provides the energy for the next step.

When this researcher was a teenager, he worked for his father, who was a builder and cabinetmaker. As he was learning the trade, his father taught him an important lesson that serves as a good example for people involved in coaching. All a carpenter really needs to know, at any moment, is where to put the next nail. He does not need to be fretting about future steps because he can read the blueprints and look at the sketches to understand the big picture. He will never accomplish the big picture goal on the blueprints until he puts the next nail in its proper place. Then he can decide where the next nail should go. With all things in their proper sequence, in their proper time, the big picture will soon become reality. It is a lesson and an example that can be passed on when working with all three groups, namely, the offenders, the targets, and the bystanders.

THREE-PART SYSTEM FOR PREVENTING AND CORRECTING WORKPLACE BULLYING

A comprehensive holistic approach to preventing and correcting bullying involves addressing the three distinct roles in all incidents: the offender, the target, and the bystanders. If a program is to become effective in changing bullying behavior, all three groups must be included and become part of the solution (Braithwaite, 1989). However, long-term, well-trained, and active bystanders can be the most important group for continual improvement of the work environment. Through education of their work community, and thereby potential future bystanders, an employer can begin to change the organizational norm from one in which bullying is attractive and acceptable, to one in which bullying is seen in a negative context by all, including offenders. It is important to encourage employers to adopt a three-part strategy consisting of stakeholder knowledge, safe reporting, and restorative practices to fully address bullying.

Stakeholder Knowledge

Companies should ensure that all participants, management, employees, board members, vendors, clients, and consultants understand the seriousness of bullying, cyberbullying, and harassment. They need to realize what potential consequences occur if bullying behavior is ignored and not corrected. They also need to know how dangerous it is to do the wrong things, that is, zero tolerance, immediate punishment, or other punitive actions without restorative practices.

Safe Reporting

Companies need a safe and secure reporting system for their stakeholders to report incidents. The system needs to be safe in the eyes of the reporter, not just the administration, if it is to be fully utilized by those needing to file reports. "Just come and tell us" is not a safe system, and neither is the "anonymous box." These systems are perceived by victims and bystanders as another way in which they can be further victimized by the offenders. Additionally, simply telling human resources or a senior manager can be ineffective because many times the information is misunderstood. For example, people who hear the reports often do not fully understand or are not trained to clarify what they are being told (Curtin, 2016). The reporters misbelieve that the company heard them or believe that the company chose to do nothing. The following examples illustrate this problem.

There is a famous case from South Hadley, Massachusetts, in which a 15-year-old recent Irish immigrant, Phoebe Prince, committed suicide after weeks of cruel bullying by her classmates. In the court case, the mother explained how six weeks before Phoebe's tragic death, she had notified the school. The school personnel testified that they only learned about the bullying two days before the tragedy and not from the mother. In reading the transcripts and in discussions with several parties who were involved in the case, it is clear that both the mother and the school personnel were telling the truth. The mother told the school how unhappy Phoebe was with the new school but did not specifically say that Phoebe was being bullied. As people frequently do not really hear each other, the school personnel did not ask whether Phoebe was being bullied and incorrectly assumed that she was just going through a new student adjustment period.

There was no safe-reporting system, so the communication was incomplete. Had there been a safe-reporting system, the mother could have used the system or the school personnel could have asked her to input into the system. The South Hadley, Massachusetts, school would then have known the extent of the negative behavior that was occurring, and the mother would have known that she had formally told them.

A second famous case involves the child molestation problem at Penn State University, in which a graduate assistant from the football program attempted to report the incident. The language used to describe what had occurred included the phrase "horsing around," which may have been interpreted by those who received the verbal reports as normal locker room banter. As there was no formal safe-reporting system, the verbal reporting was misinterpreted, and no corrective action was taken. Therefore, no one intervened, and numerous young men were physically abused until the incidents exploded in the national press and resulted in major penalties for Penn State and its president, athletic director, hall-of-fame coach, and the original offender, who is now in prison.

If Penn State had had a formal safe-reporting system available to the graduate assistant at the time of the incident, a more complete investigation could have taken place. Penn State would have had formal records to show their due diligence. The safe-reporting process would have allowed for the speedy restoration of the incident, with help for the child and his family, prosecution for the offender, and protection for the graduate assistant, coach, athletic director, and president. As those involved would have had the facts, we can assume they would not have participated in a cover up. Without a formal safe-reporting system, it appears that the persons in authority interpreted the information they were given in their own ways, minus the facts that were either confusing or unknown. Each then made a serious mistake in judgment as distorted information moved up the chain of command.

This process frequently happens in workplace organizations, with the net result that negative behavior often goes unreported and untreated. It is no coincidence that estimates show over 74 percent of American employees have reported being disengaged at work, and in a recent survey by SailPoint (2016), 27 percent of American employees stated that they would be willing to sell their logins and passwords to their company's data systems. A third of these reported they would sell them for as little as $100.

A safe-reporting system should provide for complete protection for those needing to report workplace abuse, with attention paid to assuring that there are not misperceptions about how the information is gathered, protected, and utilized. The reporters should be assured that their identities are protected and that they will not be retaliated against by the bully, the bully's supporters, or the company. A safe-reporting system can be implemented in person through a trained independent ombuds, it can be online, or it can be an outside service, provided that each system protects the identities of those reporting. The most important part of the system is the belief and reality that the system is safe for the reporters.

One system created by the Connected Learning Network (CLN) (which I developed in my role as chief executive officer of CLN) is as follows:

Online Incident/Concern Reporting System: Web-based monitored reporting system for employees, managers, and vendors whereby those affected can easily report incidents or concerns in a secure system that is accessible 24/7 via the Internet. A trained ombuds or other trained professional receives, assesses, and responds to each report. They can act immediately, if necessary, and can at any time or place, with access to the Web, check reports, compare data, input actions taken, sort and pull reports and take any corrective measures they deem necessary. They are able to "hold" reports in a temporary file as they investigate circumstances, and they easily move the report, along with their notes and actions taken, into the permanent database. The Online Incident/Concern Reporting System gives each organization a secure, Web-based, active database of all reported incidents and concerns and allows administrators to compile and compare data through multiple parameters and reports. The 4Civility System provides secure Web-based reports that will identify problems, concerns, trouble spots, bullies, victims, and bystanders. The reports will provide ongoing information, comparisons, trends, and statistical information to access the effectiveness of prevention efforts and the changing workplace environment.

This technological advance gives organizations the control and accurate information they need to monitor and improve their workplace environment. The designated mediator or ombuds can reach the system from any computer connected to the Web in a fully secured and protected system. The secured reporting system can be reached by Internet 24/7 and provides a monitoring system for the entire organization. Designed for easy adoption and operation, there is no equipment to buy, nor is there any instructional technology support needed from the organization's busy IT professionals. (4Civility Institute, 2016)

Restorative Practices

Companies and organizations should consider being trained in restorative practices to correctly address all three groups and restore them to a stable position that deals with the harm done and the obligations to rectify that harm. The restorative process should help all three groups move in a positive direction to set goals, objectives, and progressive steps to achieve their goals and objectives. The restorative practice process provides all three groups with the opportunity to establish the foundation for their own personal growth and to collectively begin to develop a shared environment of trust, respect, and dignity. Most importantly, the process can reintegrate offenders, targets, and bystanders into a functioning company with a healthy culture.

THE VALUE OF AN INDEPENDENT OMBUDS FOR SAFE REPORTING

An integral part of a safe-reporting system can be an independent ombuds. A professional independent ombuds can provide all stakeholders with a safe and truly neutral professional to help them sort through personal options. What makes a professional ombuds so valuable is that very few people ever have the opportunity to openly discuss options in a completely secure and confidential manner with a person that is truly neutral. Most people we consult in stressful situations are spouses, relatives, friends, and coworkers, all of whom have their own biases. A spouse will frequently take your interpretation of a situation and not challenge your underlying assumptions. A human resources professional might be sympathetic, but their underlying responsibility is to the organization, not the individual. Friends or coworkers might base their advice on their own agendas. Only an independent professional ombuds can provide a truly neutral environment for an employee to discuss and analyze a situation.

The ombuds will not give recommendations, but he or she will help the employee to consider all possible options and to test underlying assumptions.

If a law has been broken, the ombuds will understand the legal requirements and can begin to take action while keeping the employee's identity protected. The role of an ombuds is similar to that of an attorney or a priest in that almost all confidential information is protected. In many instances, the ombuds can help correct a negative situation without disclosing the source of the information. The most effective ombuds are truly independent and not employees of the organization. The value to a company of having a truly independent ombuds is the confidence that the company is fulfilling its obligations to help root out dangerous and negative behaviors within the organization. Their employees and other stakeholders can be assured that the organization is serious about its culture, and regulators can be assured that the company has a truly effective harassment and whistle-blower protection system.

BUILDING WORKPLACE CAPACITY FOR CIVILITY

The combination of having stakeholder knowledge of negative behaviors—including bullying, mobbing, harassment, and other destructive actions with an understanding of the consequences of either ignoring or taking wrong actions—and a safe-reporting system and a restorative system of responding will go a long way toward building workplace civility. Implementing the systems described above and helping employees to understand that they are responsible for how they treat each other and for overall workplace civility can improve employee morale and productivity. Core values that promote trust, diversity, personal and professional growth, mutual respect, and productive communications are absolute necessities in modern, innovative, and successful organizations.

Unfortunately, even the most well-intentioned corporate policies can be undermined by unmanaged conflict within the organization. Unresolved conflict is a distraction from otherwise productive use of time, energy, and resources, as it diminishes internal and external relationships and eventually impacts the organizational culture in a negative way.

To help facilitate this understanding and to foster discussions and limit wrongful assumptions, it is possible to use civility surveys (part of the CLN Safe-Reporting Software System referenced earlier):

Civility/Kindness/Compassion Survey Tool

The purpose of this brief online tool is to measure, at regular intervals, each person's and unit's perception of the work environment. The tool measures interpersonal and group relations as part of a civility, kindness, and compassion strategy. Each group member rates how they and their colleagues treat each other on a scale of 1 to 5, with a 1 being as kind and wonderful as possible and a 5 as awful, mean, and cruel. They are asked to cite any significant acts of civility, kindness, or compassion they have observed within the group. They are asked to cite any acts of meanness and also any concerns they have about questionable things, related to the group, they have seen in cyberspace.

The reports are automatically compiled and can be reviewed for information and for discussion items. Acts of special kindness can be acknowledged, and acts of negative behavior can be discussed. Giving all group members the ability to anonymously report concerns for themselves or others, coupled with the ability to cite concerns they have from the cyberworld, provides important insight into the work environment.

Group discussions based on the results encourage participants to work together to improve civility, kindness, and compassion. Often misunderstandings emerge in the reports and can be discussed in a nonthreatening informative way, thereby removing personal emotion and resentment. The reports can also serve as an early-warning system, allowing compassionate intervention before more serious incidents develop.

The most successful groups use the Civility/Kindness/Compassion surveys on a regular schedule, i.e., every 4–8 weeks. The survey takes less than 5 minutes to complete but will generate a great deal of information. The use of the surveys reminds participants that they are responsible for their work environment and how they treat and relate to each other. The anonymous nature of the instrument and its purposeful design to foster reporting on good things helps groups to redirect their collective efforts toward civility, kindness, and compassion. Regular use of the surveys will promote a positive environment and can prevent or reverse a toxic workplace. (4Civility Institute, 2016)

The civility surveys have been used in numerous organizations and have opened up positive workplace discussions and improved interpersonal understanding while reducing misconceptions and misunderstandings. Negative conflict often grows out of incorrect assumptions, with each party reinforcing their incorrect assumptions as the parties move further and further apart. Without a system for measuring and testing assumptions, misunderstandings often fester and grow, with the parties involved becoming more and more disconnected and either openly or passively aggressive toward each other. Many times, if the parties are engaged in a workplace restorative practice session, they can find their way back to the original wrongful assumptions, start over, and rebuild a positive relationship. The civility surveys provide a positive way to surface those wrongful assumptions and allow for face-saving resolutions to occur without having to proceed to formal mediation.

OTHER PROMISING WORKPLACE BULLYING INTERVENTIONS

Vanderbilt University Medical Center has developed an early-intervention protocol that has been successful in addressing and changing negative behavior at the earliest sign of dysfunction (Hickson, 2009). They commonly refer to the protocol as the "Cup of Coffee" program. Essentially, the protocol is designed to provide an informal intervention in a relaxed, nonthreatening setting at the first instance of incivility, bullying, or general harassment. The program's goal is to prevent the issue from escalating through wrong assumptions and misunderstandings while employing a graduated protocol to address and intervene in the case of harassing and bullying behaviors.

Workplace restorative practice can be a powerful tool to positively change negative environments. It should seriously be considered as an alternative to escalating disciplinary actions that only temporarily correct situations and ultimately break down, causing continued exiting or disengaged employees. In many instances of workplace bullying and incivility, employees who have other job options will exit even if the bullying was not directed at them. As they observe the bullying behavior and the negative reactions to it, they begin to seek options as they realize that their current workplace has become toxic. This phenomenon is often referred to as the "fast rats get off the ship," which means that those without immediate options, the "slow rats," are forced to stay and try to survive. As mentioned previously, there are several coping strategies for survival, and almost all are negative for both the employee and the organization.

CONCLUSION

Organizations that wish to improve their workplace culture and avoid becoming a toxic workplace should adopt a three-part strategy that includes (1) stakeholder knowledge with clear policies and plans; (2) a safe-reporting system, coupled with an independent ombuds; and (3) restorative practices to rectify harm and reintegrate offenders. Organizations should adopt an operating strategy that works to help all employees focus on their jobs and not be distracted by fear, intimidation, shame, or blame. As stated in the introduction to this chapter, harassment, intimidation, bullying, social exclusion, and other negative power imbalances should have no place in the modern workplace. However, just as in society as a whole, organizations often find they have more negative behavior than they might have expected, sometimes with tragic effect. A preferred workplace should transmit a common culture and common standards of citizenship and civility; but, unfortunately, common standards, much like common sense, are not that common.

REFERENCES

American Psychiatric Association. (2000). *Diagnostic and statistical manual of mental disorders* (4th ed., text rev.). Washington, DC: Author.

Belak, A. (2013, September). Understanding the mental health effects of bullying. Presentation at the Second Annual Symposium on Pediatric Behavioral and Mental Health, Louisville, Kentucky.

Berne, E. (1996). *Games people play: The basic handbook of transactional analysis.* New York: Ballantine Books.

Braithwaite, J. (1989). *Crime, shame and reintegration.* Cambridge, England: Cambridge University Press.

Butler, D. (2004, September 11). How a drunken rampage changed legal history. *Ottawa Citizen.* Retrieved from www.ottawacitizen.com

Christensen, C. A., & Dorn, S. (1997). Competing notions of social justice and contradictions in special education reform. *Journal of Special Education, 31*(2), 181–198.

Curtin, J-R. (2016). *An exploratory study of existing anti-bullying statutes.* Saarbrücken, Germany: Lambert Academic Publishing.

Duncan, S. (2010). Restorative justice and bullying: A missing solution in the anti-bullying laws. *New England Journal on Criminal & Civil Confinement, 37,* 701–732.

4Civility Institute. (2016). Retrieved from www.4civility.org

Harvey, L. (2010). *Restorative justice training.* Center for Planning, Policy, and Performance, Lexington, Kentucky.

Hickson, G. B. (2009). Discouraging disruptive behavior: It starts with a Cup of Coffee! Presentation at the What's Right in Health Care Conference, Chicago, Illinois.

International Institute for Restorative Practices (IIRP). (2009). *SanerSaferSchools.* Retrieved from http://www.iirp.edu/education-programs/continuing-education/projects/safer-saner-schools

Karpman, S. (1968). Fairy tales and script drama analysis. *Transactional Analysis Bulletin, 7*(26), 39–43.

Lemert, E. (1951). *Social pathology: A systematic approach to the theory of sociopathic behavior.* New York: McGraw-Hill.

Massetti, G., Swearer, S., Potter, S., & Martin, L. (2011, September). Bridging research, policy, and programming. Panel Discussion at the Second Annual Federal Partners in Bullying Prevention Summit, Washington, D.C.

Merton, R. (1957). *Social theory and social structure* (2nd ed.). New York: Free Press.

Morrison, E. W. (2002). Newcomers' relationships: The role of social network ties during socialization. *Academy of Management Journal, 45*(6), 1149–1160.

Rosenthal, R., & Jacobson, L. (1968). Self-fulfilling prophecies in the classroom: Teachers' expectations as unintended determinants of pupils' intellectual competence. In M. Deutsch, I. Katz, & A. R. Jensen (Eds.), *Social class, race, and psychological development* (pp. 219–253). New York: Holt, Rinehart, & Winston.

SailPoint. (2016). *Market pulse survey: Weak security practices leave organizations exposed.* Retrieved from https://www.sailpoint.com/identity-governance-market-pulse-survey

Sutherland, E. (1947). *Principles of criminology* (4th ed.). Philadelphia: J. B. Lippincort.
Wachtel, T., O'Connell, T., & Wachtel, B. (2010). *Restorative justice conferencing: Real justice and the conferencing handbook.* Bethlehem, PA: International Institute for Restorative Practices.
Zehr, H. (2002). *The little book of restorative justice.* Intercourse, PA: Good Books.

United Nations Intellectual History Project (UNIHP)
Geneva International Academic Network (GIAN)

Reflections on United Nations Development Ideas

À propos des idées des Nations Unies sur le développement

Proceedings of the conference
From development to international economic governance
The intellectual contributions of the United Nations
(Geneva, ICC, 24 January 2005)

&

Catalogue of the exhibition
UN ideas in the service of development
(UNOG Library Cyberspace, January-September 2005)

Note

Symbols of the United Nations documents are composed of capital letters combined with figures. Mention of such a symbol indicates a reference to a United Nations document.

All materials may be freely quoted or reprinted, but acknowledgement is requested, together with a reference to the document number.

The views expressed and the designations employed in this publication are those of the authors and do not necessarily reflect the views of the United Nations Secretariat.

Foreword / Préface

I have great pleasure in introducing this publication composed of the proceedings of the conference "From development to international economic governance: the intellectual contributions of the United Nations" and the catalogue of the "UN ideas in the service of development" exhibition, two events that took place in Geneva in 2005, the year of the 60th anniversary of the Organization.

The conference was attended by international personalities, academics and professionals to discuss the contribution of United Nations ideas to development theory and their impact in the field over the 60 years of the Organization's existence. The first five volumes of the United Nations Intellectual History Project (UNIHP) were presented to the public on this occasion and served as works of reference during the debate. The conference was co-organized by UNIHP and the Geneva International Academic Network (GIAN).

In the spirit of UNIHP, the Library of the United Nations Office at Geneva prepared an exhibition entitled "UN ideas in the service of development", that remained open to visitors from January to December 2005. Through books, articles, correspondence and rare documents held in the collections of the Library and in the archives of the United Nations Office at Geneva (UNOG), the exhibition aimed at outlining the genesis and diffusion of the ideas of some of the most important economists who had worked for the United Nations.

This publication, that has combined two different, but interlinked events, stresses the importance of UN ideas and the role of the UNOG Library in support of the history of the institution.

Sergei Ordzhonikidze
Under-Secretary-General
Director-General, United Nations Office at Geneva

C'est un très grand plaisir de présenter cette publication qui réunit les actes de la conférence « Du développement à la gouvernance du système économique mondial : les idées des Nations Unies » et le catalogue de l'exposition « Les idées des Nations Unies au service du développement », deux événements qui se déroulèrent à Genève en 2005, année du soixantième anniversaire de l'Organisation.

La conférence réunissait des personnalités internationales, des universitaires et des opérateurs pour débattre de l'apport des idées des Nations Unies à la théorie du développement et de leur impact sur le terrain au cours des soixante années d'existence de l'Organisation. Les cinq premiers volumes du Projet d'histoire intellectuelle des Nations Unies (UNIHP) ont été présentés au public à cette occasion et ont servi de référence aux débats. La Conférence était co-organisée par l'UNIHP et le Réseau universitaire international de Genève (RUIG).

Dans l'esprit du projet UNIHP, la Bibliothèque des Nations Unies à Genève réalisait l'exposition « Les idées des Nations Unies au service du développement », qui s'est tenue de janvier à décembre 2005. L'exposition retraçait l'œuvre et le rayonnement des idées de quelques-uns des plus importants économistes ayant travaillé pour les Nations Unies à travers livres, articles, lettres et documents, dont certains très rares, qui se trouvent dans les fonds de la Bibliothèque et dans les archives de l'Office des Nations Unies à Genève.

Cette publication, qui réunit deux événements différents, mais étroitement liés, met en valeur l'importance des idées des Nations Unies et le rôle de la Bibliothèque des Nations Unies à Genève comme support de mémoire à cette histoire.

Sergei Ordzhonikidze
Secrétaire général adjoint et Directeur
de l'Office des Nations Unies à Genève

Table of contents

Note 2
Préface 3

PART I

CONFERENCE REPORT
FROM DEVELOPMENT TO INTERNATIONAL ECONOMIC GOVERNANCE:
THE INTELLECTUAL ROLE OF THE UNITED NATIONS 7
Intervenants - Speakers 11
Conference objectives 13
Synthesis 14
Les objectifs du colloque 16
Synthèse 17
Introduction 19
I – Views on UN ideas and methods 25
II – A role for the UN in the economic and social field 45
III - The UN and the world economy 57
IV – Concluding remarks 65
Presentation UNIHP 66
UNIHP publications 67

PART II

EXHIBITION CATALOGUE
UN IDEAS IN THE SERVICE OF DEVELOPMENT
(UNOG LIBRARY, JANUARY-SEPTEMBER 2005) 71
Introduction 75
From the League to the United Nations 77
Early development strategies (1949-1951) 78
Technical assistance and development financing : early stages (1949-1966) 80
The evolution of the concept of development 82
Ideas from the UN regional commissions 93
The UNCTAD experience 105
UN statistics : measuring the world 113
The UNIHP volumes devoted to development 115
List of documents 121

Part 1

Conference report
From development to international economic governance:
the intellectual role of the United Nations

Part 1

Intervenants - Speakers 11

Conference objectives 13

Synthesis 14

Les objectifs du colloque 16

Synthèse 17

Introduction 19

I – Views on UN ideas and methods 25

II – A role for the UN in the economic and social field 45

III - The UN and the world economy 57

IV – Concluding remarks 65

Presentation UNIHP 66

UNIHP publications 67

Intervenants - Speakers

Gopalan Balachandran, Professor of international history and politics at the Graduate Institute for International Studies (GIIS) in Geneva.

Yves Berthelot, Director UNIHP Geneva, Senior Research Fellow at UN Institute for Training and Research (UNITAR) and former Executive Secretary of the UN Economic Commission for Europe, is the editor of the volume *Unity and Diversity in Development Ideas: Perspectives from the Regional Commissions*.

Barbara Ekwall, UN Development Division, Swiss Agency for Development and Cooperation.

Carlos Fortin, Acting Secretary-General of the UN Conference on Trade and Development (UNCTAD).

Dharam Ghai, Researcher and Advisor to the ILO, and former Director of the United Nations Research Institute for Social Development, co-authored the volume on *UN Contributions to Development Thinking and Practice*.

Victor-Yves Ghebali, Professor of Political Science at the GIIS in Geneva.

Charles Gore, Senior Economic Affairs Officer for the Special Programme for Least Developed Countries at UNCTAD.

Sir Richard Jolly, Research Associate at the Institute of Development Studies at the University of Sussex, former deputy Executive Director of UNICEF and Principal Coordinator of UNDP's Human Development Report. Mr Jolly co-authored the volume *Ahead of the Curve? UN Ideas and Global Challenges* and *UN Contributions to Development Thinking and Practice*.

Frédéric Lapeyre, Professeur à l'Institut d'études du développement de l'Université Catholique de Louvain, Belgique, est co-auteur du livre *UN Contributions to Development Thinking and Practice*.

Antoine Maurice, journaliste à la Tribune de Genève.

Jaime de Melo, Professor of economics at the University of Geneva.

Isabelle Schulte-Tenckhoff, Professeur d'anthropologie à l'Institut universitaire d'études du développement (IUED) à Genève.

Pierre de Senarclens, Professeur à l'Université de Lausanne.

Jean-Michel Servet, Professeur d'économie à l'IUED de Genève.

Richard Toye, Lecturer in History at Homerton College, Cambridge, is co-author of *UN and the Global Political Economy: Trade, Finance and Development*.

Patrick Verley, Professeur d'histoire économique à la Faculté des Sciences économiques et sociales de l'Université de Genève.

Sally-Anne Way, anthropologist and economist, Research Fellow at the Research Unit on the Right to Food of the Graduate Institute of Development Studies (GIDS) in Geneva.

Michael Windfuhr, President of Food First Information & Action Network (FIAN).

Conference objectives

On 24 January 2005, at the start of the United Nations sixtieth anniversary year, a conference was held at Geneva on the theme "From Development to International Economic Governance: The Intellectual Contributions of the United Nations".

The conference, organized by the United Nations Intellectual History Project (UNIHP) and the Geneva International Academic Network (GIAN), was intended to outline to an international and academic audience the themes raised in the first five volumes of the UNIHP series (nine more volumes are planned). The project was launched five years ago by a group of sometime United Nations experts and academics who were directly involved in developing these ideas and translating them into action.

The conference brought together international personalities and academics for dialogue and debate on the theme underlying the five volumes, namely the contributions of the United Nations to developing the ideas that have led from "the establishment of an international development policy to the organization of international economic governance".

The presentation of these five volumes was a prelude to the review to be conducted by the United Nations in 2005, in which development and economic governance will loom large. At the same time, it provided an opportunity to convey to an audience interested in these topics an overview of the United Nations contribution in this important area of modern international history.

The conference also helped to establish contacts between academics from Geneva University and United Nations research workers, facilitated by the involvement of the GIAN network established in 1999 by higher educational institutions in Geneva, namely the University, the Graduate Institute of International Studies (IUHEI) and the Graduate Institute of Development Studies (IUED), with assistance from the canton of Geneva and the Swiss Confederation and the support of international organizations. The GIAN network's mission is to establish research partnerships in international studies between academics and international institutions.

The aim was also to ensure that such collaboration should be long-lasting, result in the establishment of partnerships on the topics of mutual interest highlighted by the conference, and help to generate innovative research ideas.

The conference was extremely interesting, both in terms of the calibre of the participants (see list) and the quality of the presentations and the stimulating and sometimes lively exchanges that followed. It allowed the participants to take stock, identifying the reasons for decline of the UN influence but also discerning encouraging prospects.

Synthesis

A wide-ranging debate

The participants critically appraised action undertaken by the United Nations and the manner in which UNIHP has reported and evaluated this action. They also outlined some proposals for the future.

Assessment

No one disputes the intellectual role played by the United Nations in the economic and social fields between the 1940s and the 1960s. The Organization oversaw the development, diffusion and adoption of four big ideas - the achievement of peace through coordinated international efforts, human rights, independence (or, to put it more precisely, the right of peoples to self-determination), and development. Subsequently, the United Nations has advocated three fundamental themes, namely gender equality, respect for the environment in the name of future generations, and more recently the objective of poverty eradication, now accepted by all.

The failed implementation of the New International Economic Order (NIEO) marked the start of the decline in the intellectual leadership of the United Nations in the economic sphere. However, the Organization has continued, contrary to prevailing opinion, to underscore two basic principles: the importance of the State in managing development and the impact of the international situation on national development policies. Above all, the United Nations has highlighted the adverse effect of neo-liberal policies on social development and has prompted international financial organizations and some Governments to modify their positions.

However, one has only to attend meetings of the World Trade Organization (WTO) or the annual meetings of the World Bank and the International Monetary Fund (IMF) to see that the ideas which actuate finance or trade ministers are not those espoused by the United Nations, an Organization that they tend to bypass when shaping their countries' economic policies.

The reasons for the decline

The reasons for the decline are to be found in the duality of the United Nations, which comprises Governments on the one hand and the Secretariat on the other. The NIEO marked a line that the dominant States were not prepared to cross, that of calling the established order into question. The rich States are willing to bestir themselves to help the weakest, but not to change arrangements that suit their interests. This attitude is currently being carried to extremes, as illustrated by the rich countries' insistence that the fight against hunger or poverty is exclusively a matter for developing countries, and their refusal to consider the exogenous causes of hunger and poverty. Aid, which is in any case modest, does not help to redress the systemic injustice.

All are united in bewailing the decline in the quality of the Secretariat - many exceptions notwithstanding - which is due, on the one hand, to recruitment constraints and procedures, and on the other to States' relative lack of interest in the Organization. Moreover, pressure from States makes the leadership of the United Nations less inclined to present studies and proposals that buck the dominant intellectual trend. For the Secretariat has the double duty of serving Member States and offering up new ideas. If the Secretariat fails to perform the latter function, the Organization as a whole is weakened, or at least loses its creativity.

Richard Toye, referring to the work he has written with his father John Toye (see list of UNIHP publications on page 68) remarked: "Within international organizations, the degree of creative thinking, as opposed to synthesizing and recycling existing ideas, is inversely related to the ability of the organization's top management to exercise editorial control over the research process."

The future

The United Nations will regain its intellectual authority and influence by playing to its strengths. The Organization's main strength is its openness to the world and its consequent ability to garner ideas and experience from all quarters without an ideological filter. The Secretariat, drawing on the experience and analysis provided by the regional commissions and its national offices, could pool examples and ideas to construct new paradigms for the development and governance of the international economy. A credible response to the weaknesses in the present system would restore the United Nations' lost intellectual brilliance.

A strong personality should be charged with this task, someone who can motivate research teams throughout the system and coordinate their efforts. Coordination is the familiar mantra - but what is implied here is coordination focusing on mobilization around a common goal, a far cry from bureaucratic coordination that aims to cut costs by avoiding duplication of effort, the main upshot of which is to hobble the kind of intellectual debate that develops out of different hypotheses and experiences, leading to intellectual sterility.

Another of the strengths of the United Nations as an intergovernmental organization lies in setting goals and laying down principles for the international community and generating consensus among States that can lead to the adoption of binding obligations or guidelines within or outside the United Nations itself. This is the role it has carried out over the years. The important point is to ensure that principles, goals and consensus focus on eliminating the endogenous and exogenous causes of the evils which need to be extirpated, rather than on simply alleviating them. From this standpoint, renewed discussion of how and why inequalities develop seems to be a more pertinent approach to combating poverty than simply seeking to palliate its effects.

Goals, principles, declarations and commitments mean nothing unless they are acted upon and, as a first step, embodied in national institutions, legislation and regulations. This should be the focus of the technical assistance offered by the United Nations. The tasks of establishing the rule of law, encouraging States to adopt law-bound approaches and training citizens to exercise their rights are closely linked to the goal of capacity-building, and they provide the United Nations with an opportunity to combine principles with effectiveness.

Les objectifs du colloque

Le 24 janvier 2005, à l'ouverture de l'année du soixantième anniversaire des Nations Unies, s'est tenu à Genève un Colloque sur le thème: «Du développement à la gouvernance économique internationale: le rôle intellectuel des Nations Unies».

Organisé par le projet d'Histoire intellectuelle des Nations Unies (UNIHP) et le Réseau universitaire international de Genève (RUIG), il avait pour but de présenter à un public académique et international une réflexion sur les cinq premiers ouvrages de ce projet, qui en comptera quatorze et qui a été entrepris il y a cinq ans par une équipe d'experts des Nations Unies, anciens membres de celles-ci ou universitaires, ayant été directement associés à l'élaboration et à la mise en œuvre de ces idées.

Ce colloque rassemblait, pour un dialogue et un débat, internationaux et universitaires sur le thème majeur de ces cinq ouvrages: quel a été le rôle des Nations Unies dans l'élaboration des idées qui ont conduit «de la mise en place d'une politique internationale du développement à l'élaboration d'une gouvernance économique mondiale».

La présentation de ces cinq ouvrages a offert un prélude au bilan que les Nations Unies feront en cette année 2005 et dans lequel développement et gouvernance économique apparaîtront comme des sujets majeurs. En même temps, il a permis de communiquer à un public que ces questions intéressent, une image de l'action onusienne dans ce domaine essentiel de l'histoire du monde contemporain.

Ce colloque a également favorisé un rapprochement entre professeurs d'université genevois et chercheurs des Nations Unies, facilité par la participation du RUIG, créé en 1999 par les institutions universitaires genevoises - l'Université, l'Institut universitaire de hautes études internationales (IUHEI) et l'Institut universitaire d'études du développement (IUED) - avec le concours du Canton de Genève et de la Confédérations suisse et le soutien d'Organisations Internationales. La mission du RUIG consiste dans la création de partenariats de recherche en études internationales entre représentants du monde universitaire et des institutions internationales.

L'objectif était aussi que ce rapprochement soit durable, conduise à la constitution de partenariats sur les sujets d'intérêt commun mis en lumière par le colloque et puisse contribuer à une innovation dans ce domaine d'études,

Ce colloque a été d'un grand intérêt, tant par la haute qualification des participants que par la qualité des présentations qui ont été faites et des débats suggestifs et parfois vifs qui ont suivi. Il a permis de dresser un bilan, d'identifier les causes d'un déclin mais aussi d'entrevoir des perspectives prometteuses.

Synthèse

L'apport des débats: une présentation libre

Les débats ont apporté tant une appréciation critique de l'action de l'ONU que de la manière dont UNIHP en rendait compte et la jugeait. Ils ont aussi esquissé des propositions pour l'avenir.

Bilan

Nul ne conteste le rôle intellectuel des Nations Unies dans le domaine économique et social des années 1940 aux années 1960. Elles ont fait mûrir, partager et adopter quatre grandes idées : la paix par la concertation internationale, les droits de l'homme, l'indépendance (ou mieux le droit des peuples à disposer d'eux-mêmes) et le développement. Par la suite, elles ont promu trois thèmes essentiels: l'égalité des hommes et des femmes, le respect de l'environnement au nom des générations futures, et plus récemment elles ont fait partager par tous l'objectif d'éradication de la pauvreté.

L'échec dans la mise en œuvre du Nouvel Ordre Economique International (NOEI) a marqué le début du déclin du leadership intellectuel des Nations Unies dans le domaine économique. Cependant, elles ont continué, contre l'opinion dominante, à mettre en évidence deux vérités essentielles : l'importance du rôle de l'Etat dans la conduite du développement et l'impact de l'environnement international sur la conduite des politiques de développement nationales. Elles ont surtout mis en relief l'effet négatif de politiques néo-libérales sur le développement social et ont amené les organisations financières internationales et certains gouvernements à réviser leur discours.

Cependant, il n'est que d'assister aux réunions de l'OMC ou à l'assemblée annuelle de la Banque et du Fonds pour constater que la pensée qui anime les ministres des finances ou du commerce n'est pas celle des Nations Unies aux réunions desquelles ils ne se pressent pas, alors qu'ils façonnent la politique économique de leur pays.

Les causes du déclin

Les causes du déclin sont à rechercher dans les deux ONU : l'ONU des gouvernements et l'ONU du secrétariat. Le NOEI a marqué la limite que les Etats dominants n'étaient pas prêts à franchir : celle qui remet en cause l'ordre établi. Les Etats riches sont disposés à faire des efforts en faveur des plus faibles, pas à modifier un ordre qui leur est favorable. Cette attitude est poussée à l'extrême aujourd'hui avec l'insistance des pays riches à faire de la lutte contre la faim ou contre la pauvreté une affaire exclusive des pays en développement et leur refus de considérer les causes extérieures qui provoquent faim et pauvreté. Les aides, au demeurant modestes, ne compensent pas l'iniquité systémique. Du côté du secrétariat, chacun déplore la baisse de qualité - même si elle soufre de nombreuses exceptions - due pour une part aux contraintes et modalités du recrutement et d'autre part au relatif désintérêt des Etats pour l'Organisation. En outre, la pression des Etats rend les dirigeants de l'ONU moins disposés à mettre sur la table des études et propositions qui rompent avec la pensée dominante. Or, un secrétariat a le double devoir de servir les pays membres et de provoquer leur réflexion. Faute au secrétariat d'assumer ce second devoir, l'Organisation tout entière s'affaiblit ou, à tout le moins, perd sa créativité.

Richard Toye, s'appuyant sur l'ouvrage qu'il a écrit avec son père John Toye (voir liste des publications de l'UNIHP en page 68), remarque que « dans les organisations internationales, le degré de créativité intellectuelle, par opposition à la synthèse et au recyclage des idées existantes, est inversement corrélée avec la capacité de leur direction d'exercer un fort contrôle éditorial sur le processus de recherche. »

Perspectives

C'est en s'appuyant sur ses atouts que l'ONU retrouvera autorité intellectuelle et influence. Le principal de ces atouts est que les Nations Unies sont ouvertes à l'ensemble du monde et peuvent ainsi glaner idées et expériences de toute origine sans filtre idéologique. Le secrétariat en s'appuyant sur les expériences et analyses des Commissions régionales et de ses représentations nationales pourrait rassembler exemples et idées propres à bâtir de nouveaux paradigmes pour le développement et la gouvernance de l'économie mondiale. Une réponse crédible aux faiblesses du système actuel redonnerait à l'ONU le lustre intellectuel qu'elle a perdu.

Il faudrait en charger un esprit puissant capable de motiver les équipes de recherche disséminées dans le système et coordonner leurs efforts. Coordonner : le mot tant de fois répété est lâché. Certes, mais la coordination par la mobilisation autour d'un objectif commun dont il est question ici est tout autre que la coordination bureaucratique dont l'objectif est de faire des économies en évitant les doubles emplois et dont les résultats sont surtout d'empêcher le débat d'idées à partir d'hypothèses et de faits différents et donc de stériliser la pensée

Un autre atout des Nations Unies en tant qu'organisation intergouvernementale est d'établir des objectifs et des principes pour la communauté internationale et de générer des consensus entre les Etats qui peuvent conduire à l'adoption d'engagements contraignants ou de directives au sein ou en dehors de l'ONU proprement dite. Elle a joué ce rôle au fil des années. L'important est que principes, objectifs et consensus visent à éliminer les causes internes et externes des maux que l'on veut combattre et non seulement à en diminuer la pénibilité. Dans cette perspective, reprendre la réflexion sur le développement et les causes des inégalités semble une approche plus pertinente pour lutter contre la pauvreté que d'en pallier les effets.

Objectifs, principes, déclarations, engagements ne valent que s'ils sont mis en œuvre, et, tout d'abord, traduits dans les institutions, législations et réglementations nationales. Ce devrait être le rôle central de l'assistance technique de l'ONU. Établir les conditions de l'application du droit, encourager les Etats à adopter des approches par le droit et préparer les citoyens à exercer leurs droits, cela est intimement lié à l'objectif de renforcement des capacités et une chance pour l'ONU de joindre principes et efficacité.

Introduction

Message of Mr. Sergei Ordzhonikidze, Director-General of the United Nations Office at Geneva

It gives me great pleasure to convey my best wishes for interesting and thought-provoking discussions to all of you gathered here today. The projects that are being presented show not only the breadth and reach of ideas that were nurtured and refined by the United Nations. Importantly, they highlight the reality that sparked these ideas in the first place and inspired people within the United Nations system and beyond to strive for their implementation. And they demonstrate how these ideas played a significant role in stimulating progress and changing that reality.

The United Nations Intellectual History Project is not a theoretical exercise. It aims to provide a greater appreciation of how creative thinking is stimulated, innovative ideas are shaped and dynamic strategies implemented. The focus is on the results, not the rhetoric. The Project is as forward-looking as the ideas that it traces. In examining how the United Nations has influenced the international debate through its research, analysis and conceptual originality, the Project makes a practical contribution to strengthening the Organization's future capacity in this regard. Exploring the lessons learnt from the United Nations' role in formulating fresh ideas is thus a particularly valuable contribution to the ongoing reform of the United Nations.

Today's events provide welcome opportunities to bring these lessons to a wider audience and to use them to reflect on how the United Nations may continue to contribute as an incubator of influential ideas. I welcome the constructive collaboration with the Geneva International Academic Network in organizing this event and the active involvement of the wider academic and research community in Geneva, in particular the University of Geneva. This engagement between "International" and "Intellectual" Geneva adds particular value to the discussions.

As we celebrate the 60th anniversary of the United Nations, this clearer understanding of its intellectual impact adds an important dimension to our overall knowledge of the Organization's contribution to shaping international affairs. As mandated by the Charter, the Organization has actively sought to promote social progress and better standards of life in larger freedom. The exhibition, organized by the UNOG Library, explores United Nations ideas in the service of development in greater detail, and I invite you all to take the opportunity to benefit from it. The Chief Librarian, Mr. Pierre Le Loarer, will highlight some additional important aspects of the exhibition.

Message de Sergei Ordzhonikidze, Directeur général de l'Office des Nations Unies à Genève

C'est avec grand plaisir que j'adresse mes meilleurs vœux aux intéressants débats que vous allez mener ensemble ici aujourd'hui. Le Projet d'histoire intellectuelle des Nations Unies ne montre pas seulement l'ampleur et la portée des idées qui ont été mûries par les Nations Unies, il met, avant tout, l'accent sur la réalité qui a suscité ces idées en premier lieu et sur les personnes, au sein du système des Nations Unies et au-delà, qui ont été inspirées par ces idées et qui se sont efforcées de les mettre en œuvre. Ce Projet démontre comment ces idées ont joué un rôle significatif pour stimuler le progrès et changer cette réalité.

Le Projet UNIHP n'est pas un exercice théorique. Il a pour but d'offrir une plus grande appréciation de la manière dont la pensée créative est stimulée, les idées innovantes sont formées et des stratégies dynamiques sont mises en œuvre. L'attention est portée sur les résultats et non pas sur la rhétorique. Le Projet est autant tourné vers l'avenir que les idées qu'il formule. En examinant comment les Nations Unies ont influencé le débat international par le biais de leurs recherches, de leur analyse et de leur originalité conceptuelle, le Projet contribue de façon concrète au renforcement des capacités futures de l'organisation. Ainsi, explorer les leçons tirées du rôle des Nations Unies en formulant des idées nouvelles est une contribution de valeur à la réforme des Nations Unies en cours.

Les événements d'aujourd'hui offrent l'opportunité de porter ces leçons à la connaissance d'un public plus large et de les employer pour réfléchir à la manière dont les Nations Unies, tel un incubateur d'idées influentes, peuvent continuer à contribuer. Je me félicite de la collaboration constructive avec le Réseau Universitaire International de Genève pour l'organisation de cet événement et l'implication active de la communauté universitaire et de recherche de Genève au sens large. Cet engagement entre la Genève internationale et la Genève intellectuelle ajoute une valeur particulière aux discussions.

Alors que nous célébrons le soixantième anniversaire des Nations Unies, cette meilleure compréhension de ces impacts intellectuels ajoute une dimension importante à notre connaissance globale de la contribution de l'organisation au façonnement des affaires internationales. Telle que mandatée par la Charte, l'Organisation a activement cherché à promouvoir le progrès social et de meilleurs niveaux de vie par une plus grande liberté. L'exposition organisée par la bibliothèque de l'ONUG explore les idées des Nations Unies au service du développement et je vous invite à saisir l'opportunité de la visiter. Le bibliothécaire en chef, M. Pierre Le Loarer, soulignera quelques aspects importants de cette exposition.

Jean-Marie Dufour, Président du Réseau International Universitaire de Genève

Au nom du Réseau Universitaire International de Genève, le RUIG, je vous souhaite la bienvenue à cette Conférence sur l'histoire intellectuelle des Nations Unies. Les cinq premiers ouvrages de cette collection vous seront présentés sous le thème « Du développement à la gouvernance du système économique mondial ». Le RUIG a accueilli avec grand intérêt la proposition d'organiser en coopération avec le Projet UNIHP et la Bibliothèque de l'ONUG cette conférence. Le sujet est d'un haut intérêt au plan scientifique et politique. Il aborde la question sur le plan des idées politiques aux Nations Unies, chose qui a rarement été faite. Il peut contribuer à une meilleure connaissance des Nations Unies. Et il peut surtout restaurer un débat d'idées qui s'est affaibli mais est pourtant essentiel au progrès de la communauté internationale.

Cette question entre parfaitement dans la mission qui a été confiée au RUIG en 1999 par les institutions universitaires genevoises, la République et Canton de Genève et la Confédération : rapprocher les communautés internationale et académique sur des recherches pratiques d'intérêt commun en relations internationales dans le cadre de partenariats interdisciplinaires pour favoriser aussi un échange de connaissances et d'expériences dans un intérêt réciproque. À ce jour, cette synergie fait apparaître des résultats très intéressants et une vitalité nouvelle dans l'approche des relations internationales.

Ce début d'année est un bon moment pour tenir cette conférence. 2005 est en effet l'année du soixantième anniversaire des Nations Unies. Et nous pouvons ainsi, en préface des célébrations à venir, rendre hommage à la réflexion dont les Nations Unies ont été le cadre depuis leur création, sur des sujets cruciaux pour notre monde qui ne manqueront pas d'être évoqués dans les mois prochains et que le Secrétaire général des Nations Unies a inscrit au cœur des préoccupations de ce millénaire.

Il est également naturel que cette conférence se tienne à Genève, la Genève internationale, autre ville du monde où les Nations Unies ont une forte présence et où la réflexion et le débat sur la gouvernance économique mondiale occupent une place prééminente. C'est aussi une ville où un pôle universitaire d'excellence en relations internationales et en développement devrait voir le jour, et où réside, tant dans la communauté internationale qu'universitaire, un grand nombre d'enseignants, de chercheurs et d'opérateurs de haute compétence sur les questions dont nous allons parler. Cette conférence donnera lieu à un rapport dont nous espérons qu'il pourra être présenté à l'ECOSOC lors de sa réunion en juillet 2005.

Yves Berthelot, Directeur UNIHP Genève

Au nom des directeurs du Projet d'histoire intellectuelle des Nations Unies (UNIHP), j'ai à mon tour plaisir à vous souhaiter la bienvenue. Je commencerai par dire deux mots du Projet avant de revenir sur l'objectif de cette conférence.

Le regretté Sydney Dell eut l'idée d'une histoire intellectuelle des Nations Unies dans les années 1980, idée que Richard Jolly a reprise avec Louis Emmerij et Tom Weiss et qui est entrain de se réaliser grâce au concours de tous ceux qu'elle a séduits. Une telle histoire manquait. Il n'existait pas, en effet, d'étude historique satisfaisante de l'origine, de l'évolution et de l'impact des idées mûries au sein des Nations Unies. Il s'agit bien d'une histoire des idées et non des institutions où se sont développées ces idées. Il appartient à ces institutions d'écrire leur propre histoire - avec la dimension de plaidoyer que prennent souvent les histoires commanditées par les institutions. UNIHP n'est pas commandité par les Nations Unies : c'est un projet indépendant, qui se veut libre et critique. Les universitaires trouveront peut-être que les auteurs sont indulgents envers les Nations Unies. Peut-être, mais il est vrai que chacun en conduisant ses recherches a acquis la conviction que les Nations Unies avaient effectivement beaucoup contribué aux idées de notre temps.

Concrètement, le Projet va se traduire par onze volumes thématiques dont quatre seront présentés au cours de cette conférence et deux volumes de synthèse dont un déjà publié seront aussi présentés aujourd'hui. En outre, les témoignages oraux de soixante-treize personnalités qui ont façonné la pensée des Nations Unies ont été collectés au cours d'interviews qui seront synthétisées en un ouvrage en cours de préparation et qui seront mises à la disposition des chercheurs sous forme de CD-ROM distribué aux bibliothèques.

Le Projet a rassemblé une vingtaine d'auteurs. Des financements de l'ordre de cinq millions de dollars ont été fournis par des fondations et un certain nombre de gouvernements, dont la Suisse et le Canton et la Ville de Genève que je remercie particulièrement aujourd'hui.

La conférence de cet après-midi est la seconde d'une série de présentations qui vont avoir lieu cette année à l'occasion du soixantième anniversaire. Mais en l'organisant avec le RUIG, nous voudrions qu'elle soit le point de départ de futures recherches. Nous espérons que les thèmes abordés dans les différents livres et les questions qui restent en suspens vont donner naissance à de nouvelles recherches. Nous espérons qu'il y aura une suite à cette conférence, d'autres débats au sein des universités et instituts, et que les étudiants prendront la relève de ce qui a été commencé.

Dans la perspective de futures recherches, je voudrais mentionner le rôle important de la bibliothèque des Nations Unies à Genève. Non seulement celle-ci héberge le bureau genevois du Projet UNIHP et a fourni documents et archives au Projet, mais encore elle a préparé autour des cinq premiers ouvrages une exposition qui présente des archives et documents qui sont à la base des réflexions développées dans les ouvrages. Cette exposition montre l'extrême richesse de la bibliothèque des Nations Unies, richesse qui couvre non seulement la période des Nations Unies mais aussi la période de la Société des Nations. Aux chercheurs de l'exploiter !

Je souhaite aussi que les débats de cet après-midi inspirent ceux qui vont écrire la synthèse des ouvrages du projet et mettent en évidence le travail intellectuel des Nations Unies avec ses succès et ses faiblesses. J'espère qu'ils donneront ainsi des réponses aux jugements lapidaires et un peu sommaires qui sont souvent portés sur l'impact des Nations Unies dans le domaine économique et social. Il y a trop de critiques rapides des Nations Unies, et partager cette réflexion sur ce qui a été fait ne peut être qu'enrichissant.

Pierre Le Loarer, Bibliothécaire en chef et Président du Comité des activités culturelles de l'Office des Nations Unies à Genève

Je souhaite souligner la signification et le symbole que représente la présence dans notre bibliothèque d'une partie de l'équipe du Projet d'histoire intellectuelle des Nations Unies car c'est pour nous une manière concrète de nous mettre au service de la recherche et en ce sens de contribuer à l'effort des Nations Unies. Notre bibliothèque que certains qualifient de « trésor caché à Genève » accueille dans son fonds les documents officiels des Nations Unies dans les différentes langues mais aussi des fonds importants d'archives dont ceux de la Société des Nations. Récemment, un chercheur sur la question de l'esclavage et des traites négrières, lors d'une exposition que nous avons organisée sur l'abolition de l'esclavage, a découvert qu'il aurait pu trouver une grande partie de sa documentation dans cette bibliothèque au lieu d'aller aux Etats Unis et a découvert des documents qu'il ignorait.

L'exposition que nous présentons avec l'appui du Projet UNIHP comprend toute une série de documents - archives diverses, ouvrages et quelques illustrations — qui permettent de parcourir quelques-unes des traces de cette histoire intellectuelle des idées des Nations Unies au service du développement.

Je voudrais conclure par une petite histoire vraie. En 1932, une personnalité scientifique de premier plan fut invitée par la Société des Nations et son Institut International de Coopération Intellectuelle à un libre échange de vues avec une personnalité de son choix sur un sujet désigné à son gré. La personnalité scientifique déclara que dans l'état présent des choses la question qui lui apparaissait comme la plus importante dans l'ordre de la civilisation était la suivante : existe-t-il un moyen d'affranchir les hommes de la menace de guerre ? La conclusion de la réponse de l'intellectuel qui avait été invité à répondre fut : « Tout ce qui travaille au développement de la culture travaille aussi contre la guerre ». Le texte complet de cet échange a été publié par l'Institut International de Coopération Intellectuelle dans un petit opuscule intitulé "Pourquoi la guerre ?" paru en 1933. La personnalité scientifique qui posa cette question n'était autre qu'Albert Einstein. Et celui qui tenta de répondre à cette question était Sigmund Freud. À travers cette anecdote, je souhaite saluer l'initiative du RUIG et du Projet UNIHP qui travaillent au développement de la culture à travers l'histoire des idées et dire également que le rapport 2004 du PNUD sur le développement humain conclut également sur le caractère essentiel de la culture et de ce qui lui est liée, l'éducation.

I – Views on UN ideas and methods

The first session of the conference was presided by Victor-Yves Ghebali, GIIS. During this session, based on the five published volumes of the UNIHP series, authors of these volumes and academics from Geneva made various presentations that were followed by comments and discussions with the audience.

The interventions made by the authors and academics as well as the comments from the floor have been organised in three sections: UN ideas, Institutional dimension and methods in producing ideas, Critics of the UNIHP approach.

Victor-Yves Ghebali

Les Nations Unies ont bien analysé les obstacles au développement économique et social et proposé des politiques qui ont été prises en compte jusqu'au milieu des années 1970 : stratégies de substitution aux importations (très suivies), aide au développement (inégalement concrétisée).

Le nouvel ordre économique international, adopté mais non traduit en décisions, marque un tournant à partir duquel les Institutions de Bretton Woods prennent le leadership intellectuel et ont un impact décisif sur les politiques économiques. Les Nations Unies se limitent alors dans le domaine économique à la critique des excès du néo-libéralisme de la Banque et du FMI.

Aujourd'hui, les Nations Unies mettent en avant des thèmes importants comme la pauvreté, l'environnement ou l'égalité entre hommes et femmes. Dans ces domaines, elles ont une influence réelle, mais elles ne parviennent pas à proposer une politique économique crédible qui intègre ces dimensions. Elles ne regagneront un rôle significatif que si elles conçoivent et savent diffuser une vision du développement qui soit réaliste, différenciée (pas de « one size fits all »), équitable, respectueuse de l'environnement. Aujourd'hui le Secrétariat n'a pas pris les initiatives nécessaires et les gouvernements lui en refuseraient très vraisemblablement les moyens.

UN Ideas: Presentations and Comments

Richard Jolly: Ahead of the Curve? UN Ideas and Global Challenges

Ahead of the Curve? UN Ideas and Global Challenges begins by reminding us that the United Nations was born in San Francisco in 1945 as the most destructive war in recorded history was coming to an end. On that tragic foundation were built four powerful ideas: *peace* – the idea that sovereign states could create an international organization and procedures that would replace military aggression and war by negotiation and collective security; *independence* – the idea that people in all countries would have the right to be politically independent and make whatever national and international agreements that their citizens might choose; *development* – the idea that all countries long independent or newly so could purposefully pursue policies of economic and social advance which over time would rapidly improve the welfare and living standards of their populations; and *human rights* – the boldest idea of all, namely that every individual in every country throughout the world shares an equal claim not only to such individual, civil, and political rights as liberty and the pursuit of happiness, but also to a core of more collective economic and social freedoms.

Those four principles were built into the Charter and the early programme of work of the United Nations. Looking back we can now see the amazing vision and courage that was brought to the task. The notions that colonies were to be independent, that war was to be rejected as an instrument of foreign policy, that policies to improve standards of living were to be universally pursued and that human rights were to be there for all were ideas far ahead of the time.

At first, these four great ideas were largely pursued separately in the programmes of the UN. The most interesting point of evolution is that those ideas gradually have come together over the six decades of the UN: they have come together in terms of operations and programmes, and they have been brought together intellectually.

For all of them also, more progress has been made than was thought possible at the time. About *peace,* there was the Cold War, the absence of hot conflict, but cold confrontation. But as the report of the High Level Panel on Threats, Challenges and Change[1] has brought out, there have been more conflicts resolved by negotiations with the hand of the UN in the 1990s than in the previous two hundred years. The vision even in that area has not been chimera. *Independence* went much faster than anyone anticipated. The early vision of *development* was far ahead of what was thought reasonable in the 1940s or 1950s – but nonetheless economic progress and human advance has often exceeded expectations. In this area, the UN made the leading contributions internationally until the 1980s.

Then with debt, recession and the shift of donor attention to the Bretton Woods institutions, the UN was left on the sidelines with the result that UN's contributions in the 1980s and 1990s were those of the New York dissent and critique of the Washington consensus. The Economic Commission for Africa (ECA) preached the alternative African programme of structural adjustment[2], UNICEF, the UN Children's Fund, made the case for adjustment with a human face[3], the International Labour Organisation (ILO) struggled to hold meetings but under the threat that the US would withdraw if they went too far. For *Human Rights,* there was a surge of attention and support in the 1980s and 1990s, growing out of the Women's Conferences, of the Right to Development, and of the Convention on the Rights of the Child.

Three of these issues, peace, development and human rights, pursued almost independently for twenty to forty years, are now increasingly seen as different facets of a single core of human advance. The Right to Development[4] and the rights-based approach to development, operationally came together in the 1990s. Intellectually, human development, human security and human rights were brought together in the *Human Development Report*, a major creation of Mahbub ul Haq and Amartya Sen. In contrast, sovereign independence, largely achieved in the legal and institutional sense in the 1950s and 1960s, is now undergoing major re-thinking. Issues related to the responsibility to protect and the right to intervene are hot topics as the UN grapples with measures to tackle genocide and other egregious abuses of human rights.

In closing, I would like to underline three points: first, clearly the UN has been ahead of the curve. The reprint of our first volume will probably drop the question mark. Secondly, the US led the way for many of the UN's pioneering contributions: the role of Eleanor Roosevelt in human rights and the role of J.F. Kennedy calling for a Development Decade are only two examples. This adds to the tragedy of their present turning their

---

[1] Secretary-General's High Level Panel on Threats, Challenges and Change, *A More Secure World: Our Shared Responsibility,* report released in December 2004 (http://www.un.org/secureworld).
[2] See ECA, "African Alternative Framework to Structural Adjustment Programmes for Socio-Economic Recovery and Transformation" (A/RES/44/24).
[3] G. A. Cornia, R. Jolly, F. Stewart, *Adjustment With a Human Face – Protecting the Vulnerable and Promoting Growth,* a study by UNICEF. Oxford University Press, 1987.
[4] Adopted by General Assembly resolution 41/128 of 4 December 1986.

back on so much of the UN. Thirdly, Europe, I believe, has now a historic role to protect this heritage – human rights, rule of law, a less ideological approach to development. We need to build on this. Taken together Europe today contributes about 33% of the UN budget, 40% of peacekeeping, and over 50% of development aid. Europe needs to develop a common position on many of these issues and draw on this positive history and carry it forward.

Comment from the floor: UN has lost a sense of vision

I have the impression that the UN has lost a sense of vision, which the founding fathers had, and that this is due to the primacy of economic analysis and econometrics, that positivistic science has lessened the impact of social and cultural variables in terms of social change and development. Also, there is a loss of a vision for peace: the current notions of solutions to the planetary problems do not define solutions in terms of a peaceful alternative; they are about lessening aggression and maintaining security. A truly alternative vision has been lost. In the 1940s and 1950s, the founding fathers were adamant that we begin to think about the future of the planet in a different sense. Finally, the primacy of liberal market economy makes it difficult to move outside that box when thinking about new solutions for social change.

Reply: Richard Jolly

I do not fully agree that the UN has lost vision. *UN Voices,* the sixth volume of the Project that will be published in June, contains excerpts from the interviews of UN people active in the 1940s, 1950s and 1960s. Many of them did talk not so much about the first ten or twenty years, but the first few years just before McCarthy and the Korean War. Many we interviewed did say there was at the very beginning a vision, a sense of hope, and particularly a personal commitment that has never been recovered. This said, however, we can see that the present Secretary-General has struggled hard to re-create the vision, with the holding of the Millennium Summit, the seriousness of the pursuit of the Millennium Development Goals, and reform and strengthening of the UN. In many ways that has a number of points that the early years of the UN and its vision never quite rose to, for example the serious pursuit of human rights. The High Level Panel that integrated its proposals for peace-building and institutional change in a very realistic and creative way is also an encouraging factor.

On the primacy of neo-liberal economics, this is clearly one of the elements that many parts of the UN have been struggling against in the 1980s and 1990s, both by taking on ideologically and methodologically the extremes of the neo-liberal paradigm, by pointing to its weaknesses, and by trying to propose alternatives. The human development paradigm has attracted much attention and its influence has now spread to many parts of the UN. Also, the flirtation that WHO had with neo-liberal ideas until about two or three years ago seems to have passed with the present Director-General. This reminds us that leadership from the Directors-General and their equivalent throughout the UN is always enormously important.

Comment from the floor : Des idées ou des recettes ?

À propos de la crise des quatre concepts essentiels de l'ONU – la paix, le développement, les droits de l'homme et la souveraineté, je me demande si cette crise est circonstancielle, si ce sont des difficultés sur la route tracée par l'ONU ou si cette crise ne vient pas d'un malentendu. Dans mes souvenirs d'adolescent, l'ONU n'apparaissait pas comme le creuset d'une construction intellectuelle puissante et durable. Elle apparaissait plutôt comme le lieu d'un compromis bâtard entre diverses visions du monde incompatibles et qui n'allaient pas durer, entre les puissances dominantes d'économie capitaliste et un bloc socialiste qui essayait d'affaiblir l'ennemi avec une idéologie très cohérente. Le mot de « socialisme » qui n'a pas été mentionné a été le grand concept, la grande théorie des droits de l'homme des deux derniers siècles. Et le terme de « tiers-monde » ou de « décolonisation » a à peine été évoqué. Mais c'est peut-être cet équilibre bâtard qui a fait le succès de l'ONU : les pays qui cherchaient à se faire un peu d'espace ont profité de cet équilibre de la terreur pour gagner le maximum de liberté dans le cadre du système onusien. Maintenant que l'idéologie du grand socialisme s'est effondrée, est-ce que les valeurs de l'ONU n'apparaissent pas plutôt comme quelques faibles recettes de cuisine un peu démodées?

Reply: Richard Jolly

I would not say that the ideas of peace, sovereign independence, human rights and development are just those of socialism. I am stirred to think of the phrase of Dag Hammarskjöld that is relevant here: "The UN was created not to take us to heaven but to save us from hell." Many of the UN contributions in these areas have been less than a full vision of heaven on earth, but nonetheless have made a major impact.

Frédéric Lapeyre: UN Contributions to Development Thinking and Practice

En travaillant dans les archives pour le livre *UN Contributions to Development Thinking and Practice*, nous avons découvert l'importance des Nations Unies dans la conceptualisation du développement dès les années 1940. Les Nations Unies ont contribué à problématiser le concept de développement et à donner une vision du développement, autre que la vision dominante à l'époque qui provenait avant tout des universités américaines dans un contexte géopolitique de guerre froide. Avec le mouvement de décolonisation et sous la pression de nouveaux membres indépendants, elles vont se consacrer au développement et contribuer ainsi à l'émergence d'un nouveau champ de recherche en sciences sociales.

Dans les années 40 et 50, les Nations Unies identifient des obstacles au développement économique et recommandent des politiques pour accélérer le développement dans les pays et régions dites sous-développées. Elles vont faire avancer les débats sur le commerce international et sur la nécessité de l'assistance technique, de la solidarité et des flux financiers vers les pays du Sud. Mais j'aimerais surtout mettre l'accent sur trois contributions majeures des Nations Unies : le rôle de l'État, l'importance des facteurs externes, la réduction des inégalités.

La première contribution concerne la place de l'État dans les processus de développement. Les Nations Unies se placent dès le début dans le camp des interventionnistes. Devant l'incapacité du marché à lancer le processus de développement dans les pays sous-développés, les Nations Unies, influencées par l'héritage keynésien à la sortie de la Deuxième guerre mondiale, considèrent que l'État a un rôle-clé dans les politiques de développement. Elles mènent des travaux sur la planification qui renforcent le rôle de l'État comme moteur du développement et généralisent la planification du développement. Les nouveaux États indépendants sont mis sur le siège conducteur : c'est à eux de mener les politiques de développement. L'idée d'un rôle positif de l'État est restée un des piliers de la réflexion des Nations Unies sur le développement, idée qui revient actuellement.

La seconde contribution concerne les facteurs internes et externes du sous développement. À la fin des années 40, les principales théories sur le développement sont les théories de la modernisation, développées par les universités américaines, avec W.W. Rostow par exemple, dans lesquelles le développement est un processus de rattrapage, le passage du traditionnel au moderne.

Les Nations Unies, notamment avec le rapport de Raúl Prebisch sur les conditions économiques et les problèmes liés au développement en Amérique Latine[5] et son analyse Centre-Périphérie, remettent en question cette vision d'un rattrapage non problématique et de la dichotomie traditionnel-moderne en mettant l'accent sur les facteurs externes du sous-développement : la tendance séculière à la détérioration des termes de l'échange et le problème de la volatilité des prix des matières premières qui compliquent la tâche des pays nouvellement indépendants à planifier le développement et mener à bien des politiques économiques de développement rapide.

L'accent sur les facteurs externes marque la position des Nations Unies encore aujourd'hui avec la réflexion sur la gouvernance mondiale et une nouvelle architecture globale. Ces réflexions soulignent l'importance de prendre en compte les facteurs externes qui expliquent en partie les problèmes de développement des pays du Sud.

La troisième contribution concerne les inégalités. Dès la fin des années 40, les Nations Unies prennent en compte la nécessité de réduire les inégalités entre pays et entre régions ainsi qu'au sein des pays et des sociétés. L'assistance au développement a été centrale dans le débat sur la réduction des inégalités entre pays On connaît le Point IV de Truman, le besoin d'assistance technique, le besoin de développer les flux financiers des pays développés vers les pays sous-développés pour financer le développement. Le débat au sein des Nations Unies, notamment autour de la création de SUNFED, a porté en particulier sur la forme que devaient prendre ces flux financiers : fallait-il faire du « soft-financing » ou fallait-il attacher des contraintes fortes à ces financements ? Les pays du Sud souhaitaient un financement à faible conditionnalité, mais les Etats-Unis soutenaient la nécessité d'une forte conditionnalité.[6]

La nécessité de réduire les inégalités au sein des sociétés apparaît également dans la réflexion sur le développement. L'accent est mis sur les idées de justice sociale et de développement humain. Le rapport sur les mesures de développement économique de 1951 critiquait les classes dirigeantes et recommandait des réformes agraires radicales ainsi que la nécessité de lutter contre les inégalités dans les pays du Sud.[7] Un des objectifs de la première décennie du développement était de réduire les inégalités entre régions ainsi qu'au sein des pays en tirant les leçons des années 50 pendant lesquelles toute une partie de la population n'avait pas bénéficié des retombées positives de la croissance.

Richard Jolly: Quantifying the World: The UN Ideas on Statistics

Quantifying the World: The UN Ideas on Statistics by Michael Ward is a fascinating volume on a topic so little recognized as fundamentally important. Perhaps this is because many people have an intrinsic fear or distrust of statistics. But statistics have a deep importance. In the overview, the three editors quote Dudley Seers, who wrote: "We cannot with our own eyes and ears perceive more than a minute sample of human affairs even in our own country and a very un-random sample at that. So we rely on statistics

---

[5] Economic Commission of Latin America, The Economic Development of Latin America and Its Principal Problems. Lake Success: UN Department of Economic Affairs, 1950.
[6] See for example: V.K.R.V. Rao, "Suggestions for Creation of New International Agency for Financing Basic Economic Development", annex A, p. 129 in: UN, Methods of Financing Economic Development in Underdeveloped Countries. New York: United Nations, 1949; R. Scheyven, Special United Nations Fund for Economic Development – final report prepared in pursuance of General Assembly resolution 724B (VIII). New York: United Nations, 1954.
[7] UN Department of Economic Affairs, Measures for the Economic Development of Under-Developed Countries, report by a group of experts appointed by the Secretary-General of the United Nations. New York: United Nations, 1951.

in order to build and maintain our own model of the world. The data that are available mould out perceptions." He did not need to say that the data that is *not* available blinds our understanding of many things in the world. He went on to say: "A statistical policy, that is the policy of statistical offices, thus exerts a subtle but pervasive influence on political, social and economic development. This is why the apparently dull and minor subject of statistical priority is of crucial importance."

In this volume, Michael Ward shows how the UN from the beginning played the major international role in building up a common statistical system extending to all corners of the world. This is a truly remarkable achievement. Although the League of Nations did some work in this area, it never grappled with the major issue of statistics from all parts of the world. Looking back at any of the statistical digest in the immediate post-Second World War shows what an inadequate sample of data was available. Yet within a few years, we had national account estimates - GNP (Gross National Product) estimates - for virtually all countries of the world. Not perfectly accurate estimates, but that is a different issue.

This was a largely unsung achievement of truly worldwide significance. Anyone who has been involved in parts of the UN, realizes the difficulty of getting common definitions, of mobilizing commitment of countries to follow those definitions, to ensuring the data are collected and published on time, and then assembled into international data. For the UN to have achieved this so rapidly and so early for basic economic data is truly amazing.

The UN Statistical Office's work was not without weaknesses and omissions. The first substantive item on the agenda of the Statistical Commissions in 1946, however, was statistics on gender, women, fascinating! It is not quite clear why after that gender issues got lost for so long. In general, there was an evil coalition between developed and developing countries amounting to foot dragging with respect to social indicators, which lasted for two and a half, three decades. It was left to UNRISD in the 1960s to start pioneering a system of social indicators.[8]

Issues of environment have received more attention, but still they have not been systematically integrated into the whole system of national accounts. They have been brought in as satellite accounts. In the last two decades, city groups have taken over from the UN as the main organizing meetings where new issues are explored, and consensus points are reach to influence new ideas.

A major criticism made in the book is that: "A truly global perspective on economic and social progress and development has thus been allowed to fall by the wayside. This comes at a time when the political interest and level of debate on such questions could hardly be more intense. Having given up the crown jewels of statistical measurement and conceded control of statistical authority to institutions committed to supporting the economic and financial agenda of Western orthodoxy, the UN Statistical Office has lost much of its claim to speak for the global community and provided with required leadership to bring innovative data development into the 21st century." (Page 4) Quite a damming conclusion on a lot of what happened in the 1980s and 1990s! But, the book continues: "At the turn of the new millennium, the UN Statistical Office has moved back to centre stage to begin forging new strategies." (Page 4)

---

[8] UNRISD, *The Level of Living Index*, prepared by J. Drewnowski and W. Scott. Report n° 4. Geneva, September 1966.

I should end by quoting some of the key areas of statistical priority identified as needing action. Some points are technical, such as the difficulty of coping with global inflation —statistical techniques to assess what is being happening to global inflation. This is critically related to the measurement of international poverty. Through the poverty measurement debate (income poverty, comparisons of GNP or PPP —purchasing power parity), we know that all these issues are fundamental for our understanding as to whether things are getting better or worse in terms of income or living standards in which country and how. Yet, Ward brings out how the intellectual work by the UN to lay the foundation for proper analysis of this has been deficient.

Other statistical priorities include: global inequality which needs much greater attention; implementation of human rights —not just about countries that have ratified on which we can get all the data, but some system for measuring the extent to which countries are implementing human rights; issues of human security —nationally, community, globally; issues of sustainability and environmental monitoring. These are some of the points identified (on pages 49-50) as needing to be pushed high on the international agenda, where we need to build up a global system that does not just rely on inputs from national systems but directly gets data from the transnational corporations, from situation, households, or surveys of individuals.

Yves Berthelot : Unity and Diversity in Development Ideas : Perspectives from the UN Regional Commissions

Le livre *Unity and Diversity in Development Ideas : Perspectives from the UN Regional Commissions* présente les idées que les Commissions régionales ont développées pour répondre aux problèmes de leur région. Il permet en outre quelques remarques sur l'incidence des institutions et des circonstances sur le mûrissement des idées.

Dans le domaine des idées, les Commissions régionales ont toutes été confrontées à trois problèmes semblables auxquels elles ont apporté des réponses marquées par les circonstances : la cohésion de la région, le développement de ses pays membres, le défi de la globalisation.

La cohésion de chaque région. La Commission économique pour l'Europe (CEE) était divisée entre l'Est et l'Ouest par l'idéologie, l'ambition d'imposer au monde des modèles antagonistes et le fonctionnement de l'économie. La Commission économique pour l'Asie et l'Extrême-Orient (ECAFE, plus tard ESCAP) était divisée entre pays indépendants et colonies, pays immenses et pays minuscules. L'Afrique, l'Amérique Latine et le Moyen-Orient étaient plus homogènes, encore que les différences nombreuses de statut, de richesse et les conflits de frontière entretenaient les tensions. Gunnar Myrdal, le premier Secrétaire Exécutif de la CEE, a répondu aux divisions de l'Europe en amenant les pays à se focaliser sur des questions modestes et pratiques d'intérêt commun. Cela a donné lieu à un grand nombre de conventions et de normes dont certaines sont devenues mondiales dans le cadre de l'ONU et qui toutes furent adoptées par la Communauté européenne et devinrent parties de « l'acquis communautaire » - ce qui a facilité l'élargissement de l'Union. L'ECAFE, pour sa part, a développé des institutions panasiatiques, et notamment la Banque Asiatique de Développement. Suivant son exemple, la CEPAL a créé la Banque Inter-Américaine de Développement et la Commission Économique pour l'Afrique a poussé à la création de la Banque Africaine de Développement tout en développant des institutions sous-régionales. Voilà donc deux types de réponses au problème de l'unité : des réponses institutionnelles assez ambitieuses et des réponses pragmatiques.

Le développement. Les réflexions sur le développement sont aussi marquées par les circonstances de chaque région. L'ECAFE a été la première des institutions des Nations Unies à étudier le lien entre population et développement et à recommander de maîtriser la croissance de la population.[9] Le Fonds des Nations Unies pour la Population (FNUAP) n'a été créé que bien plus tard. La contestation des politiques d'ajustements structurels a été initiée par la Commission Economique pour l'Afrique (CEA) et par l'UNICEF en raison des graves conséquences sociales de ces politiques.[10] La CEA a en outre proposé le concept de « collective self-reliance », l'a fait adopter, mais il n'a pas été mis en œuvre. La CEE a apporté sa pierre aux réflexions académiques et gouvernementales sur la distribution des revenus et les facteurs de la croissance. Par contre, l'analyse par Raúl Prebisch de la détérioration des termes de l'échange et les politiques « d'import substitution » que la CEPAL a proposées ont eu un impact considérable sur les stratégies de développement. Elles ont été appliquées en Amérique latine et dans nombre de pays d'autres régions, avec peu de succès en Amérique latine, mais avec des résultats remarquables à Taiwan et en République de Corée, puis dans les pays d'Asie de l'Est.

La globalisation. Le troisième défi auquel ont dû faire face les Commissions régionales est celui de la globalisation. La globalisation et le « one size fits all » sous-jacent au consensus de Washington remettent implicitement en cause l'existence des Commissions régionales. Il n'y avait pas de place pour une réflexion régionale dans un monde allant vers l'unification et adoptant une manière unique de concevoir le développement. Les Commissions régionales avaient encouragé ou même suscité la création d'ensembles sous-régionaux. Ceux-ci n'avaient pas eu les effets positifs escomptés sur le développement. En effet, il est apparu, *ex-post,* que le dynamisme du commerce intra régional est dû aux échanges intra branches et non aux échanges de complémentarité qui étaient à la base des projets d'ensembles sous régionaux. Les succès de la Communauté européenne apparaissaient dus à ce que ses membres étaient déjà très industrialisés. Les Commissions ont voulu mesurer la réalité de la globalisation et ont constaté que, pour l'Europe, l'Asie et l'Amérique Latine, la tendance était en fait à l'intensification des mouvements intra régionaux de marchandises et de capitaux à long terme. Pour ces trois régions, la tendance est à la régionalisation, pas à la globalisation. L'Afrique et l'Asie de l'Ouest, qui sont moins développées, sont plus globalisées dans leurs échanges de marchandises et de capitaux. Si la globalisation est une réalité dans le domaine de modes, des pratiques, de la gestion, elle ne l'est pas en termes d'échanges et d'investissements directs. Ce constat est important pour la gestion du monde dit « globalisé » en ce qu'il souligne le rôle que devraient avoir les régions dans la gouvernance mondiale.

Trois problèmes identiques qui ont suscité des idées différentes en raison des circonstances. La diversité des Commissions régionales est à noter. Bien qu'elles aient été créées sur une période de vingt-six ans, chacune a reçu un mandat presque identique. Il est donc d'autant plus intéressant qu'en discutant des problèmes de leur région, elles aient développé des priorités différentes et qu'elles soient reconnues pour leurs contributions dans des domaines différents. La CEE est connue pour ses normes et conventions, l'ESCAP pour les institutions qu'elle a créées et pour ses activités d'assistance technique, la CEPAL pour son analyse de la détérioration des termes de l'échange et ses politiques de développement, la CEA pour ses attaques contre l'ajustement structurel, et l'ESCWA pour avoir été le bras régional des Nations Unies. Les Commissions régionales ont illustré le concept de subsidiarité et rejeté à leur manière l'idée que « one size fits all ».

---

[9] *See* UN, *Asia and the Far East Seminar on Population. Bandung, 21 November-3 December 1955*. New York: UN, 1957 (ST/TAA/SER.C/26).
[10] *See* note 2.

Sally-Anne Way: Challenges for tomorrow

From my reading of the UNIHP books on the history of UN development thinking and practice, it seems that one of the general conclusions of the books is that, while the UN institutions have been producing progressive ideas, these ideas are not always implemented in practice, particularly concepts that might challenge the relations of power that produce, and reproduce, poverty.

The books document a history that shows how, when the UN shifted from a focus on economic development towards a focus on poverty reduction, it lost intellectual leadership to the Bretton Woods institutions and the neo-liberal economic paradigm. With the UN's turn to the social, many of the UN ideas and policies became more contested and less influential; policies on how to eradicate poverty were then "politely, or less politely, ignored."[11] The reason? Powerful elites protecting their interests, an apparent aversion to policies that might challenge the status quo, and governments resisting policies that might challenge structures of power. I see this today in my own work on economic, social and cultural rights, which remain controversial and contested by many governments - because they might imply a different way of doing development.

The conclusion in the books is that development today is primarily benefiting those who are better off, rather than the very poorest. This effectively means that development is failing; or at least, it is failing the most marginalized. My question then is, why is development today not working harder to address relations of inequality and challenge structures of power that reproduce poverty? One of the books cites a quotation from Braudel, which says: "Just as a country at the centre of the world economy can hardly be expected to give up its privileges, how can one hope that dominant groups who combine capital and state power, and who are ensured of international support, will agree to play the game and hand over to someone else?"[12] But if we recognise self-interest, does this mean the necessary failure of development? If poverty persists, does this mean that the UN is left complacent in reproduction of poverty, in the reproduction of inequality? How can the benefits of development be distributed more equitably? Have we left behind the whole idea of redistribution of resources, or even challenging inequality? If so, what can we do in going forward?

Human rights is one approach, but has so far been taken up in a very limited way within the UN agencies, that does not fully address the idea of economic, social and cultural rights. There seems to be a fear of addressing the difficult questions of structural inequality; for example, for agrarian reform, we speak only about market-based land reform, which perhaps is somewhat of a tautology —how can anyone with no money buy land?

This question relates also to the book on statistics, which tries to initiate a very important discussion of the political economy of numbers – looking at why some data are chosen over others, and how the statistics shape, but are also shaped by the values and views of the dominant worldview. The book shows how development statistics at the beginning included only statistics related to economic growth and industrialisation. In many ways, statistics were euro-centric, focused on economic growth and industrialisation, reflecting a Western view of development as an evolutionary progress towards industrialisation; and never reflecting for example the importance of subsistence livelihoods.

With the shift towards more social concerns, the UN began to collect social indicators, but this was contested by governments. In the 1970s, statistics started to be collected on

---
[11] *UN Contributions to Development Thinking and Practice*, p. 136.
[12] *UN Contributions to Development Thinking and Practice*, p. 298.

poverty, health, education and other social issues, but no efforts were made to analyse the data or present recommendations. Why was this so difficult? Again, essentially because it required analysing the distribution of resources and, therefore, offered a potential challenge to the status quo. Analysis might imply recommendations of change in the current distribution of resources, and that is where we seem to be stuck. How can we go forward from this central question of challenging the structures of power that reproduce poverty? How can we make sure that the rights of the marginalized are protected and enforced? These are the questions we need to answer now.

Institutional Dimension and Methods in the Generation of Ideas

Dharam Ghai: UN methodology

I would like to focus this presentation on the methodology that the UN system has used to make its intellectual contributions, though without evaluating the efficacy of these methods. The UN intellectual approach has had three characteristics: First, the UN was open to intellectual influences and ideological currents from all parts of the world. This enabled it to keep abreast with latest thinking and to pick the most creative and relevant ideas and methodologies. This is in contrast with some other multilateral organizations such as the global financial institutions, which have been dominated by one school of thought, neo-classical economics. Precisely because of the UN breadth of vision and openness, it was able to be more creative than the Bretton Woods institutions.

The second characteristic comes from the presence of the UN at the country level. This is true of action agencies such as UNICEF, UNHCR, WFP (World Food Programme), or UNDP, but it also applies to varying degrees to other agencies. This feature of the UN system enabled agencies to have the ears and eyes close to the ground and to be sensitive to the daily realities of ordinary people's lives. This again differs from other agencies that are more headquarters-based with professionals living away from action at the country level. I think this has had something to do with UN responses to emerging problems.

Thirdly, the UN has attempted to mobilize talents and energies from different parts of the world, calling upon the best thinkers in the world to participate in its work. This is the single most important reason why the UN has been so creative.

The methods used by the UN in its intellectual work have been as follows:

1. The reliance on expert groups convened by the system. Seminal reports published in the 50s and early 60s laying out the foundation of development economics were all produced by expert groups that were able to draw on leading thinkers from around the world.

2. The setting up of Global Commissions under the UN system directly or independent and working closely with the UN system. These Commissions generated many ideas – the Brandt Commission, the Palmer Commission on Security, the Brundtland Commission on Environment and Development, the UNESCO Commission on Continuing Education, the Commission on Global Governance, the recent ILO commission on the social dimensions of globalization, etc. Many ideas were generated by these commissions and were later followed up through research and conferences.

3. The sending of multidisciplinary country missions. The best examples were ILO employment missions that pioneered employment and basic needs-oriented strategies

and other ideas, including the idea of the informal sector that was born through the mission in Kenya.
4. Global research teams. All agencies in their research programs have relied on such research teams. WIDER (World Institute for Development Economics Research) and UNRISD (UN Research Institute for Social Development) worked on the basis of setting up global teams of scholars to study thematic issues.
5. Flagship reports have been vehicles for pioneering new ideas: UNDP Human Development Report, ILO World Employment Report, UNCTAD Trade and Development Report and the reports on least developed countries... These have been used by the system to promote its research.
6. Global conferences were pioneered in the 1970s with the conference on the environment, on women, employment and other issues. The 1990s saw an upsurge of these conferences. More important than generating ideas was the role of these conferences in disseminating ideas and promoting the incorporation of these ideas in government policies.

The use of these methods does not mean that the UN did not make any contributions through its own means. In the 1950s especially, the UN had some outstanding officials, first-rate researchers and scholars working for it. Unfortunately, the galaxy of stars that was there in the 1950s has not been equalled in the subsequent period. Nevertheless, throughout the period, the UN has had a minimum critical intellectual capability through its dedicated, qualified and creative officials. Without that minimum intellectual capability, it would not have been able to play this leadership role, to identify emerging issues, or to mobilize the world's leading thinkers in an attack on social and economic development problems. Unfortunately, I feel there has been a decline in the UN system in this respect in the last few years. Unless this is redressed I fear that in the future the UN intellectual contributions will not be up to the level of the first five or six decades of existence.

Richard Toye: Creativity and managerial control

Because it is intended as a future-oriented history project and as a critical history, I would like to summarize the lessons of our book, *UN and the Global Political Economy: Trade, Finance and Development,* on the question whether the UN can offer a fertile ground for intellectual creativity in the future, and if so, how this might be achieved. It would be wrong to give too optimistic a view of the UN's contributions even though it has significant contributions to make.

At the beginning of the 1960s, Hans Singer, one of the key UN economists studied in our volume, gave a very cautious view of what it was possible for the UN Secretariat to do as an intellectual actor. He was sure that the UN had played an educational role, not only circulating ideas but also facilitating the acceptance of policies. Singer emphasized, however, that the UN Secretariat could not produce much in the way of new ideas and could not be a major producer of new ideas. Creation was not a congenial job for a Secretariat and could be dangerous. Traditionally, he said, the Secretariat has tried not to run too far ahead of possibilities and not bring matters out until states have more or less agreed. It wants to avoid frictions, rifts and disputes. This pacifying role was quite a legitimate one for the Secretariat. Its main job was to record and register change in climates of opinion and to apply new and agreed solutions to the international problems.

The implication of this view is that when members of the Secretariat did produce ideas that were genuinely new, they had to handle them very carefully, waiting for changes in climate of opinion to prepare the ground for the policy implication to become politically acceptable. In this environment, therefore, the UN Secretariat acted, when it was operating normally, more as a transmission belt than as a catalyst of new ideas. That was Singer's view.

In researching our book, we came to the conclusion that Singer's view had much truth in it, although it was not the entire story. We do argue that during its initial period in the 1940s and 1950s, a period that in terms of the UN's organization was rather chaotic, the UN did in fact demonstrate a good deal of intellectual creativity, or some parts of it did. It later declined, at least to an extent, as a vibrant centre of thinking on issues of trade, finance and development. This happened as the UN became better organized and its managers became more effective at imposing their goals. We argue that within international organizations the degree of creative thinking, as opposed to synthesizing and recycling existing ideas, is inversely related to the ability of the organization's top management to exercise strong editorial control over the research process. The managers may choose to edit out or try to prevent the articulating of ideas which either do not fit with the organization's own preconceptions or could get the organization into trouble with governments.

On the more optimistic side, the implication of this inverse relationship between management editorial control and creativity is that the UN with its comparatively light management hand and multitude of voices is more likely than some other international organizations to generate interesting new ideas. The 1990s showed some evidence of this with the UNCTAD *Trade and Development Report* and the UNDP *Human Development Report*. All the same, it is not realistic to expect that officials of the UN Secretariat, as distinct from other parts of the UN system, would be major generators of fresh ideas. If it did so in its earliest years, before successive layers of managerial control over research could solidify, this was a happy accident but not one that could be deliberately replicated today. The Secretariat can still be a purveyor and disseminator of ideas its members may be just about ready to adopt.

If the UN is to make a creative contribution in the future, however, it will be most likely to do so by nourishing its university like institutions. The setting up of the United Nations University (UNU) in 1975 laid the basis for this, but in the field of trade, finance, and development the real beginning came a decade later with the inauguration of the World Institute of Development and Economic Research (WIDER). Its history so far has not been uncontroversial, but its difficulties have never included struggles over publication of the results of research. For these reasons, it is still possible that international organizations can be creative intellectual actors and that more intellectual history of the United Nations will be written in the future.

Yves Berthelot: Le Secrétariat peut et doit prendre des initiatives

Je voudrais soutenir qu'un Secrétariat peut développer des idées, les faire mûrir par le débat intergouvernemental et finalement les faire adopter. Il y a à cela des conditions.

La première condition est que le secrétariat prenne l'initiative de mettre sur la table des études qu'il a conduites avec rigueur sans avoir le souci de dire ce que les gouvernements veulent entendre. Gunnar Myrdal a insisté sur ce point. Les grandes études auxquelles Richard Jolly et Frédéric Lapeyre se sont référés étaient de cette nature. Certains rapports annuels comme *The Trade and Development Report*, *The Economic Survey of Latin America*, *The Economic Survey of Europe* et *The Human Development Report* sont également de cette nature. Les comparaisons entre pays qui se trouvent dans les *Surveys* et le *Human*

Development Report amènent les pays à s'interroger sur leurs performances et à situer leurs politiques dans une perspective régionale. Peut-être y a-t-il moins de chefs d'agence ou de département qui soient aujourd'hui prêts à affronter les idées reçues et y a-t-il trop de texte qui n'offrent que de « l'économie diplomatique ». Pourtant, l'expérience des Commissions régionales est bien que c'est en gardant un scepticisme constructif envers l'orthodoxie du moment que peuvent émerger de nouvelles idées.

Cela dit, des analyses correctes et des propositions pertinentes n'entraînent pas toujours l'adhésion des gouvernements.[13] Il est important, comme vient de le souligner Richard Toye, de ne pas être trop loin de ce que les gouvernements peuvent accepter. Cependant, les gouvernements feront peut-être un pas d'autant plus grand qu'un état d'esprit commun (*a common mindset*) se sera développé entre eux et le secrétariat. Cela est plus facile à réaliser au niveau régional qu'au niveau mondial. Pour que cet état d'esprit puisse se créer, les Secrétariats doivent à la fois avoir la liberté de mettre sur la table des problèmes qui leur paraissaient essentiels tout en restant assez proches des préoccupations des gouvernements pour que leurs idées soient reçues et suscitent un débat intergouvernemental.

Jaime de Melo: The need for independent think tank. The winner takes all

The work of the Project made me realize even more that what is missing in Geneva is the equivalent of think-tanks or watchdogs which can be found in Washington DC. In Washington, there are the World Bank and IMF, but there are also the Centre for Global Development and the Institute for International Economics, which carry out the criticism of the work coming out of these institutions. In Geneva, the RUIG is starting to do something along these lines, but there is a great need to look into the possibility to get this critical work done. This is increasingly needed. *UN and the Global Political Economy* says that the UN has been going downhill for the past fifty years, and finds some hopes in institutions such as WIDER. But there is the need for independent institutions to look into what is happening. The same thing could be said of the World Bank and the IMF where the in-house research is often edited by the higher ups. But in Geneva, there is no critical analysis of what is being produced by reports such as the ILO *Employment Report*, or UNCTAD *Trade and Development Report*. Institutions in Geneva create a lot of data that are not available to the public. If watchdog institutions were trying to bring this out it would be beneficial.

The volume *UN and the Global Political Economy* is an intellectual history of change or the evolution of ideas in trade and development. The volume says that ideas do not spread from a vacuum and gives examples of the contributions of Kalecki and Prebisch, which were different from those put forth by the UN at the time –that is an organization largely designed by the US. How could such ideas develop and get prominence in that organization?

Finally, the book gave me the impression that the creation of ideas, which is a global public good, has the characteristic of winner-takes-all: there was one set of institutions early on, then after 1964 there was UNCTAD, and then the World Bank and the IMF took over and from then virtually no substitute. Is that really the case?

---

[13] Ainsi, la CEE montrait en 1955 que l'Europe payait son pétrole trop cher, car les Etats-Unis imposaient que le prix du brut FOB au départ du Moyen-Orient soit aligné sur celui du brut au départ du Golfe du Mexique. Mais surtout, elle jugeait que la répartition du profit entre pays d'origine et grandes compagnies était inéquitable et non-durable. Il a fallu dix-huit ans pour que les pays s'en rendent compte. ECE, *The Price of Oil in Western Europe*, prepared by the Secretariat, ECE. Geneva: United Nations, 1955 (E/ECE/205).

Since 1996 when the WTO was created, the amount of work done in the area of trade by the World Bank alone is in the order of ten or one hundred times more than what the WTO has done. In that sense it is a "winner-takes-all" situation. There was an opportunity for the WTO to take the intellectual leadership for the world trading system, but it did not happen. The World Bank is twenty or thirty million dollars worth of money from bilateral donor agencies to do research and other projects, why is it that there has not been more granted to the WTO or other institutions? You describe it in your book: the rich countries put their money into the World Bank and IMF; the G77 does not do the same, as they do not have any money.

Richard Toye

About "winner-takes-all", the inevitability of the decline of UN ideas, or the likelihood that the World Bank and the Washington consensus will always retain all the territory: first, the winner-takes-all idea is a bit of an exaggeration. We have to consider the wider picture of UN contributions in other areas where the picture may be more positive than in trade, finance and development. Also winner-takes-all may not be quite right, because if the ideas of the Washington consensus had achieved total intellectual hegemony, none of us would be sitting here questioning it. There has always been a battle. Even when the UN was producing various ideas in the 1940s and 1950s, it was not the case of the UN being the winner and then later being defeated by another set of forces. The two sets of forces were long-standing. There may be, therefore, a sort of on-going challenge rather than necessarily it being a winner-takes-all situation.

Why was it that some of these more original ideas could come about, given that the UN was designed largely by the Americans, with some inputs from others, but essentially it reflected the Americans view? In terms of what they believed it was important that the UN had economic functions so that economic security could complement military security. But they had a rather orthodox idea of how this could come about through the creation of free trade and payments regimes. Yet, having created this organization, unorthodox ideas did spring up within it and were widely articulated. Therefore, the advocacy of modest reform whilst hoping for the wider forces of history to change may be all one can say.

Richard Jolly

The volume as a whole shows that the ideas were in many cases marginalized in the 1980s and 1990s by the shift of the industrial countries to give most attention to the Bretton Woods institutions. But more recently the Bretton Woods have been shifting backwards when they have seen that many of the ideas of the Washington consensus have not worked out. Some of the shift back has been to take on ideas that parts of the UN were promoting very strongly in the 1980s and 1990s.

The suggestion that some of the stronger institutions or groups in Geneva should look more consistently at issues of the UN is a lovely idea. Why not within Europe have some stronger networks that could take this on? While there is darkness in Washington, Europe has a particular role to keep alive many of these important ideas. Within Europe there should be more of a coherent network of people looking at research, criticising in a creative way, making suggestions, interacting. That could be the Third UN interacting with the First and Second.

Some Critics of the UN Intellectual History Project

Patrick Verley: Du bon et du moins bon

Le projet UNIHP est un projet d'histoire intellectuelle et non pas un projet d'histoire des idées, c'est-à-dire qu'il ne se contente pas de suivre le développement logique des concepts. L'histoire intellectuelle étudie le rapport entre les représentations et la réalité dans leur double dimension : la réalité permet la représentation qui opère ensuite un *feedback* sur la réalité. Ainsi, les idées fondent les pratiques au travers des institutions qui les portent. Cela est expliqué dans l'introduction méthodologique de *Ahead of the Curve?* et correspond à la pratique des historiens qui travaillent dans le champ des idées. Ce qui nous intéresse, ce sont les conditions d'émergence des idées et leur diffusion. Si je peux faire un rapport avec l'histoire des techniques, la même relation existe entre invention et innovation. L'important au plan économique est l'innovation, c'est à dire l'application d'une invention à une échelle suffisamment large pour qu'elle ait un effet sur l'économie. De même pour les idées, l'important est de comprendre les processus d'acceptation d'une idée à une échelle suffisamment large ou à un niveau suffisamment stratégique pour qu'elle puisse exercer une influence sur la réalité au travers des représentations et des pratiques des dirigeants.

Quant à savoir s'il y a des idées nouvelles, une phrase tirée d'un article de Ngaire Woods[14] dit qu'en fait, il y a très peu d'idées nouvelles. Peut-être le Projet aurait-il pu insister sur l'énorme continuité avec les travaux historiques de la Société des Nations (SdN), avec des hommes qui sont restés les mêmes et qui ont continué à travailler au cours des années 1940. Les sigles changent mais les hommes restent, et les idées restent aussi largement les mêmes. La rupture dans l'histoire intellectuelle est sans doute davantage dans les années 1930 que lors de cette date fatidique de 1945.

Donc, qu'y a-t-il de nouveau ? C'est souvent de l'ancien mis dans une nouvelle perspective ou de l'innovation latérale, c'est à dire qu'une idée est appliquée à un contexte qui n'est pas celui dans lequel elle est originellement née. Les rapports de 1949 et de 1951 font apparaîtrent des idées nouvelles qui sont de l'ancien mais qui sont quand même nouvelles.[15]

Les facteurs d'instabilité du cycle sont bien connus. Il y a eu les travaux de Mitchell, la synthèse de Haberler en 1938.[16] On a tout dit et tout étudié : les variations de stock, l'influence des déséquilibres externes, etc. Sur la variation des prix des matières premières il y a eu des centaines de pages écrites dans les années 1930. Il en va de même avec le consensus sur le keynésianisme et les politiques conjoncturelles : à partir de 1938, les économistes qui sont dans le vent vont dans cette direction.

Cependant c'est là où le rôle de l'institution est considérable parce qu'elle met les hommes dans une position qui favorise un changement de perspective. L'ancien devient alors nouveau parce que les idées sont replacées dans une autre perspective géographique, par exemple: au lieu de parler d'instabilité de la conjoncture dans les pays industriels, on l'étudie désormais dans l'ensemble du monde et dans les pays qui sont les exportateurs primaires. Même si les études de la SdN dans les années 1920 avaient révélé l'instabilité qu'engendrait dans les pays exportateurs primaires la baisse des prix

---

[14] Ngaire Woods, "Economic Ideas and International Relations: Beyond Rational Neglect", *International Studies Quarterly*, 39, 2, 1995, 161-180.
[15] UN, "National and International Measures for Full-Employment," report by a group of experts appointed by the Secretary-General of the United Nations. Lake Success: United Nations, December 1949, and UN, *Measures for Economic Development*.
[16] Arthur Burns & Wesley Mitchell, *Measuring Business Cycles*, 1946.

des matières premières, facteur de déséquilibre de leur balance des paiements courants, le sujet restait local car l'attention se focalisait sur les pays du centre de l'économie internationale.

De même, lorsque la perspective temporelle change en passant d'un horizon de court terme au long terme, il est possible d'innover : le problème de l'instabilité était posé dans le cadre de l'étude du business cycle, désormais il est posé dans le cadre du problème du développement – ce que les travaux de Hans Singer et Raúl Prebisch ont fait.

On pourrait également insister sur le caractère révolutionnaire du fait de dire que le plein emploi est un devoir des États démocratiques. C'est une phrase extraordinairement nouvelle parce que le volontarisme de l'Etat qui avait permis de réaliser le plein emploi dans les années 1930 avait été le fait des Etats autoritaires, qui avaient isolé leurs économies pour se libérer des contraintes externes. On évoque toujours l'Allemagne, mais il y a aussi l'Amérique Latine. Les économistes latino-américains se souvenaient bien, vingt ans plus tard, de la réussite économique du Brésil de Getúlio Vargas. Le libéralisme, tel qu'on l'affirme dans les années 1940 - comme chez Friedrich Hayek - est le refus du communisme et du fascisme. Dire donc que le plein emploi est un devoir (aussi) pour les États démocratiques est un changement de perspectives et une idée nouvelle, même si le consensus keynésien à partir de 1938-1939 y incitait.

J'apprécie dans le Projet ce fait d'essayer de voir le jeu des idées, de permettre de comprendre que le nouveau est en général de l'ancien remis dans une autre dimension. Mais je regrette qu'il n'y ait pas d'histoire des échecs, des idées qui ne réussissent pas. Et je n'approuve pas dans *Ahead of the Curve ?* ce choix de sélectionner les idées qui sont encore importantes pour le XXIe siècle. C'est faire de l'histoire téléologique que de penser que les bonnes idées sont celles qui réussissent et ignorer qu'il y a, dans l'histoire, des bifurcations, des moments où reste ouvert tout le champ des possibles et où donc les choses auraient pu se passer autrement. Et ce n'est pas obligé que ce soient les meilleures idées qui l'emportent car il y a les jeux d'institutions, les jeux de personnes, et tout simplement le hasard. Il est intéressant de faire l'expérience des idées qui n'ont pas réussi, qui ont raté. Comprendre pourquoi elles ne s'imposent pas nous apporterait beaucoup.

Comment from the floor: Too many authors from the normal intellectual circles

What have been the attempts by the Project's organizers to engage researchers and thinkers from outside the "normal" intellectual circles and to outreach to the developing countries in order to see what their views of the UN are? As analysis is shaped by the context in which one lives, a greater outreach towards the South may have brought a different view on some of the issues. For example, *UN and the Global Political Economy* analyses UNCTAD saying that the New International Economic Order (NIEO) was not realistic to be implemented within today's international economic relations, and therefore it failed. But one could say that it failed because it did not realize its objectives, not because it was too idealistic.

Richard Jolly

The Project has certainly tried to be sensitive to this. About one third of the authors of the volumes are from developing countries. For example, in *Women, Development and the UN: A Sixty Year Quest for Equality and Justice,* a volume just completed but not published yet, Devaki Jain explicitly has taken a view from the South for her analysis of what was going on or not going on in the UN at different times in relation to gender and women.

Richard Toye

It is a spot on question and a fair critique of what we were trying to do. The real issue here, as a historian, is that in terms of the sources for the studying the UN history or the history of the international economy or any international organizations, there is a structural bias in the sources against the developing countries, because developing countries being poor and under-developed do not have good archival preservation systems. They tend not to have freedom of information laws. So even if the material is being preserved, it may well not being preserved systematically. It may be very difficult to get to. We had these problems very much in mind when trying to write the book. The question was how to get around it. We don't claim to have got around it completely successfully. But the oral history is a crucial contribution here to try and get to individuals whose voices might otherwise not be recorded. We struggled against these forces, and I think it is worth continuing to try.

Comment from the floor: Too much on Secretariat not enough on delegates

I deplore too much a focus on the UN Secretariat and not on the delegates. The UN intellectual history is not made only by Secretariat's contributions, but an important infusion of ideas is taking place through the intergovernmental machinery, and studying this process would be interesting and useful as well.

Richard Jolly

The Project volumes refer to two United Nations: the UN of governments and the UN of the secretariat staff. A third UN could be considered: the UN of NGO voices, because both NGOs and certainly many distinguished academics from the outside have all contributed to many of the ideas addressed. Some of this comes up in *UN Voices* to be published soon: in the interviews, mostly with staff members or others from the UN, not government people, the way government views have affected what has happened or what has not happened emerges as an important point.

Isabelle Schulte-Tenckhoff : Perspective évolutionniste ou approche holistique

Au-delà de l'intérêt du Projet d'histoire intellectuelle des Nations Unies, j'ai été frappée par la vision évolutionniste qui sous-tend l'ensemble des volumes. En tant qu'anthropologue, j'aimerais soulever un problème non pas d'idées en soi ou d'idée du développement, mais de perspective, voire de paradigme. J'aimerais aussi faire un plaidoyer pour un changement de paradigme selon la perspective de l'anthropologie. Car la vision évolutionniste qui sous-tend les volumes affecte la perspective critique des ouvrages, telle qu'elle transparaît du rejet d'une approche purement quantitative du développement axée sur la croissance, de la notion de développement humain ou encore de la prise en compte d'une certaine diversité, régionale ou autre.

Si l'ONU a problématisé le développement dans une logique spatio-temporelle particulière, l'idée d'une progression dans le temps, d'une séquence unilinéaire de changements cumulatifs et inéluctables produit dans les volumes en question une méthodologie axée sur des raisonnements en termes de cause à effet, des raisonnements basés sur des analogies, voire même sur l'idée de résidus, en vue de reconstruire les transformations ayant abouti à la modernité, au développement, à l'individu et aux sociétés développées. Des notions comme « pays en transition », « pays sous-développés », etc. renvoient à une vision évolutionniste qu'il faut interroger.

Pour ce faire, je voudrais rappeler quatre principes de l'anthropologie socioculturelle pour voir s'ils peuvent nous aider à arriver à un changement de paradigme. Premièrement l'anthropologie socioculturelle défend une approche holistique qui tient compte des aspects historiques, politiques et économiques pour arriver à une description complète des phénomènes sociaux et culturels. Ce principe se retrouve en partie dans les volumes, notamment l'idée que le développement ne se ramène pas à ses aspects purement économiques.

Un deuxième principe consiste à prendre comme point de mire de l'analyse les relations sociales, ce contexte humain auquel on fait référence quand on parle de développement humain, mais sans pour autant considérer ce contexte comme une évidence, comme allant de soi. On cherche plutôt à remettre en cause ou à déconstruire les concepts et les revendications liés au social afin d'exposer les intérêts, les rapports de pouvoir, les interdépendances structurelles, les interprétations mises en jeu, en l'occurrence ceux qui se rapportent aux théories et à la pratique du développement.

Le troisième principe de l'anthropologie socioculturelle exige que l'on se méfie des interprétations et des définitions imposées de manière exogène ou fondées sur un ensemble exogène de catégories de pensées. Appliqué à la question du développement, cela signifie aborder le développement en tenant compte des interprétations et des discours de part et d'autre, des « développeurs » comme de ceux qui sont visés par le développement, y compris les discours élaborés par les organisations multilatérales.

Le quatrième principe est celui de la maîtrise de la comparaison qui consiste à briser la logique d'antériorité de ce qui est non-développé ou sous-développé et qui, prétendument, exige un rattrapage.

La question est donc de savoir quels enseignements tirer de ces quatre principes pour retracer l'histoire intellectuelle des Nations Unies en matière de développement, même si l'intégration d'une telle perspective signifie secouer quelques idées, voire même exige un renversement de perspective. Un « paradigme shift » ne s'impose-t-il pas pour donner tout son relief à ce développement humain qui occupe une place centrale dans les ouvrages ?

Gopalan Balachandran: The contribution of the South in UN development thinking

As the UNIHP project also does in greater or lesser measure, I too understand a history of ideas not merely in terms of the internal histories of their postulates, manipulations, and derivations, but as an inquiry that looks into the contexts of the formation of ideas and their development, that is sensitive to the political and social uses of ideas by academics, political and social movements, and institutions, and that is aware of the constraints within which these ideas are defined, reproduced, appropriated, refashioned, etc.

But there is another assumption in this project that for me is a little worrisome: the assumption of the United Nations as a progenitor of development ideas, as an autonomous site at which some of these ideas were developed and reproduced. No explicit claims are made, but implications of this nature are suggested through a combination of silences and contextualisation.

It is evident that one of the objectives of the volumes of this project dealing with development is to reclaim the UN's intellectual role, if not its ascendancy in this sphere from the World Bank and IMF. This is an aspiration that many will warmly endorse.

But I believe the way the project defines the UN is self-defeating in relation to this objective because it does not leverage the UN's true strengths. The UN can never rival the World Bank or the IMF as an economic policy 'research' institution because its political constitution and institutional dynamics are so different, and it lacks the internal and external incentive structures and disciplinary mechanisms of these institutions.

What is true for the UN is also true for UN-funded research institutions (such as the WIDER) because unless their ideas and proposals mimic those produced by the Bretton Woods twins or the WTO, the push and jostle of politics will ensure that they are modified or mediated out of existence before they arrive in New York. The UN's greatest intellectual asset is not its ability to provide finished policy templates that acquire canonical power from being reinforced by political and financial power, but, compared especially to the Bretton Woods institutions and the WTO, its sheer plurality and inclusiveness, and therefore its access to a wider and more diverse body of development experiences.

These experiences and the UN's access to them are not unmediated since states, UN organizations themselves, and in recent decades a variety of non-state actors, help transmit and translate these experiences to the UN system. But the mediations too are diverse and multiple. Thus, for example, the UN was able, especially in the 1960s and the 1970s when it was transformed by the agency of the developing countries, to gain access to more voices and develop a more rounded and nuanced perspective on development issues than institutions that filter real experiences through regnant economic (and institutional) orthodoxies or serve entrenched political-economic interests. Therefore, a history of the UN conceived in a way as to deny its plurality and diversity and its enormous responsiveness and capacity for learning impoverishes both the institution and our appreciation of its successes and understanding of its failures.

It is clear to anyone familiar with the history of the UN that it learnt quickly and on the whole well, and transformed itself greatly during the 1960s and 1970s. As already mentioned neither could have happened without the active and coordinated self-agency of the countries and institutions of the South. But these volumes appear to me to convey the assumption that the latter were merely passive objects of UN assistance and mute recipients of its ideas and initiatives, rather than sources of creative ideas and experiences and active contributors themselves to the UN's body of knowledge. Is this a bias that comes from the nature of available sources and historical materials? Or is it more a bias of vision, of perspective?

Probably both. But the bias of vision is more fundamental. It may even be getting encoded in institutional memory, and is therefore in urgent need of correction. In the mid-1990s, the former UN Secretary-General, Boutros Boutros-Ghali, declared in a policy paper on the agenda for democratization that the UN had taken the lead in supporting colonies that wished to overthrow colonialism. The UN, he said, was similarly there to support countries that were moving towards democracy.

Was the UN there for the developing countries at the inception of postcolonial modernization? An honest answer would be no, not really. The UN may have been thinking about development issues since its earliest years, but it is important to remember that for more than a decade after it was established, it was far from being the universal institution that we see today. The precise political and institutional, as opposed to accidental, roots of the research and activities relating to development that were carried on at the UN, not to mention their ability to make a difference, remain moot, because in the 1950s there were not many developing countries in the UN. This was not merely because decolonization had yet to get seriously under way, or because non-industrial countries had yet to recognize they were 'un' or 'under-developed', and that it was not entirely beyond them to redress their condition.

The real reason was more fundamental, and political, and deserves to be recalled. In the mid-1950s for one reason or another, even countries that had thrown off colonialism for some years, such as Indonesia and Ceylon, found the doors of the UN shut to them. One of the volumes refers to the Bandung Conference as a founding moment of non-alignment. Apart from this being a common error—many old bridges had to be broken, and new ones built and crossed between the Afro-Asian movement and the non-aligned movement—we need to remember that a major concern at Bandung was the exclusion of many Asian countries from the UN. The issue figured explicitly in the resolution of the Bandung Conference, while in the run up to the event there was much speculation in the Western media that Afro-Asian countries would decide to abandon the UN and set up a rival Afro-Asian entity. So at least until the mid-1950s the UN was regarded as a Western club from which the Afro-Asian countries were largely excluded, and the Bandung Conference was partly a protest against that.

It was therefore a fortunate accident that in its earliest years the UN became a site at which a number of important and influential ideas were produced. Many of these ideas came into the UN along with their authors, and some such as Kalecki's on the means of financing economic development went out with them. They did not originate or germinate within the UN—this is true of both Singer and Prebisch's work. But, the fact that Prebisch and Singer are identified with the ECLA nevertheless testifies to the important role that the UN played in developing and ventilating these arguments. It is doubtful whether, absent the agency of the UN, these arguments would have generated the same amount of resonance around the world.

What the Prebisch-Singer or Singer-Prebisch story tells us is that the UN was more a midwife than a parent. (In saying this, I do not mean to underestimate the role of the midwife.) Thus, it is no diminution of the UN's role to say that its contribution to development thinking really represented a mediated institutional articulation of ideas developing within and outside it, reflecting on the experiences of non-industrial countries and the challenges facing them. But it is well to remember that communities around the world respect midwives only when they are seen to regard motherhood and childbirth with humility even if not awe, not when they are seen to view them as opportunities to exercise or display their power over mother and child.

II – A role for the UN in the economic and social field

Antoine Maurice summed up the first session and moderated the discussion panel during the second session of the Conference. Issues discussed included poverty, the capacity of the UN to regulate the world economy, and reforms of the UN. Antoine Maurice launched the debate on issues of poverty, inequalities, redistribution, and social justice –terms used successively by the UN in the field of development.

Poverty Reduction or Development Strategies

Richard Jolly: Evolution of the UN thinking on poverty

Over the years the UN has contributed to key issues in poverty by defining the objectives, identifying key elements of strategy, and indicating some modalities in order to make progress in reducing and eventually ending poverty.

In defining objectives, the early years of the UN focused on unemployment. This focus influenced by the Keynesian perspective was built into the Charter and into the IMF and the World Bank: their policies ought to be guided by helping countries maintain full-employment. In the UN, in 1951, this approach to employment as a means of improving living standards and reducing poverty in developing countries was seen to be misconceived. The question was not how to move to full-employment within an existing economic structure, but how to change that economic structure and move to accelerated economic growth. In the 1960s, with the Development Decade, the focus shifted not to growth, but to growth plus change. The documents of the time show a strong emphasis on change, including land reform and some of the dimensions of more equal distribution and equality. International action was seen as a vital complement to national action from the beginning. In the 1970s, gender came in and the UN played an important role with all the other seven major global conferences of the decade. The volume on gender shows the close links between gender issues and the many women working in the informal sector. I do not think the UN has ever fallen for the thesis that "growth is ultimately what it is all about", and yet it is quite difficult to find times in the World Bank and the IMF when the main message was not "growth is what it is mostly about."

On modalities, in the early 1960s, UNICEF brought in a number of distinguished economists - Jan Tinbergen, Hans Singer, Alfred Sauvy and V.K.R.V.Rao and others - who outlined ways to bring issues of children into development planning. Unless this was done, they argued, the ending of child poverty and attention to other issues of children would never be adequately brought into development planning. That was an interesting and early recognition of the need for people focused, comprehensive planning.

About goals, now we have the Millennium Development Goals. But let us remember that it was the UN that in 1960-1961, and UNESCO more precisely, that held major regional conferences to set goals with quantified targets for education expansion by 1980. Different parts of the UN over the years have formulated time-bound quantitative targets. The record of achievement is much better than cynics often quote; however far from perfect. The Bretton Woods institutions have opposed goals almost all the way through, and changed only in the past five years. In the 1980s, they had goals as adjustment programmes, but they were goals focused on economic means rather than goals focused on ends. And outcomes.

Also, the UN has played a major role in statistics, although coming to social indicators rather late. Finally, many parts of the UN have stressed participation and empowerment as critical elements of reducing poverty from very early days. Looking at the UN's work in human rights, its work related to indigenous people, we see how this issue of marginalized people and what the world might try and do about has long been seen as part of the whole issue, including how to empower people in those situations. These are some of the dimensions that have been important to UN's concerns with poverty over the years.

Michael Windfuhr: The necessity for a rights-based approach in fighting hunger

Food First Information & Action Network (FIAN) is a non-governmental organization with consultative status at the UN. It is a human rights organization focusing on the right to food, which is an important component of poverty reduction. As a Millennium Development Goal, hunger is linked to the first goal "Eradicate extreme poverty and hunger." When addressing poverty, one has to consider hunger.

The recent documents of the Millennium Task Force on Hunger[17] present astonishing data which are important for the overall poverty debate: of all those who are hungry, 50% are farmers, small-holder farmers, two-thirds of whom are living on marginal lands. These farmers are marginalized in a double sense. First, they are marginalized from the political process living in very remote areas, and they have no access to markets, to credits or to secure assets. Another 22% of the hungry are landless labourers trying to sell their labour in rural areas. This is already more than 70% of the hungry who have no access to assets, and any way of livelihood. These people are also marginalized in the poverty discourse: we talk more and more about how growth can be made pro-poor, but many economic policies are hurting these groups hard when they are already marginalized. When markets open up while European surpluses are dumped on their markets, the poor are doubly hurt.

Keeping this in mind and looking at the report of Jeffrey Sachs, the result of the Millennium Project and its Task Forces[18], we can see that a rights-based approach is basically missing. In the agricultural sector, for example, the report is not talking about a rights-based approach at all. But, because of the particular situation and the marginalization of these groups, we have to take such an approach more seriously, especially in the coming month towards the Special Session of the General Assembly.

Amartya Sen told us that development policies try to increase people's capabilities, while human rights or rights-based approaches are concerned with people's entitlement. In particular for poor people today, the entitlement approach, that is, one's ability to hold governments accountable when they are not properly guaranteeing security in land tenure for example, is extremely important. You can train someone to be a perfect farmer, but if land titles are not secure, either because of a civil war or because there is not security of land tenanting, persons, families, or poverty-ridden women who have particular problems with access will not make it. So we need to take this rights-based approach very seriously. Only a combination of increasing capabilities through development policies and secure entitlements through a rights-based approach can adequately challenge poverty. That is the only way if we want to move on with the Millennium Development Goals.

Pierre de Senarclens: Divisions politiques et stratégies confuses ne laissent à l'ONU que l'humanitaire

Il a déjà été rappelé que les racines de la pauvreté étaient essentiellement politiques aussi bien dans nos sociétés qu'à l'échelle internationale. À l'origine de la pauvreté on

---
[17] See http://www.unmillenniumproject.org/documents/Hunger-highres-complete.pdf (14 April 2005).
[18] Millennium Project, Investing in Development: A Practical Plan To Achieve the Millennium Development Goals, report to the UN Secretary-General. See http://www.unmillenniumproject.org/reports/fullreport.htm (14 April 2005)

trouve toujours des relations de pouvoir entre classes sociales à l'intérieur d'une société. Les pauvres sont exclus par leur éducation, par leur niveau de santé, et par toutes sortes d'aléas déterminés par les structures sociales. Aujourd'hui, de plus en plus, la pauvreté a des origines transnationales ou internationales, où s'exercent évidemment là aussi des relations de pouvoir. Le Burkina Faso, par exemple, un pays exportateur de coton - c'est à peu près la seule chose qu'il exporte -, est confronté au coton subventionné des Etats Unis. Il s'agit là d'un problème essentiellement politique. On ne peut pas réduire la question des relations internationales à cet exemple du commerce, mais c'est un exemple illustratif.

En ce qui concerne les Nations Unies, elles ont toujours été excellentes pour déterminer des normes. La Déclaration Universelle de 1948, par exemple, contient le droit à l'éducation, le droit au travail, etc. Les objectifs que devaient s'assigner les sociétés nationales et la communauté internationale ont été inscrits en lettre de feu. Mais à l'intérieur des Nations Unies, et du système des Nations Unies, il y a toujours eu des divergences fondamentales sur les stratégies à mettre en œuvre pour réaliser ces objectifs. Les Soviétiques avaient une position, les Occidentaux en avaient une autre. Dans le camp occidental, certains mettaient l'accent sur le marché, d'autres sur l'intervention étatique.

Ces divisions ont donné lieu à un langage de plus en plus confus quand il s'agissait de définir des stratégies de développement. La première Décennie du Développement tient en une résolution de deux pages. La première stratégie du développement dix ans plus tard est un très long texte, long parce qu'il n'y a pas d'entente sur ce que la stratégie doit être. La deuxième stratégie devient absolument illisible, sans parler de la troisième. Moins il y a d'entente, plus le texte est long, plus les considérations sont confuses.

En fin de compte, dans les années 1980, avec le poids grandissant des néo-libéraux qui prônent que l'état doit avoir un rôle minime et que la charité doit combler le vide, les Nations Unies sont devenues une organisation qui gère l'humanitaire. Gérer l'humanitaire, ce n'est pas s'occuper de la pauvreté, mais des conséquences de la pauvreté. Ce n'est pas donner une stratégie de développement mais résoudre les problèmes issus d'une absence de stratégie et d'une absence de débat sur la stratégie. Et, effectivement, l'humanitaire a pris une ampleur considérable dans le discours des Nations Unies.

Les objectifs du Millénaire eux-mêmes sont des objectifs humanitaires. Ils sont camouflés en objectifs de développement, mais il y a une absence totale de consensus sur la stratégie pour réduire la pauvreté, pour atteindre les objectifs d'éducation, de santé, d'égalité des genres, etc. Par contre, on s'accorde sur les objectifs. Dans les pays très pauvres, aujourd'hui tout le monde dit la même chose sur ce qu'il faut faire : plus d'éducation, meilleurs services de santé, soutien à la société civile, bonne gouvernance, etc. Mais en fin de compte, il n'y a plus de stratégie de développement.

Tout le monde fait très bien les choses. Au Burkina, les coopérations nationales s'entendent bien et font un excellent travail. La Banque Mondiale aussi fait du très bon travail. Mais personne ne fait plus ce que l'on appelait du développement. À la question sur ce que le Burkina va faire pour s'intégrer dans le marché mondial, les réponses sont que c'est très compliqué, qu'ils n'ont pas d'eau, pas d'électricité, qu'on ne peut pas faire de textile parce que les entrants sont trop lourds, qu'il y a la concurrence. Personne ne sait comment le Burkina ou le Mali ou n'importe quel autre pays pauvre va pouvoir s'en sortir.

La seule réponse réaliste est d'admettre que ces pays vont être assistés pendant les cent prochaines années. Mais comme on ne s'accorde pas sur cette assistance, les petits projets vont continuer pour soutenir la société civile, pour construire des programmes d'alphabétisation ou des pistes qui désenclavent des villages, et pendant ce temps 80% de la population burkinabé n'est pas alphabétisée. Ceux qui le sont oublient ce qu'ils ont appris parce qu'ils sont alphabétisés dans la langue française que les parents ne comprennent pas. Et dans les villages, qui constituent les 80% de la population, il n'y a pas d'eau, pas d'électricité, pas de sanitaire, etc. C'est la misère la plus absolue qu'on essaie de soulager par des processus qui soutiennent une économie de subsistance. Tout ceci est l'aboutissement d'un consensus qui a l'avantage de fixer des objectifs mais pas de les atteindre.

Jean-Michel Servet: Lutte contre la pauvreté versus lutte contre les inégalités

Les ouvrages du Projet UNIHP montrent un déséquilibre entre pauvreté et inégalité qui me semble tout à fait significatif des politiques au sein de l'organisation des Nations Unies. Le contenu même des politiques mélange les questions d'inégalité et les questions d'insuffisance de revenu.

La Charte des Nations Unies dans son article 1 fait référence aux différences de race, de sexe, de langue et de religion. En ce qui concerne le genre, des choses intéressantes furent faites. Mais il ne s'agit pas d'un groupe social, il s'agit d'une catégorie statistique. Pour le travail des enfants, les réalisations sont beaucoup plus ambiguës pour une raison claire : les intérêts économiques en jeu. Le développement et le travail des enfants sont conceptuellement liés.

Ainsi, même si la Charte des Nations Unies affirme primordial l'objectif d'une lutte contre les inégalités sociales, depuis plus d'un demi-siècle l'action des divers programmes et organisations s'est essentiellement focalisée sur « la lutte contre la pauvreté » ; les objectifs du Millénaire en sont le dernier avatar.

Ceci provient d'une approche essentiellement économiste du processus de développement et de la croyance selon laquelle les inégalités naissent de la pauvreté. Les inégalités sont elles-mêmes définies sur des critères de revenus (comme l'indicateur publié du coefficient de Gini, indicateur d'inégalité de revenus) et de capacités d'accès à des services comme l'éducation ou la santé, dont les privatisations et les dérégulations ont pour objectif de rendre cet accès partiellement ou totalement payant. J'ai vu en Inde des gens qui avaient fait le collège universitaire et qui étaient en servitude. Cela veut dire que l'approche internationale, et l'ouvrage sur les statistiques le montre, tend à produire pour chaque pays des catégories statistiques qui sont des données macro-économiques décomposées mais qui ne sont en rien des groupes sociaux. Mettre en valeur les inégalités serait grandement s'ingérer dans les politiques nationales parce que ce serait révéler, au-delà d'inégalités économiques, les discriminations et les marginalisations qui produisent la pauvreté.

L'insuffisance des revenus est une des conséquences des discriminations, des marginalisations et des exclusions, en un mot des inégalités sociales ; elle n'en est pas la cause première. Ce sont les inégalités et les discriminations qui entraînent la pauvreté. Ce sont les différences ethniques, les différences de caste, de religion ou même de lieu d'habitation au sein de nos villes modernes qui provoquent cela.

Quelques chiffres : est-ce simplement une question économique qu'en Inde les balayeurs de la fonction publique soient constitués pour 44% de populations issues de groupes tribaux qui ne dépassent pas 25% dans la population indienne ? En Chine, les minorités ethniques représentent 9% de la population chinoise, elles représentent 43% des Chinois en position de pauvreté absolue. L'incidence de la pauvreté est de 5,3% parmi les couples mariés aux Etats-Unis, elle est de 45% parmi les mères célibataires d'origine afro-américaine. Les Tziganes en Europe sont 8 à 10 millions de personnes dont une large fraction est en situation de discrimination. Un exemple de discrimination en France : une étude a été faite sur les discriminations à l'emploi à partir de faux CV envoyés pour l'emploi. Les discriminations ne sont pas religieuses, de sexe ou de race, mais tiennent à l'adresse qui figure sur le document envoyé. C'est une discrimination par quartiers qui se produit aujourd'hui en France.

Pour finir j'aimerais citer Victor Hugo qui écrit dans Quatre vingt treize : « Vous voulez rendre la misère supportable, ce qu'il faut c'est la supprimer. »

Charles Gore: Beyond internal factors, the international dimension

I would like to address the following question: what and how can the UN contribute in the future to the field of poverty? My comments will be based on my experience in UNCTAD. In contrast to the work on human development which has been emphasized as the key UN contribution thus far in the meeting, UNCTAD research has focussed on the growth model underlying the Washington consensus and has sought to reconstruct an alternative growth model. Most of that work has examined middle-income countries, but my own role is as Team Leader of The Least Developed Countries Report.[19] This has analyzed not only the growth model in the poorest countries in the world but also the question of income poverty in more detail.

Essentially, research work in UNCTAD is applied research that addresses specific problems and specific political debates. But underlying this applied work, there are certain deeper conceptual moves. These address issues beyond the question of the state versus markets, which is the issue normally emphasized in the critique of the Washington Consensus.

The first critical issue is to identify what is meant by the *international* analysis of poverty. Most poverty analyses have focused on the national level. Moreover most of the global discourse is attributing national poverty trends to national factors and national policies. This is a form of explanation that I would call «methodological nationalism».

A main challenge - and this is where I think the UN can make a contribution to the field of poverty - is to get out of this methodological nationalism. In this regard it is worth noting that although the distinction between internal and external is very important, it actually also sustains a methodologically nationalist perspective because it allows thinking about internal factors alone. We should rather think about global and national factors and move toward a multilevel analysis of the causes of poverty. We are trying to develop such a multilevel analysis, incorporating both national factors and international relations, and then apply it to specific problems in our work in the Least Developed Countries Report.

The second key issue, and important area of contribution, is the question of the global ethics that underpins poverty analysis. As mentioned earlier, the rights-based and human development approach are currently the major ethical perspectives considered in the UN at the moment. But there are different ethical perspectives on global justice. The evaluation of these different perspectives of what is meant by global justice is a key arena through which we can see why poverty defined in certain ways and why different ways of reducing poverty are more important or less important.

The third key issue and conceptual area, besides moving beyond methodological nationalism and examining different conceptions of global justice, is the attempt

---
[19] www.unctad.org/ldcs (29 May 2005)

to construct a new international development consensus. From the perspective of UNCTAD, what happened at the beginning of the 1980s was not merely a swing away from states to markets as the major agent of development. It was the breakdown of a development consensus in which development in the South was seen as also being good for the North because development and growth of import capacity in the South promoted full employment in the North. A critical issue now is how we can reconstruct a new international development consensus. The Millennium Development Goals (MDGs) can be understood as an attempt to do that. But we are actually just beginning to test whether those in the South and those in the North are actually behind these Goals and whether they will be realized. The security issue is also now being brought up as the basis for a new North-South development consensus. So the question of constructing a new international development consensus remains relevant.

These three conceptual moves enable new forms of thinking, out of the box of states versus markets and beyond the shift from economic growth to human development. Through these three creative moves the UN can make an important contribution in the future in the field of poverty. But to achieve these kinds of moves, various practical things can be done. One of them, statistics, is extremely important. Very powerful numbers are now being created on the world income distribution. They show, for example, that the bottom 40% of the population gets 5% of the global income. Also an important side-effect of the MDGs has been the statistical effort which is being made to monitor progress through various standardized indicators. This effort seeks to create a global space of comparison in which to measure and compare well-being in different parts of the world. More investment in these global databases is very important as it changes the way we see the world.

A second point which I would stress is that in my experience in UNCTAD the greatest advances in our research have come from multi-country research projects, which take about three to five years to conduct and usually have received funding from donors. These multi-country research projects can have major benefits. They are important if the UN is to continue to make an innovative evidence-based research contribution.

Finally, it is important to multiply the outlets for the research of the UN system. A work like The Least Developed Countries Report has to go through a vetting process. I have never felt that this is very heavy. For example, instead of calling the LDC Report 2002 *Escaping the International Poverty Trap*, it was called *Escaping the Poverty Trap*. If the levels of research output were multiplied beyond flagship reports, people would get many documents that are discussion papers or research papers with named authors. This would do much to revive a research culture within the UN system.

Antoine Maurice

Je vous rejoins tout à fait sur le besoin de trouver des canaux de distribution de cette énorme somme de travail qui est faite aux Nations Unies : la télévision, la radio, les nouveaux médias pourraient être plus utilisés. Il y a tout un travail de résumé qui est souvent mal reçu par les universitaires qui ont l'impression qu'on casse la pensée, mais en réalité ce sont des choses très utiles.

Yves Berthelot: La lutte contre la pauvreté une diversion des stratégies de développement

Je partage le point de vue que la lutte contre la pauvreté doit être insérée dans une stratégie de développement et non s'y substituer. Je partage également le point de vue que les facteurs externes sont importants. Trop souvent, les politiques de lutte contre la pauvreté ne sont que des palliatifs. S'attaquer aux causes impliquerait des stratégies de développement nationales et une certaine remise en cause de l'ordre international. La communauté internationale a fait de la lutte contre la pauvreté une affaire propre à chaque pays qu'elle est prête à soutenir par quelques aides peu coûteuses. Elle n'est pas prête à remettre en cause les modes de vie des plus riches ni les règles du jeu qui leur sont favorables, ni à financer les investissements qui seraient nécessaires.

Le refus de se remettre en cause des pays de l'OCDE trouve une illustration dans les débats sur les directives volontaires relatives à la mise en œuvre du droit à l'alimentation auxquels Michael Windfuhr et moi avons participé comme représentant d'un ensemble d'ONG. Nous avons été frappé par la résistance des pays de l'OCDE à admettre qu'une des causes de la faim provenait de leurs politiques agricoles et des règles du commerce mondial. Ils voulaient cantonner la mise en œuvre du droit à l'alimentation à des politiques nationales dans les pays qui en souffraient. Cette opposition a été en partie levée. Mais, les gouvernements n'ont pas voulu franchir l'obstacle créé par les contradictions qui existent entre les différents principes et règles adoptées internationalement. À la FAO, on ne peut remettre en cause les accords de l'OMC même s'ils sont un obstacle au droit à l'alimentation. Le problème des conflits entre les règles et principes adoptés internationalement n'est pas résolu et est, à mon avis, un défi pour les Nations Unies dans le futur.

J'ajouterai deux remarques sur les stratégies de développement. Tout d'abord, je ne crois pas qu'il faille sous-estimer la croissance. Actuellement, la croissance n'est plus un objectif, mais le résultat d'une bonne gouvernance. Sans doute parce que la croissance prise comme objectif demande des interventions de l'État et des investissements importants. Cependant, la pauvreté a diminué dans les pays où la croissance est soutenue alors qu'elle continue à augmenter dans les pays sans croissance. La croissance peut être plus égalitaire et plus respectueuse de l'environnement, mais elle ne doit pas être négligée.

Ma deuxième remarque concerne le partenariat public privé si souvent prêché dans les discours et parfois imposé comme conditionnalité. J'ai eu l'occasion d'interviewer des organisations de la société civile, des maires et des entreprises sur ce qu'il faudrait faire pour que tous, et surtout les pauvres, aient accès aux services essentiels. Tous s'accordent à dire qu'il serait sans doute bon de développer des partenariats entre les différents acteurs, mais que cela demande beaucoup de temps et entraîne de multiples tensions. Tous insistent pour dire que pour que ces partenariats soient possibles et durables et, tout simplement, pour que chaque acteur puisse jouer pleinement son rôle, il faut clarifier les droits et responsabilités de chacun d'eux. Les autorités locales ne savent pas si elles peuvent lever des impôts, compter sur des transferts de l'État, emprunter sur le marché national, sur le marché international. Dans les instances internationales, on recommande de consulter les organisations de la société civile, mais sur le terrain celles-ci ne sont que rarement libres de proposer des politiques alternatives. Sauf dans quelques « success stories » qui sont répétées à l'envi. Les Nations Unies pourraient encourager les pays à clarifier les droits et responsabilités des différents acteurs et à les inscrire dans les règles et lois nationales. Dans les stratégies de développement, cela permettrait aux citoyens d'exercer leurs droits comme le demandait Michael Windfuhr et à tous les acteurs d'assumer leur rôle.

Comment from the floor

I used to work in ECE as Economic Analyst. About methodological nationalism, it is perfectly logical to accept a new level of consensus. The world consensus now is to have free markets, free flows of capital, and liberalized trade. If countries follow the IMF in establishing macro-economic stability, everything will be all right. If there are problems, it is their fault. So to challenge and to get out of methodological nationalism, you have to come back to the argument between states and markets, because that is essentially what the neo-liberal consensus is about.

I agree that growth is important. Growth is a vector; it has direction as well as quantity. Shifting from one direction to another is what politics is about. The extent to which national preferences are reflected in such a shift is extremely important. But, that is what is being undermined essentially by the preferences of the G7 countries. That is why they are extending the agenda of the WTO into non-trade areas. This means that countries will not be able to do what the G7 countries did themselves, which now are being forbidden. One of the neo-liberal embarrassments is South-East Asia. They try to get out of this embarrassment by saying that Japan did intervene and had open oriented import protection –there is a distinction from the Latin American version-, and that it did not have any effect. So by trying to get out of methodological nationalism, you come back to challenging the basic neo-liberal consensus on trade and investment.

Comment from the floor: The lack of coordination, an obstacle to poverty reduction

As an evaluator in the UN system, the first evaluation I was on was with Codex Alimentarius, which was created by WHO and FAO[20]. For this evaluation, I went to three different offices of the UN system and each one of them conflicted with each other. UNCTAD created projects, in Ghana with women poultry farmers for example, which were involved with developing cooperatives, and at the same time the standards that were set by Codex Alimentarius, another UN agency, meant that those products could never go to market. Out of that evaluation I learnt that members of the UN system do not view themselves as a system. What I have been hearing discussed here are outcomes, but it is important if we want to have an intellectual history of the UN that we look at how the UN works itself.

Through an evaluation of linkages and coordination between UN agencies, specifically the programmes and funds, the specialized agencies being included, I found out how little the UN system is coordinated. So if we look at what the UN system has done, unless we investigate the working methods of the UN system and where they currently are, I don't think we are going to have any place to move, because the actual working methods conflict with the actual goals that are being stated. And I see that as part of the problem with poverty reduction.

Antoine Maurice : Coordination or coherence?

Les Nations Unies sont-elles capables d'entamer les réformes nécessaires, pas nécessairement les plus spectaculaires qui se trouvent dans le domaine politique et dont on parle souvent, mais celles qui ont trait à un meilleur fonctionnement du système, à une meilleure gestion du système et davantage de coordination ?

---

[20] *For more information, see: http://www.codexalimentarius.net/web/index_en.jsp (20 April 2005).*

A role for the UN in the economic and social field

Pierre de Senarclens: Les Nations Unies, un système non coordonnable

Les premières résolutions de l'ECOSOC qui avaient pour mission de coordonner le système datent de 1947, et depuis lors je ne crois pas qu'il y ait eu une année dans l'histoire des Nations Unies où la problématique de la coordination n'ait pas été martelée par différents gouvernements. Mais ces mêmes gouvernements ne sont pas coordonnés. Les administrations nationales ont toutes leurs politiques : une vis-à-vis de l'UNESCO, une autre sur la santé, quelqu'un est envoyé au PNUD, quelqu'un d'autre à l'UNICEF, etc. Il n'y a pas de coordination à l'intérieur des États. Et comme pour une bonne partie des États occidentaux, les Nations Unies n'ont pas véritablement d'importance parce que les vraies questions se décident ailleurs, les diplomates ont beaucoup de marge de manœuvre. Mais ils sont là pour trois ou quatre ans et ont leurs propres agendas.

Il y a donc un problème à l'intérieur des administrations nationales. Mais le péché originel des Nations Unies est d'avoir créé un système qui n'est pas coordonnable dans la mesure où chaque institution a ses propres organes constitutifs. De telle sorte que ce qui est débattu à la Deuxième Commission, à l'ECOSOC ou à la CNUCED ne sera pas nécessairement ce qui se fera à l'UNESCO, à la FAO ou à l'OMS. Au Burkina Faso, où il y a 80% pour cent d'analphabètes, tout le système des Nations Unies semble d'accord sur ce qu'il faut faire, mais dans le bâtiment des Nations Unies il n'y a pas de représentant de l'UNESCO. C'est vous dire que le système tel qu'il a été créé n'est pas coordonnable. Il faut abandonner toute espérance qu'il n'y ait jamais une coordination dans le système des Nations Unies, c'est impossible.

Yves Berthelot: Mauvaise et bonne coordination

Attention, la coordination pour la coordination est absurde ! La coordination devient en outre dangereuse si son objet est d'éviter que se développent des idées divergentes ou non orthodoxes. La coordination ne doit pas avoir pour objet d'imposer telle ou telle doctrine ou des approches identiques dans des pays différents.

Bien entendu, il y a des coordinations positives. Dans le domaine des idées sur le développement, il pourrait être fort utile qu'une personnalité, comme Joseph Stiglitz ou Amartya Sen, soit chargée aux Nations Unies de développer de nouveaux paradigmes sur le développement, en coordonnant collecte d'expériences, recherches et jugements contradictoires de l'ensemble du système. Alors les Nations Unies pourraient retrouver une place de choix dans le débat intellectuel.

Richard Jolly: Ambiguities in the advocacy for coordination

Coordination is often presented as something the UN must do more of – and without more of it, there will be disaster. A large part of the intellectual history actually shows the reverse: it is when the UN or some parts of the UN have broken away from the consensus of the time that new ideas have emerged. This is not a recipe for total proliferation, endless UN multiplications pursuing their narrow interests at country level. If there were to be one international view on any particular issue, it would be intellectually and organizationally stifling, especially if it had to be reached by consensus.

Often when governments, that is UN type 1, argue for this, they are in fact putting forward reasons for cutting some part of the UN. This is well described in the chapter on ECE. In 1948, Walt Rostow, the distinguished US economist, and the US State Department argued that the ECE should run the Marshall Plan, because they had the people and the expertise.[21] The decision with US influence went otherwise. Thus was the OECD created. A parallel example came again in 1980-90. Which agency should overview the transition in the former Soviet Union? Again OECD decided to set up a separate body rather than work through the ECE, that part of the UN that already had several decades of experience analysing both East and West Europe. As regards the substance of strategy during transition, it took until 2000 before the World Bank recognized[22] what was written in the 1990 report of ECE.[23]

The moral? We need to think twice about the arguments for coordination. Many people argue that the virtue of the private sector is competition. And yet allowing a little bit of competition between different bodies of the UN is seen as a sign of sin, weakness, hopelessness and inefficiency. The test should be valued added, not duplication. Often two or more agencies can be working in the same broad area, each contributing more than one would produce if acting alone.

Comments from the floor: A need for coordination

The problem of coordination in the system is real. All the agencies fall over one another's feet in developing countries, and it was the same thing in Eastern Europe and the former Soviet Union for the ECE. There is also another more in-house problem: if you compare the office of the Secretary-General of the UN with the president of the World Bank or the IMF, coordination is very weak in the first, while in the latter is mind-blowing at times.

Marrack Goulding, who was sent as the Secretary-General's Special Representative to Bosnia or Serbia, in his book *Peacemonger*,[24] confesses his embarrassment going there without having been briefed. He did not know the ins and outs of the economy, of the ethnic conflicts and diversity. Later, I asked him why he did not ask us in ECE: we could have set a seminar up for him. He said he did not know about us, he did not know we existed. There is another example of a general sent off to Rwanda who had to go get himself a map of Rwanda; nobody could supply him with one at the UN. This sort of lack of coordination, lack of knowledge of what is available within the system is extremely embarrassing.

The UN has come under attack from the Bush administration, the Republicans in Congress and others. It is no secret that they would like to get rid of the UN system over time. The Bretton Woods institutions are increasingly doing things the UN used to do, and are perceived, at least by the shareholders, as doing them very effectively. That is why IDA is continuing to get increased funding and the UNDP is not. And the message is basically: either you coordinate amongst yourselves, UN agencies, especially at the country level, or your utility, your usefulness will not be recognized and you will become less and less important.

The example of the Burkina Faso shows the real issue. In the 1990s, that country had among the highest level of GDP growth in Africa, averaging 5-6% consistently, based on structural adjustments begun in 1990. The question is: what happened with that growth? This is about re-distributive policies, ensuring that growth benefits the poor and as wide a part of the population as possible. The World Bank has new instruments for helping

---

[21] *Unity and Diversity in Development Ideas*, pp.59-62
[22] World Bank Group, *Entering the 21st Century – World Development Report 1999-2000*. New York: Oxford University Press, 2000
[23] UN ECE, *Economic Survey of Europe in 1990-1991*. Geneva: UN ECE, 1991.
[24] Marrack Goulding, *Peacemonger*. London: John Murray, 2002.

countries do this. The poverty reduction strategies are increasingly government owned documents; they are formulated and implemented by the governments in collaboration with civil society and with the NGO community, both in the formulation and the implementation of these strategies. This is an ongoing process. The first generation of poverty reduction strategies is not as good as the second generation, and the third hopefully will be even better, and there will be more interactions with civil society.

In recent discussions at the Human Rights Commission, a rights-based approach to development is increasingly taken into account. Last year, as representative of the World Bank to the UN and the WTO, I was part of a task force sponsored by the UN Commission on Human Rights where for the first time economists from the IMF, the WTO, the World Bank, and UNCTAD were brought together with human rights lawyers and experts from the Commission and from academic institutions to try to define a set of recommendations and actions supporting the right to development or a rights-based approach to development. The results of this task force will be submitted to the working group, subsequently to the ECOSOC and eventually we hope to the General Assembly, depending on the reactions of member states.

Increasingly, institutions like the World Bank, even the WTO, and the IMF are looking at a rights-based approach to development as a possible tool for meeting the MDGs and for poverty alleviation. What we are trying to do with the Human Rights Commission is to make operative some of the concepts that have been debated for the past five or ten years.

On globalization and the weakening of the state, in many respects we do not have a choice. Today, 70 to 80% of the population are in rural areas. In 15-20 years, 60 to 70% of the population will be living in cities. We will have megalopolises of 20-30-40 million people with problems we have not begun to think about yet. One of the implications, however, is that in those megalopolises, municipal governments will be increasingly called on to provide services, to ensure an enabling environment for employment, to provide education, health, etc. This also means they will get more power to tax. Fiscal authority and other forms of taxing authority will pass from the state level to municipalities and sub-national levels of government. That is already beginning to happen in certain parts of the world, in certain countries. That is an inevitable process and it will probably produce a weakening of the state, and it is not necessarily going to be a bad thing.

Michael Windfuhr: The issue is coherence of policies

The Millennium Development Task Force has shown that in the year 2015 more than half of the world population will still be in rural areas. We should not forget this, because the downward trends in investment in agricultural and rural development, which has gone down by half in the last ten years, is something that has to be addressed. The sooner we see everybody living in cities, the less we look at those who are actually poor, and we will not reach the Millennium Development Goals this way.

While the nation state is weakening in a process that cannot just be reversed, social movements are calling for food sovereignty. We have to think about what is being lost when the nation-state is weakened. If the state's distributive and re-distributive functions are lost, what can replace them? What would be a mechanism to deal with these issues? What would be an adequate replacement?

We can call for more coherence. But in Europe, for example, there is a Maastricht treaty provision on the coherence of policies. And, when agricultural traders come in saying that coherence also means to adjust a development policy to their agricultural export needs, coherence can lead into the wrong direction in terms of development. Coherence is not a positive thing *per se*; what matters is the direction it is given. We have to discuss the content, the way in which we are building coherence.

We have a proliferation of international instruments, and we have obligations under human rights conventions, environmental treaties, international economic policies, WTO rules and so forth, but where there is a conflict between these rules, what do we do? We have 182 objectives in the plan of action of the World Food Summit, which are not all coherent, so which are to be followed? At the national level, Supreme Courts make decisions when there are conflicting interests, and determine the extent of the parties' protection and rights.

Internationally, we are missing this type of regulation. Some support a rights-based approach to guarantee the assets of small farmers, while others support, for macro-economic purposes, a liberal scheme in order to get more foreign direct investments. How to deal with these conflicts? We have to determine priorities and go much more into the details of the direction of coherence.

To some extent, human rights are binding the nation-state so that it does not harm individuals. But with globalization, the nation-state itself is loosing the power to regulate. So, how to deal with those who give the direction? How to find binding human rights rules? For example, how to put European –German or French- agro-exports to Africa under human rights binding rules. There is no extra-territorial obligation at the moment. There are no human rights rules for inter-governmental agencies or for private actors. We are starting with the Global Compact or the UN rules of conduct for TNCs. The discussion is on whether inter-governmental organizations can be bound through their membership to human rights standards? We are trying to find something universally accepted –like human rights- and how to make it binding for all relevant actors, not only the nation-states.

It is necessary to discuss the adequate level of economic openness, but also policy spaces. The economy has to protect certain people. Right now things are out of balance: we have a very radical opening, but we lost some agencies that can care for people, through affirmative action for example. The right to undertake affirmative action has been lost and we have to regain it. The point is not to be against openness, it is about a good balance between the two directions. We have to take care of those who are marginalized. Without this at the centre of our concern, we will lose out.

III - The UN and the world economy

Antoine Maurice

Ces commentaires nous conduisent au thème de la capacité de l'ONU, lorsqu'on se tourne vers l'avenir, de réguler l'économie mondiale. Est-ce une capacité résiduelle, une capacité qui croît ?

Carlos Fortin: A feasible future: UN-governments setting goals and reaching consensus, UN secretariat helping and reconstructing its intellectual capacity

Even though I may appear pedantic, I think we could benefit from some definitional exercise. For one thing, when we talk about the UN we are talking at least about two quite different things. First, we have a group of governments, which are present through intergovernmental structures, some standing like the General Assembly, ECOSOC, or UNCTAD, and others conferences held on a one-time basis. Then, we have the Secretariat that is a continuing body of individuals and work. The volume *The UN and Global Political Economy* refers to both but mostly to the Secretariat. So I think we should separate out what the UN can do with the world economy as an intergovernmental body and as a Secretariat that has its own program of work and its own mandates.

Secondly, what do we mean by managing or regulating the world economy? There are at least three different meaning. First, the establishment of international binding commitments and disciplines, obligations of states vis-à-vis each other –the GATT 1994 is one such body. Secondly, commitments entered into by governments vis-à-vis international organizations – like the labour conventions, or IMF programmes when governments agree to certain policies. Thirdly, intervention by the international community in the world economy – for example, UNCTAD Common Fund and the Integrated Programme for Commodities are an effort of the international community as a whole to intervene in commodity markets.

So what can the UN as an intergovernmental body and as a Secretariat do about these three things? My answer is simple: very little. When it comes to international binding commitments, with the possible exception of environmental agreements, there are no instances of the UN being the locus of entering into formal commitments and disciplines that can be enforced in the way in which those of the WTO are. In the case of trade it is quite clear: the WTO is the place where rules are promulgated, and commitments are entered into. They are monitored and adjudicated if there is a dispute. I don't see the UN as an intergovernmental body having much of a role there.

Neither do I see much a role for the UN as an intergovernmental body in getting governments to agree to commitments as far as domestic policies are concerned vis-à-vis the UN. I am using the UN in the sense of UN proper excluding the specialized agencies because some of those do have some of these powers. This clearly is the province of the IMF and the World Bank. They are the ones who discuss policy and get governments to agree to certain policy guidelines. The question of intervention by the international community in the world economy is essentially taken up by the predominant approach that is to let the markets operate. So I do not see much of a role for the UN in those three areas.

But I do see a role for the UN as an intergovernmental body in two ways. First, in establishing goals and principles for the international community and for the international economy. The UN has been quite active in doing so with the Millennium Development Goals, the Millennium Summit, the Millennium Declaration, or the Monterey consensus on financing for development. These are goals to be achieved and guiding principles. Not necessarily strategy to implement those goals or to pursue those principles, but at least the normative element is present.

Secondly, the UN has a role in generating some consensus that may later lead to action by other organizations. In that respect, UNCTAD was particularly active when the Generalized System of Preferences was discussed and agreed. But it was implemented in the GATT through the enabling clause. The definition of services in Article one of GATT was discussed in UNCTAD, and it was agreed formally in the WTO. These are not irrelevant. It is a contribution to the design of the world economy and the world system through a work that is preparatory to the negotiation of binding commitments or to the entry into binding obligations.

The Secretariat is there essentially to animate this process at the intergovernmental level, to do analysis and research, to explore policy options and proposals, to put forward ideas. It does that very effectively. UNCTAD *Trade and Development Report* is a good example of an effort at being ahead of the curve in thinking about the global economy. The *Human Development Report* was a pioneer in bringing the social dimension in. This has been done and will continue to be done. It is a very important contribution especially because it has a more critical view of the prevailing orthodoxy. It is useful to have a questioning, an inquisitive voice in the global debate to keep those who are promoting the orthodoxy up to date. But is that enough? It is a contribution, but a modest one.

The same book substantiates my basic proposition, which is that the UN Secretariat has been most successful when it has created ideology —in a neo-Marxian sense of a set of propositions which are a partial reflection of reality, partial in the sense of being incomplete and being partial to a particular set of social actors whose interests are reflected in those propositions and whose contribution is sought to move forward the implementation of those ideas. Ideology in that sense has an analysis, good but incomplete, agents who have interests and power, and policy. This is what Prebisch was about. His genius (the book makes quite clear that he was not a great theoretician, he took from others) was to put the convergence of those three things to work. He articulated an understanding of what was happening in Latin America, which was defensible if not true. He identified the social agent, the emerging industrial bourgeoisie of Latin American, and gave them a set of policies, import substitution. That approach has dominated the thinking of Latin America in the post-war period.

Can the Secretariat do something similar today? I have doubts. Even Prebisch documented the terrible difficulties he faced. And it is much more difficult today. But we should still try to recapture this. The book suggests to do top class research analysis, to bring new ideas, but universities and others already do that. What is unique about the UN is this combination of intellectual analysis, of policy formulation and action with real agents. If we can bring that back into our work, even if we cannot do another Prebisch, we can get closer to what the founders of the UN had in mind and to what probably Prebisch had in mind.

Barbara Ekwall: Perspectives from a new member country, Switzerland

I will not present the official positions of Switzerland on the issues discussed here today because these positions have not been consolidated yet.

I would like to offer some elements of reflection about the challenges that the UN will be facing this year and in the longer term. Five years ago when governments adopted the Millennium Declaration and committed to the Millennium Development Goals for

2015, the mood was one of confidence. Today, five years later, it is quite different. We wonder where we are going with respect to these goals.

The FAO recently published the *State of Food Insecurity in the World*.[25] The number of undernourished people is growing being now at 852 million. In a world of plenty there is so much misery. The report shows that extreme poverty is increasing in a number of countries and regions, but that progress has been achieved in some countries, especially in Asia. That means it is possible to do better, to find solutions. Finally, the report shows the cost of extreme poverty: five million children die from hunger each year, not because of tsunami or conflict. Malnutrition creates lifelong physical and cognitive deficiencies, which cost billions in prejudice. Children pay their whole life for malnutrition suffered in their early years and no school or health centre will remedy what was caused at that age. This is challenge number one for the United Nations system.

About reforms and linking history to the future, we know business as usual will not work and adjustments will not do it. We need innovative ideas, and new, creative solutions to the new situation we are facing. Five heads of agencies will change this year. Will the new personalities be willing to do the necessary reforms? What will be their contributions to ideas and the realization of these ideas? What kind of leadership will the UN have?

Regarding development financing and new mechanisms for financing development. It is not possible within the political systems to increase ODA as the world community has committed itself to. We need to reflect on new mechanisms. The financial architecture is also a challenge as the Bretton Woods institutions are increasingly involved in a work traditionally done by UN agencies. So, what is our vision of the UN system, the Bretton Woods and UN funds and programmes in 20-25 years?

The challenge of the Millennium +5 review will be to open new doors and lead to new commitments and concrete solutions for reaching the MDGs. In his Millennium Project report, Jeffrey Sachs insists that: "the year 2005 should inaugurate a decade of bold action." Will that happen?

It is important not only to have goals but also strategies, and even more important is that existing or new strategies be coherent. In many respects the UN reflects the organization of national governments. The need for more coherence within the UN system should be taken as a mirror of the need for more coherence in our own countries, between our own policies.

Many countries are important for the UN. We talked this afternoon about the importance the US has had in defining new activities or creating new ideas. Today, the attitude of the US towards the UN is a source of preoccupation, because of its impact on the capacity of the UN to fulfil its mandate in the areas of peace, development and human rights. These are the challenges.

To end on a positive note, I would like to mention some of the strengths of the UN: it has a high credibility; it is a bearer of values; its universality, the participation of all countries on equal footing; from its work in the field, the UN can identify new developments and help new ideas and creative solutions emerge. These new approaches help us in turn to understand differently the realities. These are comparative advantages that must be maintained.

---

[25] See: http://www.fao.org/sof/sofi/index_en.htm (20 April 2005).

Pierre de Senarclens: Pas d'intérêt des gouvernements pour débattre économie à l'ONU

Le problème des Nations Unies, c'est que dès 1947 le système a été marginalisé. Les décisions se sont prises ailleurs, pour des raisons liées à la guerre froide. Cela vaut aussi pour les institutions de Bretton Woods qui ont eu un rôle très marginal jusque dans les années 1980. Il y a eu le Plan Marshall, l'OECE, le processus d'intégration européenne, et d'autres institutions dans lesquelles ont été mis en œuvre un certain nombre d'objectifs des Nations Unies.

Etant marginalisé, le système a peu de ressources. Et quand il y a peu de ressources, il n'y a rien à coordonner. Coordonner un système qui a 4% de l'assistance publique au développement – sans parler des institutions de Bretton Woods, ce n'est pas coordonner grand chose et c'est condamner ces institutions à produire davantage des normes ou des idées importantes, stimulantes et critiques, mais leur rôle effectif est limité. Une institution marginalisée fait des Commissions pour étudier des problèmes et aboutir à la décision de créer une nouvelle instance qui va elle-même faire des rapports pour créer une autre instance, etc. Cela mobilise l'essentiel de l'activité des diplomates, qui cherchent à être président d'une commission ou à placer l'un de leurs ressortissants au Secrétariat. Ce sont des effets pervers de la marginalisation. Les difficultés des Nations Unies viennent de là.

De plus comme les diplomates ont de moins en moins de rôle traditionnel et qu'ils ne sont pas toujours adaptés au multilatéralisme, ils n'interviennent plus sur la substance. Il n'y a donc plus ces « check-and-balance » qui permettent de redresser une organisation qui fonctionne mal ou dont le directeur général n'est pas très bon. Les organisations fonctionnent bien quand il y a de gros intérêts derrière, quand elles sont contrôlées par les donateurs. Mais sans ces gros intérêts, la politique du « chien crevé » ou du « fil de l'eau » peut durer très longtemps. Il est impossible de réformer une institution en crise parce que les gouvernements ne s'y intéressent plus. Ils ne veulent pas d'interpellation au parlement, pour la Suisse. Ils ne prennent pas de positions importantes dans l'organisation. Donc le « check-and-balance » n'existe pas, les diplomates ne sont pas en mesure de l'apporter et sont surmenés par tous ces comités et toutes ces négociations, et la question de la substance perd beaucoup de son importance.

Tout ce qui permettrait de créer un organe dans lequel on pourrait assumer à la fois les fonctions du G7 et les fonctions d'intégrer des grands pays ou des pays en développement dans un lieu où les choses importantes sont discutées, serait un élément essentiel de la réforme des Nations Unies. En fait, il faut transformer les règles du jeu et le mode de fonctionnement des Nations Unies.

Actuellement les Etats-Unis veulent détruire le système des Nations Unies et comme l'Union Européenne n'a pas de politique étrangère, il n'y a pas de relais à cette déliquescence du soutien des Nations Unies. Il faudrait créer une structure au niveau des Nations Unies où les gens qui ont la possibilité d'agir, où les ministres des finances ou de l'éducation, viennent discuter comme dans le cadre des Conseils de la Commission Européenne où les décideurs importants sont mobilisés. Mais simplement avoir des instances où un ministre se déplace pendant deux heures pour faire un discours qui sera répercuté dans la presse est une perte de temps.

Michael Windfuhr: Human rights as an instrument of regulation

On the issue of strategy, why is a widespread strategy of such an importance, and where are we to redefine or rethink some of the work the United Nations has done? First, let me say that the nation-state is an important actor. We have to analyse what we are loosing if we loose the nation-state. In political science we know there are three kinds of policies: regulative, distributive that is distributing growth, and re-distributive. Only a very closed nation-state would be able to have re-distributive policies because a society has to be willing to pay for those who are worse off. Even in the European Union there is not much readiness to pay for the worst off, at least not more than 1% of the GNP.

At the international level, re-distributive policies and even distributive policies become even more problematic, so we are left with regulative policies. For example, the WTO is quite effective in regulating food ingredients, in adopting sanitary regulations. But we have so few institutions that can distribute or re-distribute. And we do not ask the nation-state any longer to do so, and there is nothing else replacing it. This creates in terms of human rights a real problem. Who is to implement distribution or re-distribution?

This is why the rights-based approach is so important. It comes down to what we can duly demand from a nation-state. And we can demand much more than we often do. We should not move too fast to the global level, because then we give leeway to all the unwilling governments that do not give land rights to women, or marginalize part of their population because they are minorities, or old people, or because they do not count in voting. We have to make governments accountable, giving people the right to go to court. This is why we face all these resistance when we talk about the right to food, particularly from developing countries.

On the other hand, we also have to think about what kind of international conditions the nation-state needs, and here I see three major challenges. First, without the nation-state we lose a policy-space to define objectives for poverty reduction. The main demand concerning food issues made by the social movements at Porto Alegre is food sovereignty. That is the motto of Via Campesina, the worldwide rural farmer movement. They argue they have no longer control of what is happening locally, everything is defined either by the WTO or by structural adjustment policies —now called poverty reduction strategy plans.

Decisions are made elsewhere and there is no much policy-space left. If a country wants to deliberately combat discrimination against marginalized groups, it is impossible because trade rules stipulate that everybody has to be treated in the same way. On the contrary, human rights rules would promote "affirmative action" for the structurally disadvantaged. So on one level, the question is how to re-regain certain areas where states need flexibility to deal with marginalized groups and to give them some policy-space back. We are just beginning to recall the food sovereignty.

Secondly, we are giving a lot of policy advice to developing countries. For this, the UN system is quite effective. In Africa, numerous consultants advise how to change land-owning structures, for example. Land laws have been changed in Uganda in 1995, and in Angola recently. All the land is rigidly divided and registered into cadastre and traditional land rights are destroyed just to get more foreign direct investment into the countries. For plantations or mining companies all come in through foreign direct investments.

In one of the better off countries, Ghana, two thirds of the FDI are for mining corporations, which create tremendous problems, expelling people, changing river course. 70% of FDI in Ghana has been given to one region as concessional area for mining companies. A consultant from the World Bank has written the new mining laws in Ghana, and UN people have written all the land policy reforms. We give a lot of policy advice. So why are we talking about poverty reduction? We have to be more critical particularly from a pro-poor perspective on what policy advice really means.

Finally, I would like to address the issue of trade-offs. The understanding of the economic mainstream is that trade-offs are needed, so some people are worse off, but there will be world growth and in the long run we will all be better off. What to say about marginalized people? What would be their future role in society? If 75% of the poor are rural people living in marginal areas, what type of structural change or ideal do we envisage for them as future? How many trade-offs can we allow?

That is where human rights are important, because they tell us under certain conditions trade-offs are not allowed. You cannot expel 30,000 people for just one dam without giving them adequate compensation. We have to discuss which trade-offs are possible and which are not. When it comes to minimum economic, social and cultural standards, we have to be much more clear-cut on the limits of trade-offs. We cannot take it for granted that in the end everything will be fine and just ask how to make trade more pro-poor.

Yves Berthelot: La dimension régionale dans la gouvernance mondiale

Pour l'avenir des Nations Unies, Carlos Fortin a défini des perspectives raisonnables : il est en effet important que celles-ci continuent à produire des idées et à définir des principes et des normes. Mais une plus grande attention devrait être apportée à leur mise en œuvre. Cela pourrait se faire en réorientant l'ensemble des modestes moyens d'assistance technique des Nations Unies vers la mise en place de lois et règles conformes aux principes adoptés, ce qui donnerait aux citoyens plus de moyens d'exercer leurs droits.

Sur la gouvernance et les régions, je voudrais partir du constat fait par les Commissions régionales que je rappelais dans ma première intervention, à savoir que plus une région est développée et plus les pays de la région commercent entre eux. Une des conclusions à en tirer est que l'échelon régional dans une gouvernance équilibrée du monde devrait avoir plus d'importance qu'il n'en a aujourd'hui.

À l'intérieur des Nations Unies, le niveau régional pourrait définir, et il le fait dans certains cas, des règles et des normes adaptées à la région et qui n'ont pas besoin d'être mondiales. Le principe de subsidiarité est un bon principe. Après les crises en Asie et ailleurs, il a été un moment envisagé de développer des règles prudentielles. Cela ne s'est finalement pas fait car il est très compliqué de développer de telles règles au niveau mondial. C'est faisable régionalement et certaines régions l'ont fait. L'idée, avancée par le Japon et reprise par José Antonio Ocampo alors qu'il était à la tête de la CEPALC, qu'il faudrait des IMF régionaux n'est pas déraisonnable. Ces institutions, plus proches de leurs membres, les connaîtraient mieux et surtout pourraient décider d'intervenir plus rapidement que l'organisation mondiale pour éviter la contagion ou qu'une crise de liquidités se transforme en crise de solvabilité.

Les grandes régions des Nations Unies ont un rôle dans l'analyse économique, la définition de politiques et la négociation de normes. Les Commissions régionales assument tout ou partie de ces responsabilités selon la volonté des gouvernements. Les départements régionaux des agences et programmes pourraient dans leur domaine jouer des rôles identiques, mais se contentent souvent de gérer l'assistance technique régionale. Il est clair que le principe de subsidiarité devrait être appliqué plus systématiquement à la définition des politiques et des normes.

Quant à la mise en œuvre des politiques et des normes, les États en ont la responsabilité qu'ils peuvent déléguer à des entités régionales comme l'Union Européenne, le MERCOSUR, l'ASEAN, etc. Ici le concept-clé est celui de la délégation d'autorité que les pays membres de l'Union Européenne pratiquent dans certains domaines, mais que les autres regroupements ne pratiquent guère. Ainsi, quand l'UE négocie un accord commercial avec l'ASEAN, par exemple, elle se retrouve en face de douze ministres qui sont loin de parler d'une seule voix. Si les différentes entités régionales se voyaient déléguer responsabilités et autorité, elles seraient à même de négocier entre elles et de faire appliquer les principes, normes et politiques qui doivent être mondiaux et laisseraient se développer en leur sein des politiques nationales ou régionales plus adaptées aux circonstances locales. C'est un plaidoyer pour que, demain, la dimension régionale soit effectivement prise en compte dans la gouvernance mondiale.

IV – Concluding remarks

Richard Jolly

I hope this conference will inspire other meetings to look at the UN record and at where should the UN be going. I hope when one looks at the volumes, one has some antidote to extreme UN pessimism. Of course there is pessimism in Washington, which is based on the Bush administration sees as "Realpolitik". But Europe's role is to keep alive the flame of belief in internationalism and in the many good ideas of the UN, many of which came from Washington and the US governments over the years.

Antoine Maurice

Une phrase du *Monde* d'aujourd'hui (24 janvier 2005) dit : « Le système de la presse ne vit pas dans la pensée unique mais dans un monde unique où tous s'accordent à trouver un événement digne d'intérêt et un autre négligeable ». Florence Aubenas qui s'est beaucoup penchée sur la question de l'homogénéité de la presse écrivit ceci. Les livres du Projet UNIHP et les discussions d'aujourd'hui ont montré qu'on n'était pas dans ce genre de monde et c'est réjouissant. On est dans un monde globalisé mais on est dans un monde où l'agenda, les points qui semblent importants ne relèvent pas d'une pensée unique ou d'un agenda unique.

Jean-Marie Dufour

Les présentations et les commentaires semblent avoir ouvert des pistes de recherche qui nous intéressent au RUIG. Chaque année le RUIG ouvre un concours de projets de recherche fondés sur des partenariats entre le monde académique et les organisations internationales qui sont des partenariats interdisciplinaires et dont les travaux doivent être « action oriented ». Je voudrais donc faire appel aux universitaires et aux membres des organisations internationales pour qu'ils poursuivent le dialogue qui s'est noué aujourd'hui et créent ensemble des projets, constituent des équipes de recherche, et fassent des propositions au RUIG. Après cinq ans d'expérience, ces projets sont appréciés tant du côté universitaire où ils apportent une vue nouvelle de la vie internationale, que du côté des organisations internationales où ils apportent une connotation nouvelle dans l'analyse et l'appréciation du fonctionnement de ces institutions. Nous pensons qu'une action qui va dans ce sens est propre à assurer à ce que nous appelons la Genève internationale une dimension de rayonnement supplémentaire en Suisse, en Europe et dans le monde.

Enfin, l'exposition « Les idées des Nations Unies au service du développement » à la Bibliothèque de l'Office des Nations Unies à Genève présente des documents très intéressants sur ce sujet qui nous préoccupe et montre la richesse des archives de la Bibliothèque.

Je remercie les auteurs et les participants de l'université de Genève, de HEI et de l'IUED, les membres des organisations internationales, et tous nos auditeurs qui ont apporté la résonance nécessaire à cette conférence

UNIHP Presentation

The United Nations Intellectual History Project (UNIHP)

A future oriented intellectual history of the UN in the world economy:

Development ideas and concepts in action

There is no adequate historical study of the origins and evolution of the history of ideas cultivated within the UN and on their impact on wider thinking and international action. Although certain aspects of the UN economic and social activities have been the subject of books and articles, there is no comprehensive intellectual history of the world organisation's contributions to setting the past, present and future development agenda, nor comprehensive intellectual history for the economic and social fields.

UNIHP is tracing the origin and analysing the evolution of key ideas and concepts about international economic and social development born or nurtured under UN auspices. The motivation behind these ideas as well as their relevance, influence, and impact are being assessed against the backdrop of socio-economic situation of individual countries, the global economy, and major international developments.

UNIHP Publications

Ahead of the Curve?

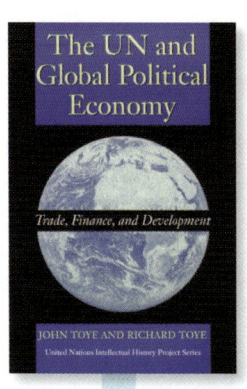

The UN and Global Political Economy

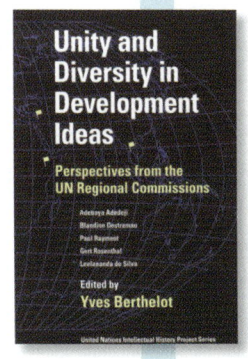

Unity and Diversity in Development Ideas

Quantifying the World

UN Contributions to Development Thinking and Practice

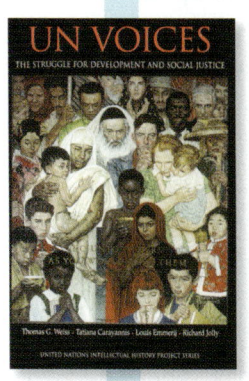

UN Voices

UNIHP Publications

The volumes of the UNIHP series are published in English by Indiana University Press, IUP.

Ahead of the Curve? UN Ideas and Global Challenges, *Louis Emmerij, Richard Jolly, Thomas G. Weiss (2001 ; 2nd edition 2003 ; A Choice Outstanding Academic Book of 2003).*

■*French translation:*
En avance sur leur temps ? Les Nations Unies face aux défis mondiaux (Blonay, Switzerland : Van Diermen - ADECO ; Geneva : Nations Unies, 2003).

■*German translation:*
Der Zeit voraus ? Vereinte Nationen : Ideen und globale Herausforderungen (Blonay, Switzerland : Van Diermen - ADECO ; Geneva : Nations Unies, 2003).

■*Arabic translation (Al Ahram, Cairo: 2003).*
سباق مع الزمن؟ أفكار الأمم المتحدة في مواجهة التحديات العالمية

Unity and Diversity in Development Ideas: Perspectives from the UN Regional Commissions, edited by Yves Berthelot with contributions from Adebayo Adedeji, Yves Berthelot, Leelananda de Silva, Paul Rayment, Gert Rosenthal, and Blandine Destremeau (2004).

Quantifying the World: UN Contributions to Statistics, Michael Ward (2004).

UN Contributions to Development Thinking and Practice, Richard Jolly, Louis Emmerij, Dharam Ghai, and Frédéric Lapeyre (2004).

The UN and Global Political Economy: Trade, Finance, and Development, John Toye and Richard Toye (2004).

UN Voices: The Struggle for Development and Social Justice, Thomas G. Weiss, Tatiana Carayannis, Louis Emmerij, and Richard Jolly (2005).

Women, Development, and the UN: A Sixty-Year Quest for Equality and Justice, Devaki Jain (2005).

Human Security and the UN: A Critical History, S. Neil MacFarlane and Yuen Foong-Khong (2006).

FORTHCOMING:

The Human Rights Ideas at the United Nations: the Political History of Universal Justice, Sarah Zaidi and Roger Normand (2007).

The UN and Development Cooperation, Olav Stokke (2007).

The UN and the Global Commons: Development without Destruction, Nico Schrijver (2007).

The UN and Transnationals, from Code to Compact, Tagi Sagafi-Nejad and John Dunning (2007).

The UN and Global Governance: An Idea and its Prospects, Ramesh Thakur and Thomas G. Weiss (2007).

The Intellectual History of Preventive Diplomacy at the United Nations: the Journey of an Idea, B.G. Ramcharan (2007).

The United Nations: A History of Ideas and Their Future, Richard Jolly, Louis Emmerij, and Thomas G. Weiss (2007).

Also published under the aegis of UNIHP: **The Power of UN Ideas: Lessons from the First 60 Years: A Summary of the Books and Findings from the United Nation Intellectual History Project,** Richard Jolly, Louis Emmerij, and Thomas G. Weiss (New York : UNIHP, 2005).

The UNIHP is supporting **The Oxford Handbook on the UN,** edited by Thomas G. Weiss and Sam Daws, to be published by Oxford University Press in 2007.

Part 2

Exhibition catalogue
UN ideas in the service of development
(UNOG Library, January-September 2005)

Part 2

Introduction 75

From the League to the United Nations 77

Early development strategies (1949-1951) 78

Technical assistance and development financing : early stages (1949-1966) 80

The evolution of the concept of development 82

Ideas from the UN regional commissions 93

The UNCTAD experience 105

UN statistics : measuring the world 113

The UNIHP volumes devoted to development 115

List of documents 121

Introduction

The exhibition *UN Ideas in the Service of Development* is the outcome of cooperation between researchers from the United Nations Intellectual History Project (UNIHP) and the Library and Archives of the United Nations Office at Geneva.

The exhibition presents United Nations contributions to social and economic development from the organization's early years, with the inheritance from the League of Nations, to the challenges of today. The exhibition displays annotated drafts, working documents, personal letters, memos, and photos, as well as UN documents and various publications. The exhibition also shows the contributions of personalities such as Gunnar Myrdal, Jan Tinbergen, Wassily Leontief, or Raúl Prebisch.

UN Ideas in the Service of Development explores when and where, within the UN system, analyses about development issues were made and ideas emerged: when and where policies were proposed and institutions created, addressing issues of development financing, technical assistance, international trade, commodity prices, the special situation of least developed countries, economic transition, etc.

Through the years, the increasing emphasis on the social aspects of development is glaring. The work of the Regional Commissions in this area, as well on reconstruction, population, women, and regional integration has been tremendous, as has been the work on statistics done in various UN organs in developing, for example, input-output tables for national accounting, population or human development indexes, and general principles of official statistics.

The exhibition places these ideas and initiatives in their historical context through significant events, such as the first Afro-Asian Conference at Bandung, decolonization, the creation of the Non-Aligned Movement and the Group of 77, the oil shocks, the debt crisis, structural adjustment policies, and globalization.

The many proposals and commitments made within the UN system represent a huge potential for change. The gap between this potential and what has actually been implemented can be surprising. Proposals taking the human dimensions of development into consideration or the need for time for appropriate institutions to develop were elaborated, and too often disregarded. But creative thinking has not been lacking. Even since the 1980s, when the Bretton Woods Institutions took the leadership in economic policy decisions, UN criticism of the neo-liberal excesses of these institutions and its repeated calls for reducing poverty and improving fairness and sustainability in the development process have not been ignored.

The exhibition *UN Ideas in the Service of Development* and this catalogue have been realized by Sophie Theven de Gueleran, Research Fellow at the UNIHP project in Geneva, and by Cristina Giordano, Chief of the General Reference Unit, in cooperation with the team of the Archives and the UN Documents Collection of the Library of the United Nations Office at Geneva.

From the League to the United Nations

The League of Nations had begun addressing many of the issues that will later be crucial to social and economic development. The "Bruce" report, *The Development of International Cooperation in Economic and Social Affairs* (1939), considered measures to expand the League's machinery for dealing with economic and social problems and to promote participation by all nations in efforts to solve these problems.

The report recommended the establishment of a new League Central Committee for Economic and Social Questions made up of Governments and experts that would direct the work of existing committees on these matters. The League's Twentieth Assembly accepted this proposal and set up an organizing committee to implement it. The extension of the war in Europe, however, prevented the realization of this plan.

The comprehensive set of provisions found in Chapters IX, "International Economic and Social Cooperation", and X, "The Economic and Social Council", of the Charter of the United Nations found its origins in the recommendations of this report.

Related documents

League of Nations, *The Problem of Nutrition: Interim Report of the Mixed Committee on the Problem of Nutrition* (Geneva, 1936).

League of Nations, *The Development of International Cooperation in Economic and Social Affairs: Report of the Special Committee* (Geneva, 1939, Series of League of Nations Publications. General. 1939.3).

Chapter IX, "International Economic and Social Cooperation", and Chapter X, "The Economic and Social Council" *in* Charter of the United Nations and Statute of the International Court of Justice (New York, 2003, DPI/511 Reprint).

United Nations, *Economic Report: Salient Features of the World Economic Situation 1945-1947* (New York, 1948, Sales No. E.48.II.C.1).

United Nations, *Preliminary Report on the World Social Situation, 1952. With Special Reference to Standards of Living* (New York, 1952, Sales No. E.52.IV.11)

Early development strategies (1949-1951)

From the beginning, the United Nations turned its attention to development problems such as development financing, technical assistance, international trade for economic development, industrialization for diversification out of primary commodities, as well as land reform and the distribution of national income. Both internal and external factors of underdevelopment were taken into account: the deteriorating terms of trade of primary commodities and the short-term volatility of commodity prices – a critical problem for economic development and planning.

The 1949 Secretariat study, *Post-War Price Relations in Trade Between Under-developed and Industrialized Countries,* addressed the problem of high prices of goods such as machinery and equipment imported by the under-developed countries relative to prices of primary products, and called for further study of the prices of capital goods, their relative trends, and those of primary products.

To this era belong the three seminal reports:

National and International Measures for Full Employment (1949) addressed measures required for full employment in economically developed countries. The report stressed that the object of a full-employment policy in its international aspects was to "create conditions under which any particular country will so behave in its international economic relations as not to prevent other countries from maintaining the stability and prosperity of their economies", and proposed measures for bringing about a new equilibrium in world trade, and for the stabilization of the flow of international trade and investment for economic development.

Measures for the Economic Development of Under-developed Countries (1951) addressed the problem of reducing unemployment and underemployment in under-developed countries. The report recommended that underdeveloped countries set in place an institutional framework conducive to economic development, and to create employment opportunities through industrialization and land reforms. At the international level, recommendations included measures for developed countries concerning commercial policies and terms of trade, and measures for the UN and other international agencies concerning technical assistance and the strengthening of resources available for development financing.

Measures for International Economic Stability (1951) analysed alternative ways of dealing with the problem of reducing the international impact of recessions. The vulnerability of underdeveloped countries to external economic fluctuations required concerted international action to reduce fluctuations in the volume of trade and in the prices of primary commodities to moderate the swings in the terms of trade of underdeveloped countries. To enable these countries to maintain their programmes of economic development in the face of fluctuations, the report recommended measures such as long-term agreements on quantity and prices, with quotas, fixed prices, and buffer stocks to help reduce fluctuations in world markets, as well as adequate capital flow for a steady international flow of goods and services to borrowing countries and a steady volume of exports for foreign economic development.

Early development strategies emphasized public intervention as key in the development process, specifically in raising savings and investment. Development planning was the necessary tool in setting and realizing goals. Early reports also addressed inequalities within countries and stressed that the benefits of economic development had to be widely distributed and not serve the wealth and power of a few. While analysing the preconditions for development, these reports strongly criticized the ruling classes and land tenure in developing countries.

Related documents

United Nations, *Post-War Price Relations in Trade Between Under-developed and Industrialized Countries* (New York, 1949, E/CN.1/Sub.3/W.5).

United Nations, *National and International Measures for Full Employment : Report by a Group of Experts appointed by the Secretary-General of the United Nations. B. Ronald Walker, Chairman; J.M. Clark, Nicholas Kaldor, Arthur Smithies, and Pierre Uri* (Lake Success, New York, 1949, document from UNOG Archives ARR 14/1360, Box 69, Folder I/3/10, Sub Folder "Rostow").

United Nations, *Measures for the Economic Development of Under-developed Countries: Report by a Group of Experts Appointed by the Secretary-General of the United Nations* (New York, 1951, Sales No. E.51.II.B.2).

United Nations, *Measures for International Economic Stability*: *Report by a Group of Experts appointed by the Secretary-General* (New York, 1951, Sales No. E.51.II.A.2).

Letter dated 1 March 1950 from Walt Rostow, Special Assistant to the Executive Secretary of the UN Economic Commission for Europe, to Gunnar Myrdal, Executive Secretary of the ECE (document from UNOG Archives ARR 14/1360, Box 69, Folder I/3/10, Sub Folder "WW Rostow").

Technical assistance and development financing : early stages (1949-1966)

International aid was soon perceived as essential to the development of underdeveloped countries. United Nations programmes of technical assistance began in 1948 to address the need to transfer skills and knowledge in economic surveys and policy, fiscal administration, statistics, expert training, social welfare, housing, town and country planning, child welfare, and other aspects of economic and social development.

President Truman's Four Points (Programme for World Economic Progress Through Cooperative Technical Assistance) of his inaugural address in January 1949 raised the need for technical assistance to the top of the international agenda. The Expanded Programme for Technical Assistance (EPTA) was established by the General Assembly in August 1949 to coordinate and promote efforts.

Since 1946, the importance of development of projects not immediately self-liquidating that could not be financed from the country's own resources or for which loans could not be obtained on business principles was recognized. The first proposal for a new development financing agency was made by V.K.R.V. Rao, Chair of the Sub-Commission on Economic Development in 1949. In 1950, the General Assembly recognized that the volume of private capital flowing into underdeveloped countries could not meet their financial needs for development, and that these needs could only be met with an increased flow of international public funds.

After examining the recommendation of the 1951 report *Measures for the Economic Development of Under-developed Countries* to establish an International Development Authority, ECOSOC prepared the plan for a Special UN Fund for Economic Development (SUNFED). This capital fund for grants-in-aid and low-interest, long-term loans was to help underdeveloped countries accelerate their development and finance non-self-liquidating projects.

From 1949 to 1955, developing countries tried to influence the establishment of SUNFED, but powerful countries hostile to soft financing preferred bilateral aid, stronger conditionality, and financial agencies where they had a blocking vote. Thus, SUNFED was set aside (though the World Bank took up the idea later through the creation of IDA) and in 1958 the creation of the Special Fund was approved.

In 1966, to face the increasing demand for development assistance, the activities of EPTA and the Special Fund were merged into the United Nations Development Programme (UNDP), the largest multinational assistance effort to provide developing countries with expert services, training and pre-investment assistance in the economic and social fields.

Related documents

United States, Department of State, *Point Four: the Truman "Point Four" Program for World Economic Progress Through Cooperative Technical Assistance* (Washington, D.C., U.S. Government Printing Office, 1949, UNOG Archives document ARR 14/1360, Box 85, Folder II/3/9, Sub Folder "Technical Assistance. Regional Commissions").

United Nations. Economic and Social Council, *Economic Development of Under-Developed Countries*. Resolution 222 (IX), 14 and 15 August 1949, *Official Records of the Economic and Social Council, Ninth Session, Supplement No.1* (E/1553).

United Nations, *General Approach to the Operation of the Programme. Categories of Under-Developed Countries and Possible Criteria for Priorities* (New York, 1950, TAB/R.2).

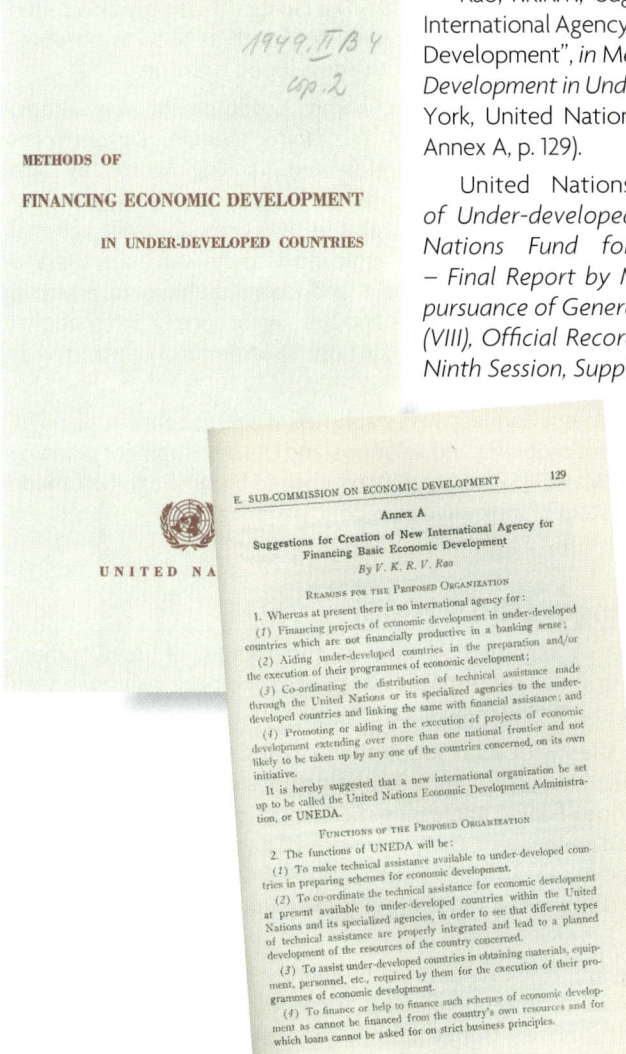

Rao, V.K.R.V., "Suggestions for Creation of New International Agency for Financing Basic Economic Development", in *Methods of Financing Economic Development in Under-developed Countries* (New York, United Nations, 1949, Sales No. E.49.II.B.4, Annex A, p. 129).

United Nations, *Economic Development of Under-developed Countries. Special United Nations Fund for Economic Development – Final Report by Mr R. Scheyven, prepared in pursuance of General Assembly resolution 724 B (VIII), Official Records of the General Assembly, Ninth Session, Supplement No. 19* (A/2728).

Statement by Secretary-General, U Thant, at Opening Meeting of Governing Council of United Nations Development Programme (New York, 10 January 1966, press release SG/SM/427-DEV/6).

Telex message dated 18 December 1965 informing of change in cable prefixes effective 1 January 1966 due to TAB (Technical Assistance Board) and SPUN (Special UN Fund) being consolidated into the United Nations Development Programme (Document from UNOG Archives GX 10/1/146 (36341)).

The evolution of the concept of development

THE 1960s: FIRST DEVELOPMENT DECADE

The resolution on the first United Nations Decade of Development resulted from a proposal made by United States President Kennedy in 1961 to expand and coordinate measures required for national self-sustaining growth and social advancement. Each underdeveloped country was to increase its annual rate of growth of national income to a minimum of 5 per cent by the end of the Decade. The General Assembly also called for the increase of development assistance and capital to "reach as soon as possible" one per cent of the combined national incomes of the developed countries.

The importance of national planning for economic development was almost universally recognized at the time. Chapter II of *The United Nations Development Decade: Proposals for Action*, "The approach to development planning", written by Hans Singer, stated that the purpose of a development plan was to provide a programme of action for the achievement of targets based on available resources, and that national and sectoral objectives were more likely to be achieved if they were defined and translated into action programmes. Economic, social and demographic data essential for formulating development plans were collected, and the significance of international trends was analysed. Country after country was making use of some form of planning as a tool for achieving its national economic goals.

The Committee for Development Planning was established in 1965 to consider planning trends in the world, development problems and solutions, and UN development planning activities. At its first session in May 1966, the Committee, chaired by Jan Tingerben, made a proposal for a worldwide system of indicative economic planning.

Hans W. Singer (1910- 2006)

Sir Hans Singer is regarded as one of the fathers of development economics, working in the interests of poor people and poor countries both as an economist and as a United Nations official.

Singer, who studied with Schumpeter then Keynes, treated economics as a moral science whose "intellectual rigour combines with its potentiality for good". Early in his teaching at the New School, he was addressing the "vicious circles of poverty", the role of the State in economic development, the importance of human capital, and above all, the terms of trade. His name is inextricably linked with Prebisch, who relied heavily on Singer's work for the first documentation of the declining terms of trade of primary commodities.

After working for the Pilgrim Trust Unemployment Enquiry in the United Kingdom, Singer joined the UN Department of Economic and Social Affairs, where he was in charge of developing countries, moving from the study of unemployment and poverty in developed countries to poverty in developing countries.

While at the UN, between 1947 and 1969, Singer held many different positions and was part of major initiatives such as the Special United Nations Fund for Economic

Development (SUNFED), which led to the creation of the soft-loan arm of the World Bank; the UN Development Programme; the United Nations Industrial Development Organization (UNIDO); the African Development Bank, and changing the focus of UNICEF from an emergency fund to an organization concerned with the long-run interests of children. He played a major role in the World Employment Programme launched in 1969 by the ILO – heading the first mission to Kenya – and in the World Food Programme.

Singer always dissented from the popular view that food aid was dangerous because it discouraged domestic production and reinforced Governments' neglect of agriculture. It all depends on how food aid is used. Singer was also always a campaigner for a greater flow of aid to developing countries, and a harsh critic of the activities of the International Monetary Fund and the World Bank.

When he retired from the UN in 1969, Singer joined the Institute of Development Studies (IDS) at Sussex as Professorial Fellow.

Jan Tinbergen (1903-1994)

Dutch economist Jan Tinbergen worked for the Bureau of Statistics and Planning in the Netherlands. He advised developing countries' Governments and international organizations such as the League of Nations, the World Bank, the European Coal and Steel Community, and various UN agencies.

Tinbergen was the first to analyse the business cycle as a complete dynamic model of interrelated variables represented in a quantitative form. His book *Business Cycles in the United States, 1919-1932* (1939), modelling the interplay of different facets of the American economy, provided the raw material for later development of business cycle theory and for creating a new branch of macroeconomics.

He started working with Ragnar Frisch in the 1930s to draw a plan to fight the causes of the Depression and keep unemployment under control, developing economic policy models with multiple targets and instruments. With other economists and statisticians, they also created the science of econometrics, the merging of statistics and economic analysis, which enabled economists to use concrete statistical instruments. In 1969, they won the first Nobel Prize in Economics for their dynamic models for the analysis of economic processes.

In the 1950s, Tinbergen turned to the problems of developing countries, studying methods for long-term development planning. He developed models for the optimal distribution of production and investments throughout an economy, and for educational planning.

In 1966, he became Chairman of the UN Committee on Development Planning. His concern with the distribution of power and income among individuals and nations – the highest priority in research and policymaking — greatly influenced the drafting of a proposal for the UN International Development Strategy for the Second Development Decade. The proposal, however, was accepted only half-heartedly and after a rewriting that omitted the commitment to social justice.

Related documents

Letter dated 27 February 1962 from Walter Hecht, Acting Chief of the Regional Commissions Section, to E.M. Chossudovsky, Economic Commission for Europe, transmitting Hans Singer's first draft of the chapter on development planning for the report on the United Nations Development Decade (UNOG Archives document GX 10/1/129 (30216)).

Letter dated 27 April 1962 from W.R. Malinowski, Secretary of the Economic and Social Council, to Vladimir Velebit, Executive Secretary of the Economic Commission for Europe, transmitting a copy of the final internal draft of the report on the United Nations Development Decade (UNOG Archives document GX 10 10/1/129 (30216)).

United Nations, *The UN Development Decade: Proposals for Action. Report of the Secretary-General* (New York, 1962, Sales No. E.62.II.B.2).

Projections at the International Level *in* Committee for Development Planning. Report on the First Session (2-11 May 1966), *Official Records of the Economic and Social Council, Forty-first Session, Supplement No. 14* (E/4207/Rev.1, p.5).

Journal of Development Planning, No.1 (November 1969). (New York, Sales No. E.69.II.B.24).

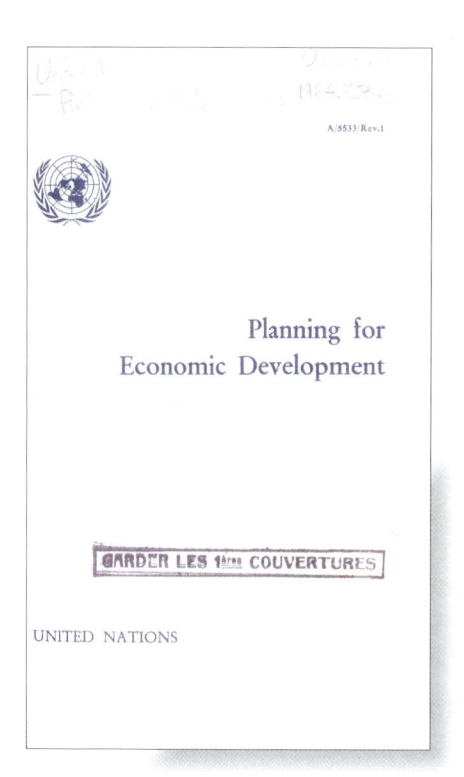

United Nations, *Planning for Economic Development: Report of the Secretary-General Transmitting the Study of a Group of Experts* (New York, Sales No. E.64.II.B.3).

The rights-based approach

Civil and political rights strongly supported by Western powers have made rapid progress, whereas economic, social, and cultural rights, a demand of the South, have been lagging.

As an example of social rights, the right to food has long existed, but once it is adopted, a right has to be interpreted and given a legal basis so that people can make use of it. The Committee on Economic, Social and Cultural Rights made its General Comment No. 12 on the right to adequate food in 1999. This general comment spells out that States cannot deprive people of their right to adequate food, that this right has to be protected, and that policies to make food available in quantity and quality, accessible and affordable have to be undertaken.

By enabling people to make use of the law in upholding their rights, this rights-based approach to basic needs promotes the progress of democracy. It also defines the obligations of States to give priority to problems for which a right exists and to undertake policies so that no one is deprived of this right.

Related documents

Universal Declaration of Human Rights (New York, 1998, DPI/876/Rev.2).

Letter dated 22 November 1950 from Gunnar Myrdal, Executive-Secretary of the United Nations Economic Commission for Europe, to Gordon Fraser, Chief of Radio Diffusion, UNESCO, transmitting "The economic implications of the Universal Declaration on Human Rights", a radio script by Gunnar Myrdal for the UNESCO broadcast on the Universal Declaration of Human Rights (UNOG Archives document ARR 14/1360, Box 22, Folder "Radio").

United Nations, General Assembly, *International Covenant on Economic, Social and Cultural Rights, International Covenant on Civil and Political Rights and Optional Protocol to the International Covenant on Civil and Political Rights.* Resolution 2200(XXI), 16 December 1966, *Official Records of the General Assembly, Twenty-first Session, Supplement No. 16* (A/6316).

Letter dated 17 July 1972 from Robert J. Crooks, Officer-in-Charge of the Department of Economic and Social Affairs, to Janez Stanovnik, Executive Secretary of the Economic Commission for Europe, requesting each regional economic commission to include in its agenda the consideration of "The question of the realization of the economic, social and cultural rights contained in the Universal Declaration of Human Rights, taking into account special problems relating to human rights in developing countries", according to ECOSOC resolution 1689(LII) (UNOG Archives document GX 10/1/129/30216).

United Nations, General Assembly, *Charter of Economic Rights and Duties of States.* Resolution 3281 (XXIX), 12 December 1974, *Official Records of the General Assembly, Twenty-ninth Session, Supplement No. 31* (A/9631).

United Nations, General Assembly, *Declaration on the Right to Development.* Resolution 41/128, 4 December 1986, *Official Records of the General Assembly, Forty-first Session, Supplement No. 53* (A/41/53).

United Nations, *The Committee on Economic, Social and Cultural Rights* (Geneva, 1996, Human Rights Fact Sheet No. 16 (Rev.1)).

The 1970s: Basic needs and social approach to development

In the early years, it was assumed that poverty and employment problems in developing countries would be rapidly overcome by accelerating economic growth. This was the central thesis of the First Development Decade, with United Nations system efforts geared to raising productivity and removing the obstacles to growth in developing countries. The conventional wisdom, however, that higher levels of employment and improved living standards for all would automatically result from growth was questioned in the mid-1960s. Rapid growth of aggregate output did not by itself reduce poverty and inequality and create sufficient employment.

In 1969, the International Labor Organization (ILO) launched the World Employment Programme (WEP) with a new employment-oriented approach to development, focusing on the creation of more productive and remunerative jobs. The WEP promoted analyses of the interrelationships between employment and other aspects of economic and social development, such as income distribution, technologies, labor-intensive public works, population, education, international trade and migration, poverty, multinational enterprises, and applying these findings to development policies. Social objectives – a more equitable distribution of income and wealth, increases in employment, improved nutrition and housing - were included in the International Development Strategy for the Second UN Development Decade.

The 1975 World Employment Conference called for the adoption of a basic-needs approach to development, aiming at a specific minimum standard of living before the end of the century by increasing the volume and productivity of employment. The satisfaction of basic needs – the minimum standard of living a society should set for the poorest groups of its people - implies meeting the minimum requirements for personal consumption of goods and services: food, shelter, clothing; access to essential services, such as safe drinking water, sanitation, transport, health and education; and an adequate remuneration for each working person, which are social, economic and cultural rights. The Conference underlined that redistributive measures and the redirection of investment necessary for more and better employment should be combined with more equitable access to public services to reduce underemployment, inequality and poverty.

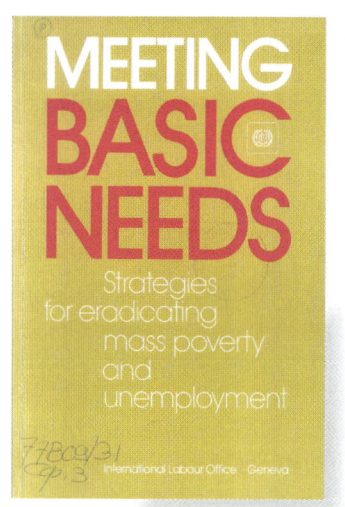

Related documents

ILO, The World Employment Programme: Report of the Director-General to the International Labour Conference (Geneva, 1969).

ILO, Employment, Growth and Basic Needs: A One-World Problem (Geneva, 1976).

ILO, Meeting Basic Needs: Strategies for Eradicating Mass Poverty and Unemployment (Geneva, 1976).

The 1980s: The "lost decade" for development

The 1980s were marked by the debt crisis and a global trend in favour of economic liberalization that had major impact on development policies pursued by developing countries and on their capacity to influence the shaping of international economic policies.

From the mid-1970s, oil-importing developing countries faced the rise in oil prices, the decline or slowdown in foreign demand for their exports and a deterioration of their terms of trade with the industrial countries. Debt service rose, and the debt structure changed, with a reduced share of concessional and official debt and an increased proportion of private loans.

To deal with the debt problem, the Bretton Woods institutions and major industrial countries advocated stabilization and structural adjustment policies. In return for debt rescheduling, indebted countries had to pursue policies to balance budgets and correct prices through reduced public spending, increased revenue, devaluation, trade and financial liberalization, deregulation of domestic markets and privatization. With growing neo-liberal influence, the objectives of poverty reduction and growth were to be achieved by relying on market forces and private enterprise, and restricting the role of the State to a minimum.

Employment and basic-needs strategies and the NIEO promoted by the UN and incorporated in the Third Development Decade Strategy were swept off the global and national agendas. The balance of political forces shifted from weakened popular institutions, impoverished working and middle classes, to foreign investors and creditors and domestic groups linked to the international economy. The power of the State declined and foreign creditors influenced decision-making on social and economic policies.

UNCTAD was the first organization to underline that the debt problem would not be solved without debt cancellations. In the face of this new situation, the UN (mainly UNICEF, ECA and UNRISD) provided evidence of the negative impact of stabilization and adjustment policies on growth, income distribution, poverty, child welfare, health. Alternative approaches were proposed that advocated the need for well targeted policies of the State for stimulating economic growth, encouraging structural reforms of the economy, and improving health and education. Sceptical that price liberalization would promote adjustment and growth, they underlined the structural roots of poverty.

Related documents

"Third Development Decade: The Slowdown"", *UN Chronicle Perspective* (New York, 1984, DPI/828).

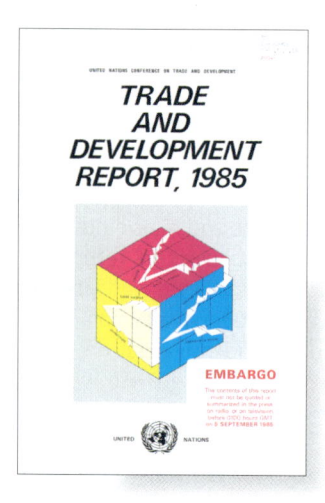

"Debt, Development and the World Economy", in *Trade and Development Report, 1985* (Geneva, 1985, Sales No. E.85.II.D.16, Part II, pp. 62-148).

United Nations, General Assembly, *Strengthened International Economic Cooperation Aimed at Resolving External Debt Problems of Developing Countries.* Resolution 41/202, 8 December 1986, *Official Records of the General Assembly, Forty-first Session, Supplement No. 53* (A/41/53).

Cornia, Giovanni Andrea, Jolly, Richard, Stewart, Frances (eds.), *Adjustment With a Human Face,* a Study by UNICEF (Oxford, England, Clarendon Press, 1987-1988, 2 vols.).

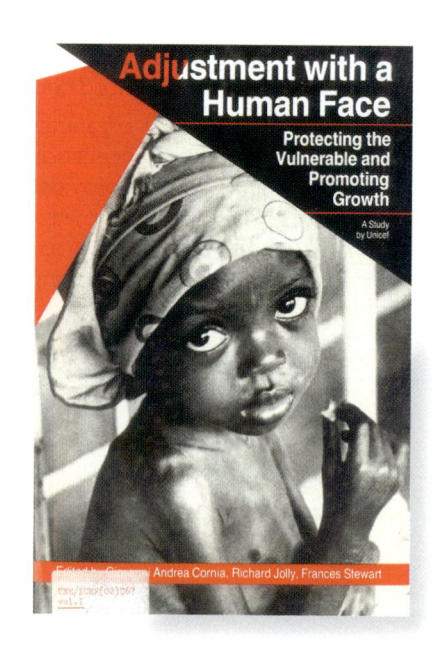

The transition process and the shock therapy

At the fall of the Berlin Wall, the United Nations Economic Commission for Europe (UN-ECE) was the best-informed UN entity on the actual situation of the economies of the European Communist bloc. It doubted that shock therapy would be best adapted to assure the transition of these centrally planned economies to market economies. UN-ECE considered that transition would be a long process and socially costly. It considered that a market economy could not work properly without strong institutions and that building these institutions would take time. The *2000 World Bank report* finally insisted on the importance of institutions in economic transition and development, as had the 1990 *Economic Survey of Europe*.

In economics, shock therapy refers to the sudden release of price and currency controls, withdrawal of State subsidies, immediate trade liberalization, and privatization. According to Sachs, its foremost proponent, shock therapy traces its roots from the economic liberalization programme undertaken by post-war West Germany in the late 1940s. During 1947 and 1948, price controls and government support were withdrawn over a very short period - this had the effect of kick-starting the German economy. Germany had previously had a highly authoritarian and economic interventionist Government and seemingly overnight threw off these restrictions and became a developed market economy. These free-market reforms became the basis of the neo-liberal economic theory.

As a result, during the early 1990s, the Bretton Woods institutions and the OECD, as well as numerous self-declared "experts", recommended to countries of Eastern Europe and those issued from the dismantlement of the Soviet Union to release all price controls, subsidies, sell off State assets and float their currencies in order to shake off the economic lethargy of the Communist era. The shocks took the form of sudden radical changes to the structure and incentives within economies.

The effects were primarily negative with unemployment rates jumping above 20 per cent, poverty spreading, and crime increasing. Income distribution worsened. Then the economies of Central Europe recovered more rapidly for one main reason: the perspective of joining the European Union gave a direction to the reforms that were maintained despite many political changes of majorities resulting from democratic elections. Reforms in the Russian Federation and part of Southern Europe were not sustained and changed direction.

Related documents

"The Death of the Old Order. As Communist Rule Crumbles, Is a New Germany Rising?", *U.S. News & World Report* 107: 20-24, 20 November 1989, No. 20.

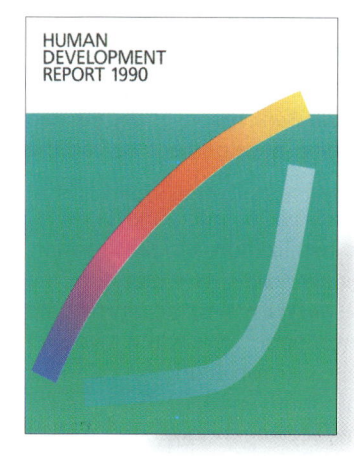

"Human Development Indicators", *in Human Development Report 1990,* published for the United Nations Development Programme (New York; Oxford, England, Oxford University Press, 1990, pp. 123-180).

United Nations Economic Commission for Europe, *Economic Survey of Europe in 1990-1991* (New York, 1991, Sales No. E.91.II.E.1).

Copenhagen Declaration on Social Development *in The Copenhagen Declaration and Programme of Action : World Summit for Social Development* [6-12 March 1995] (New York, 1995, DPI/1707, pp. 1-35).

Coleman, Stephen (ed.), *The E-Connected World: Risks and Opportunities* (Montreal; Kingston, Canada, McGill-Queen's University Press, 2003).

Mahbub Ul Haq (1934-1998) initiated the Human Development Report and promoted the idea of an Economic Security Council.

Amartya Sen (1993), 1998 Nobel Laureate in Economics, worked on the formulation of the Human Development Report

The 1990s: globalization

The pace of globalization generated hopes and illusions. The assumption, considered as a dogma, was that well-functioning markets and privatization would suffice to take advantage of the globalization of commercial and financial flows and not only create wealth, but also resolve problems of human welfare. The social issues were not addressed per se and most States took measure to let market forces operate more freely and privatized public enterprises and services. Some countries were able to take advantage of the new opportunities at the price of growing internal inequality. But for most of the countries, globalization failed to deliver on its promise of rapid growth and poverty reduction. New social tensions and even civil strife arose with declining living standard for millions of people.

Considered as obstacles to progress, social and economic instruments were banned and eventually institutions eroded or dismantled. Power was transferred to institutions ignoring the social implications of their actions, while passing responsibility for absorbing the damage to non-governmental agencies or to weakened communities. The imperatives of global forces undermined communities and families.

The UN drew attention to the negative impact of globalization, proposed policies to limit the social damages, but also suggested measures to take advantage of the opportunities created by commercial and financial liberalization. Efforts were made to rein in the extremes of current policy prescriptions, to evolve more balanced approaches that emphasized a stronger government role and policies to tackle unemployment and poverty. There was a strong upsurge of interest in human rights and good governance. The UN also convened a series of international conferences on some of the most critical social and economic problems. These conferences contributed to building a blueprint for goals, strategies, and policies for global social and economic development. Though the Bretton Woods institutions adopted many of the ideas generated by the UN system, their core macroeconomic approach remained unaltered.

In 2000, on the occasion of UNCTAD X, the UN Regional Commissions did an interesting statistical exercise to measure the reality of globalization. They considered the evolution of intraregional trade in the global trade of each UN region. Contrary to what globalization suggested, the share of intraregional trade increased while interregional trade decreased for the four more developed regions: North America, Europe, Asia, and Latin America. The trend is the same for foreign direct investments. The world witnessed more regionalization than globalization. This underlined the importance of regional institutions in the management of the global economy.

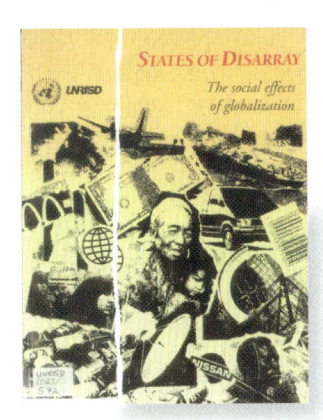

Related documents

UN Research Institute for Social Development, *States of Disarray: the Social Effects of Globalization: an UNRISD Report for the World Summit for Social Development*. (Geneva, 1995).

2000: Millennium Development Goals

In the UN Millennium Declaration, heads of State and Government asserted their responsibility for and attachment to fundamental values in international relations and national governance, and committed themselves to achieve a number of objectives in order to improve the lot of the poorest by 2015 and 2020.

In parallel, calls to make the world safer, fair, ethical, inclusive and prosperous for the majority, not just for a few, within and between countries are being increasingly voiced, implying the need to rethink globalization and governance on the basis of social and environmental priorities. The dominant perspective on globalization must shift from a narrow preoccupation with markets to a broader preoccupation with people, empowering local communities, making governments accountable, and establishing fair global rules and pro-people international institutions.

This evolution was inspired by the many UN studies and reports that were prepared for the global conferences of the 1990s and the Conference on the Least Developed Countries and, also, the yearly *Human Development Report* and the flagship publications of UNCTAD, *The Trade and Development Report*, and of the Regional Commissions, *The Economic Surveys*.

Related documents

IMF, OECD, UN, *A Better World For All: Progress Towards the International Development Goals* (Washington, D.C. ; Paris ; New York, 2000).

Sachs, J.D., "Investing in Development: a Practical Plan to Achieve the Millennium Development Goals". Full-text available online at:
http://www.unmillenniumproject.org/reports/fullreport.htm .

ILO. World Commission on the Social Dimension of Globalization. *A Fair Globalization: Creating Opportunities for All* (Geneva, 2004).

Narayan, Deepa [et al.] *Voices of the Poor: Can Anyone Hear Us?* (Oxford, England; New York, Oxford University Press for the World Bank, 2000).

Annan, Kofi. *We the Peoples: the Role of the United Nations in the 21st Century* (New York, 2000, Sales No. E.00.I.16).

United Nations, *United Nations Millennium Declaration: Millennium Summit, New York, 6-8 September 2000* (New York, 2000, DPI/2163).

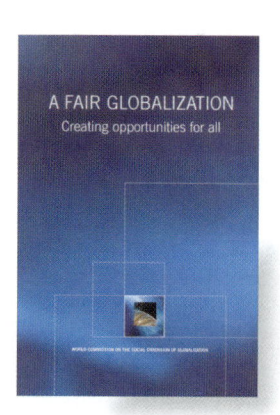

United Nations Conference on Trade and Development, *The Least Developed Countries Report 2002: Escaping the Poverty Trap* (New York and Geneva, 2002, Sales No. E.02.II.D.13).

Tallaway, Mervat, "Mounting Challenges to Reach the MDG Goal of Poverty Reduction: a Regional Perspective", *Regional Commissions Development Update*, No. 16, July 2004, p.1.

Ideas from the UN regional commissions

Economic Commission for Europe

The UN Economic Commission for Europe (UN-ECE) was created in 1947 and took over the functions of the "E-Organizations" created in 1945 to organize the supply and equitable distribution of basic materials, especially coal, and remove the bottlenecks in the transport system.

Under Gunnar Myrdal's leadership, the ECE sought a middle way between the neo-classical approach and the Marxist alternative, which continental Western Europe translated into the so called "social market economy" of the 1950s and 1960s. The Secretariat believed in indicative planning and State intervention to correct market failure and guide economic development. Gunnar Myrdal established, under the sole authority of the Executive Secretary, the publication of an independent annual report not negotiated by Member States: *The Economic Survey of Europe*. It proved to be a valuable source of information on Eastern European countries during the Cold War, not only for Western Europe, but for those countries themselves. *The Survey*, still published today, permits comparisons between all the European countries and presents independent views on major European economic problems.

ECE developed studies on a variety of issues, such as the factor of growth, the reform of planning, the oil price discrepancy between producers and consumers, etc. The most famous addressed the steel overproduction capacities in Europe, which led to the Coal and Steel Agreement that is at the origin of the European Community and then the European Union. In 1990, ECE questioned the prevailing shock therapy theories and underlined the importance of institutions.

For more than 50 years, the ECE sustained the idea of an undivided Europe. By addressing issues of common interest to both East and West, it developed an important set of conventions and norms on transport, environment and energy, each of which served to bridge the two parts during the Cold War and later facilitated the integration of Central Europe into the European Union. Today the normative work of ECE embraces all of Europe and links with the United States and Canada.

Two Nobel Prizes at the Economic Commission for Europe: Gunnar Myrdal (1898-1987) and Nicholas Kaldor (1908-1986)

Gunnar Myrdal (1898-1987) was a Swedish economist, sociologist and politician – twice senator in Sweden's Parliament, Minister of Trade and Commerce, and first Executive-Secretary of the UN Economic Commission for Europe (1947-1957). Myrdal is regarded as a major theorist in international relations and development economics.

In 1974, Gunnar Myrdal and Friedrich Hayek were awarded the Nobel Prize in Economics for "their pioneering work in the theory of money and economic fluctuations and for their analysis of the interdependence of economic, social, and institutional phenomena".

Among Myrdal's writings, *An American Dilemma: The Negro Problem and Modern Democracy* (1944), a staunch criticism of the "separate but equal doctrine", played a role in the outlawing of racial segregation in public schools in the United States. *The Political Element in the Development of Economic Theory* (1930) discussed the foundations of political economy and the development of economics. *Asian Drama: An Inquiry into the Poverty of Nations* (1968), a 10-year study of the economic concerns and vested interests of southern Asia that accounted for its social conditions, emphasized the importance of human capital and a wider distribution of agricultural land for economic development in this region.

A British economist born in Budapest, **Nicholas Kaldor** was Professor of Economics at the London School of Economics and later at Cambridge. He was Economic Advisor to the Labour Party and Fiscal Advisor to the Treasury and to several overseas Governments. He held a variety of senior appointments within the UN and served on various experts committees. In 1947, he directed the Research and Planning Division of the UN Economic Commission for Europe.

Kaldor, an outspoken critic of monetarist policy, is best known for forging, together with Joan Robinson, the core of the Cambridge School and its offshoots – the Neo-Ricardian and post-Keynesian schools. He applied his skills to development policy. Among his policy advice to developing countries was the "Expenditure Tax" scheme (1955) as opposed to income tax policy, which was implemented in India and Sri Lanka, and the Bancor "Commodity Reserve Currency" scheme (1964) developed with Jan Tinbergen, which is yet to be taken up.

Related documents

Mende, T., "The Marshall Plan and Europe: the need for Old World initiative in saving is pointed up by activities of the European Economic Commission", *New York Herald Tribune*, 15 June 1947.

Hamilton, Thomas J., "Role for UN seen in Marshall Plan – Use of Economic Commission would bolster prestige, it is argued by some", *New York Times*, 29 June 1947.

"UN group makes another bid for role in implementing Marshall Aid Program", Special to the New York Times, *New York Times*, 29 June 1947.

United Nations Economic Commission for Europe, *Survey of the Economic Situation and Prospects of Europe* (Geneva, 1948, Sales No. E.48.II.E.1).

Letter dated 11 October 1948 from Nicholas Kaldor, Director of the Research and Planning Division of the Economic Commission for Europe, to Paul A. Baran, Federal Reserve Bank of New York, providing explanation about discrepancies between Table 25 of the Survey and Table 6 of the East-West Trade Report (UNOG Archives document GX/18/8/1/4/2907).

United Nations Economic Commission for Europe, *The Challenge of European Reconstruction Based on a Survey of the Economic Situation and Prospects of Europe*, annotated draft paper of the ECE Secretariat (July 1948, UNOG Archives document ARR 14/1360, Box 67, Folder I/3/1, Sub Folder "History").

Dabernat, René, « Un haut fonctionnaire des Nations Unies à Moscou – Une « médiation commerciale » est tentée entre l'Est et l'Ouest : M. Myrdal expose au « Monde » le sens de sa mission », *Le Monde*, 27 avril 1950.

United Nations Economic Commission for Europe, *The Financing of European Exports to the Under-Developed Countries*, annotated draft paper of the ECE Secretariat (document from UNOG Archives ARR 14/1360, Box 1, Folder «Finance» Aug 1950 Files No. 2).

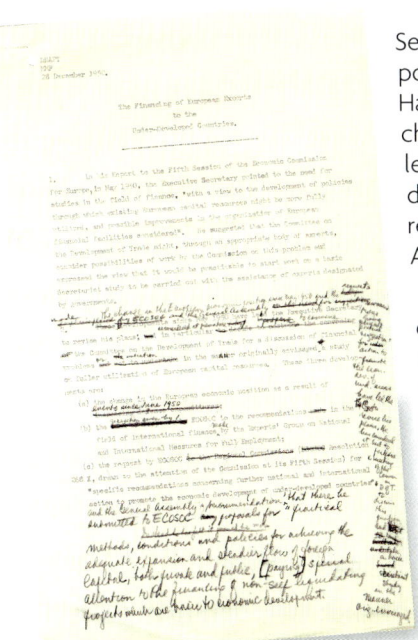

Câble du 19 décembre 1951 de Gunnar Myrdal, Secrétaire Exécutif de la Commission économique pour l'Europe (CEE), à Jean Monnet, Président de la Haute Autorité de la Communauté européenne du charbon et de l'acier (CECA), proposant de comparer les activités de la CECA et celles de la CEE dans les domaines du charbon, acier, transport, habitat et recherche économique (UNOG Archives document ARR 14/1360, Box 67, Folder I/3/3).

Lettre du 25 novembre 1952 de F. Vinck, Directeur de la Division du Marché des Services, Haute Autorité de la Communauté européenne du charbon et de l'acier (CECA), à Gunnar Myrdal, Secrétaire exécutif de la CEE, l'informant que, suite à sa nomination à la CECA, il ne pourra plus assumer la présidence du Comité du charbon de la CEE (UNOG Archives document ARR 14/1360, Box 67, Folder I/3/3).

United Nations Economic Commission for Europe, *ECE: the First Ten Years 1947-1957*. (Geneva, 1957, E/ECE/291).

Economic and Social Commission for Asia and the Pacific (former ECAFE, Economic Commission for Asia and the Far East)

In 1947, ECAFE was the only economic organization for the region. Its creation responded to the need for economic reconstruction in war-devastated countries. But with only three sovereign States members of the UN (China, India and the Philippines), the Commission had difficulties expressing the region's demands. There was the hope, however, that ECAFE would play a key role in channelling assistance from developed countries to the Asian region. The Colombo Plan (1951), adopted by seven independent Asian countries and later extended to other former British colonies, pointed in the same direction as the Marshall Plan for Europe, and made estimates of the capital and technical assistance needs of the Asian region.

In the early years, membership and the composition of the Commission was an issue. Access by some non-self-governing territories to associate membership (without voting rights) resulted in tense situations. For ECAFE to be representative of Asian countries' interests, its regional members had to have a determining influence in the decision-making process, while Western powers' influence in the region opposed the purpose of ECAFE as an instrument of Asian aspirations.

In 1951, the Executive Secretary, Dr. P.S. Lokanathan, submitted a memorandum, *Future of the Commission,* to the ECAFE session in Lahore, proposing that non-regional members should exercise restraint in voting on matters predominantly concerning the region. This led in 1960 to the Lahore Declaration according to which only countries in the region were to decide on substantive issues while non-regional members could express their opinions but refrain from voting.

Until the mid-1970s, ECAFE was the major regional organization where economic issues were discussed. Then, the Asian Development Bank, established by ECAFE in the 1960s, emerged as a rival for regional economic cooperation and development, with strong analytical capacities and resources to back its prescriptions. Countries of the region also shifted attention to their own subregional organizations. ECAFE (renamed in 1974 the Economic and Social Commission for Asia and the Pacific) became a forum for developing common regional positions on social and environmental aspects of development.

Related documents

Asian Relations; being Report of the Proceedings and Documentation of the First Asian Relations Conference, New Delhi, March-April, 1947 (New Delhi, Asian Relations Organization, 1948).

United Nations Economic Commission for Asia and the Far East, *Economic Survey of Asia and the Far East, 1947* (Shanghai, 1948).

Round-up of the First Session of ECAFE, Omnipress 61 from Shanghai (UNOG Archives document ARR 14/1360, M.134/47, Box 83, Folder II/3/3).

Lokanathan, P.S., "ECAFE, the Economic Parliament of Asia", *The Indian Year Book of International Affairs* (Madras, India) 2:3-26, 1953.

«La Chine décide de participer à la Conférence asiatico-africaine; Taïwan, la plus grande île de Chine; Le Nord-Est, notre base industrielle», *Bulletin d'information de la Légation de la République Populaire de Chine* (Berne, 10 mars 1955, UNOG Archives document GX/10/1/11/1638).

«Final Communiqué of the Asian-African Conference Held at Bandung from 18th to 24th April 1955», *Asian-African Conference Bulletin*, No. 9, 24 April 1955, pp. 2-3.

«Some Groups of Delegates About Their Work», *Asian-African Conference Bulletin*, No. 7, 22 April 1955, pp. 8-9.

The Colombo Plan: Cooperative Economic Development in South and Southeast Asia. (Colombo, Colombo Plan Information Unit, Bureau for Technical Cooperation, 1955).

United Nations Economic Commission for Asia and the Far East, *Future of the Commission: Note by the Executive Secretary* (Bangkok, 1951, E/CN.11/278).

Letter dated 9 April 1951 from P.S. Lokanathan, Executive Secretary of the Economic Commission for Asia and the Far East, to Gunnar Myrdal, Executive Secretary of the Economic Commission for Europe, requesting information on European countries in view of increasing trade exchanges in iron and steel and iron and steel products between the ECAFE and ECE regions (UNOG Archives document ARR 14/1360, Box 83, Folder II/3/3).

Economic Commission for Latin America and the Caribbean (former ECLA, Economic Commission for Latin America)

Under the leadership of Raúl Prebisch, ECLA had a great impact on development thinking in its pioneering years. The core of ECLA's original analysis and proposals for the region are condensed in Prebisch's *The Economic Development of Latin America and Its Principle Problems* (1949) and in the Commission's *Economic Survey of 1948*. These documents consider the secular deterioration in the terms of trade of Latin American economies; the asymmetrical relations between the developed countries of the centre and the developing countries of the periphery, and the perverse structural effects these asymmetrical relations have on domestic patterns of production, consumption, and savings. Proposals stressed the need to industrialize with protection against imports of manufactured goods, the importance of technological progress, and the role of the state in development. The subsequent *structuralist* theories on the structural obstacles to development were built on these seminal ideas.

The military regimes that later took over in numerous Latin American countries were hostile to the Commission. Influenced by events in its host country, the now ECLAC secretariat was adversely affected by the advent of the Pinochet regime in the 1970s. ECLAC's original conceptual framework was increasingly discredited, especially the sustainability of industrialization based on import substitution.

In the 1980s, the Commission abandoned holistic frameworks and turned its attention to the crisis and the short term, addressing debt overhang and hyperinflation, and calling for debt alleviation. In the 1990s, the Commission began promoting open regionalism, and made important studies showing the interactions between political, economic and social factors.

Raúl Prebisch (1901-1986)

Argentinean, international and development economist, Raúl Prebisch was a professor of Economic Policy at the National University of Buenos Aires, and assumed several important positions in the Argentine public sector (Director of Department of Statistics, the National Bank, Under-Secretary for Finance).

In 1948, Prebisch joined the United Nations Economic Commission for Latin America, and from 1950 to 1963 was the Executive Secretary of the Commission. He then served as Secretary-General to the United Nations Conference on Trade and Development (UNCTAD), before returning to Argentina to work with the democratic Government elected in 1983.

Prebisch's views on international trade and development had a significant impact on ideas and policy making not only in Latin America and the Caribbean but also throughout the developing world, and contributed to the United Nations' effort towards a fairer international economic order.

From an analysis of export and import price indices for the 1876-1947 period, Prebisch concluded that the gains of international trade and specialization had not been equitably distributed, and that the industrialized countries had reaped far greater benefits than the less developed regions. As a result, he argued that Latin America should embark upon its own process of industrialization through protection, exchange controls and planning in order to decrease its dependency on imports. Industrialization thus became the primary means of growth for most Latin American nations during the post- World War II period.

Prebisch's writings include: *Towards a Dynamic Development Policy for Latin America* (1963); *The Crisis of Argentine Development*; and *The Economic Development of Latin America and Its Principal Problems* (1950). This last, known as «El Manifiesto», thrust him into the position of ECLA Executive Secretary.

Related documents

United Nations, *Economic Survey of Latin America, 1948; prepared by the Secretariat of the Economic Commission for Latin America* (Lake Success, New York, 1949, Sales No. E.49.II.G.1).

First draft of part II of ECLA's economic survey of Latin America (note in pencil on cover: "Latin America and the world economy")(Division of Economic Stability and Development, Latin American Unit, 28 March 1949, UNOG Archives document GX 20/3 (6803)).

United Nations Economic Commission for Latin America, *The Economic Development of Latin America and Its Principal Problems* (Lake Success, New York, 1950, Sales No. E.50.II.G.2).

Letter dated 16 February 1952 from Raúl Prebisch, Executive-Secretary of the Economic Commission for Latin America to Gunnar Myrdal, Executive-Secretary of the Economic Commission for Europe, concerning the possibilities of entering into practical action for expanding trade between Latin America and Europe (UNOG Archives document GX 20/2/4785).

« M. Raul Prebish *[sic]* critique les discriminations tarifaires accordées par le Marché commun à certains pays en voie de développement », *Le Monde*, 26 août 1965.

United Nations, *Towards a Dynamic Development Policy for Latin America* (New York, 1963, Sales No. E.64.II.G.4).

Cardoso, Fernando Henrique, Faletto, Enzo. *Dependencia y desarrollo en América Latina: ensayo de interpretación sociológica*, Decimaoctava edición. Mexico, D.F, Siglo Veintiuno, 1983.

Sunkel, Osvaldo, *La dimensión ambiental en los estilos de desarrollo de América Latina,* Santiago de Chile, CEPAL, PNUMA, 1981 (Sales no.81.II.G.66).

Furtado, Celso. *La fantaisie organisée: le développement est-il encore possible?*, Paris, Publisud, 1991.

Economic Commission for Africa

The Economic Commission for Africa (ECA) was established in 1958 with 10 independent African countries. Its inaugural session was the first major gathering of Africans to discuss African problems. Members wished to use the Commission to promote decolonization and pan-Africanism. Full political liberation was regarded as a precondition for achieving this. The Organization of African Unity (OAU), created in 1963, took over the struggle for decolonization.

The failure to launch a process of development despite adherence to orthodox development models stimulated a critical analysis of their appropriateness in the African situation and the search for an African development paradigm. The 1976 *"Revised Framework of Principles for the Implementation of the New International Economic Order in Africa"* exposed the inadequacy of existent theories for transforming the economy of the continent, questioning trade and foreign investments as engines of growth. The "Framework" identified means to bring about strategic changes, and proposed increased self-reliance, and internal and autonomous processes of growth and diversification. Self-reliance – freeing national economies from excessive external dependence - was to be the basis of new national economic strategies. And a new African regional economic order was to achieve collective self-reliance and intra-African economic integration. Economic policies and strategies, however, were not changed and most countries became more and more dependent on a few agricultural or mineral commodities and on foreign aid.

In the 1980s, Africa's GDP per capita, food self-sufficiency, industrial output and share of world trade declined, exacerbated by the second oil shock, a world depression, the debt crisis, droughts and widespread violence. ECA soon pointed to the perils of pursuing structural adjustment programs (SAPs) in Africa as they promoted adjustment to a system perpetuating a mono-cultural and excessively dependent economy. Any programme for Africa's recovery should be based on social and human priorities. Education, health, welfare and all related social sectors were indispensable components of national policy and regional collaboration. In 1989, the *African Alternative Framework to SAPs* (AAF-SAP) addressed necessary changes in production, income level and distribution, spending for basic needs, and institutions. Successive programmes and initiatives for Africa have included commitments from both Africa, for policy reforms, and the international community, for assistance and debt relief. But, they have all suffered the same fate: failure of the international community to fulfil their obligations and lack of breakthrough in debt relief and cancellation; and failure of the African Governments in designing and conducting appropriate reforms.

In the second half of the 1990s, ECA ceased to advocate radical changes in economic policy as those adopted in the previous decade and never implemented. It initiated a programme of sensitization of Governments regarding key structural issues like regionalization, communication or HIV/Aids. It initiated also dialogues between finance ministers of Africa and ministers for cooperation from donor countries. It gave full support to the New Partnership for Africa's Development (NEPAD), a political initiative of African Heads of State for regional peace, reforms designed by the African themselves, and mutual support.

Related documents

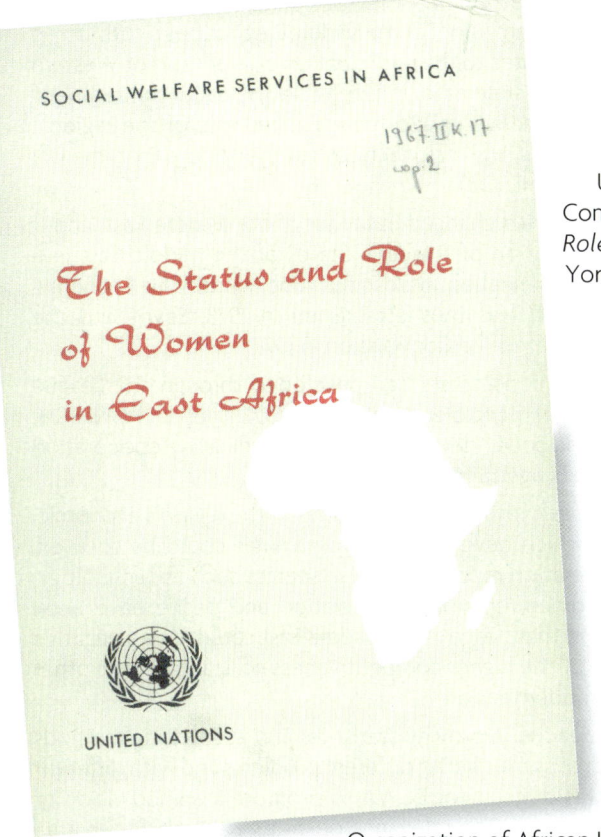

United Nations Economic Commission for Africa, *The Status and Role of Women in East Africa* (New York, 1967, Sales No. E.67.II.K.17).

Organization of African Unity, *Lagos Plan of Action for the Economic Development of Africa 1980-2000* (Geneva, International Institute for Labour Studies, 1981).

United Nations, General Assembly, *United Nations Programme of Action for African Economic Recovery and Development 1986-1990*. Resolution S-13/2, 1 June 1986, *Official Records of the General Assembly, Thirteenth Special Session, Supplement No. 2* (A/S-13/16).

United Nations Economic Commission for Africa, *The Khartoum Declaration: Towards a Human-Focused Approach to Socio-Economic Recovery and Development in Africa*. Resolution 631 (XXIII), 15 April 1988, *Official Records of the Economic and Social Council, 1988, Supplement No. 13* (E/1988/37-E/ECA/CM.14/42).

United Nations Economic Commission for Africa, *African Alternative Framework to Strutural [sic] Adjustment Programmes for Socio-Economic Recovery and Transformation (AAF-SAP)* (Addis Ababa, 1989, E/ECA/CM.15/6/Rev.3-A/44/315 Annex).

Economic and Social Commission for Western Asia (former UN Economic and Social Office in Beirut)

The establishment of an economic commission for the Middle East had been considered since 1947, but the opposition of Arab States to the participation of Israel and of Western countries to any discrimination led to a stalemate. In the 1960s, the decentralization of UN social and economic development activities and the enhanced role of the regional commissions led to the endorsement of a UN regional body for the Middle East, the UN Economic and Social Office in Beirut (UNESOB).

In the 1970s, the balance of power had changed in favour of the Middle East, and it was argued that the lack of representation of the Arab States of the Middle East in a regional commission constituted discrimination against the Arab world. The Economic Commission for Western Asia (ECWA) was thus established in 1973. Egypt and the Palestinian Liberation Organization entered the Commission in 1977.

Awareness of the region's economic interests had developed through the League of Arab States, the Organization of Arab Petroleum Exporting Countries and UNESOB. ECWA was to promote economic and social development by coordinating cooperation among the countries of the region, UN agencies and regional bodies.

ECWA has provided member States with surveys and studies of the region's economic, social and technical problems on which development programmes could be focused, policy suggestions made, and cooperation recommended in sectors such as technology, industry and trade. Population, women, economic integration and peace have been critical issues. Several studies showed that peace in the Middle East could have a negative impact on local industries because of the higher competitiveness of Israel. On the other hand, though, this could promote modernization.

The Commission also took the lead in improving statistical and accounting methods for international comparisons. With countries facing different problems and with different development needs, however, it was difficult for ECWA to promote a unified vision of regional development and gain legitimacy. The relevance of the UN agenda for an area boosted by oil revenues was questioned, and ideas put forward by ECWA often collided with those of the oil-producing countries.

More generally, the Commission has been the regional arm of the UN, providing input to ECOSOC and the General Assembly and supporting member countries in complying with the norms and policies adopted by these two bodies.

Related documents

United Nations, General Assembly, *Decentralization of the Economic and Social Activities of the United Nations and Strengthening of the Regional Economic Commissions and the United Nations Office in Beirut*. Resolution 1941 (XVIII), 11 December 1963, *Official Records of the General Assembly, Eighteenth Session, Supplement No. 15* (A/5515).

United Nations Economic and Social Office in Beirut, *Studies on Selected Development Problems in Various Countries in the Middle East, 1970* (New York, 1970, Sales No. E.70.II.C.1).

United Nations, Economic and Social Council, *Establishment of an Economic Commission for Western Asia*. Resolution 1818 (LV), 9 August 1973, *Official Records of the Economic and Social Council, Fifty-fifth Session, Supplement No.1* (E/5400).

United Nations Economic Commission for Western Asia, *Report on the First Session (3-8 June 1974). Official Records of the Economic and Social Council, Fifty-seventh Session, Supplement No.10* (E/5539-E/ECWA/9).

United Nations Economic and Social Commission for Western Asia, *Survey of Economic and Social Developments in the ESCWA Region, 1998-1999. Part II, Economic Development in the ESCWA Region during the Last 25 Years* (New York, 1999, E/ESCWA/ED/1999/5/Add.1).

Les problèmes de la recherche démographique dans les pays desservis par l'UNESOB: document rédigé par le Bureau des affaires économiques et sociales de l'ONU à Beyrouth *(UNESOB)*. (Beyrouth, 1971, E/CN.9/AC.13/R.32, en français seulement).

Population Bulletin of the United Nations Economic Commission for Western Asia, No. 6, January 1974 (Beirut, ECWA).

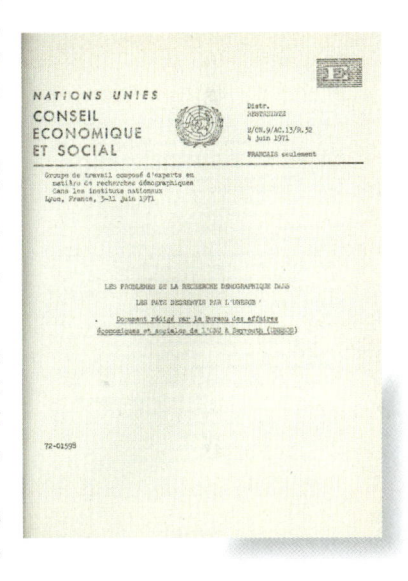

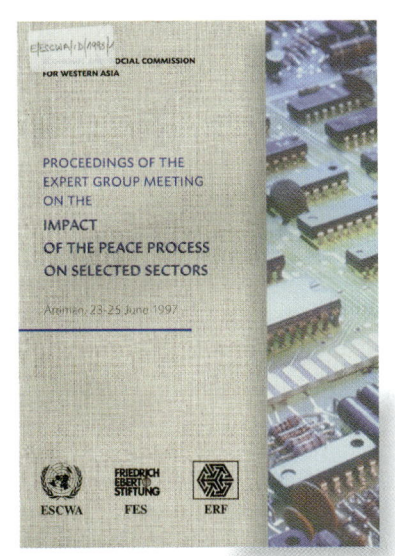

United Nations Economic Commission for Western Asia, *Economic Integration in Western Asia* (London, Frances Pinter, 1985).

United Nations Economic and Social Commission for Western Asia, *Arab Women in the Manufacturing Industries* (Studies on Women and Development, No.19, New York, 1995, E/ESCWA/ID/1994/5/Rev.1).

United Nations Economic Commission for Western Asia, *Proceedings of the Expert Group Meeting on the Impact of the Peace Process on Selected Sectors, Amman, 23-25 June 1997* ([Amman], 1998, E/ESCWA/ID/1998/1).

The UNCTAD experience

The creation of the United Nations Conference on Trade and Development (Geneva, Spring 1964)

The holding of a Conference on Trade and Development was decided in August 1962 to consider the implications of the UN development goals for international trade and aid, and find a way towards an international economic order that would facilitate the growth of developing countries.

The Conference considered that equitable and mutually advantageous international trade would promote economic and social progress in all countries, and that the economic development of the developing countries depended largely on a substantial increase in their share of international trade.

The Conference identified existing trends in world trade as intensifying the difficulty of reaching growth objectives. It addressed the issue of primary commodity exports and the deterioration in the terms of trade between declining prices of primary commodity exports and increasing prices of imports of manufactured goods and equipment. Developing countries' dependence on primary commodity exports was reducing their capacity to import, while capital imports that filled the trade gap resulted in external debt servicing that was becoming a severe burden.

As for solutions, the Conference suggested inward-looking industrialization, substitution policy within the regional groupings, and the promotion of exports of manufactures. A new trade policy for development had to be established and translated into action through effective international machinery in order to result in a more rational and equitable international division of labour with adjustments in world production and trade.

UNCTAD was established as a permanent organ of the General Assembly for deliberation and negotiation in the field of trade and development.

The role of Wladyslaw R. Malinowski (1909-1975)

Polish economist and statistician Malinowski was adviser to the Polish delegation to the International Labour Conference in Philadelphia and to the International Monetary and Financial Conference at Bretton Woods before joining the UN Secretariat. Through his various UN appointments he sought to bring about effective solutions to the economic and social problems of Third World. He was instrumental in the establishment of the regional economic commissions, and headed the Regional Commissions Section of the Department of Economic and Social Affairs. He advocated the Commissions' strengthening and autonomy in social and economic matters. He was also Secretary of ECOSOC and of the Second Committee (Economic and Financial) of the General Assembly.

As Executive Assistant to the Secretary-General of the UNCTAD Conference, Malinowski shared with Prebisch the credit for the institution of UNCTAD as a permanent feature of the UN. He played a role in defining the nature and operation of UNCTAD, which was to respond to the economic concerns of developing countries, to give them a full part in decision-making, and to lead to the negotiation of concrete agreements. Operationally, Malinowski resisted the introduction of weighted-voting and the consensus principle, which were unfavourable to developing countries.

Malinowski was advisor to the first three Secretaries-General of UNCTAD. He headed the Division of Invisibles dealing with the economic aspects of maritime transport, insurance and transfer of technology. The adoption in 1974 of the UN Convention on a Code of Conduct for Liner Conferences, a binding agreement regulating liner conferences and safeguarding developing countries' interests, crowned Malinowski's contributions to UNCTAD. Under his direction, the Division also sowed the seeds for an International Code of Conduct on the Transfer of Technology.

Related documents

United Nations, Economic and Social Council, *United Nations Conference on Trade and Development: Interim Report of the Preparatory Committee on Its First Session* (New York, 1963, E/3720-E/CONF.46/PC/3).

Letter dated 26 February 1963 from Jacob L. Mosak, Director, Bureau of General Economic Research and Policies, to Vladimir Velebit, Executive Secretary, Economic Commission for Europe, transmitting the Interim report of the Preparatory Committee on its first session, which includes the draft agenda for the United Nations Conference on Trade and Development (UNOG Archives document GX 18/12/1/51 (31245).

United Nations Economic Commission for Europe, Principles, rules and practices of foreign trade between countries having different social and economic systems to the World Conference on Trade and Development, annotated draft paper by the Research and Planning Division, ECE, for the World Conference on Trade and Development (UNOG Archives document ARR 14/1360, Box 26, Folder «File 2 UNCTAD 3rd Meeting»).

Letter dated 24 April 1963 from Raúl Prebisch, Secretary-General, United Nations Conference on Trade and Development, to Vladimir Velebit, Executive Secretary, Economic Commission for Europe, discussing cooperation among the Regional Commissions, specialized agencies and Headquarters for a successful trade conference (UNOG Archives document GX 18/12/1/51 (31245).

United Nations Conference on Trade and Development, *Towards a New Trade Policy for Development: Report by the Secretary-General of the United Nations Conference on Trade and Development* (Geneva, 1964, Sales No. E.64.II.B.4).

United Nations Conference on Trade and Development (Geneva, 23 March-16 June 1964). *Proceedings of the Conference. Vol. 1, Final Act and Report* (New York, 1964, Sales No. E.64.II.B.11).

«Les recommandations de la Conférence mondiale du commerce n'ont pas été suivies d'effets», déclare M. Prebisch», *Le Figaro*, 25 août 1965.

«Un an après sa réunion – Le bilan de la conférence internationale du commerce paraît médiocre», *Le Figaro*, 25 août 1965.

United Nations Conference on Trade and Development, *Trade and Development Report, 1981* (New York, 1981, Sales No. E.81.II.D.9).

The Generalized System of Preferences (GSP)

Within UNCTAD in the 1960s, developing countries won acceptance for the principle of preferential treatment for their exports in the markets of industrialised countries. Export-oriented industrialization could promote employment, production and greater export earnings, while reducing developing countries' dependence on trade in primary products whose slow growth and price instability contributed to chronic trade deficits. However, only industrialized countries' markets were large enough to provide such growth stimulus.

A system of generalized, non-reciprocal preferences was devised in which developed countries would lower their custom duties on imports from developing countries, giving their producers a price advantage over other foreign producers, and the ability to compete with them domestically. This was an extension of the infant industry argument, helping developing countries overcome export markets' difficulties from high initial costs.

As one unified system with identical concessions granted across-the-board by all developed countries was unfeasible, the GSP became a system of individual national schemes in which developed countries determined preferential concessions, based on common goals and principles to provide developing countries with broadly equivalent opportunity for expanded export growth. With the first scheme implemented in 1971 by the European Economic Community, the GSP was complete in 1976 when the US scheme became operational.

In 1971, the GATT Council adopted the "Enabling Clause" to give the GSP a 10-year legal status allowing exception from the Most-Favoured-Nation treatment. In 1979 with the Tokyo Round, the Enabling Clause became a permanent GATT legal status. While developed countries were looking for stability in the operation of the system, developing countries continued to press for broader product and country coverage and greater preferential tariff reduction. The system continued to evolve during its first decade.

The GSP has contributed to freer market access and to trade expansion for developing countries that have received increasing trade preferences for their exports. Individual GSP schemes, however, failed to give full effect to the principles and objectives of the preferences as originally conceived, with many products subjected to exemptions and restrictions. With the reduction of tariffs resulting from GATT and WTO negotiations, GSP schemes progressively lost their interests for developing countries. Today, they remain important to least developed countries.

Related documents

Letter dated 9 December 1969 from Manuel Pérez-Guerrero, Secretary-General of UNCTAD, to Janez Stanovnik, Executive Secretary of the Economic Commission for Europe, with attached Appendix 1 of documentation for a Generalized System of Preferences: "Degree of determination of a gravitational model without breakdown by commodities, with an assumption of equilibrium of trade balances" (UNOG Archives document GX 18/12/1/51 (31245)).

United Nations Conference on Trade and Development, *The Generalized System of Preferences: report by UNCTAD Secretariat* (Geneva, 1971, TD/124).

Photo: Gamani Corea (Sri Lanka) to succeed Manuel Pérez-Guerrero (Venezuela) as Secretary-General of UNCTAD on 1 April 1974 (UNOG Photo Library, UN 124,608).

The Integrated Programme for Commodities (IPC)

The role of commodities in developing countries' economies, as generator of employment, income and foreign exchange, was one of the principal concerns that led to the establishment of UNCTAD in 1964. The Committee on Commodities, specifically, was to promote integrated commodity policies and international stabilization agreements at a time when the international financial institutions and bilateral donors were encouraging supply expansion of primary commodities, thus contributing to structural oversupply.

In the mid-1970s, with the oil crisis, the influence of OPEC on international economic relations, and the establishment of the New International Economic Order (NIEO), UNCTAD made proposals for changes in the international economic system placing commodity export earnings at the core of economic development. This led during UNCTAD IV in 1976 to the adoption of the Integrated Programme for Commodities (IPC) and a financial institution, the Common Fund for Commodities (CFC). This was an attempt to address problems of international commodity trade, the short-term instability of commodity markets, and the longer-term development issues within an integrated framework of principles, objectives and instruments.

IPC objectives included achieving price levels remunerative for producers and equitable to consumers by reducing price fluctuations and ensuring market access and reliability of supply, helping expand commodity processing in developing countries, improving marketing and distribution systems, and promoting diversification of exports.

The Common Fund and beyond

The Common Fund for Commodities (CFC) was to be a key instrument in attaining Integrated Programme for Commodities (IPC) objectives, helping to improve market structures in commodity trade through compensatory financing facilities for dealing with the short-term negative impacts of shortfalls in developing countries' commodity export earnings, and financing buffer stocks and other commodity measures. By providing an assured source of funding, CFC would promote the negotiations of International Commodity Agreements on a wide range of commodities.

The CFC finally agreed on at UNCTAD IV in 1976 was much less ambitious. First, CFC was not empowered to intervene to support prices in emergency situations on commodity markets not covered by International Commodity Agreements. Secondly, with a modest amount of capital and most of its resources derived from deposits made by participating international commodities organizations, CFC would have had only a modest influence as a new independent financial institution. But, this so-called "First Window" never materialized.

A "Second Window" was included to finance measures other than buffer stock operations, such as research and development, diversification and productivity to improve the structural conditions of commodity markets and enhance the long-term competitiveness of particular commodities. This "Second Window" entered into force at the end of the 1980s.

Stressing the need for producer-consumer dialogue to tackle individual IPC commodity problems, UNCTAD established Inter-governmental Groups with government and industry experts from both producing and consuming countries. These groups helped improve market transparency, review market situations, correct supply-demand imbalances, and monitor prices, thus contributing to market stability and a more equitable distribution of the costs of instability.

Failures of Commodity Agreements further shook the belief in buffer stocks and export quotas, and other policy issues took over UNCTAD policy agenda in the 1990s. More recently, UNCTAD contributed to the establishment of the Sustainable Commodity Initiative to improve the social, environmental and economic sustainability of commodities production and trade by developing global, multi-stakeholder, market-based strategies for action on a sector-by-sector basis. The first product to be taken up, in 2003, was coffee.

Related documents

United Nations, General Assembly, *Permanent Sovereignty over Natural Resources.* Resolution 1803 (XVII), 14 December 1962, *Official Records of the General Assembly, Seventeenth Session, Supplement No. 17* (A/5217).

United Nations Conference on Trade and Development, *Problems of Raw Materials and Development: Report by the Secretary General of UNCTAD Prepared for the Sixth Special Session of the General Assembly* (New York, 1974, TD/B/488).

United Nations, General Assembly, *Declaration on the Establishment of a New International Economic Order*. Resolution 3201 (S-VI), 1 May 1974, *Official Records of the General Assembly, Sixth Special Session, Supplement No. 1* (A/9559).

United Nations Conference on Trade and Development, *Review of the Implementation of the Recommendations of the Conference. An Overall Integrated Programme for Commodities: note by the Secretary-General of UNCTAD* (Geneva, 1974, TD/B/498).

United Nations Conference on Trade and Development, *Agreement establishing the Common Fund for Commodities* (Geneva, 1980, TD/IPC/CF/CONF/24).

United Nations Conference on Trade and Development, *Commodity issues: a Review and Proposals for Further Action: Report by the UNCTAD Secretariat* (Geneva, 1983, TD/273).

The current commodity crisis and its implications for the world economy. In Commodity Issues: a Review and Proposals for Further Action: Report by the UNCTAD Secretariat (Geneva, 1983, TD/273, chapter I, pp.1-12).

The least developed countries

The international community has recognized differences between developing countries, and the need for those at the earliest stage of development to receive preferential treatment and financial resources, and for special national and international policy targets and measures to achieve them.

Based on indicators agreed on by the Committee for Development Planning (per capita GDP, manufacturing share, adult literacy rate), 42 countries were given LDC status between 1971 and 1990. The World Bank never recognized this category and continues to distinguish between countries on the basis of per capita GDP only. Since 1991, new indicators as well as inclusion and graduation rules for the triennial review of the LDC list have been adopted. UNCTAD secretariat has been advocating a reform of the graduation rule so that a country would exit the LDC category only if it meets all three graduation criteria – income, human development, and economic structure.

UNCTAD work on criteria for identifying LDCs, on their development needs and national efforts, and on international measures in their favor provided the basis for three decennial programmes of action for LDCs adopted by the first (Paris, 1981), second (Paris, 1990), and third (Brussels, 2001) UN Conferences on the Least Developed Countries (UNLDC).

UNCTAD has emphasized the necessity of international support measures (aid, debt relief, trade concessions) for LDCs to achieve any progress out of poverty. In the 1980s, ODA (official development assistance) targets and increased concessionary financing to LDCs were proposed, but ODA and private capital flows declined. UNLDC 1990 adopted differentiated ODA commitments based on each group of donors' previous achievements. However, both the quantity and quality of development financing to LDCs deteriorated in the 1990s. UNLDC 2000 underlined the aid requirements in relation to the Millennium Development Goals and urged the donor community to implement previous commitments.

With debt servicing frustrating development efforts, UNCTAD has recommended a comprehensive debt relief strategy coupled with an aid strategy. In 1996, the Bretton Woods institutions initiated a debt relief strategy with the Highly Indebted Poor Countries, which could not create, however, the conditions for sustained economic growth to rise above unsustainable indebtedness. Regarding trade, UNCTAD has adopted special measures within its initiatives on market access, international commodity policies and supply capacities. The WTO has maintained differential treatment for LDCs.

Related documents

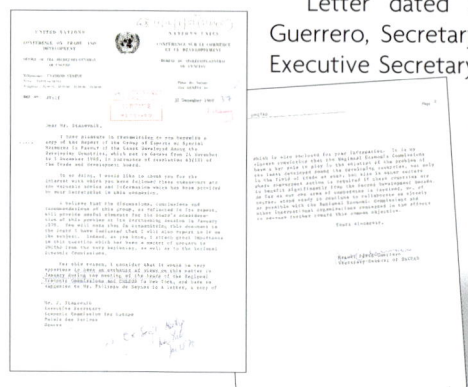

Letter dated 31 December 1969 from Manuel Pérez-Guerrero, Secretary-General of UNCTAD to Janez Stanovnik, Executive Secretary of the Economic Commission for Europe, transmitting a copy of the Report of Experts on Special Measure in Favour of the Least Developed Countries and envisaging cooperation between UNCTAD and the Regional Commissions on the issue of the least developed countries (UNOG Archives document GX/18/12/1/51 (31245)).

United Nations Conference on Trade and Development, *Special Measures in Favour of the Least Developed Among the Developing Countries: Report of the Group of Experts on Special Measures in Favour of the Least Developed Among the Developing Countries held at the Palais des Nations, Geneva from 24 November to 5 December 1969* (Geneva, 1969, TD/B/288).

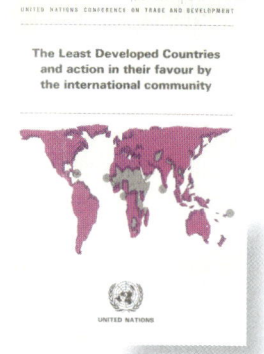

«Characteristics of the Least Developed Among Developing Countries» *in Committee for Development Planning. Report on the Seventh Session (22 March-1 April 1971). Official Records of the Economic and Social Council, Fifty-first Session, Supplement No. 7* (E/4990, chap. II, pp. 13-14).

"The Substantial New Programme of Action for the 1980s for the Least Developed Countries", *in The Least Developed Countries and Action in Their Favour by the International Community: Selected Documents of the United Nations Conference on the Least Developed Countries* (Paris, 1-14 September 1981) (New York, 1983, Sales No. E.83.I.6, Pt. 1, pp. 1-22).

United Nations Conference on Trade and Development, *Paris Declaration and Programme of Action for the Least Developed Countries for the 1990s* (New York, 1992, Sales No. E.91.II.D.20).

United Nations Conference on Trade and Development, *The Least Developed Countries, 1984 report prepared by the UNCTAD Secretariat* (New York, 1984, Sales No. E.84.II.D.25, Vol. I).

UN statistics : measuring the world

The UN Statistical Commission was established in 1946. It progressively developed a system of statistics – concepts, indicators, framework, norms, standards - that has permitted it to measure economic and social performance and to make comparison among countries.

According to Michael Ward, "The creation of a universally acknowledged statistical system and of a general framework guiding the collection and compilation of data according to recognized standards, both nationally and internationally, is one of the great and mostly unsung success of the UN Organization".[26]

The UN's early statistical work was to develop a system of national accounts, a framework that was then revised regularly and the type of statistical data necessary to fill it. This system was influenced by the vision of the economic priorities of the 1940s: production and employment. The gross national product rapidly became the only instrument to measure growth, per capita GDP and to indicate welfare.

The attempts to develop statistics that would better reflect the situation of different group of people within a country or to shed light on specific problems (satellite accounts, social accounts) were not systematically pursued and generalized to all countries because of the resistance of some countries and the cost of such instruments.

The statistical system developed by the UN reflects the fact that it is an intergovernmental organization. The statistics are national and a vision of the world is provided by the addition of national data. This may be insufficient to measure global phenomena such as air and water pollution.

The United Nations is not the only source of statistical indicators; the "City Groups" have developed several instruments over the last decades. But, the UN remains the place where these instruments are recognized and made universal.

The contribution of Wassily Leontief (1906-1999)

Wassily Leontief's name has been associated with a particular type of quantitative economics: input-output analysis. Input-output was partly inspired by the Marxian and Walrasian analysis of general equilibrium via inter-industry flows. Input-output analysis has been a mainstay of economics and economic policy and planning throughout the world for the past half-century. It was at Harvard in 1932 that Leontief began constructing an empirical example of his input-output system. Novel, this system inspired large-scale empirical work. It has been used for economic planning throughout the world, in Western, socialist or Third World countries. For his development of input-output, Leontief won the Nobel memorial prize in 1973.

Born and raised in Russia, Leontief obtained his PhD in economics in Berlin. In addition to his teaching positions, he served as economic consultant to many institutions: the United States Departments of Labor and of Commerce; the Science Advisory Council of the Environmental Protection Agency; the UN Secretary-General's Consultative Group on the Economic and Social Consequences of Disarmament; and the UNDP Transportation section.

Leontief's other contributions include the «composite commodities» theorem, the stress on fixed nominal wages in interpreting Keynes's theory, his analysis of international

---

[26] Michael Ward, Quantifying the World, UN Ideas and Statistics, Indiana University Press, Bloomington, 2004, p. 2

trade, the wage contract, and findings on the American labour-intensive rather than capital-intensive export goods - the «Leontief Paradox» - which brought into question the validity of the conventional factor-proportions theory of international trade. As a critic, Leontief's repeated admonishment of economics for its misuse of mathematics and quantitative methods and the lack of relevance and realism in its theorizing are both still pertinent.

Related documents

United Nations, *Yearbook of International Trade Statistics, 1950, 1st issue* (New York, 1951, Sales No. E.51.XVII.2).

United Nations Economic Commission for Asia and the Far East, *Conference of Asian Statisticians*. Resolution 21 (XIII), 25 March 1957, *Official Records of the Economic and Social Council, Twenty-fourth Session, Supplement No. 2* (E/2959-E/CN.11/454).

United Nations Economic Commission for Asia and the Far East, *Report of the Conference of Asian Statisticians (First Session)* ([s.l.], 1957, E/CN.11/456-E/CN.11/ASTAT/Conf.1/3).

United Nations Economic Commission for Asia and the Far East, *Quarterly Bulletin of Statistics for Asia and the Far East*, vol. 1, no. 1, Sept. 1971 (Hong Kong, Sales No. E.71.II.F.22).

Letter dated 18 September 1961 from Wassily Leontief, Chairman of the 3rd International Input-Output Conference, to Vladimir Velebit, Executive Secretary of the Economic Commission for Europe, thanking him for the hospitality and services provided to the International Input-Output Conference by the Economic Commission for Europe (UNOG Archives document GX 2/6/1/101 (28141)).

International Conference on Input-Output Techniques, Palais des Nations, Geneva, September 11-15, 1961. A selective bibliography of books, documents and studies on input-output techniques, including items available for consultation in the UNOG Library (UNOG Archives document GX 2/6/1/101 (28141), ME/242/61).

Lettre datée 1 juin 1961 de R. Dumas, de l'Office statistique des Communautés européennes, à M. Barrie N. Davies, Chef de la Section des statistiques, Division des Etudes et des Programmes, Commission économique pour l'Europe, en demandant de lui faire parvenir tous les documents de la Conférence des statisticiens européens, relatifs aux tableaux input-output (UNOG Archives document GX 2/6/1/101 (28141)).

Table 1, Input-Output Relations, Egypt, 1954 in *Structural Interdependence and Economic Development: Proceedings of an International Conference on Input-Output Techniques*, Geneva, September 1961. Edited by Tibor Barna, in collaboration with William I. Abraham amd Zoltán Kenessey. (London, Macmillan & Co., 1963).

United Nations Economic Commission for Europe, *Fundamental Principles of Official Statistics in the Region of the Economic Commission for Europe*. Decision C (47). 15 April 1992. (New York, E/CN.3/1993/26).

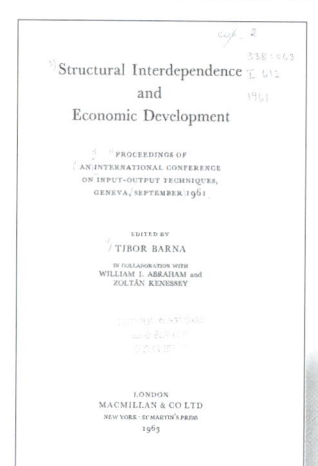

The UNIHP volumes devoted to development

Ahead of the Curve? UN Ideas and Global Challenges, **Louis Emmerij, Richard Jolly, and Thomas G. Weiss (IUP, 2001)**

In the early period, the United Nations insisted on the need of an *international development framework* to assist *national* economic and social policies. This idea was ahead of its time, but the action taken – namely the Marshall Plan - took place outside the UN and was limited to the industrial world. In the 1940s, development was not a concern for academics: the UN put it on the world agenda. Industrial countries were to encourage capital flows to developing countries to stimulate the rapid growth of production and real incomes, so that the world economy as a whole could attain a steady rate of growth and permit needed structural adjustments without a contraction of world trade. It was proposed to negotiate commodity agreements in order to reduce the deterioration of their terms of trade. The World Bank was invited to make loans to avoid recession and the IMF to give support to overcome temporary difficulties in the balance of payments of developing countries. The underdeveloped countries were invited to promote agrarian reforms, to encourage savings, and to transfer labour forces from low-productivity rural areas to higher-productivity urban areas.

The 1970s were creative in that new ideas for development policies were launched (employment and basic needs oriented development strategies). The UN also played an important role in influencing population policies, and putting environmental and gender issues firmly on the map. It was less successful in channelling the debate on the New International Economic Order to a productive middle ground, though the NIEO can be considered the first real attempt to put international governance on the table.

The 1980s were a difficult decade for the UN. Attention shifted to the Bretton Woods institutions and neo-liberal economic and financial policies – a recycled version of trickle-down economics. The reaction of the UN was too timid and too disordered. ECA reacted for Africa in proposing the concept of collective self-reliance for the region. UNICEF drew attention on the dramatic consequences on mothers and children of structural adjustment policies. We had to wait until the 1990s for a reaction in the shape of the Human Development Reports and the UNCTAD Trade and Development reports. The Millennium Development Goals, launched in 2000, are part of this reaction of the UN to take the initiative again.

Good ideas do not always win out and being ahead of the curve can mean that time has not come. This was illustrated by the policies proposed for the transition economies in 1989-1990, drawing attention on the importance of institutions and proposing a gradual approach. But "shock therapy" won the day for political and financial reasons.

The UN has done better in economic and social development than is sometimes thought. Very often it has been ahead of the curve. It has travelled a long and productive road with occasional big bumps. The road ahead looks bumpy too, but not more so than the one that the Organization has left behind.

Richard Jolly

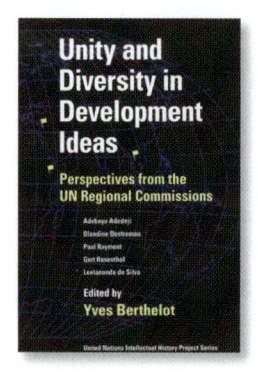

Unity and Diversity in Development Ideas – Perspectives from the UN Regional Commissions, **edited by Yves Berthelot (IUP, 2004)**

Ideas moved back and forth between global entities and Regional Commissions, and were mutually stimulating. Creative, the Regional Commissions developed ideas that responded to the needs of their members and, sometimes, to those of the global community.

Because they discussed the concerns of their regions, they each developed a different set of priorities and made intellectual contributions in different domains: the Economic Commission for Europe (ECE) created bridges between East and West while Europe was split by the Cold War by negotiating norms and conventions on matters of common interests. Some of these norms were progressively adopted worldwide. The Economic Commission for Asia and the Far East (now ESCAP) created institutions such as the Asian Development Bank to give unity to its immense region. The Economic Commission for Latin America (ECLAC) analysed the deterioration of the terms of trade and conceived development paradigms that influenced the whole developing world. The Economic Commission for Africa (ECA) challenged the structural adjustment policies and proposed the concept of collective self-reliance. Receptive, the Regional Commissions adopted global views or principles and advocated them in their region: the Economic and Social Commission for West Asia (ESCWA) took up the issue of gender equality and population for which it became the "regional arm" of the UN.

Because countries of a same region share, in diverse degrees, geographical vicinity, a history of disputes and reconciliations, intertwined cultures, similarities in their economic problems and common interests vis-à-vis the rest of the world, the Regional Commissions were able, through the analyses produced by their secretariats and the debates they organized, to create a common mindset among Governments and between the Governments and the Secretariat that permitted them to address problems, to nurture consensus around ideas and policies to solve them. Creating such a mindset may prove, for an institution, a criterion of relevance even more important than the ideas produced.

Looking ahead, the Regional Commissions have the potential to make two major contributions. First, *Unity and Diversity in Development Ideas* shows that the more a region is developed, the more it generates regional trade and financial flows. Globalization goes hand in hand with regionalization, and regional entities should be central instruments of global governance. Second, in the world of ideas, the Regional Commissions, their member States and secretariats have developed common mindsets and accumulated experiences, which could provide the building blocks for a bottom-up process to improve development thinking. However, the pieces need to be brought together. Who will have the talent, the modesty, the courage and the leadership skills to do that? A Myrdal or a Prebisch could have done it, but even they would have a much more difficult task today in overcoming the institutional complexity and bureaucratic obstacles – a major constraint on substantive work in the present-day UN. The question remains open but it will need to be answered if the UN is to recover an influential and constructive role in economic policy in the future.

Yves Berthelot

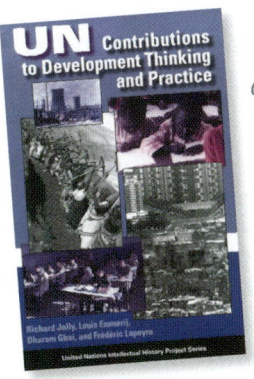

UN Contributions to Development Thinking and Practice, **Richard Jolly, Louis Emmerij, Dharam Ghai, and Frédéric Lapeyre (IUP, 2004)**

The United Nations may not have invented the discipline of development economics but it made much the greatest contribution to its establishment as a critical area of study in the early years of its creation.

Among the key development ideas advanced, four may be highlighted here. These related to the role of trade in development and the secular decline in the commodity terms of trade, the imperative of industrialization to bring about balanced and rapid growth, the need for resource transfers from rich to poor countries to enhance capital accumulation and the contribution of technical assistance to economic development.

The 1960s saw further development of these ideas, especially in relation to planning. In 1961, the UN published the First Development Decade Plan. The decade also witnessed the creation of the World Food Programme and of UNCTAD.

The 1970s witnessed a shift in UN development thinking in favor of equitable distribution of benefits of growth. Four aspects of equity were addressed: equity among different socio-economic groups within a country and equity among countries and generations and between men and women. To address the enormous inter-country inequalities in wealth and power, the UN pioneered a set of ideas under the New International Economic Order (NIEO).

In the 1980s, marked as they were by the onset of the debt crisis, UN agencies were largely eclipsed. They ended up either endorsing the policies of the financial agencies, or at best, offering low-key critiques of policies relating to debt servicing and stabilization. UNICEF and ECA work on the social impact of stabilization and adjustment policies was exceptional and influential. Likewise, the ECE did valuable but less known work in foreseeing the disastrous social and economic consequences for Eastern and Central Europe of the "big bang" neo-liberal policies advocated by the OECD and the international financial agencies.

One of the conclusions of the work done so far under the UNIHP is that the vitality and quality of UN contributions to development ideas and action were at their peak during the first three decades of the post-war period and have suffered a decline in the last two. Several economists and lawyers, among those of other disciplines, who worked for the UN system in its early years, enjoyed world reputations and were leading authorities in their areas. In its later years, the UN system never succeeded in attracting such a galaxy of stars to work for it as full-time officials.

Dharam Ghai

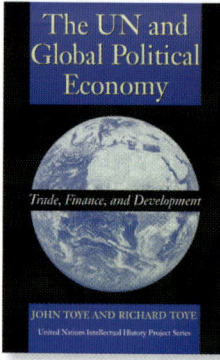

The UN and Global Political Economy – Trade, Finance, and Development, **John Toye and Richard Toye (IUP, 2004)**

We argue that in international organizations the degree of creative thinking – as opposed to the synthesizing and recycling of existing ideas – is inversely related to the ability of their top management to exercise strong editorial control over the research process, control that is often exercised for the purpose of preaching a doctrine supposed to promote the aims of the organization.

The implication of this inverse relation is that the United Nations, with its light hand and multitude of voices, is more likely than some other international organizations to generate interesting new ideas. The 1990s showed some evidence of this in the UNCTAD *Trade and Development Report* and the UNDP *Human Development Report*.

All the same, we acknowledge that it is not realistic to expect that officials of the Secretariat, as distinct from other parts of the UN system, will be a major generator of fresh ideas. That it did so in its earliest years, before successive layers of managerial control over research could solidify, was a happy accident, but not one that could be deliberately replicated today. The Secretariat can still be a purveyor and a disseminator of ideas that its members are just about ready to adopt.

If the UN is to make a creative contribution in future, however, it will be most likely to do so by nourishing its university-like institutions. The setting up of the United Nations University in 1975 laid a basis for this, but in the field of trade, finance and development the real beginning came a decade later with the inauguration of WIDER, the World Institute of Development Economics Research in 1985. Its history to date has not lacked controversy, but its difficulties have never included struggles over publication of the results of research.

Richard Toye

Quantifying the World – UN Ideas and Statistics, **Michael Ward (IUP, 2004)**

The United Nations has played a crucially important and mostly unsung role in unifying such quantitative approaches by standardising and coordinating the process of international official data compilation. It has achieved this through establishing the sound foundations of common concepts and definitions. It has introduced well ordered and logical standard classifications, implemented universally recognized statistical methodologies and recommended good practice. These conform with both theory and empirical observation concerning the relationship between individual and institutional behaviour and how they react to different events and phenomena. In creating a uniform and accepted statistical system, the UN has provided a form of international language that has helped to establish the necessary common ground to enable nation to talk to nation about the strategic issues affecting them while also contributing to the exchange of ideas concerning policy and priorities.

Quantifying the World traces the evolution of statistical ideas since 1945 and their practical application through the evolving inter-relationship of official data and policy objectives. The book explores the economic, social and environmental dimensions of development over the past six decades and recounts how the UN Statistical Office established the early conceptual foundations on which to measure world phenomena. The UN set out to monitor in a consistent way not only national output and well-being but also global change. The book reviews the economic, social and environmental dimensions of this process and how the statisticians have handled these various challenges. It draws attention to some missed opportunities for measuring critical concerns such as the increase in international poverty, the problem of global inflation and the growing economic and social inequality both within counties and across the world. These issues are related to the inner tensions between the UN and its Member States about what events and societal characteristics should and should not be measured by an international agency.

Michael Ward

List of documents

League of Nations, *The Development of International Cooperation in Economic and Social Affairs: Report of the Special Committee* (Geneva, 1939, Series of League of Nations Publications. General. 1939.3).. 77

United Nations, *Measures for the Economic Development of Under-developed Countries: Report by a Group of Experts Appointed by the Secretary-General of the United Nations* (New York, 1951, Sales No. E.51.II.B.2)... 79

Rao, V.K.R.V., "Suggestions for Creation of New International Agency for Financing Basic Economic Development", *in Methods of Financing Economic Development in Under-developed Countries* (New York, United Nations, 1949, Sales No. E.49.III.B.4, Annex A, p. 129)... 81

United Nations, *Planning for Economic Development: Report of the Secretary-General Transmitting the Study of a Group of Experts* (New York, Sales No. E.64.II.B.3)................................ 84

United Nations, General Assembly, *Declaration on the Right to Development*. Resolution 41/128, 4 December 1986, *Official Records of the General Assembly, Forty-first Session, Supplement No. 53* (A/41/53)... 85

ILO, Meeting Basic Needs: Strategies for Eradicating Mass Poverty and Unemployment (Geneva, 1976)... 86

"Debt, Development and the World Economy", in *Trade and Development Report, 1985* (Geneva, 1985, Sales No. E.85.II.D.16, Part II, pp. 62-148)... 88

Cornia, Giovanni Andrea, Jolly, Richard, Stewart, Frances (eds.), *Adjustment With a Human Face: a Study by UNICEF* (Oxford, England, Clarendon Press, 1987-1988, 2 vols.)................ 88

"Human Development Indicators", *in Human Development Report 1990*, published for the United Nations Development Programme (New York; Oxford, England, Oxford University Press, 1990, pp. 123-180)... 90

UN Research Institute for Social Development, *States of Disarray: the Social Effects of Globalization: an UNRISD Report for the World Summit for Social Development*. (Geneva, 1995).. 91

ILO. World Commission on the Social Dimension of Globalization. *A Fair Globalization: Creating Opportunities for All* (Geneva, 2004)... 92

United Nations, *United Nations Millennium Declaration: Millennium Summit, New York, 6-8 September 2000* (New York, 2000, DPI/2163).. 92

United Nations Economic Commission for Europe, *The Financing of European Exports to the Under-Developed Countries*, annotated draft paper of the ECE Secretariat (document from UNOG Archives ARR 14/1360, Box 1, Folder «Finance» Aug 1950 Files No. 2). 95

«Final Communiqué of the Asian - African Conference Held at Bandung from 18th to 24th April 1955», *Asian-African Conference Bulletin*, No. 9, 24 April 1955, pp. 2-3........................ 97

United Nations Economic Commission for Latin America, *The Economic Development of Latin America and Its Principal Problems* (Lake Success, New York, 1950, Sales No. E.50.II.G.2).. 99

United Nations Economic Commission for Africa, *The Status and Role of Women in East Africa* (New York, 1967, Sales No. E.67.II.K.17). 101

List of documents

Les problèmes de la recherche démographique dans les pays desservis par l'UNESOB: document rédigé par le Bureau des affaires économiques et sociales de l'ONU à Beyrouth *(UNESOB)*. (Beyrouth, 1971, E/CN.9/AC.13/R.32, en français seulement). 103

United Nations Economic Commission for Western Asia, *Proceedings of the Expert Group Meeting on the Impact of the Peace Process on Selected Sectors, Amman, 23-25 June 1997* ([Amman], 1998, E/ESCWA/ID/1998/1).. 103

United Nations Conference on Trade and Development, *Towards a New Trade Policy for Development: Report by the Secretary-General of the United Nations Conference on Trade and Development* (Geneva, 1964, Sales No. E.64.II.B.4). 106

Photo: Gamani Corea (Sri Lanka) to succeed Manuel Pérez-Guerrero (Venezuela) as Secretary-General of UNCTAD on 1 April 1974 (UNOG Photo Library, UN 124,608). 107

United Nations Conference on Trade and Development, *Commodity issues: a Review and Proposals for Further Action: Report by the UNCTAD Secretariat* (Geneva, 1983, TD/273). 110

Letter dated 31 December 1969 from Manuel Pérez-Guerrero, Secretary-General of UNCTAD to Janez Stanovnik, Executive Secretary of the Economic Commission for Europe, transmitting a copy of the Report of Experts on Special Measure in Favour of the Least Developed Countries and envisaging cooperation between UNCTAD and the Regional Commissions on the issue of the least developed countries (UNOG Archives document GX/18/12/1/51 (31245)). 112

"The Substantial New Programme of Action for the 1980s for the Least Developed Countries", *in The Least Developed Countries and Action in Their Favour by the International Community: Selected Documents of the United Nations Conference on the Least Developed Countries* (Paris, 1-14 September 1981) (New York, 1983, Sales No. E.83.I.6, Pt. 1, pp. 1-22)... 112

Letter dated 18 September 1961 from Wassily Leontief, Chairman of the 3rd International Input-Output Conference, to Vladimir Velebit, Executive Secretary of the Economic Commission for Europe, thanking him for the hospitality and services provided to the International Input-Output Conference by the Economic Commission for Europe (UNOG Archives document GX 2/6/1/101 (28141)). 114

Table 1, Input-Output Relations, Egypt, 1954 *in Structural Interdependence and Economic Development: Proceedings of an International Conference on Input-Output Techniques*, Geneva, September 1961. Edited by Tibor Barna, in collaboration with William I. Abraham amd Zoltán Kenessey. (London, Macmillan & Co., 1963). 114